POSITIVE PSYCHOLOGY

This volume is a comprehensive review of theoretical and empirical contributions to positive psychology. It provides a scientific understanding of how human strengths help people psychologically and physically, showing how stressful circumstances do not inexorably lead to negative prognoses. It examines how individuals confront challenges, appreciate others, and regard daily experiences as meaningful. Many of the chapters also challenge the negative, disease-model approach that dominates much of the research concerning health and well-being. Chapters also address applications and future directions for the field. The broad scope makes it a key resource for undergraduates, graduates, researchers, and practitioners in social, clinical, and positive psychology.

Dana S. Dunn is Professor of Psychology at Moravian College, Bethlehem, Pennsylvania. His research interests include the social psychology of disability and the scholarship of teaching and learning. He is the author of over 150 articles, chapters, and book reviews, and author or editor of over 30 books.

Frontiers of Social Psychology

Series Editors:

Arie W. Kruglanski, University of Maryland at College Park
Joseph P. Forgas, University of New South Wales

Frontiers of Social Psychology is a series of domain-specific handbooks. Each volume provides readers with an overview of the most recent theoretical, methodological, and practical developments in a substantive area of social psychology, in greater depth than is possible in general social psychology handbooks. The editors and contributors are all internationally renowned scholars whose work is at the cutting edge of research.

Scholarly, yet accessible, the volumes in the *Frontiers* series are an essential resource for senior undergraduates, postgraduates, researchers, and practitioners and are suitable as texts in advanced courses in specific subareas of social psychology.

Published Titles

Forthcoming Titles

For continually updated information about published and forthcoming titles in the *Frontiers of Social Psychology* series, please visit: www.routledge.com/psychology/series/FSP

POSITIVE PSYCHOLOGY

Established and Emerging Issues

Edited by Dana S. Dunn

Routledge
Taylor & Francis Group

NEW YORK AND LONDON

First published 2018
by Routledge
711 Third Avenue, New York, NY 10017

and by Routledge
2 Park Square, Milton Park, Abingdon, Oxon, OX14 4RN

Routledge is an imprint of the Taylor & Francis Group, an informa business

© 2018 Taylor & Francis

Library of Congress Cataloging-in-Publication Data
Names: Dunn, Dana, editor.
Title: Positive psychology: established and emerging issues / edited by Dana Dunn.
Description: New York, NY: Routledge, 2018. | Series: Frontiers of social psychology | Includes bibliographical references and index.
Identifiers: LCCN 2017013029 | ISBN 9781138698659 (hard back: alk. paper) | ISBN 9781138698666 (paper back: alk. paper) | ISBN 9781315106304 (ebook)
Subjects: LCSH: Positive psychology.
Classification: LCC BF204.6 .P6597 2018 | DDC 150.19/88—dc23
LC record available at https://lccn.loc.gov/2017013029

ISBN: 978-1-138-69865-9 (hbk)
ISBN: 978-1-138-69866-6 (pbk)
ISBN: 978-1-315-10630-4 (ebk)

Typeset in Bembo
by codeMantra

In Memory of Gordy Weil

CONTENTS

CONTRIBUTING AUTHORS

Lara B. Aknin, Simon Fraser University

Erica J. Boothby, Yale University

Laura C. Bouchard, University of Miami, Coral Gables

Charles S. Carver, University of Miami, Coral Gables

Kaiyuan Chen, Texas A&M University

Andrew G. Christy, Texas A&M University

Margaret S. Clark, Yale University

Bella DePaulo, University of California, Santa Barbara

Dana S. Dunn, Moravian College

Barbara L. Fredrickson, University of North Carolina, Chapel Hill

Regina Frey, University of Nebraska, Lincoln

Katherine B. Hanniball, Simon Fraser University

Samantha J. Heintzelman, University of Virginia

Joshua A. Hicks, Texas A&M University

Jaime L. Kurtz, James Madison University

Ellen J. Langer, Harvard University

Khoa D. Le Nguyen, University of North Carolina, Chapel Hill

Tim Lomas, University of East London

Fred Luthans, University of Nebraska, Lincoln

Maria G. Mens, Carnegie Mellon University

Christelle T. Ngnoumen, Harvard University

Acacia C. Parks, Hiram College

Cynthia L. S. Pury, Clemson University

Grace Rivera, Texas A&M University

Lindsey Root Luna, Hope College

Shawn Saylors, Comprehensive Soldier and Family Fitness, Columbia, SC

Michael F. Scheier, Carnegie Mellon University

Laurie A. Schreiner, Azusa Pacific University

Karrie A. Shogren, University of Kansas

Mariya Smirnova, University of California, Irvine

Louis Tay, Purdue University

Charlotte vanOyen Witvliet, Hope College

Michael L. Wehmeyer, University of Kansas

Dylan Wiwad, Simon Fraser University

PREFACE

Positive psychology is the science of understanding human strengths and the practice of promoting these strengths to help people psychologically and physically (e.g. Bolt & Dunn, 2016). Psychology has grown to accept the view that stressful circumstances do not inexorably lead to negative prognoses. Positive psychology explores factors that make life worth living and those strengths that enable individuals to confront challenges, appreciate others, and regard daily experiences as meaningful. Still a relatively new subfield of psychology, positive psychology provides a distinct contrast to the negative focus of the disease-model approach that traditionally dominated much of the discipline. Following an overview chapter, this book has three sections that outline the main areas of inquiry in positive psychology (e.g. Seligman & Csikszentmihalyi, 2000): positive subjective experiences; positive traits and states; and positive institutional perspectives, coupled with new directions in positive psychological research.

This volume provides a comprehensive overview of established and emerging issues in the field of positive psychology. Internationally recognized, respected scholars who have made solid theoretical and empirical contributions to the study of positive psychology and social psychology contributed to the book. As you will see, they crafted fine chapters that link classic or established perspectives and theories in positive and social psychology to new research and directions that promote human well-being. I was honored to work with them during the course of this project.

I am grateful to Paul Dukes and his colleagues at Taylor and Francis for ushering the manuscript through production and into print. I thank Moravian College for granting me a sabbatical leave in spring 2017, a reflective break that enabled me to finish the project and to begin some new ones. The book is dedicated to my friend, Gordy Weil, a positive psychologist in his own right, one who left us all too soon.

References

Bolt, M., & Dunn, D. S. (2016). *Pursuing human strengths: A positive psychology guide*. New York: Worth.

Seligman, M. E. P., & Csikszentmihalyi, M. (2000). Positive psychology: An introduction. *American Psychologist, 55*, 5–14. doi:10.1037/0003-066X.55.1.5.

1

PUTTING POSITIVE PSYCHOLOGY INTO PERSPECTIVE

Dana S. Dunn

> Happiness is the meaning and the purpose of life, the whole aim and end of human existence.
>
> *(Aristotle, 384–322 BCE)*

In retrospect, perhaps, it is no surprise that a discipline dedicated to the study of factors affecting mental and physical health would eventually examine the positive qualities that make life worth living. Yet it took a quite a while for the discipline's *zeitgeist* to shift from dealing with negative states and traits— reacting to and alleviating distress and dysphoria—to promoting prevention via the identification and cultivation of beneficial behaviors (e.g. Seligman, 1999). However, what could be described as something of a sea change did occur, and positive psychology morphed from an idea to a movement to an established subfield in psychology in a relatively short period of time. Journal articles, monographs, textbooks, conferences, graduate degrees, and even dedicated journals—the *Journal of Happiness Studies, The Journal of Positive Psychology*—now espouse the strengths and benefits associated with positive psychology. In large part, positive psychology is the study of positive subjective states, traits, and institutions that enable people to flourish—to enjoy high levels of well-being and low levels of mental illness (Keyes, 2009)—in their daily lives. As these burgeoning resources attest, pursuing and living a good life is a worthy goal (Franklin, 2010).

Though now well established in mainstream psychology, positive psychology is not without its critics (Richardson & Guignon, 2008). The late stress and coping theorist, Richard Lazarus (2003), for example, wondered whether the field would be a fad, mostly because in his view its message was not a terribly new one. To be fair, it is sometimes hard not to wonder whether at least some work in positive psychology is not merely "old wine in new bottles"; for example, the late social psychologist, Alice Isen, established that positive affect had a variety of beneficial effects for people (e.g. Isen, 1987) long before the term "positive psychology" was even coined. And at least one subfield of psychology—humanistic psychology—sees positive psychology as treading on its intellectual turf (Friedman, 2014; Schneider, 2011; Waterman, 2014), while acknowledging the respective subfields' reliance on distinct views of humanity, the construal of well-being, and particular empirical methods (Waterman, 2013).

I am confident, however, the scholarship in this book will convince readers that positive psychology is not a passing fancy or mere "happiology" (e.g. Seligman, 2011), that the subfield does not offer overly simplistic—or, worse, solipsistic—views of people and their lives. We know that positive interventions can promote happiness and other beneficial states (e.g. Quoidbach, Mikolalczak, & Gross, 2015; Seligman, Steen, Park, & Peterson, 2005). Thus, the aim of this edited book is twofold: To provide readers with current perspectives on established, key subject areas in positive psychology, and to introduce them to emerging topical areas where positive psychology is making constructive inroads. As a result, chapters in this book are spread among three parts: positive subjective experiences, positive traits and states, and positive institutional perspectives and new directions. We will review the contents of each part in turn.

Positive Subjective Experiences

Human experience is inherently subjective: We know our own experiences and we guess, assume, or posit the experience of other people (e.g. Wegner & Gilbert, 2000). Positive subjective experiences are those favorable states that people associate with "being happy" and "feeling good" about themselves and their place in the world. The chapters in Part I of the book explore various approaches to understanding and explicating the benefits that can be accrued from positive subjective experiences.

Current perspectives on *subjective well-being* (SWB) are the focus of the chapter by Heintzelman and Tay. SWB is a more comprehensive indicator than the more familiar construct of "happiness," and the authors review definitional and assessment issues, benefits and validated promotional triggers, and possible future directions for research. Le Nguyen and Fredrickson discuss *emotions and well-being* in the next chapter, linking positive emotions to the well-known broaden-and-build theory, including evidence indicating how positive emotions promote well-being and its components, such as resilience. The authors also examine connections between positive emotions and health, emotional contingencies linked to dosage, emotion type, and cultural influences, as well as evidence-based ways to pursue happiness and well-being.

Kurtz discusses the growing psychosocial literature concerning *savoring*, arguing that people's ability to focus on, value, and even amplify pleasure associated with particular experiences has beneficial consequences. Although some people are predisposed to savor more than others, savoring is elicited by predictable factors found in the environment; besides considering future directions for research, Kurtz also considers various techniques that boost enjoyment of activities and special moments. Having more money might not lead to greater happiness, but as Hanniball, Aknin, and Wiwad show in the next chapter, there are decided strategies for *spending money well* that lead to positive subjective states. Part I closes with a chapter by Boothby and Clark, who demonstrate that there is something quite positive and beneficial about *close relationships*. They show that the mere presence (i.e. no interaction) of a familiar, close partner can dampen perceived threats and challenges, and amplify pleasures.

Positive Traits and States

An important claim made by Peterson and Seligman (2004) in their book, *Character Strengths and Virtues*, is that many positive traits can be learned. In other words, it need not be the case that by the luck of the draw some people are blessed with a positive demeanor that promotes well-being while others struggle to cope with tepid outlooks on the world. Some beneficial character-istics can be learned, even later in life. And, fortunately, research in positive psychology suggests that there are behavioral steps people can take to adjust their cognitive and emotional outlooks regarding ongoing experiences. In Part II of the book, researchers consider how positive traits and states can influence well-being.

In the opening chapter of Part II, Langer and Ngnoumen examine how *mindfulness*—a desirable mental state where awareness is focused on the present moment—can enhance health and well-being. As the authors show, a substan-tial body of research demonstrates that mindfulness promotes positive affect and creativity, diminishes stress, heightens quality of life, and improves physi-cal health and psychological outlooks. In the next chapter, Bouchard, Carver, Mens, and Scheier discuss how *optimism*—the expectation that future occur-rences will generally be positive—favorably influences people's physical and mental conditions. These investigators highlight how optimism affects goal pursuit, the values attached to particular goals, and an individual's confidence in achieving desired ends. Part II's third chapter explores how forgiving peo-ple for their transgressions can impact both physiological and emotional well-being. In doing so, vanOyen Witvliet and Root Luna present forgiveness as a moral response for challenging relational injustice. The final chapter in Part II, which was written by Pury and Saylors, focuses on courage and courageous actions as positive psychological constructs. They define features constituting courage, indicating how it is similar to, but distinct from, related constructs, and review social psychological concepts that render brave actions as understandable and representative of courage.

Positive Institutional Perspectives and New Directions

To date, most empirical and theoretical investigations of positive psychological phenomena focus on positive subjective states, traits, and related phenomena. Less research deals with positive psychology's third pillar (Peterson, 2006), the role of positive institutions in people's growth and development. Positive institutions are settings or organizations that impart civic virtues, encourage individuals to be conscientious citizens, and promote the collective good. Two important positive institutional settings, the workplace and the university campus, are discussed in this third part. The opening chapter by Luthans and Frey explores the role of positive psychological capital or *PsyCap* in the workplace. The authors review how PsyCap influences workers' attitudes, actions, and performance at work, as well as the development of beneficial psychological resources linked to employment. In the next chapter, Schreiner considers what factors allow students to thrive academically during college and in their postgraduate life. *Student success and well-being* is much more than solid grades and degree completion; indeed, Schreiner argues successful student growth is dependent on a process of academic, psychological, and social engagement during their college years.

The remaining chapters here cover emerging topical areas in positive psychology, many of which build bridges between other areas of psychology, such as social psychology, clinical psychology, and rehabilitation psychology, to the established areas of positive psychology. In their chapter, Christy, Rivera, Chen, and Hicks address the role of finding *meaning in life* and how doing so influences positive psychological functioning and outcomes. A chapter by Dunn outlines recent advances concerning positive psychological factors linked to the experience of *disability*, rehabilitation services, and psychosocial outcomes. DePaulo, a social psychologist, offers a positive psychological perspective on *single life*, presenting powerful evidence that, despite the ways single people are frequently stereotyped, stigmatized, and ignored, they nonetheless lead happy lives, reporting and showing markers of high levels of well-being.

Does positive psychology have implications for *clinical interventions*? In their chapter, Smirnova and Parks argue that findings from positive psychology have beneficial clinical applications that can be used to ameliorate depression and other negative symptoms that some people experience. A chapter by Wehmeyer and Shogren shares applications of the *self-determination* construct to both positive psychology and social psychology. Self-determination, a general psychological construct, is an account of human agency and volition, one where self and other caused action are attributed to human will. In this volume's closing chapter, Lomas discusses *applied positive psychology* within the context of a multidimensional, meta-theoretical model designed to promote human well-being.

Positive Psychology in Perspective

In many ways, the rapid rise of research in positive psychology is remarkable. As the chapters in this book attest, positive psychology has emerged as a viable, exciting, and even dynamic subfield of psychology. In formal terms, positive psychology is a little less than 20 years old (though psychological research stipulating salutary approaches to understanding mental health and physical well-being appeared long before, if not in such an organized way). Yet readers will likely view much of the discussion in the chapters in the first two parts of this book as scientifically mature or maturing—a base of established data and theory are allowing investigators to make confident claims about positive perspectives on behavior. Chapters in Part III offer readers the pleasure of discovering new areas of inquiry that push positive psychology in new empirical directions. The contributors to this book and I very much hope readers—researchers, students, interested lay people—will not only learn from the collective work presented herein but will apply some of it to their own lives. And we will be gratified if some readers use ideas and findings from the present chapters to plan their own positive psychological investigations.

References

Franklin, S. S. (2010). *The psychology of happiness: A good human life*. New York: Cambridge University Press.

Friedman, H. (2014). Are humanistic and positive psychology really incommensurate? *American Psychologist, 69*, 89–90. doi:10.1037/a0034865.

Isen, A. M. (1987). Positive affect, cognitive processes, and social behavior. In L. Berkowitz (Ed.), *Advances in experimental social psychology* (Vol. 20, pp. 203–253). San Diego, CA: Academic Press. doi:10.1016/S0065-2601(08)60415-3.

Keyes, C. M. (2009). Toward a science of mental health. In S. J. Lopez & C. R. Snyder (Eds.), *Oxford handbook of positive psychology* (2nd ed., pp. 89–95). New York: Oxford University Press.

Lazarus, R. S. (2003). Does the positive psychology movement have legs? *Psychological Inquiry, 14*, 93–109.

Peterson, C. (2006). *A primer in positive psychology*. New York: Oxford University Press.

Peterson, C., & Seligman, M. E. P. (2004). *Character strengths and virtues: A handbook and classification*. Washington, DC: American Psychological Association.

Quoidbach, J., Mikolalczak, M., & Gross, J. J. (2015). Positive interventions: An emotion regulation perspective. *Psychological Bulletin, 141*, 655–693. doi:10.1037/a0038648.

Richardson, F. C., & Guignon, C. B. (2008). Positive psychology and philosophy of social science. *Theory & Psychology, 18*, 605–627.

Schneider, K. (2011). Toward a humanistic positive psychology: Why can't we just get along? *Existential Analysis, 22,* 32–38.

Seligman, M. E. P. (1999). The president's address. *American Psychologist, 54,* 559–562.

Seligman, M. E. P. (2011). *Flourishing: A visionary new understanding of happiness and well-being.* New York: Free Press.

Seligman, M. E. P., Steen, T. A., Park, N., & Peterson, C. (2005). Positive psychology progress: Empirical validation of interventions. *American Psychologist, 60,* 410–421.

Waterman, A. S. (2013). The humanistic psychology-positive psychology divide: Contrasts in philosophical foundations. *American Psychologist, 68,* 123–133. doi:10.1037/a0032168.

Waterman, A. S. (2014). Further reflections on the humanistic psychology-positive psychology divide. *American Psychologist, 69,* 92–94. doi:10.1037/a0034966.

Wegner, D. M., & Gilbert, D. T. (2000). Subjective experience in social cognition and behavior. In H. Bless & J. P. Forgas (Eds.), *Social psychology: The science of human experience* (pp. 1–9). Philadelphia, PA: Psychology Press.

PART I

Positive Institutional Perspectives and New Directions

2

SUBJECTIVE WELL-BEING

Payoffs of Being Happy and Ways to Promote Happiness

Samantha J. Heintzelman and Louis Tay

The desire to be happy is a near-universal motivation. Additionally, reflections aimed to describe the features of happiness, debates about its foundations, and disagreements about its moral value and impact on individuals and societies have been prominent for centuries in diverse fields such as philosophy, theology, literature, and politics. Recent decades have seen an ascent of happiness into the psychological arena as well. The science of happiness in psychology has taken great strides by establishing robust measures of happiness and providing evidence regarding the antecedents and consequences of this experience (De Neve, Diener, Tay, & Xuereb, 2013; Diener, Inglehart, & Tay, 2013). This effort has enabled psychology to add valuable insights to inform our conceptualizations of happiness and strategies to maximize this experience.

These burgeoning scientific findings regarding happiness have infiltrated domains of great import. Particularly, there has been a growing emphasis by many governments (e.g. United Kingdom, France, Bhutan, and the United States) and international organizations (e.g. Organisation for Economic Co-operation and Development [OECD], United Nations) on systematically assessing the happiness of people across the world. Whereas traditional indicators of a nation's prosperity focused on economic markers such as gross domestic product (GDP), conceptualizations of a successful society now increasingly include an assessment of the overall happiness of its citizens (Diener & Seligman, 2004; Tay, Chan, & Diener, 2014). The increased utilization of such measures has provided valuable insights into wide-ranging policy issues, illuminating the features of societal practices that make for happier nations (Diener, Oishi, & Lucas, 2015).

In this chapter, we will review the rapidly growing body of psychological research on subjective well-being (SWB; the preferred scientific conceptualization of the more colloquial term "happiness," which we define below) before offering prospective insights into some directions the study of happiness can take in the years ahead.

Defining and Measuring Happiness

SWB is defined as the overall evaluation a person makes regarding his or her life and emotional experience. SWB is an umbrella term for a multifaceted construct (Diener, 1984) comprised of life satisfaction, which is a broad cognitive appraisal regarding one's life, and affective feelings, which include abundant positive feelings and minimal negative feelings (Diener & Emmons, 1984). While SWB represents a more scientifically precise term for this construct, we will also use the more approachable, "happiness," when referring to life satisfaction, positive affect, and low negative affect.

The three components of SWB, life satisfaction, positive affect (PA), and negative affect (NA), are distinct (e.g. Pavot & Diener, 1993). These constructs are separable in factor analyses (Diener, Emmons, Larsen, & Griffin, 1985), and they share differential associations with other variables, in terms of both antecedents and outcomes. For example, PA is more strongly tied to social relationships (Tay & Diener, 2011) and positively linked to sociability (Berry & Hansen, 1996), whereas life satisfaction is more affected by factors such as health, income, and the quality of one's work (Diener, Tay, & Oishi, 2013; Kahneman & Deaton, 2010; Schimmack & Oishi, 2005). As such, these facets of SWB can, and ought to be, measured as separate constructs.

Self-report measures have been developed and validated to do so. Life satisfaction is most commonly measured using the five-item Satisfaction with Life Scale (SWLS; e.g., "I am satisfied with my life"; Diener, Emmons, Larsen, & Griffin, 1985), though single-item measures (e.g. present day life satisfaction; Cantril, 1965) have also been employed to measure life satisfaction. The SWLS has demonstrated strong reliability, predictive validity, and discriminant validity to measures of emotional well-being, as well as a degree of temporal stability while remaining sensitive to changes over time (Diener et al., 2013; Pavot & Diener, 1993; Pavot, Diener, Colvin, & Sandvik, 1991).

PA and NA can also be measured with self-report scales that ask participants to indicate the extent to which they experience certain emotions. The Positive and Negative Affect Schedule (PANAS; Watson, Clark, & Tellegen, 1988) represents the first common measure used to assess PA and NA. The PANAS measures PA by asking participants to rate the extent to which they feel certain emotions (e.g. active, enthusiastic, proud for PA, upset, afraid, guilty for NA) over a set time frame to assess either trait or state affect. This measure demonstrated reliability and validity beyond other measures of affect that preceded it (e.g. Gray & Watson, 2007) and was used extensively for several decades. However, the scale has also been the subject of a variety of critiques. For example, consider that the scale includes terms that are not clearly emotions (Diener, Smith, & Fujita, 1995), that happiness is underrepresented among these items (Egloff, 1998), that some of the items seem to be culturally specific (Thompson, 2007), and that the scale seems to inappropriately confound affective valence with approach motivation (Harmon-Jones, Harmon-Jones, Abramson, & Peterson, 2009).

The Scale of Positive and Negative Experience (SPANE) has been forwarded more recently to overcome these concerns in the measurement of PA and NA (Diener et al., 2010). This scale consists of six items for each PA and NA, half of which are general in nature (positive, pleasant, good, happy, joyful, contented for PA; negative, unpleasant, bad, sad, afraid, angry for NA). This feature of the SPANE allows it to capture positive and negative feelings of varied forms, arousal levels, and cultural situations (Diener et al., 2010). Indeed, this scale's reliability and validity has now been demonstrated across various cultures, including Portuguese (Silva & Caetano, 2013) and Japanese (Sumi, 2014) samples. Furthermore, the SPANE shows incremental validity beyond the PANAS in predicting life satisfaction, depression, and general well-being (Jovanović, 2015).

Given the internal and experiential nature of affective experiences and satisfaction judgments, research in this area has traditionally relied on self-report measures. Still there are some limitations to this method, including the effect of cultural norms on self-reports (Diener, Suh, Smith, & Shao, 1995), the influence of current moods on general SWB ratings (Diener, Sandvik, Pavot, & Gallagher, 1991), and socially desirable response patterns (Heintzelman, Trent, & King, 2015). Given these concerns, alternative strategies for assessing SWB constructs have been pursued.

For one, informant reports have been used as an alternative measure of SWB. Informant reports of SWB seem to represent a broad summary of the emotions expressed by the target over time, and are less subject to reporting biases as targets are likely more honest with their true feelings with their close others than to a researcher (Sandvik, Diener, & Seidlitz, 1993). Another alternative SWB measurement examines the ease of recalling positive vs. negative events. Happy people recall more positive than negative life events compared to unhappy people (Diener et al., 1991; Pavot, Diener, Colvin, & Sandvik, 1991). The relative number of positive to negative life events participants recall in set amounts of time can indicate the accessibility of positive and negative memories (Seidlitz & Diener, 1993). Conclusions from research including self-reports and these alternative measurement techniques together suggest that self-reports of SWB are valid; however, the inclusion of additional non-self-report measures can provide a more integrative account of these constructs (Sandvik et al., 1993).

Payoffs of Happiness

The advent of measurement strategies to assess SWB opened a field of work aimed at identifying the consequences of happiness. An ever-expanding body of research suggests that happiness is not only the phenomenological experience of good, but it also has wide-ranging individual and societal benefits in domains including physical health, social relationships, productivity, and prosociality (De Neve et al., 2013; Diener & Tay, 2012; Lyubomirsky, King, & Diener, 2005).

Health and Longevity

First, happiness is associated with health and longevity (see reviews by Chida & Steptoe, 2008; Cohen & Pressman, 2006; Diener & Chan, 2011; Howell, Kern, & Lyubomirsky, 2007; Lyubomirsky, King, & Diener, 2005; Pressman & Cohen, 2005). For example, happier people self-report better health, take fewer sick days, and are hospitalized less than their unhappy counterparts (Graham, Eggers, & Sukhtankar, 2004).

Work examining the causal direction of these relationships suggests that positive moods improve physiological health indicators such as cortisol, blood pressure, and immune system parameters (Barak, 2006; James, Yee, Harshfiled, Blank, & Pickering, 1986; Kuykendall & Tay, 2015; Marsland, Pressman, & Cohen, 2007; Schnall et al., 1990). Whereas negative emotions have detrimental effects on cardiovascular, immune, and endocrine system functioning, positive emotions seem to help these systems (Edwards & Cooper, 1998; Kiecolt-Glaser, McGuire, Robles, & Glaser, 2002; Steptoe, Wardle, & Marmot, 2005).

At the cardiovascular level, a number of studies suggest happiness relates to healthier hearts. For example, positive feelings correlate with healthier heart rate variability (Bhattacharyya, Whitehead, Rakhit, & Steptoe, 2008) and lower ambulatory heart rate (Steptoe et al., 2005). Childhood stress and adversity predicts elevated markers of inflammation years later (Slopen, Kubzansky, McLaughlin, & Koenen, 2013), and chronic inflammation takes a toll on the cardiovascular system over time. Conversely, positive emotions protect against cardiovascular disease (Boehm, Peterson, Kivimaki, & Kubzansky, 2011), are associated with lower rates of strokes in senior citizens (Ostir, Markides, Peek, & Goodwin, 2001), and negatively predicted heart disease risk in a prospective study (Davidson, Mostofsky, & Whang, 2010). Causally, a positive mood induction following a stressful experience brought participants' cardiovascular systems back to baseline more quickly compared to controls (Fredrickson & Levenson, 1998).

SWB is also related to stronger immune functioning and recovery processes (see Marsland et al., 2007, for a review). For example, participants exposed to a cold virus experienced more cold symptoms, measured with various objective markers including mucus production and congestion, if they were low in positive feelings at the beginning of the study (Cohen, Doyle, Turner, Alper, & Skoner, 2003). Furthermore, an optimistic outlook predicts quicker recovery following major surgery (Scheier et al., 1989), and wound healing after an injury is hindered by stress (Christian, Graham, Padgett, Glaser, & Kiecolt-Glaser, 2006). Happiness is also related to surviving fatal diseases such as end-stage renal disease (Devins, Mann, Mandin, & Leonard, 1990), recurrent breast cancer (Levy, Lee, Bagley, & Lippman, 1988), and spinal cord injuries (Krause, Sternberg, Lottes, & Maides, 1997) for longer periods of time.

In addition to the physiological processes (e.g. inflammation, sleep disturbances) underlying the relationships between happiness and health and longevity, these associations are also driven by various positive health behaviors (Steptoe, Dockray, & Wardle, 2009). Happier people are more likely to engage in healthy behaviors such as eating a healthier diet (Blanchflower, Oswald, & Stewart-Brown, 2013), exercising more (Grant, Wardle, & Steptoe, 2009), seatbelt use (Goudie, Mukherjee, De Neve, Oswald, & Wu, 2014), and lower rates of smoking (Strine et al., 2008).

SWB is also related to living longer. In one longitudinal study, researchers examined autobiographies written by a group of nuns around the time they took their vows, when they were in their early twenties. They found that those who demonstrated more positive emotions in their writings lived approximately ten years longer than those with less positive essays, despite their nearly identical living conditions throughout life and the many decades that elapsed between the time of writing and the time of death (Danner, Snowdon, & Friesen, 2001).

A number of subsequent studies have shown that SWB relates to a longer life. Indeed, Chida and Steptoe (2008) examined this relationship across over 50 studies. Synthesizing these findings in meta-analyses, they found relationships between SWB and decreased mortality in a sample of 28 studies of participants with established diseases and an even stronger relationship in a sample of 26 studies of initially healthy participants (Chida & Steptoe, 2008). Well-being reduces all-cause morality (Maier & Smith, 1999); living a happier life is associated with living a healthier and longer life.

Social Relationships

SWB is also associated with better social relationships. Happier people spend more time socializing and engaging in social activities than less happy people (Berry & Hansen, 1996) and are more popular and likable (Boehm & Lyubomirsky, 2008). Diener and Seligman (2002) found that the happiest 10 percent of a sample were all highly social and had the strongest social and romantic relationships than less happy people. Further, in a meta-analysis of 286 findings, SWB was strongly predicted by quantity and quality of contact with one's friends (Pinquart & Sörensen, 2000). A similar pattern emerges at the societal level. A world survey of 123 nations found that positive feelings at the nation level were related to good social relationships across sociocultural regions (Tay & Diener, 2011). There now exists a body of experimental and longitudinal research suggesting that this relationship is bidirectional; while having high-quality relationships boosts SWB, so too does having high SWB lead to stronger social relationships (Lyubomirsky, King, & Diener, 2005).

In experiments, participants who are induced to be in a positive mood (compared to negative or neutral moods) are more sociable with a confederate (Isen, 1970), see new people as more likable (Baron, 1987), and express greater social interests, such as being with friends or going to a party (Cunningham, 1988a). Similarly, children put in a good mood showed better social skills and were more confident in their social behaviors compared to controls (Kazdin, Esveldt-Dawson, & Matson, 1982). Positive mood inductions made participants more talkative and self-disclosing compared to negative mood inductions (Cunningham, 1988b). Furthermore, in a study that monitored participants' everyday conversations, happy participants spent around 25 percent less time alone and about 70 percent more time talking when they were with others compared to less happy participants (Mehl, Vazire, Holleran, & Clark, 2010). Not only does happiness make people more social, but it makes them more socially appealing as well. For instance, in one study, outside observers rated the social interactions happy people had with strangers as better, compared to unhappy people (Berry & Hansen, 1996).

The effects of happiness on sociability extend to the existence, quality, and duration of romantic relationships as well. Longitudinal work demonstrating the link between happiness and marriage (see Lyubomirsky, King, & Diener, 2005, for a review) suggests that happier people are more likely to become married (e.g. Lucas, Clark, Georgellis, & Diener, 2003), be happy in those marriages (Headey & Veenhoven, 1989), stay married (Stutzer & Frey, 2006), and in the event of a divorce, to be remarried (Spanier & Furstenberg, 1982). This does not mean that romantic relationships will always lead to greater happiness, as there are critical moderating factors such as the quality of the relationship (Tan & Tay, 2015). Research on single people also suggests that marriage is not essential to happiness (see DePaulo, this volume).

Productivity

Happier people are more likely to hold "better" jobs, those that were rated by observers as having more autonomy, meaning, and variety (Staw, Stutton, & Pelled, 1994). Happier people are also more satisfied with their jobs (Connolly & Viswesvaran, 2000), and job satisfaction has important consequences for job-related outcomes. The meta-analytic correlation between job satisfaction and job performance is a moderately strong 0.30 (Judge, Thoresen, Bono, & Patton, 2001). Furthermore, analysis across multiple studies that have cross-lagged relationships show that this effect runs from job attitudes to performance (Riketta, 2008). Job satisfaction is also negatively associated with work withdrawal, intention to quit, and turnover (Podsakoff, LePine, & LePine, 2007).

Employees high in SWB get better performance reviews from their supervisors, demonstrate better financial performance (Peterson, Luthans, Avolio, Walumbwa, & Zhang, 2011), and are absent from work less (Pelled & Xin, 1999) than employees lower in SWB. SWB also contributes to patterns of thinking and behaving that are valued by many employers, such as creativity (Amabile, Barsade, Mueller, & Staw, 2005; George & Zhou, 2007). Happier workers are also better negotiators as positive emotions promote cooperation and collaboration, rather than withdrawal or competition, in negotiations (e.g. Carnevale, 2008; Forgas, 1998) and tend to reach better joint solutions (Carnevale & Isen, 1986). Higher SWB is also related to higher income (Judge, Piccolo, Podsakoff, Shaw, & Rich, 2010) and future income (De Neve & Oswald, 2012; Diener, Nickerson, Lucas, & Sandvik, 2002; Graham et al., 2004).

The SWB of a company's workers also predicts important business metrics including greater productivity and profitability. Job satisfaction within a manufacturing plant predicts that plant's productivity (Bockerman & Ilmakunnas, 2012). Furthermore, work units with high employee satisfaction showed improvements in revenue, sales, and profit (Harter, Schmidt, Asplund, Killham, & Agrawal, 2010). American companies rated among the best to work for demonstrated increased equity value compared to industry benchmarks, resulting in higher annual returns (Edmans, 2012).

Prosociality

There is growing evidence, as well, that SWB is linked to prosociality. Happiness is associated with the inclination to help others (Feingold, 1983). SWB predicts participating in volunteer work and spending more time volunteering (Oishi, Diener, & Lucas, 2007; Thoits & Hewitt, 2001) and the frequency of blood donations (Priller & Schupp, 2011). Furthermore, time spent in a good mood, in studies using experience sampling or daily diary methodologies, is associated with the amount of time helping others (Lucas, 2001). Aknin, Dunn, and Norton (2012) provide evidence suggesting that prosocial spending (i.e. spending money on others) is tied to happiness in a bidirectional manner: Giving to others increases happiness, and happy people are more likely to give to others (see also Hanniball, Aknin, & Wiwad, this volume).

Experimental research has shown that people induced to feel happy, compared to sad or neutral, contribute more money to charity or needy children (e.g. Cunningham, Steinberg, & Grev, 1980) and donate blood (O'Malley & Andrews, 1983). In one study, children in a positive mood condition gave more money away to classmates compared to children in a negative mood condition (Rosenhan, Underwood, & Moore, 1974). These manipulations also make participants more likely to agree to help experimenters by completing an additional experiment (e.g. Aderman, 1972).

Happiness is also associated with better citizenship in the workplace. Employees in a good mood are more likely to engage in "organizational citizenship behaviors" (i.e. voluntary behaviors beyond their job requirements) (Spector & Fox, 2002; Williams & Shiaw, 1999) and show lower deviant workplace behaviors such as stealing and inefficiency (Judge, Scott, & Ilies, 2006). In one study, inexperienced sales staff members at a department store were more helpful to a customer if their previous interaction (with a confederate) was pleasant, compared to neutral or unpleasant (Forgas, Dunn, & Granland, 2008).

Promotion of Happiness: Scientifically Validated Ways to Improve Happiness

Given the wide-ranging benefits of happiness across a variety of life domains, finding ways to increase happiness is an important personal and societal goal. A prerequisite of such pursuits is a working understanding of the sources of happiness.

Sources of Happiness

Happiness, like most psychological states, is multiply determined. Departing from previous suggestions that levels of trait SWB were fully determined genetically (Lykken & Tellegen, 1996), contemporary research provides a more restrained conclusion: Genes are among the factors influencing a person's SWB, while both life circumstances and intentional activities also play important, and perhaps larger roles. A recent meta-analysis produced an average heritability estimate of 0.40 with a great deal of variability between studies (Nes & Roysamb, 2015). In addition to leaving a large portion of variability in SWB unaccounted for by one's genes, heritability estimates also do not consider how environmental actions or personal actions can alter a trait (Roysamb, Nes, & Vitterso, 2014). It is clear, then, that a meaningful portion of the variance in SWB depends on other factors.

Circumstances also influence happiness. Prominent nation-level differences in happiness, which are partially explained by important societal factors such as income, corruption, laws, and standards of equity (Diener, Diener, & Diener, 1995; Oishi, Kesebir, & Diener, 2011; Tay, Herian, & Diener, 2014), illustrate this point. Individual-level differences in SWB are also predicted by life circumstances such as marital status and positive social relationships (e.g. Diener, Gohm, Suh, & Oishi, 2000).

However, humans tend to adapt to the circumstances in their lives. An early study of lottery winners were found to be no happier than matched controls and, furthermore, they rated their daily activities as *less* enjoyable than controls (Brickman, Coates, & Janoff-Bulman, 1978). The "hedonic treadmill" was proposed based on these findings to explain adaptation to positive events by highlighting a shifting standard of comparison for general life evaluations. Subsequent research has demonstrated adaptation to other major life events including marriage (Lucas et al., 2003) and meta-analyses across these events showed consistent evidence of hedonic adaptation, though the rate of this process differed by event (Luhmann, Hofmann, Eid, & Lucas, 2012).

Despite this tendency to adapt, some events can still cause long-lasting changes in happiness (Lucas, 2007). For example, people do not seem to completely adapt to some negative events such as disability and unemployment (Anusic, Yap, & Lucas, 2014). Indeed, even after such situations are resolved (i.e. reemployment), there is evidence suggesting "scarring" effects, as the affected individual's SWB levels fail to return to pre-event levels (Clark, Georgellis, & Sanfey, 2001). In sum, life circumstances and large events are related to SWB, though to a lesser extent than is often expected.

Although happiness is partially determined by one's genes and significant life circumstances, personal choices, and patterns of thoughts and behaviors are of utmost importance in this regard. Research at both the individual and societal levels suggests that SWB is malleable (Tay & Kuykendall, 2013) and a vastly expanding literature showing that brief experimental manipulations can increase SWB has emerged (Parks & Schueller, 2014; Quoidbach, Mikolajczak, & Gross, 2015). That happiness is driven, in large part, by our everyday activities opens the door to intentional actions to improve SWB.

Personal Applications

Research demonstrates reliable increases in SWB stemming from a number of such activity interventions. In a seminal study of positive activity manipulations, Seligman and colleagues (2005) randomly assigned participants to complete a control activity, or one of five positive activities, for a week. They measured SWB before and after the activity week, and 1 week, 1 month, 3 months, and 6 months later. Two of the activities, using one's character strengths in new ways and writing about three good things, increased happiness through the 6-month assessment, and the gratitude visit activity, in which participants wrote and delivered a letter of gratitude to an impactful person in their lives, elicited increases in happiness that lasted 1 month. Further, continuing to practice an assigned exercise beyond the 1-week activity related to greater long-term benefits (Seligman, Steen, Park, & Peterson, 2005). Finally, two of the conditions did not affect happiness, highlighting that simply engaging in *any* positive action is not automatically effective. Lyubomirsky and Layous (2013) have outlined a model to identify features of positive activities (e.g. longer duration, variety, habit development) and individuals (e.g. motivation, effort) that promote effective SWB interventions. Furthermore, they argue that person–activity fit is essential for happiness changes.

Fortunately, there are many activities to choose from that subsequent research has shown are effective for increasing SWB. Among these are performing acts of kindness (Lyubomirsky, Sheldon, & Schkade, 2005), savoring experiences (Bryant & Veroff, 2007), counting blessings to cultivate a grateful mindset (Emmons & McCullough, 2003) and expressing gratitude to others (Lyubomirsky, Dickerhoof, Boehm, & Sheldon, 2011), imagining one's best possible self for the future (King, 2001), interacting with strangers or "weak ties" (Sandstrom & Dunn, 2014), and sharing our positive experiences with others (Lambert et al., 2013). There is also a flourishing literature suggesting benefits of mindfulness practice for SWB (Brown & Ryan, 2003). Taken together, two independent meta-analyses of SWB intervention studies suggest effect sizes of $r = 0.29$ (Sin & Lyubomirsky, 2009) and $r = 0.34$ (Bolier et al., 2013).

Workplace Applications

Interventions targeting the SWB of workers have been implemented at the organizational level and have been shown to promote both the general happiness of workers as well as job satisfaction and other positive workplace behaviors (see also Luthans & Frey, this volume). For example, interventions focused on goal-setting, resource-building, and happiness led to increases in positive feelings in workers compared to controls (Ouweneel, Le Blanc, & Schaufeli, 2013). Furthermore, interventions targeted at stress management are effective in doing so according to moderate to large meta-analytic effect sizes (Richardson & Rothstein, 2008). Additionally, workplace resilience interventions seem to have a small to moderate effect on positive outcomes, but these effects seem to diminish over time and require continued practice (Vanhove, Herian, Perez, Harms, & Lester, 2016).

Other techniques that are seemingly less relevant to one's job also garner benefits for work-relevant outcomes. One technique, loving-kindness meditation, which involves meditative contemplation on positive feelings for the self and others, has been shown to significantly effect job satisfaction compared to waitlist controls (Hülsheger, Alberts, Feinholdt, & Lang, 2013). A three-day expressive writing intervention in which workers wrote about their deepest thoughts and feelings led to greater positive emotions and less workplace incivility compared to a control condition (Kirk, Schutte, & Hine, 2011). Considering the importance of happiness for successful and productive workers and initial evidence suggesting that interventions in workplace settings can increase employee SWB, it is wise for organizations to continue allocating resources in pursuit of strategies to increase worker SWB in the long run.

Societal and Community Applications

As we mentioned at the outset of this chapter, societies are increasingly using measures of happiness as an indicator of national prosperity (Diener & Seligman, 2004; Diener & Tay, 2015; Tay et al., 2014). Researchers can now leverage this data to gain insight into societal policies and community features that promote happiness at larger group levels. Diener et al. (2015) recently reviewed characteristics of happy societies based on research leveraging cross-national comparisons. They highlighted a number of features of happy nations, including economic development and wealth; political freedoms and efficient and effective governments low in corruption; strong protections of human rights; progressive taxation policies; and generous income security, unemployment, and healthcare programs (Diener et al., 2015).

Furthermore, steps can be taken at the narrower community level to promote the happiness of locals. For one, lower levels of pollution in one's local area on a given day are associated with greater SWB (Levinson, 2012) and policies that reduce pollution can be important for the SWB of local citizens (Luechinger, 2009; MacKerron & Mourato, 2009). Furthermore, people tend to be happier when they are in natural green spaces compared to in urban settings (MacKerron & Mourato, 2013), and the presence of green space areas in one's community is associated with SWB (Hartig, Evans, Jamner, Davis, & Garling, 2003; Velarde, Fry, & Tveit, 2007). Thus, adding green spaces to community areas is among the ways to structure communities to make for happier citizens.

Prospective Research Directions

Although much has been learned about SWB over the past 30 years, and especially in the past decade, there are many promising directions for future research, both topically as well as methodologically and statistically. First, we suggest, and anticipate, that future research should/will continue to uncover nuances in understanding the effectiveness of different intervention techniques to increase happiness, and to sustain these gains over long periods of time. In addition, it is important for work to be done to examine the underlying mechanisms driving happiness changes to hone more effective strategies for improvements in this area moving forward. For example, the general model proposed by Lyubomirsky and Layous (2013) of how positive activity can lead to increased well-being will need to be tested rigorously in terms of both moderators (e.g. person–activity fit) and mediators (e.g. specific types of positive thoughts or feelings).

Second, we see the field of SWB research expanding to include a process-oriented view of happiness where we are concerned not merely about the levels of happiness but also the ebb and flow of it over time. Future work toward a further understanding of the determinants and consequences of the trajectories of happiness and unhappiness is warranted to complement the existing body of work focused on such effects on current levels of SWB. This focus will enable us to understand the growth and recovery of SWB, in lieu of different practices and life events. To achieve this, it will require the use of more time-sensitive measures and methodologies, such as experience sampling.

Lastly, we also anticipate and encourage a methodological and statistical shift, mirroring the field of psychology and other social sciences, toward a big data approach to happiness measurement and tracking. Researchers have already begun leveraging big data for SWB research, for example, by examining language used on Twitter to characterize SWB across US counties (Eichstaedt et al., 2013; Schwartz et al., 2016). This will enable the use of multiple methods to compare community and national levels of well-being in conjunction with more macro socio-economic conditions (e.g. corruption levels, culture, unemployment). Further, the use of social media, for instance, can give rise to nuanced information over time which may not be captured by large-scale community or national surveys that are usually administered over longer intervals (e.g. yearly). This will require SWB researchers to broaden their methodological expertise or build collaborative efforts in multidisciplinary teams to advance the measurement of well-being in societies.

References

Aderman, D. (1972). Elation, depression, and helping behavior. *Journal of Personality and Social Psychology, 24*, 91–101.

Aknin, L. B., Dunn, E. W., & Norton, M. I. (2012). Happiness runs in a circular motion: Evidence for a positive feedback loop between prosocial spending and happiness. *Journal of Happiness Studies, 13*, 347–355.

Amabile, T. M., Barsade, S. G., Mueller, J. S., & Staw, B. (2005). Affect and creativity at work. *Administrative Science Quarterly, 50*, 367–403.

Anusic, I., Yap, S. C., & Lucas, R. E. (2014). Testing set-point theory in a Swiss national sample: Reaction and adaptation to major life events. *Social Indicators Research, 119*, 1265–1288.

Barak, Y. (2006). The immune system and happiness. *Autoimmunity Reviews, 5*, 523–527.

Baron, R. A. (1987). Interviewer's moods and reactions to job applicants: The influence of affective states on applied social judgments. *Journal of Applied Social Psychology, 17*, 911–926.

Berry, D. S., & Hansen, J. S. (1996). Positive affect, negative affect, and social interaction. *Journal of Personality and Social Psychology, 71*, 796–809.

Bhattacharyya, M. R., Whitehead, D. L., Rakhit, R., & Steptoe, A. (2008). Depressed mood, positive affect, and heart rate variability in patients with suspected coronary artery disease. *Psychosomatic Medicine, 70*, 1020–1027.

Blanchflower, D. G., Oswald, A. J., & Stewart-Brown, S. (2013). Is psychological well-being linked to the consumption of fruit and vegetables? *Social Indicators Research, 114*, 785–801.

Bockerman, P., & Ilmakunnas, P. (2012). The job-satisfaction-productivity nexus: A study using matched survey and register data. *Industrial & Labor Relations Review, 65*, 244–262.

Boehm, J. K., & Lyubomirsky, S. (2008). Does happiness lead to career success? *Journal of Career Assessment, 16*, 101–116.

Boehm, J. K., Peterson, C., Kivimaki, M., & Kubzansky, L. (2011). A prospective study of positive psychological well-being and coronary heart disease. *Health Psychology, 30*, 259–267.

Bolier, L., Haverman, M., Westerhof, G. J., Riper, H., Smit, F., & Bohlmeijer, E. (2013). Positive psychology interventions: A meta-analysis of randomized controlled studies. *BMC Public Health*, *13*, 119.

Brickman, P., Coates, D., & Janoff-Bulman, R. (1978). Lottery winners and accident victims: Is happiness relative? *Journal of Personality and Social Psychology*, *36*, 917.

Brown, K. W., & Ryan, R. M. (2003). The benefits of being present: Mindfulness and its role in psychological well-being. *Journal of Personality and Social Psychology*, *84*, 822–848.

Bryant, F. B., & Veroff, J. (2007). *Savoring: A new model of positive experience.* Mahwah, NJ: Erlbaum Publishers.

Cantril, H. (1965). *The pattern of human concerns.* New Brunswick, NJ: Rutgers University Press.

Carnevale, P. J. (2008). Positive affect and decision frame in negotiation. *Group Decision and Negotiation*, *17*, 51–63.

Carnevale, P. J., & Isen, A. M. (1986). The influence of positive affect and visual access on the discovery of integrative solutions in bilateral negotiations. *Organizational Behavior and Human Decision Processes*, *37*, 1–13.

Chida, Y., & Steptoe, A. (2008). Positive psychological well-being and mortality: A quantitative review of prospective observational studies. *Psychosomatic Medicine*, *70*, 741–756.

Christian, L. M., Graham, J. E., Padgett, D. A., Glaser, R., & Kiecolt-Glaser, J. K. (2006). Stress and wound healing. *Neuroimmunomodulation*, *13*, 337–346.

Clark, A. E., Georgellis, Y., & Sanfey, P. (2001). Scarring: The psychological impact of past unemployment. *Economica*, *68*, 221–241.

Cohen, S., Doyle, W. J., Turner, R. B., Alper, C. M., & Skoner, D. P. (2003). Emotional style and susceptibility to the common cold. *Psychosomatic Medicine*, *65*, 652–657.

Cohen, S., & Pressman, S. D. (2006). Positive affect and health. *Current Directions in Psychological Science*, *15*, 122–125.

Connolly, J. J., & Viswesvaran, C. (2000). The role of affectivity in job satisfaction: A meta-analysis. *Personality and Individual Differences*, *29*, 265–281.

Cunningham, M. R. (1988a). What do you do when you're happy or blue? Mood, expectancies, and behavioral interest. *Motivation and Emotion*, *12*, 309–330.

Cunningham, M. R. (1988b). Does happiness mean friendliness? Induced mood and heterosexual self-disclosure. *Personality and Social Psychology Bulletin*, *14*, 283–297.

Cunningham, M. R., Steinberg, J., & Grev, R. (1980). Wanting to and having to help: Separate motivations for positive mood and guilt induced helping. *Journal of Personality and Social Psychology*, *38*, 181–192.

Danner, D. D., Snowdon, D. A., & Friesen, W. V. (2001). Positive emotions in early life and longevity: findings from the nun study. *Journal of Personality and Social Psychology*, *80*, 804–813.

Davidson, K. W., Mostofsky, E., & Whang, W. (2010). Don't worry, be happy: Positive affect and reduced 10-year incident coronary heart disease: The Canadian Nova Scotia Health Survey. *European Heart Journal*, *31*, 1065–1070.

De Neve, J. E., Diener, E., Tay, L., & Xuereb, C. (2013). The objective benefits of subjective well-being. In J. Helliwell, R. Layard, & J. Sachs (Eds.), *World Happiness Report 2013.* New York: UN Sustainable Development Solutions Network.

De Neve, J. E., & Oswald, A. J. (2012). Estimating the influence of life satisfaction and positive affect on later income using sibling fixed effects. *Proceedings of the National Academy of Sciences*, *109*, 19953–19958.

Devins, G. M., Mann, J., Mandin, H. P., & Leonard, C. (1990). Psychosocial predictors of survival in end-stage renal disease. *Journal of Nervous and Mental Disease, 178,* 127–133.

Diener, E. (1984). Subjective well-being. *Psychological Bulletin, 95,* 542–575.

Diener, E., & Chan, M. (2011). Happy people live longer: Subjective well-being contributes to health and longevity. *Applied Psychology: Health and Well-being, 3,* 1–43.

Diener, E., Diener, M., & Diener, C. (1995). Factors predicting the subjective well-being of nations. *Journal of Personality and Social Psychology, 69,* 851–864.

Diener, E., & Emmons, R. A. (1984). The independence of positive and negative affect. *Journal of Personality and Social Psychology, 47,* 1105–1117.

Diener, E., Emmons, R. A., Larsen, R. J., & Griffin, S. (1985). The satisfaction with life scale. *Journal of Personality Assessment, 49,* 71–75.

Diener, E., Gohm, C. L., Suh, E., & Oishi, S. (2000). Similarity of the relations between marital status and subjective well-being across cultures. *Journal of Cross-Cultural Psychology, 31,* 419–436.

Diener, E., Inglehart, R., & Tay, L. (2013). Theory and validity of life satisfaction scales. *Social Indicators Research, 112,* 497–527.

Diener, E., Nickerson, C., Lucas, R. E., & Sandvik, E. (2002). Dispositional affect and job outcomes. *Social Indicators Research, 59,* 229–259.

Diener, E., Oishi, S., & Lucas, R. E. (2015). National accounts of subjective well-being. *American Psychologist, 70,* 234–242.

Diener, E., Sandvik, E., Pavot, W., & Gallagher, D. (1991). Response artifacts in the measurement of subjective well-being. *Social Indicators Research, 24,* 35–56.

Diener, E., & Seligman, M. E. P. (2002). Very happy people. *Psychological Science, 13,* 81–84.

Diener, E., & Seligman, M. E. P. (2004). Beyond money: Toward an economy of well-being *Psychological Science in the Public Interest, 5,* 1–31.

Diener, E., Smith, H., & Fujita, F. (1995). The personality structure of affect. *Journal of Personality and Social Psychology, 69,* 130–141.

Diener, E., Suh, E. M., Smith, H., & Shao, L. (1995). National differences in reported subjective well-being: Why do they occur? *Social Indicators Research, 34,* 7–32.

Diener, E., & Tay, L. (2012). A scientific review of the remarkable benefits of happiness for successful and healthy living. *Report of the Well-Being Working Group, Royal Government of Bhutan: Report to the United Nations General Assembly, Well-Being and Happiness: A New Development Paradigm,* UN, New York.

Diener, E., & Tay, L. (2015). Subjective well-being and human welfare around the world as reflected in the Gallup World Poll. *International Journal of Psychology, 50,* 135-149.

Diener, E., Tay, L., & Oishi, S. (2013). Rising income and the subjective well-being of nations. *Journal of Personality and Social Psychology, 104,* 267–276.

Diener, E., Wirtz, D., Tov, W., Kim-Prieto, C., Choi, D. W., Oishi, S., & Biswas-Diener, R. (2010). New well-being measures: Short scales to assess flourishing and positive and negative feelings. *Social Indicators Research, 97,* 143–156.

Edmans, A. (2012). The link between job satisfaction and firm value, with implications for corporate social responsibility. *The Academy of Management Perspectives, 26,* 1–19.

Edwards, J. R., & Cooper, C. L. (1988). The impacts of positive psychological states on physical health: A review and theoretical framework. *Social Science and Medicine, 12,* 1447–1459.

Egloff, B. (1998). The independence of positive and negative affect depends on the affect measure. *Personality and Individual Differences, 25,* 1101–1109.

Eichstaedt, J. C., Schwartz, H. A., Kern, M. L., Dziurzynski, L., Lucas, R. E., Agrawal, M., … Ungar, L. H. (2013). *Characterizing geographic variation in well-being using tweets.* Seventh International AAAI Conference on Weblogs and Social Media. Boston, MA.

Emmons, R. A., & McCullough, M. E. (2003). Counting blessings versus burdens: An experimental investigation of gratitude and subjective wellbeing in daily life. *Journal of Personality and Social Psychology, 84,* 377–389.

Feingold, A. (1983). Happiness, unselfishness, and popularity. *Journal of Psychology, 115,* 3–5.

Forgas, J. P. (1998). On feeling good and getting your way: Mood effects on negotiator cognition and bargaining strategies. *Journal of Personality and Social Psychology, 74,* 565–577.

Forgas, J. P., Dunn, E., & Granland, S. (2008). Are you being served? An unobtrusive experiment of affective influences on helping in a department store. *European Journal of Social Psychology, 38,* 333–342.

Fredrickson, B. L., & Levenson, R. W. (1998). Positive emotions speed recovery from the cardiovascular sequelae of negative emotions. *Cognition and Emotion, 12,* 191–220.

George, J. M., & Zhou, J. (2007). Dual tuning in a supportive context: Joint contributions of positive mood, negative mood, and supervisory behaviors to employee creativity. *Management Journal, 50,* 605–622.

Goudie, R. J., Mukherjee, S., De Neve, J. E., Oswald, A. J., & Wu, S. (2014). Happiness as a driver of risk-avoiding behaviour: Theory and an empirical study of seatbelt wearing and automobile accidents. *Economica, 81,* 674–697.

Graham, C., Eggers, A., & Sukhtankar, S. (2004). Does happiness pay? An exploration based on panel data from Russia. *Journal of Economic Behavior & Organization, 55,* 319–342.

Grant, N., Wardle, J., & Steptoe, A. (2009). The relationship between life satisfaction and health behaviour: A cross-cultural analysis of young adults. *International Journal of Behavioral Medicine, 16,* 259–268.

Gray, E. K., & Watson, D. (2007). Assessing positive and negative affect via self-report. In J. A. Coan & J. J. B. Allen (Eds.), *Handbook of emotion elicitation and assessment* (pp. 171–183). New York: Oxford University Press.

Harmon-Jones, E., Harmon-Jones, C., Abramson, L., & Peterson, C. K. (2009). PANAS positive activation is associated with anger. *Emotion, 9,* 183–196.

Harter, J. K., Schmidt, F. L., Asplund, J. W., Killham, E. A., & Agrawal, S. (2010). Causal impact of employee work perceptions on the bottom line of organizations. *Perspectives on Psychological Science, 5,* 378–389.

Hartig, T., Evans, G. W., Jamner, L. D., Davis, D. S., & Garling, T. (2003). Tracking restoration in natural and urban field settings. *Journal of Environmental Psychology, 23,* 109–123.

Headey, B., & Veenhoven, R. (1989). Does happiness induce a rosy outlook? In R. Veenhoven (Ed.), *How harmful is happiness? Consequences of enjoying life or not* (pp. 106–127). Rotterdam, The Netherlands: Universitaire Pers Rotterdam.

Heintzelman, S. J., Trent, J., & King, L. A. (2015). Revisiting desirable response bias in well-being reports. *The Journal of Positive Psychology, 10,* 167–178.

Howell, R. T., Kern, M. L., & Lyubomirsky, S. (2007). Health benefits: Meta-analytically determining the impact of well-being on objective health outcomes. *Health Psychology Review, 1,* 83–136.

Hülsheger, U. R., Alberts, H. J. E. M., Feinholdt, A., & Lang, J. W. B. (2013). Benefits of mindfulness at work: The role of mindfulness in emotion regulation, emotional exhaustion, and job satisfaction. *Journal of Applied Psychology, 98,* 310–325.

Isen, A. M. (1970). Success, failure, attention and reaction to others: The warm glow of success. *Journal of Personality and Social Psychology, 15,* 294–301.

James, G. D., Yee, L. S., Harshfield, G. A., Blank, S. G., & Pickering, T. G. (1986). The influence of happiness, anger, and anxiety on the blood pressure of borderline hypertensives. *Psychosomatic Medicine, 48,* 502–508.

Jovanović, V. (2015). Beyond the PANAS: Incremental validity of the scale of positive and negative experience (SPANE) in relation to well-being. *Personality and Individual Differences, 86,* 487–491.

Judge, T. A., Piccolo, R. F., Podsakoff, N. P., Shaw, J. C., & Rich, B. L. (2010). The relationship between pay and job satisfaction: A meta-analysis of the literature. *Journal of Vocational Behavior, 77,* 157–167.

Judge, T. A., Scott, B. A., & Ilies, R. (2006). Hostility, job attitudes, and workplace deviance: Test of a multilevel model. *Journal of Applied Psychology, 91,* 126–138.

Judge, T. A., Thoreson, C. J., Bono, J. E., & Patton, G. K. (2001). The job satisfaction-job performance relationship: A qualitative and quantitative review. *Psychological Bulletin, 127,* 376–407.

Kahneman, D., & Deaton, A. (2010). High income improves evaluation of life but not emotional well-being. *Proceedings of National Academy of Sciences, 107,* 16489–16493.

Kazdin, A. E., Esveldt-Dawson, K., & Matson, J. L. (1982). Changes in children's social skills performance as a function of preassessment experiences. *Journal of Clinical Child Psychology, 11,* 243–248.

Kiecolt-Glaser, J. K., McGuire, L., Robles, T. F., & Glaser, R. (2002). Emotions, morbidity, and mortality: New perspectives from psychoneuroimmunology. *Annual Review of Psychology, 53,* 83–107.

King, L. A. (2001). The health benefits of writing about life goals. *Personality and Social Psychology Bulletin, 27,* 798–807.

Kirk, B. A., Schutte, N. S., & Hine, D. W. (2011). The effect of an expressive-writing intervention for employees on emotional self efficacy, emotional intelligence, affect, and workplace incivility. *Journal of Applied Social Psychology, 41,* 179–195.

Krause, J. S., Sternberg, M., Lottes, S., & Maides, J. (1997). Mortality after spinal cord injury: An 11-year prospective study. *Archives of Physical Medicine and Rehabilitation, 78,* 815–821.

Kuykendall, L., & Tay, L. (2015). Employee subjective well-being and physiological functioning: An integrative model. *Health Psychology Open, 2,* 1-11.

Lambert, N. M., Gwinn, A. M., Baumeister, R. F., Strachman, A., Washburn, I. J., Gable, S. L., & Fincham, F. D. (2013). A boost of positive affect: The perks of sharing positive experiences. *Journal of Social and Personal Relationships, 30,* 24–43.

Levinson, A. (2012). Valuing public goods using happiness data: The case of air quality. *Journal of Public Economics, 96,* 869–880.

Levy, S. M., Lee, J., Bagley, C., & Lippman, M. (1988). Survival hazard analysis in first recurrent breast cancer patients: Seven-year follow-up. *Psychosomatic Medicine, 50,* 520–528.

Lucas, R. E. (2001). Pleasant affect and sociability: Towards a comprehensive model of extraverted feelings and behaviors. *Dissertation Abstracts International, 61*(10-B), 5610.

Lucas, R. E. (2007). Adaptation and the set-point model of subjective well-being: Does happiness change after major life events? *Current Directions in Psychological Science, 16*, 75–79.

Lucas, R. E., Clark, A. E., Georgellis, Y., & Diener, E. (2003). Reexamining adaptation and the set point model of happiness: Reactions to changes in marital status. *Journal of Personality and Social Psychology, 84*, 527–539.

Luechinger, S. (2009). Valuing air quality using the life satisfaction approach. *The Economic Journal, 119*, 482–515.

Luhmann, M., Hofmann, W., Eid, M., & Lucas, R. E. (2012). Subjective well-being and adaptation to life events: A meta-analysis. *Journal of Personality and Social Psychology, 102*, 592–615.

Lykken, D., & Tellegen, A. (1996). Happiness is a stochastic phenomenon. *Psychological Science, 7*, 186–189.

Lyubomirsky, S., Dickerhoof, R., Boehm, J. K., & Sheldon, K. M. (2011). Becoming happier takes both a will and a proper way: An experimental longitudinal intervention to boost well-being. *Emotion, 11*, 391–402.

Lyubomirsky, S., King, L. A., & Diener, E. (2005). The benefits of frequent positive affect: Does happiness lead to success? *Psychological Bulletin, 131*, 803–855.

Lyubomirsky, S., & Layous, K. (2013). How do simple positive activities increase well-being? *Current Directions in Psychological Science, 22*, 57–62.

Lyubomirsky, S., Sheldon, K. M., & Schkade, D. (2005). Pursuing happiness: The architecture of sustainable change. *Review of General Psychology, 9*, 111–131.

MacKerron, G., & Mourato, S. (2009). Life satisfaction and air quality in London makes a better life? The determinants of subjective well-being in OECD countries. *Ecological Economics, 68*, 1441–1453.

MacKerron, G., & Mourato, S. (2013). Happiness is greater in natural environments. *Global Environmental Change, 23*, 992–1000.

Maier, H., & Smith, J. (1999). Psychological predictors of mortality in old age. *Journal of Gerontology, 54B*, 44–54.

Marsland, A. L., Pressman, S. D., & Cohen, S. (2007). Positive affect and immune function. In R. Ader (Ed.), *Psychoneuroimmunology* (pp. 761–779). San Diego, CA: Elsevier Publications.

Mehl, M. R., Vazire, S., Holleran, S. E., & Clark, C. S. (2010). Eavesdropping on happiness: Well-being is related to having less small talk and more substantive conversations. *Psychological Science, 21*, 539–541.

Nelson, D. W. (2009). Feeling good and open-minded: The impact of positive affect on cross cultural empathic responding. *The Journal of Positive Psychology, 4*, 53–63.

Nes, R. B., & Roysamb, E. (2015). The heritability of subjective well-being: Review and meta-analysis. In M. Pluess (Ed.), *The genetics of psychological well-being: The role of heritability and genetics in positive psychology.* (pp. 75–96). Oxford: Oxford University Press.

Oishi, S., Diener, E., & Lucas, R. (2007). The optimum level of well-being: Can people be too happy? *Perspectives on Psychological Science, 2*, 346–360.

Oishi, S., Kesebir, S., & Diener, E. (2011). Income inequality and happiness. *Psychological Science, 22*, 1095–1100.

O'Malley, M. N., & Andrews, L. (1983). The effect of mood and incentives on helping: Are there some things money can't buy? *Motivation and Emotion, 7*, 179–189.

Ostir, G. V., Markides, K. S., Peek, M. K., & Goodwin, J. S. (2001). The association between emotional well-being and the incidence of stroke in older adults. *Psychosomatic Medicine, 63,* 210–215.

Ouweneel, E., Le Blanc, P. M., & Schaufeli, W. B. (2013). Do it yourself: An online positive psychology intervention to promote positive emotions, self-efficacy, and engagement at work. *The Career Development International, 18,* 173–195.

Parks, A. C., & Schueller, S. M. (Eds.). (2014). *The Wiley-Blackwell handbook of positive psychological interventions.* Chichester: Wiley-Blackwell.

Pavot, W., & Diener, E. D. (1993). Review of the satisfaction with life scale. *Psychological Assessment, 5,* 164–172.

Pavot, W., Diener, E. D., Colvin, C. R., & Sandvik, E. (1991). Further validation of the satisfaction with life scale: Evidence for the cross-method convergence of well-being measures. *Journal of Personality Assessment, 57,* 149–161.

Pelled, L. H., & Xin, K. R. (1999). Down and out: An investigation of the relationship between mood and employee withdrawal behavior. *Journal of Management, 25,* 875–895.

Peterson, S. J., Luthans, F., Avolio, B. J., Walumbwa, F. O., & Zhang, Z. (2011). Psychological capital and employee performance: A latent growth modeling approach. *Personnel Psychology, 64,* 427–450.

Pinquart, M., & Sörensen, S. (2000). Influences of socioeconomic status, social network, and competence on subjective well-being in later life: A meta-analysis. *Psychology and Aging, 15,* 187–224.

Podsakoff, N. P., LePine, J. A., & LePine, M. A. (2007). Differential challenge stressor-hindrance stressor relationships with job attitudes, turnover intentions, turnover, and withdrawal behavior: A meta-analysis. *Journal of Applied Psychology, 92,* 438–454.

Priller, E., & Schupp, J. (2011). Social and economic characteristics of financial and blood donors in Germany. *DIW Economic Bulletin, 6,* 23–30.

Pressman, S. D., & Cohen, S. (2005). Does positive affect influence health? *Psychological Bulletin, 131,* 925–971.

Quoidbach, J., Mikolajczak, M., & Gross, J. J. (2015). Positive interventions: An emotion regulation perspective. *Psychological Bulletin, 141,* 655–693.

Richardson, K. M., & Rothstein, H. R. (2008). Effects of occupational stress management intervention programs: A meta-analysis. *Journal of Occupational Health Psychology, 13,* 69–93.

Riketta, M. (2008). The causal relation between job attitudes and performance: A meta-analysis of panel studies. *Journal of Applied Psychology, 93,* 472–481.

Rosenhan, D. L., Underwood, B., & Moore, B. (1974). Affect moderates self-gratification and altruism. *Journal of Personality and Social Psychology, 30,* 546–552.

Roysamb, E., Nes, R. B., & Vitterso, J. (2014). Well-being: Heritable and changeable. In K. M. Sheldon & R. E. Lucas (Eds.), *Stability of happiness: Theories and evidence on whether happiness can change* (pp. 9–36). Amsterdam, The Netherlands: Academic Press.

Sandstrom, G. M., & Dunn, E. W. (2014). Social interactions and well-being: The surprising power of weak ties. *Personality and Social Psychology Bulletin, 40,* 910–922.

Sandvik, E., Diener, E., & Seidlitz, L. (1993) Subjective well-being: The convergence and stability of self-report and non-self-report measures. *Journal of Personality, 61,* 317–342.

Scheier, M. F., Matthews, K. A., Owens, J. F., Magovern, G. J., Lefebvre, R. C., Abbott, R. A., & Carver, C. S. (1989). Dispositional optimism and recovery from coronary artery bypass surgery: The beneficial effects on physical and psychological well-being. *Journal of Personality and Social Psychology*, *57*, 1024–1040.

Schimmack, U., & Oishi, S. (2005). The influence of chronically and temporarily accessible information on life satisfaction judgments. *Journal of Personality and Social Psychology*, *89*, 395–406.

Schnall, P. L., Pieper, C., Schwartz, J. E., Karasek, R. A., Schlussel, Y., Devereux, R. B., ... Pickering, T. G. (1990). The relationship between "job strain," workplace diastolic blood pressure, and left ventricular mass index: Results of a case-control study. *JAMA*, *263*, 1929–1935.

Schwartz, H. A., Sap, M., Kern, M. L., Eichstaedt, J. C., Kapelner, A., Agrawal, M., ... Ungar, L. H. (2016). Predicting individual well-being through the language of social media. *Pacific Symposium on Biocomputing*, *21*, 516–527.

Seidlitz, L., & Diener, E. (1993). Memory for positive versus negative life events: Theories for the differences between happy and unhappy persons. *Journal of Personality and Social Psychology*, *64*, 654–664.

Seligman, M. E., Steen, T. A., Park, N., & Peterson, C. (2005). Positive psychology progress: Empirical validation of interventions. *American Psychologist*, *60*, 410–421.

Silva, A. J., & Caetano, A. (2013). Validation of the flourishing scale and scale of positive and negative experience in Portugal. *Social Indicators Research*, *110*, 469–478.

Sin, N. L., & Lyubomirsky, S. (2009). Enhancing well-being and alleviating depressive symptoms with positive psychology interventions: A practice-friendly meta-analysis. *Journal of Clinical Psychology*, *65*, 467–487.

Slopen, N., Kubzansky, L. D., McLaughlin, K. A., & Koenen, K. C. (2013). Childhood adversity and inflammatory processes in youth: A prospective study. *Psychoneuroendocrinology*, *38*, 188–200.

Spanier, G. B., & Furstenberg, F. F. (1982). Remarriage after divorce: A longitudinal analysis of well-being. *Journal of Marriage and the Family*, *44*, 709–720.

Spector, P. E., & Fox, S. (2002). An emotion-centered model of voluntary work behavior: Some parallels between counterproductive work behavior and organizational citizenship behavior. *Human Resource Management Review*, *12*, 269–292.

Staw, B. M., Sutton, R. I., & Pelled, L. H. (1994). Employee positive emotion and favorable outcomes at the workplace. *Organization Science*, *5*, 51–71.

Steptoe, A., Dockray, S., & Wardle, J. (2009). Positive affect and psychobiological processes relevant to health. *Journal of Personality*, *77*, 1747–1776.

Steptoe, A., Wardle, J., & Marmot, M. (2005). Positive affect and health-related neuroendocrine, cardiovascular, and inflammatory processes. *Proceedings of National Academy of Sciences*, *102*, 6508–6512.

Strine, T. W., Mokdad, A. H., Dube, S. R., Balluz, L. S., Gonzalez, O., Berry, J. T., ... Kroenke, K. (2008). The association of depression and anxiety with obesity and unhealthy behaviors among community-dwelling US adults. *General Hospital Psychiatry*, *30*, 127–137.

Stutzer, A., & Frey, B. S. (2006). Does marriage make people happy, or do happy people get married? *Journal of Socio-Economics*, *35*, 326–347.

Sumi, K. (2014). Reliability and validity of Japanese versions of the flourishing scale and the scale of positive and negative experience. *Social Indicators Research*, *118*, 601–615.

Tan, K., & Tay, L. (2015). Relationships and well-being. In R. Biswas-Diener & E. Diener (Eds.), *Noba textbook series: Psychology*. Champaign, IL: DEF Publishers. Retrieved from www.nobaproject.com.

Tay, L., Chan, D., & Diener, E. (2014). The metrics of societal happiness. *Social Indicators Research, 117*, 577–600.

Tay, L., & Diener, E. (2011). Needs and subjective well-being around the world. *Journal of Personality and Social Psychology, 101*, 354–365.

Tay, L., Herian, M. N., & Diener, E. (2014). Detrimental effects of corruption on subjective well-being: Whether, how, and when. *Social Psychological and Personality Science, 5*, 751–759.

Tay, L., & Kuykendall, L. (2013). Promoting happiness: The malleability of individual and societal-level happiness. *International Journal of Psychology, 48*, 159–176.

Thoits, P. A., & Hewitt, L. N. (2001). Volunteer work and well-being. *Journal of Health and Social Behavior, 42*, 115–131.

Thompson, E. R. (2007). Development and validation of an internationally reliable short-form of the positive and negative affect schedule (PANAS). *Journal of Cross-Cultural Psychology, 38*, 227–242.

Vanhove, A. J., Herian, M. N., Perez, A. L. U., Harms, P. D., & Lester, P. B. (2016). Can resilience be developed at work? A meta-analytic review of resilience-building programme effectiveness. *Journal of Occupational and Organizational Psychology, 8*, 278–307.

Velarde, M. D., Fry, G., & Tveit, M. (2007). Health effects of viewing landscapes: Landscape types in environmental psychology. *Urban Forestry & Urban Greening, 6*, 199–212.

Watson, D., Clark, L. A., & Tellegen, A. (1988). Development and validation of brief measures of positive and negative affect: The PANAS scales. *Journal of Personality and Social Psychology, 54*, 1063–1070.

Williams, S., & Shiaw, W. T. (1999). Mood and organizational citizenship behavior: The effects of positive affect on employee organizational citizenship behavior intentions. *Journal of Psychology, 133*, 656–668.

3
POSITIVE EMOTIONS AND WELL-BEING

Khoa D. Le Nguyen and Barbara L. Fredrickson

In comparison to the negative feelings that we typically try to avoid, less is known about the positive emotions that we seek. Most people recognize that fear, anger, and sadness are bitter medicines that are sometimes necessary, as they come with the urges to "fight, flight, or freeze" that have ensured the survival of the human species. In contrast, positive emotions have long been thought to be sweet candies with unknown nutritional value. They are pleasant, yet their functions and mechanisms of action have remained mysterious. After a rich history of studying mostly negative emotions (e.g. Ekman, 1992; Izard, 1977), psychologists in the late 1990s began to wrestle with neglected questions such as "What evolutionary functions do positive emotions serve?" "What are the mechanisms of actions of positive emotions?" and "What purposes do positive emotions serve beyond providing pleasure?"

The ensuing research has revealed that positive emotions serve a wide range of essential human needs. Happier people have better physical health, live longer (Pressman & Cohen, 2005) and are more successful (Lyubomirsky, King, & Diener, 2005), creative (Isen, Daubman, & Nowicki, 1987), and socially connected (Cavanaugh, Bettman, & Luce, 2015). Moreover, everyday positive emotions are not merely the reflection of health and superior psychological functioning, but rather play an active role in cultivating well-being through multiple pathways (for a review, see Fredrickson, 2013). The broaden-and-build theory of positive emotions (Fredrickson, 1998, 2001) proposes that these pleasant feelings create measurable changes, ranging from calming cardiac activity to broadening visual attention and action urges. These changes, as they accumulate over time, are theorized to build up a person's durable biopsychosocial resources, such as their cardiac vagal tone, resilience, spirituality, mindfulness, creativity, and prosociality. Such resources, in turn, may help a person benefit even more from subsequent positive emotions, thereby creating a self-sustaining, upward spiral toward well-being—a counterpart to the downward spirals of anxiety and depression well-known to clinical psychologists (Garland et al., 2010).

An increasing body of research has supported the broaden-and-build theory by shedding light on the causal effect of positive emotions on well-being via biological and psychological pathways (e.g. Fredrickson, 2013; Pressman & Cohen, 2005). The effects of positive emotions on well-being are also complex, as they appear to vary across individuals, situations, and cultures. For example, research on bipolar disorder reveals that excessive positive emotions and overvaluation of happiness are related to poor mental health (Gruber, Mauss, & Tamir, 2011). Cross-cultural studies also suggest that whether or not a person reaps the benefits of positive emotions depends on cultural context (Leersnyder, Kim, & Mesquita, 2015). For example, positive affect predicts lower levels of healthy biomarkers for Japanese individuals who are socially disconnected, but seems to benefit Americans in general (Yoo, Miyamoto, & Ryff, 2016). These developments reveal how researchers have incorporated psychological and cultural perspectives into a nuanced, well-rounded understanding of how positive emotions affect people's lives.

In this chapter, after outlining our working definition of positive emotions, we provide an overview of the broaden-and-build theory, which offers a framework for understanding the relationship between positive emotions and well-being. Next, we review the empirical evidence for the theory, including that on how positive emotions "build" various components of well-being, such as psychological resilience. We then take a closer look at the relations between positive emotions and physical health, touching both on health behaviors and plausible biological mechanisms. We then explore how the effects of positive emotions are contingent on dosage, specific types of emotions, and cultural context. Finally, we offer evidence-based strategies to help individuals pursue happiness and well-being, and close with suggestions for future research.

Broaden-and-Build: Theory and Evidence

Emotions are a subclass of affective phenomena. Affect is a neurophysiological state that is subjectively experienced as being pleasant versus unpleasant (valence) and being sleepy versus activated (arousal). An emotion is an affective episode comprised of multiple, loosely coupled components such as affect, the attribution of affect to a prior event, cognitive appraisal, thought patterns, facial movements, and action urges (Russell, 2003). In this chapter, we use "emotion" to refer to this multicomponent affective phenomenon, although we may use "emotion" and "affect" interchangeably when referring to a group of emotions that share the same affect. By "positive emotions," we mean emotions that are generally perceived as both pleasant and desirable. These emotions include, but are not limited to, amusement, awe, contentment, joy, gratitude, hope, elevation, curiosity, love, and pride.

Using this definition of positive emotions, the broaden-and-build theory first hypothesizes that such emotions "broaden" cognition and attention. Ample evidence has shown that negative emotions narrow attention and cognition, and trigger specific action tendencies (Frijda, Kuipers, & Ter Schure, 1989; Schmitz, De Rosa, & Anderson, 2009). Moreover, repeated and prolonged negative emotions can cause "wear and tear" on the body (McEwen, 1998). The broaden-and-build theory proposes that positive emotions function as complements to narrowing and depleting negative emotions. Rather than prompting specific action tendencies and fixation on thoughts centered on self-preservation, positive emotions expand the range of ideas and action urges, and increase flexibility to switch between thoughts and behaviors (Fredrickson, 1998, 2001). In contrast to "fight, flight, or freeze," positive emotions facilitate approaching, exploring, as well as other-focused thoughts and prosocial behaviors.

Decades of research have provided evidence that certain types of positive emotions may broaden individuals' thoughts–action repertoire and enhance their cognitive flexibility (Fredrickson, 2013). Positive emotions that broaden tend to have a low motivational component and be associated with "liking" something (e.g. amusement, contentment) whereas highly motivational emotions associated with "wanting," such as desire, appear to the narrow scope of attention (Harmon-Jones, Gable, & Price, 2013). The former has been demonstrated to enhance the breadth of visual attention in lab experiments that use cognitive tasks (Fredrickson & Branigan, 2005; Rowe, Hirsch, & Anderson, 2007) and eye-tracking (Wadlinger & Issacowirtz, 2006). An fMRI study found that induced positive affect enhanced perceptual encoding of peripheral brain areas in the parahippocampal place area, indicating an expanded visual field of view, whereas induced negative affect had the opposite effect (Schmitz et al., 2009). These results suggest that the broadening process takes place at an early selection stage of visual inputs.

In addition to expanding visual awareness, laboratory experiments have also shown that positive emotions broaden thoughts in various ways. They increase the breadth of people's action urges (Fredrickson & Branigan, 2005), generate more inclusive categorization (Isen & Daubman, 1984), enhance creativity by enlarging conceptual space and creating more connections between ideas (Rowe et al., 2007), and promote openness to new experiences (Kahn & Isen, 1993) and information, including negative information that could benefit the self (Reed & Aspinwall, 1998). Similarly, positive emotions also "open up" social thoughts and behaviors. Studies have shown, for instance, that pleasant affect increases inclusivity in social categorization (Dovidio, Gaertner, Isen, & Lowrance, 1995), enhances recognition of distinctive outgroup faces (Johnson & Fredrickson, 2005), promotes self-other overlap (Waugh & Fredrickson, 2006), and fosters trust (Dunn & Schweitzer, 2005).

The second hypothesis of the broaden-and-build theory proposes that, over time, the cognitive openness and behavioral flexibility associated with positive emotions help individuals "build" enduring biopsychosocial resources that are conducive to long-term survival and flourishing. The theory provides a framework that connects hedonic well-being, or momentary pleasant feelings, to eudaimonic well-being, a more enduring form of well-being associated with meaning and purpose, or otherwise transcending self-interest to connect to something larger (Fredrickson, 2016).

Accumulating evidence supports this hypothesis, documenting that positive emotions build long-term personal resources, such as psychological resilience, the ability to bounce back from adversity (Fredrickson, Cohn, Coffey, Pek, & Finkel, 2008; Tugade & Fredrickson, 2007). The broadened and flexible thinking that positive emotions engender appears to pave the way for adaptive coping strategies, such as positive appraisal, problem-focused coping, or finding positive meaning (Folkman & Moskowitz, 2000; Tugade & Fredrickson, 2004). Crucially, the relationship between positive emotions and "broad-minded" coping is reciprocal, with each enhancing the other to form an upward spiral of improving resilience and emotional well-being (Fredrickson & Joiner, 2002). Over longer timespans, this reciprocal dynamic "builds" individuals' enduring coping resources that can be drawn on later, when adversity inevitably arises.

Additional evidence that positive emotions are active ingredients that cultivate resilience comes from a diary study; over a period of one month, individuals' day-to-day experiences of positive emotions predicted increases in their resilience and life satisfaction over the same time span (Cohn, Fredrickson, Brown, Mikels, & Conway, 2009). Mediational analyses further revealed that daily positive emotions predicted increased life satisfaction through associated increases in resilience. This pattern of results suggests that positive emotions do not simply reflect life satisfaction, but, more significantly, day-to-day pleasant feelings help build resources for adapting to life's challenges, which in turn makes life more satisfying.

Initial causal evidence for the build hypothesis comes from a longitudinal experiment (Fredrickson et al., 2008) in which participants were randomly assigned to attend a 6-week workshop on loving-kindness meditation (LKM), a traditional practice centered on cultivating friendly warm-heartedness, or to a monitoring waitlist control group. Diary data suggest that participants in the LKM group experienced increases in daily positive emotions over eight weeks, which in turn predicted increases in personal resources such as resilience, mindfulness, and purpose in life. These gains in resources, in turn, predicted increases in life satisfaction and decreases in depressive symptoms. Further causal evidence for the build hypothesis suggests that positive emotions also augment social resources, which can buffer individuals from stress. People who self-generated positive emotions via LKM, for instance, show heightened levels of social support (Fredrickson et al., 2008) and greater perceptions of social connectedness (Kok et al., 2013). In short, positive emotions spur the development of both psychological and social resources for coping, fostering greater resilience to life's ups and downs.

Positive Emotions and Physical Heath

Beyond building psychological resilience, positive emotions may also build behavioral and biological resources that benefit physical health (Kok et al., 2013). Ample evidence has shown that positive emotions and related constructs, such as subjective well-being, are linked to better health, greater longevity, and various beneficial biological processes (Boehm & Kubzansky, 2012; Chida & Steptoe, 2008; Pressman & Cohen, 2005). Positive emotions may help to improve health via two pathways: by promoting positive health behaviors, or more directly, by altering the body's biophysiological processes and resources.

Positive emotions are associated with a range of positive health behaviors, such as better sleep quality (Ong et al., 2013) and engagement in enjoyable restorative activities, such as vacationing or pursuing hobbies (Pressman et al., 2009). In the United States as well as in many European and Asian countries, higher life satisfaction—a close correlate of trait positive emotions (see Cohn et al., 2009)—predicts less smoking, more physical activity, and (in some continents) more sun protection and greater fruit intake (Grant, Wardle, & Steptoe, 2009). Although these associations do not allow causal inferences, lagged analyses in one diary study find that today's fruit and vegetable consumption predict increases in tomorrow's positive affect (White, Horwath, & Conner, 2013). Further research, particularly experimental evidence, is needed in this area (Cameron, Bertenshaw, & Sheeran, 2015).

New evidence regarding whether positive emotions affect positive health behavior comes from research on positive spontaneous thoughts and passion. This research draws insights from behavioral neuroscience, which categorizes the human reward system into a "liking" system, responsible for the enjoyment of an activity, and a "wanting" system, responsible for motivating activity engagement (Berridge, 2007). Positive emotions experienced during a positive health behavior, or "liking," may act as cues that trigger subsequent motivation, or "wanting," to engage in that health behavior. Recent research suggests that spontaneous thoughts about a particular behavior that are imbued with pleasant affect may function as "wanting" cues that automatically motivate subsequent engagement in that behavior. In a cross-sectional study, for instance, greater harmonious passion for an activity such as reading or taking part in a sport (as opposed to obsessive passion for it) was associated with greater positivity of spontaneous thoughts about that activity (Rice & Fredrickson, 2016). In another study in the same paper, positive spontaneous thoughts about physical activity (e.g. exercises or muscle-strengthening activities) accounted for (mediated) the association between harmonious passion for physical activity and people's daily physical activities over the ensuing two weeks (Rice & Fredrickson, 2016). These findings suggest that spontaneous thoughts laden with pleasant affect may function as a causal mechanism that links positive emotions to the maintenance of positive health behaviors.

Positive emotions may also improve physical health more directly by impacting the body's biophysiological systems, such as habitual cardiovascular activity. Dispositional levels of positive emotions have been associated with one such biological resource: cardiac vagal tone (Oveis, Cohen, Gruber, Shiota, & Haidt, 2009). Cardiac vagal tone is an index of autonomic flexibility, the capacity of the parasympathetic nervous system to adapt to changing environments by modulating attention, arousal, respiration, and heart rate (Friedman & Thayer, 1998; Porges, 1995). Although cardiac vagal tone is often considered a stable trait-like resource (Oveis et al., 2009), correlational evidence from a 9-week longitudinal study has shown that day-to-day increases in positive emotions predict increases in cardiac vagal tone at end of study (Kok & Fredrickson, 2010). In the same study, participants had been randomly assigned to learn LKM or to serve in a waitlist control group (Kok et al., 2013). Although all participants, regardless of experimental conditions, had shown a relation between increased positive emotions and increased cardiac vagal tone (Kok & Fredrickson, 2010), compared to the control group, those randomized to learn LKM showed greater increases in positive emotions, which in turn predicted greater increases in cardiac vagal tone. Moreover, higher baseline cardiac vagal tone appeared to allow participants in the LKM group to generate daily positive emotions to a greater degree. This mutually enhancing relationship between positive emotions and cardiac vagal tone may reflect an upward spiral of increasing emotional well-being and this biological index of physical health. Such an upward dynamic over time may augment stable physiological resources, such as vagal function, which in turn facilitate social functioning (Porges, 1995) and protect individuals against the risk of cardiovascular disease (Thayer & Lane, 2007). In short, positive emotions may also improve physical health through helping individuals to build beneficial biological resources.

Positive Emotions Across Cultures

The effects of positive emotions on well-being may depend on a person's cultural context. Cultures have different conceptions of well-being, and as such, well-being appears to be attained by pursuing diverging goals (Ryff et al., 2014; Uchida, Norasakkunkit, & Kitayama, 2004). In European-American individualist societies, well-being is linked to the pursuit of personal happiness, independence, and achievement. In contrast, in East Asian collectivist countries, such as Japan or China, well-being involves maintaining interdependence and social harmony, even at the cost of individuals' positive emotions.

Due to the differences in cultural goals and conceptions of well-being, people in collectivistic and individualistic societies tend to value and regulate positive feelings differently. Emotions like pride and happiness are more often considered to be good in a Western context, as they fit with the goal of personal fulfillment. Compared to East Asians or Asian Americans, European Americans tend to value high arousal positive emotions such as joy, enthusiasm, excitement, and pride (Tsai, 2007; Tsai, Knutson, & Fung, 2006). Therefore, they more frequently strive to maximize such positive emotions and minimize negative emotions (Ryff et al., 2014). In contrast, in an East Asian context, personal pride and happiness are perceived to potentially invite jealousy and disharmony in social relationships, thereby decreasing well-being. Relative to European Americans, East Asians, and Asian Americans tend to value low arousal positive affect, such as calmness and serenity (Tsai et al., 2006). Therefore, they more frequently strive to balance positive and negative emotions to achieve moderation (Ryff et al., 2014). They appear to do this by engaging in less hedonic emotion up-regulation after negative events (Miyamoto, Ma, & Petermann, 2014) or by feeling more concerned and responsible for others' emotions in a self-success situation (Miyamoto, Uchida, & Ellsworth, 2010) compared to European Americans. Consistent with these findings, North Americans, relative to East Asians, report feeling more pleasant in response to daily events (Mesquita & Karasawa, 2002).

Because high arousal positive affect is not as highly valued in East Asian collectivistic societies, there exists a general consensus that positive emotions seem to play a lesser role in judgments of life satisfaction in East Asian compared to Western cultures (Diener, Scollon, Oishi, Dzokoto, & Suh, 2000; Oishi, 2002; however, see Oishi, Diener, Choi, Kim-Prieto, & Choi, 2007 for opposite findings on daily satisfaction). Compared to East Asians, Westerners tend to remember more positive than negative events, rely more on positive and less on negative aspects of life in their judgment of life satisfaction, and report higher global life satisfaction. Similarly, although positive emotions are associated with lower levels of depression symptoms among Caucasian Americans, this relationship diminishes among second-generation Asian Americans and becomes non-significant among immigrant Asian participants (Leu, Wang, & Koo, 2011). Further research is needed, however, to assess the degree to which symptoms of depression are different across these cultures (Chentsova-Dutton et al., 2007).

Culture may also moderate the relationship between positive emotion and physical health. A cross-sectional study examined social connectedness, positive emotions, and biomarkers of good health such as HDL (high-density lipoprotein) and DHEA-S (dehydroepiandrosterone-sulfate) in mid-life Japanese and American adults (Yoo et al., 2016). The study found that Japanese participants who reported high positive emotions but low social connectedness displayed lower HDL and DHEA-S, whereas American participants with greater positive emotions showed high HDL levels independently of social connectedness. Moreover, in Japanese individuals with high social connectedness, positive emotion did not predict healthy biomarker levels. These results suggest that, in East Asian cultures, social connection may impact health more so than positive emotions.

Why might positive emotions have a weaker effect on well-being among East Asians? The types of positive emotions may moderate the relationship between positive emotions and well-being. For example, low arousal positive emotions, which are more valued in East Asian cultures (Tsai, 2007) may be important in predicting well-being in such cultures. However, widely used emotion scales such as the Positive and Negative Affect Schedule (PANAS; Watson, Clark, & Tellegen, 1988) emphasize high arousal emotions rather than low arousal ones, and thus may fail to capture important cross-cultural variation positive emotions (Nemanick & Munz, 1994). In fact, discrepancies between the ideal and actual levels of high arousal and low arousal positive emotions have been found to predict depression symptoms for European-American, Chinese-American, and Chinese participants (Tsai et al., 2006).

Beyond arousal, if a positive emotion experienced in a prototypical cultural context fits the cultural goals (i.e. to promote independence in Western societies versus interdependence in East Asian countries), the emotion is more likely to enhance well-being. A correlational study examined whether culture-emotion fit during different situations in prototypical culture contexts predicted psychological well-being across three cultures: American, Hong Kong, and Belgian (De Leersnyder, Kim, & Mesquita, 2015). Work is often considered a prototypical context for American culture, which emphasizes independent and self-assertive norms. By contrast, family is often considered a prototypical context for Korean participants, whose culture emphasizes adjustment and relatedness norms. Belgian society is unique in that it has both independent norms for the work context and interdependent norms for the family context. Participants were asked to report their emotional patterns in autonomy-promoting versus relatedness-promoting situations for each context, and their emotional patterns were compared against the average emotional pattern of their respective cultural groups in the same situations, to compute individuals' culture-emotion fit indexes. The results showed that well-being was predicted by culture-emotion fit in self-promoting situations at work for Americans; in relatedness-promoting situations at home for Koreans; and in both types of situations for Belgians. Therefore, whether positive emotions serve the pursuit of cultural goals and values appears to shape the degree to which positive emotions predict well-being.

The notion of emotional fit can be extended to the individual, too, as people also endorse different values and desire to feel emotions congruent with those values (Tamir et al., 2015). For example, those who identify with self-transcendent values, such as benevolence, want to feel love, trust, and empathy, whereas those who hold self-enhancement values, such as power, want to feel self-focused emotions of pride, anger, and contempt. Given that value systems vary across individuals, it is important for research to examine how specific value-emotion fit mediates the effects of positive emotions on well-being.

In conclusion, despite the numerous benefits of positive emotions, their contributions to well-being appear to vary across cultures. The more a culture values positive feelings and personal happiness versus emotional moderation and social harmony, the more positive emotions enhance the life satisfaction and physical health of that culture's members. In addition, positive emotions that fit with a culture's goals and values—for example, promoting autonomy and personal achievement in Western individualistic societies, or maintaining social relationships and interdependence in East Asian collectivistic societies—are more effective at building well-being.

The Negative Side of Positive Emotions

In addition to cultural contexts, other factors influence whether positive emotions are salubrious or harmful. Extreme levels, inappropriate type, and excessive desire of pleasant feelings may actually undermine well-being. Extreme and persistent positive emotions can signal poor psychological functioning, specifically a higher risk of bipolar disorder and mania (Gruber, 2011). People with high mania risk exhibit more intense positive emotional and physiological responses to positive stimuli (Gruber, Johnson, Oveis, & Keltner, 2008). Their elevated positive emotions tend to be self-focused emotions, such as joy and pride (Gruber & Johnson, 2009). Finally, they experience and perceive positive emotions in inappropriate contexts, such as in response to neutral and negative film clips (Gruber et al., 2008) or to a stranger's touches that convey negative emotions (Piff, Purcell, Gruber, Hertenstein, & Keltner, 2012). Such positive emotion disturbance may be initiated by biased attention to positive stimuli, motivation focused on attaining pleasant feelings (Gruber, 2011), and fast, varied thinking (Pronin & Jacobs, 2008). It is maintained by a greater tendency to up-regulate positive emotions (e.g. through positive rumination) and relatively ineffective attempts to down-regulate positive emotions (Gruber, 2011). As an aspect of bipolar disorder, a severe mental illness, positive emotion disturbance may thus be as harmful as negative mood disturbance.

Moreover, not all positive emotions are equally beneficial. Pride, a valued positive emotion in independent cultures, such as American culture, has been shown to have two facets: authentic pride and hubristic pride (Tracy & Robins, 2007). Authentic pride refers to feeling confident and accomplished, based on specific goal attainments or successes. It is linked to desirable characteristics such as agreeableness, genuine self-esteem, conscientiousness, and extraversion. In contrast, hubristic pride refers to feeling arrogant and conceited based on one's global beliefs about their good qualities and strengths. This emotion may be maladaptive as it is associated with self-aggrandizing narcissism and shame-proneness. Thus, although subjectively pleasant, hubristic pride may lead to antisocial attitudes and behaviors, which may increase social isolation and decrease well-being.

The excessive desire to attain positive emotions may also cause negative consequences. Valuing happiness is paradoxically associated with lower well-being and more loneliness and depressive symptoms both in healthy samples (Mauss, Tamir, Anderson, & Savino, 2011) and in samples of individuals with major depressive disorder (Ford, Shallcross, Mauss, Floerke, & Gruber, 2014). This negative association may result from the way people pursue happiness. Because well-being is associated with individual accomplishment in American culture, individuals who highly value happiness may pursue positive emotions by taking less socially engaging actions (e.g. they are less likely to seek happiness through spending time with family and friends), thereby paradoxically becoming more lonely and unhappy (Ford et al., 2015). As reviewed in the prior section, however, this paradox may not necessarily emerge in other cultural contexts. Research has found, for example, that the inverse association between valuing happiness and well-being in the US became non-significant in Germany and positive in Russia and East Asia (Ford et al., 2015). Moreover, only in Russia and East Asia, valuing of happiness was positively associated with socially engaged conceptions of happiness. Importantly, socially engaged conceptions of happiness positively predict well-being regardless of cultures. This finding suggests that the well-being of those who highly value happiness may be decreased by a socially disengaged pursuit of happiness, and increased by relatedness-promoting behavior.

Excessively valuing happiness may also make people more aware and critical of the discrepancy between their current and ideal state of happiness, thereby reducing positive emotions. Compared to control participants, those who were manipulated to value happiness showed less positive emotion in response to a happy film clip, whether measured implicitly or explicitly (Mauss et al., 2011). In this experiment, disappointment in one's feelings mediated the effect of valuing happiness on explicitly expressed positive emotions. In countries in which positive emotions are more socially valued, such as the United States, people tend to report higher life satisfaction and more frequent positive emotions (Bastian, Kuppens, Roover, & Diener, 2014). However, those who report frequent negative emotions do not get a positive boost from living in societies that value positive feelings. Perhaps the salient culture norm of happiness leads to more frequent social comparison, which has been shown to disproportionately worsen the emotions of less happy people (Lyubomirsky & Ross, 1997). In other words, unhappy individuals who value the cultural ideal of happiness may experience frequent disappointment as they often compare their well-being to that of others.

Applications and Future Direction

Applications

Throughout this chapter, we have reviewed evidence that positive emotions are not only sources of momentary pleasure ("sweet candy" experiences), but that they are also vital nutrients for human mental and physical well-being. However, the desire for positive emotions is not necessarily sufficient to attain happiness and may even backfire (Mauss et al., 2011). Nevertheless, as happiness is both a goal and an instrument for success (Lyubomirsky et al., 2005), it seems that it would be worthwhile to proactively pursue positive emotions. Recent research has shown that "prioritizing happiness"—organizing everyday activities and making life decisions to naturally experience positive emotions—may be an effective strategy to pursue happiness (Catalino, Algoe, & Fredrickson, 2014). Those who use this strategy report less depressive symptoms, more frequent day-to-day positive emotions and greater psychosocial resources, such as self-compassion, resilience, mindfulness, and positive relations with others. A longitudinal study with 408 Filipino secondary school students found that prioritizing positivity in second grade predicted positive emotions in third grade, which in turn predicted life satisfaction during fourth grade (Datu & King, 2016). Based on the research on prioritizing positivity, rather than attempting to feel happy in all situations, individuals may pursue happiness more effectively by choosing to enter situations that naturally generate pleasant emotions. For example, a person may make time to regularly experience pleasant activities, whether it be a hobby, dinner with family, exercise, or other desired leisure activities.

Using the same "prioritizing positivity" strategy, individuals can also allocate their time to practicing empirically tested methods that may promote positive emotions. Two examples are two ancient practices: loving-kindness meditation and mindfulness meditation. During the former, the meditators offer kind wishes for another's safety, happiness, health, and peace in order to generate other-focused positive emotions; during the latter, the meditators practice attending to their present conscious experience with an open and non-judgmental attitude. Longitudinal experiments have shown that these two practices increase daily positive emotions and psychological well-being over time (Fredrickson et al., 2008; Fredrickson et al., 2016; Kok et al., 2013). Several other practices that have been strongly backed by intervention studies to increase positive emotions include doing acts of kindness, guided relaxation imagery, and imagining one's best self (for a review of effective positive interventions, see Quoidbach, Mikolajczak, & Gross, 2015).

When and where positive emotions are felt is also important. It may be beneficial to "choose" to feel emotions that fit cultural norms and values (De Leersnyder et al., 2015). For example, if one lives in a culture that values interdependence, he or she should aim to promote socially engaging emotions, such as compassion and love, in non-work contexts, while down-regulating pride and personal joy, since these emotions may potentially disrupt social relationships. In contrast, in Western cultures where self-expression and agency are socially acceptable and desirable, it is to some extent good for well-being to feel contextually appropriate self-promoting emotions such as authentic pride and personal joy at work. In this context, however, it is important to be cognizant of the difference between authentic and hubristic pride, given the deleterious effect of the latter on relationships and health. It is also important in Western cultures to balance self-promoting emotions, such as pride and joy with socially engaging emotions, such as love, trust, and gratitude, as focusing exclusively on the former at the cost of the latter may decrease social engagement and well-being (Ford et al., 2015).

Future Research Directions

Much research has been done on the downward spirals triggered by depression and anxiety, and comparably less is known about its counterpart, the upward spirals triggered by positive emotions. According to the broaden-and-build theory, the cascade of positive cognition, biological, and behavioral changes created by instances of positive emotions are theorized to form a cycle, generating an increase in future positive emotions and co-occurring changes that lead to an upward-spiraling accumulation of well-being resources. More research is needed to examine the various links in, and forms of, this upward spiral model.

One such link is the biological mechanisms that mediate the effect of positive emotions on health. Future studies should examine the pathways through which positive emotions increase cardiac vagal tone and promote cardiovascular health. Recently, more research is being conducted on the relationship between psychosocial processes and the shifts in the body's biological systems at the cellular and molecular levels (Slavich & Cole, 2013). How positive emotions influence health at such levels is new territory to explore. It is also important to understand whether and how positive emotions enhance health by promoting healthy behaviors. Our research team is investigating how positive emotions during positive health behaviors (e.g. physical activity) serve as an implicit learning cue that motivates future engagement in the same activity (Rice & Fredrickson, 2016; Van Cappellen, Rice, Catalino, & Fredrickson, 2016).

Conclusion

Over the past two decades, the science of positive emotions and well-being has grown exponentially from virtually no studies to filling two recent handbook volumes: *Handbook of Positive Emotions* (Kirby, Shiota, & Tugade, 2014) and *Positive Emotions: Integrating the Light Sides and Dark Sides* (Gruber & Moskowitz,

2014). The broaden-and-build theory provides an overarching framework for how positive emotions affect well-being: They expand people's momentary cognitive flexibility and build their durable biopsychosocial resources. Supporting this theoretical framework, accumulating evidence reveals a cascade of cognitive, biological, and behavioral mechanisms through which positive emotions contribute to psychological resilience, physical health, and general well-being. Although the pursuit of positive feelings is a delicate art (Catalino et al., 2014), one that is contoured by individual beliefs and cultural and social contexts, we argue that it is a worthwhile endeavor due to the multitude of benefits felt through positive emotions. Future research on positive emotions will not only help to further develop the science of emotion, but also stands to improve lives.

References

Bastian, B., Kuppens, P., De Roover, K., & Diener, E. (2014). Is valuing positive emotion associated with life satisfaction? *Emotion, 14,* 639–645.

Berridge, K. C. (2007). The debate over dopamine's role in reward: The case for incentive salience. *Psychopharmacology, 191,* 391–431.

Boehm, J. K., & Kubzansky, L. D. (2012). The heart's content: The association between positive psychological well-being and cardiovascular health. *Psychological bulletin, 138,* 655–691.

Cameron, D. S., Bertenshaw, E. J., & Sheeran, P. (2015). The impact of positive affect on health cognitions and behaviours: A meta-analysis of the experimental evidence. *Health Psychology Review, 9,* 345–365.

Catalino, L. I., Algoe, S. B., & Fredrickson, B. L. (2014). Prioritizing positivity: An effective approach to pursuing happiness? *Emotion, 14,* 1155–1161.

Cavanaugh, L. A., Bettman, J. R., & Luce, M. F. (2015). Feeling love and doing more for distant others: Specific positive emotions differentially affect prosocial consumption. *Journal of Marketing Research, 52,* 657–673.

Chentsova-Dutton, Y. E., Chu, J. P., Tsai, J. L., Rottenberg, J., Gross, J. J., & Gotlib, I. H. (2007). Depression and emotional reactivity: Variation among Asian Americans of East Asian descent and European Americans. *Journal of Abnormal Psychology, 116,* 776–785.

Chida, Y., & Steptoe, A. (2008). Positive psychological well-being and mortality: A quantitative review of prospective observational studies. *Psychosomatic Medicine, 70,* 741–756.

Cohn, M. A., Fredrickson, B. L., Brown, S. L., Mikels, J. A., & Conway, A. M. (2009). Happiness unpacked: Positive emotions increase life satisfaction by building resilience. *Emotion, 9,* 361–368.

Datu, J. A. D., & King, R. B. (2016). Prioritizing positivity optimizes positive emotions and life satisfaction: A three-wave longitudinal study. *PAID, 96,* 111–114.

De Leersnyder, J., Kim, H., & Mesquita, B. (2015). Feeling right is feeling good: Psychological well-being and emotional fit with culture in autonomy-versus relatedness-promoting situations. *Frontiers in Psychology, 6,* 630.

Diener, E., Scollon, C. K. N., Oishi, S., Dzokoto, V., & Suh, E. M. (2000). Positivity and the construction of life satisfaction judgments: Global happiness is not the sum of its parts. *Journal of Happiness Studies, 1,* 159–176.

Dovidio, J. F., Gaertner, S. L., Isen, A. M., & Lowrance, R. (1995). Group representations and intergroup bias: Positive affect, similarity, and group size. *Personality and Social Psychology Bulletin, 21,* 856–865.

Dunn, J. R., & Schweitzer, M. E. (2005). Feeling and believing: The influence of emotion on trust. *Journal of Personality and Social Psychology, 88,* 736–748.

Ekman, P. (1992). An argument for basic emotions. *Cognition & Emotion, 6,* 169–200.

Folkman, S., & Moskowitz, J. T. (2000). Positive affect and the other side of coping. *American Psychologist, 55,* 647–654.

Ford, B. Q., Dmitrieva, J. O., Heller, D., Chentsova-Dutton, Y., Grossmann, I., Tamir, M., ... Bokhan, T. (2015). Culture shapes whether the pursuit of happiness predicts higher or lower well-being. *Journal of Experimental Psychology: General, 144,* 1053–1062.

Ford, B. Q., Shallcross, A. J., Mauss, I. B., Floerke, V. A., & Gruber, J. (2014). Desperately seeking happiness: Valuing happiness is associated with symptoms and diagnosis of depression. *Journal of Social and Clinical Psychology, 33,* 890–905.

Fredrickson, B. L. (1998). What good are positive emotions? *Review of General Psychology, 2,* 300–319.

Fredrickson, B. L. (2001). The role of positive emotions in positive psychology: The broaden-and-build theory of positive emotions. *American Psychologist, 56,* 218–226.

Fredrickson, B. L. (2013). Positive emotions broaden and build. *Advances in Experimental Social Psychology, 47,* 1–53.

Fredrickson, B. L. (2016). The eudaimonics of positive emotions. In J. Vitterso (Ed.), *The Handbook of Eudaimonic Wellbeing.* New York: Springer.

Fredrickson, B. L., Boulton, A. J., Firestine, A. M., Van Cappellen, P., Algoe, S. B., Brantley, M. M., ... Salzberg, S. (2016). Positive emotion correlates of meditation practice: A comparison of mindfulness meditation and loving-kindness meditation. *Mindfulness,* 1-11.

Fredrickson, B. L., & Branigan, C. (2005). Positive emotions broaden the scope of attention and thought-action repertoires. *Cognition & Emotion, 19,* 313–332.

Fredrickson, B. L., Cohn, M. A., Coffey, K. A., Pek, J., & Finkel, S. M. (2008). Open hearts build lives: Positive emotions, induced through loving-kindness meditation, build consequential personal resources. *Journal of Personality and Social Psychology, 95,* 1045–1062.

Fredrickson, B. L., & Joiner, T. (2002). Positive emotions trigger upward spirals toward emotional well-being. *Psychological Science, 13,* 172–175.

Fredrickson, B. L., & Levenson, R. W. (1998). Positive emotions speed recovery from the cardiovascular sequelae of negative emotions. *Cognition and Emotion, 12,* 191–220.

Friedman, B. H., & Thayer, J. F. (1998). Autonomic balance revisited: Panic anxiety and heart rate variability. *Journal of Psychosomatic Research, 44,* 133–151.

Frijda, N. H., Kuipers, P., & Ter Schure, E. (1989). Relations among emotion, appraisal, and emotional action readiness. *Journal of Personality and Social Psychology, 57,* 212–228.

Garland, E. L., Fredrickson, B., Kring, A. M., Johnson, D. P., Meyer, P. S., & Penn, D. L. (2010). Upward spirals of positive emotions counter downward spirals of negativity: Insights from the broaden-and-build theory and affective neuroscience on the treatment of emotion dysfunctions and deficits in psychopathology. *Clinical Psychology Review, 30,* 849–864.

Grant, N., Wardle, J., & Steptoe, A. (2009). The relationship between life satisfaction and health behavior: A cross-cultural analysis of young adults. *International Journal of Behavioral Medicine, 16,* 259–268.

Gruber, J. (2011). Can feeling too good be bad? Positive emotion persistence (PEP) in bipolar disorder. *Current Directions in Psychological Science*, *20*, 217–221.

Gruber, J., & Johnson, S. L. (2009). Positive emotional traits and ambitious goals among people at risk for mania: The need for specificity. *International Journal of Cognitive Therapy*, *2*, 176–187.

Gruber, J., Johnson, S. L., Oveis, C., & Keltner, D. (2008). Risk for mania and positive emotional responding: Too much of a good thing? *Emotion*, *8*, 23–33.

Gruber, J., Mauss, I. B., & Tamir, M. (2011). A dark side of happiness? How, when, and why happiness is not always good. *Perspectives on Psychological Science*, *6*, 222–233.

Gruber, J., & Moskowitz, J. T. (Eds.). (2014). *Positive emotion: Integrating the light sides and dark sides*. New York: Oxford University Press.

Harmon-Jones, E., Gable, P. A., & Price, T. F. (2013). Does negative affect always narrow and positive affect always broaden the mind? Considering the influence of motivational intensity on cognitive scope. *Current Directions in Psychological Science*, *22*, 301–307.

Isen, A. M., & Daubman, K. A. (1984). The influence of affect on categorization. *Journal of Personality and Social Psychology*, *47*, 1206–1217.

Isen, A. M., Daubman, K. A., & Nowicki, G. P. (1987). Positive affect facilitates creative problem solving. *Journal of Personality and Social Psychology*, *52*, 1122–1131.

Izard, C. E. (1977). *Human emotions*. New York: Plenum.

Johnson, K. J., & Fredrickson, B. L. (2005). "We all look the same to me": Positive emotions eliminate the own-race bias in face recognition. *Psychological Science*, *16*, 875–881.

Kahn, B. E., & Isen, A. M. (1993). The influence of positive affect on variety seeking among safe, enjoyable products. *Journal of Consumer Research*, *20*, 257–270.

Kirby, L. D., Shiota, M. N., & Tugade, M. M. (Eds.). (2014). *Handbook of Positive Emotions*. New York: Guilford Press.

Kok, B. E., Coffey, K. A., Cohn, M. A., Catalino, L. I., Vacharkulksemsuk, T., Algoe, S. B., ... Fredrickson, B. L. (2013). How positive emotions build physical health: Perceived positive social connections account for the upward spiral between positive emotions and vagal tone. *Psychological Science*, *24*, 1123–1132.

Kok, B. E., & Fredrickson, B. L. (2010). Upward spirals of the heart: Autonomic flexibility, as indexed by vagal tone, reciprocally and prospectively predicts positive emotions and social connectedness. *Biological Psychology*, *85*, 432–436.

Leu, J., Wang, J., & Koo, K. (2011). Are positive emotions just as "positive" across cultures? *Emotion*, *11*, 994–999.

Lyubomirsky, S., King, L., & Diener, E. (2005). The benefits of frequent positive affect: Does happiness lead to success? *Psychological Bulletin*, *131*, 803–855.

Lyubomirsky, S., & Ross, L. (1997). Hedonic consequences of social comparison: A contrast of happy and unhappy people. *Journal of Personality and Social Psychology*, *73*, 1141–1157.

Mauss, I. B., Tamir, M., Anderson, C. L., & Savino, N. S. (2011). Can seeking happiness make people unhappy? Paradoxical effects of valuing happiness. *Emotion*, *11*, 807–815.

McEwen, B. S. (1998). Stress, adaptation, and disease: Allostasis and allostatic load. *Annals of the New York Academy of Sciences*, *840*, 33–44.

Mesquita, B., & Karasawa, M. (2002). Different emotional lives. *Cognition and Emotion*, *16*, 127–141.

Miyamoto, Y., Ma, X., & Petermann, A. G. (2014). Cultural differences in hedonic emotion regulation after a negative event. *Emotion*, *14*, 804–815.

Miyamoto, Y., Uchida, Y., & Ellsworth, P. C. (2010). Culture and mixed emotions: Co-occurrence of positive and negative emotions in Japan and the United States. *Emotion, 10,* 404–415.

Nemanick, R. C., & Munz, D. C. (1994). Measuring the poles of negative and positive mood using the positive affect negative affect schedule and activation deactivation adjective check list. *Psychological Reports, 74,* 195–199.

Oishi, S. (2002). Experiencing and remembering of well-being: A cross-cultural analysis. *Personality and Social Psychology Bulletin, 28,* 1398–1406.

Oishi, S., Diener, E., Choi, D. W., Kim-Prieto, C., & Choi, I. (2007). The dynamics of daily events and well-being across cultures: When less is more. *Journal of Personality and Social Psychology, 93,* 685–698.

Ong, A. D., Exner-Cortens, D., Riffin, C., Steptoe, A., Zautra, A., & Almeida, D. M. (2013). Linking stable and dynamic features of positive affect to sleep. *Annals of Behavioral Medicine, 46,* 52–61.

Oveis, C., Cohen, A. B., Gruber, J., Shiota, M. N., Haidt, J., & Keltner, D. (2009). Resting respiratory sinus arrhythmia is associated with tonic positive emotionality. *Emotion, 9,* 265–270.

Piff, P. K., Purcell, A., Gruber, J., Hertenstein, M. J., & Keltner, D. (2012). Contact high: Mania proneness and positive perception of emotional touches. *Cognition & Emotion, 26,* 1116–1123.

Porges, S. W. (1995). Orienting in a defensive world: Mammalian modifications of our evolutionary heritage. A polyvagal theory. *Psychophysiology, 32,* 301–318.

Pressman, S. D., & Cohen, S. (2005). Does positive affect influence health? *Psychological Bulletin, 131,* 925–971.

Pressman, S. D., Matthews, K. A., Cohen, S., Martire, L. M., Scheier, M., Baum, A., & Schulz, R. (2009). Association of enjoyable leisure activities with psychological and physical well-being. *Psychosomatic Medicine, 71,* 725–732.

Pronin, E., & Jacobs, E. (2008). Thought speed, mood, and the experience of mental motion. *Perspectives on Psychological Science, 3,* 461–485.

Quoidbach, J., Mikolajczak, M., & Gross, J. J. (2015). Positive interventions: An emotion regulation perspective. *Psychological Bulletin, 141,* 655–693.

Reed, M. B., & Aspinwall, L. G. (1998). Self-affirmation reduces biased processing of health-risk information. *Motivation and Emotion, 22,* 99–132.

Rice, E. L., & Fredrickson, B. L. (2016). Of passions and positive spontaneous thoughts. *Cognitive Therapy and Research, 1–12.* doi:10.1007/s10608-016-9755-3.

Rowe, G., Hirsh, J. B., & Anderson, A. K. (2007). Positive affect increases the breadth of attentional selection. *Proceedings of the National Academy of Sciences, 104,* 383–388.

Russell, J. A. (2003). Core affect and the psychological construction of emotion. *Psychological Review, 110,* 145–172.

Ryff, C. D., Love, G. D., Miyamoto, Y., Markus, H. R., Curhan, K. B., Kitayama, S., … Karasawa, M. (2014). Culture and the promotion of well-being in East and West: Understanding varieties of attunement to the surrounding context. In G. A. Fava & C. Ruini (Eds.), *Increasing psychological well-being in clinical and educational settings* (pp. 1–19). Netherlands: Springer.

Schmitz, T. W., De Rosa, E., & Anderson, A. K. (2009). Opposing influences of affective state valence on visual cortical encoding. *The Journal of Neuroscience, 29,* 7199–7207.

Slavich, G. M., & Cole, S. W. (2013). The emerging field of human social genomics. *Clinical Psychological Science, 1,* 331–348.

Tamir, M., Schwartz, S. H., Cieciuch, J., Riediger, M., Torres, C., Scollon, C., … Vishkin, A. (2015). Desired emotions across cultures: A value-based account. *Journal of Personality and Social Psychology, 111,* 67–82.

Thayer, J. F., & Lane, R. D. (2007). The role of vagal function in the risk for cardiovascular disease and mortality. *Biological Psychology, 74,* 224–242.

Tracy, J. L., & Robins, R. W. (2007). The psychological structure of pride: A tale of two facets. *Journal of Personality and Social Psychology, 92,* 506–525.

Tsai, J. L. (2007). Ideal affect: Cultural causes and behavioral consequences. *Perspectives on Psychological Science, 2,* 242–259.

Tsai, J. L., Knutson, B., & Fung, H. H. (2006). Cultural variation in affect valuation. *Journal of Personality and Social Psychology, 90,* 288–307.

Tugade, M. M., & Fredrickson, B. L. (2004). Resilient individuals use positive emotions to bounce back from negative emotional experiences. *Journal of Personality and Social Psychology, 86,* 320–333.

Tugade, M. M., & Fredrickson, B. L. (2007). Regulation of positive emotions: Emotion regulation strategies that promote resilience. *Journal of Happiness Studies, 8,* 311–333.

Uchida, Y., Norasakkunkit, V., & Kitayama, S. (2004). Cultural constructions of happiness: Theory and emprical evidence. *Journal of Happiness Studies, 5,* 223–239.

Van Cappellen, P., Rice, E. L., Catalino, L. I., & Fredrickson, B. L. (2016). Positive affective processes underlying positive health behavior change. *Psychology & Health, 12,* 1–21.

Wadlinger, H. A., & Isaacowitz, D. M. (2006). Positive mood broadens visual attention to positive stimuli. *Motivation and Emotion, 30,* 87–99.

Watson, D., Clark, L. A., & Tellegen, A. (1988). Development and validation of brief measures of positive and negative affect: The PANAS scales. *Journal of Personality and Social Psychology, 54,* 1063–1070.

Waugh, C. E., & Fredrickson, B. L. (2006). Nice to know you: Positive emotions, self-other overlap, and complex understanding in the formation of a new relationship. *The Journal of Positive Psychology, 1,* 93–106.

White, B. A., Horwath, C. C., & Conner, T. S. (2013). Many apples a day keep the blues away–Daily experiences of negative and positive affect and food consumption in young adults. *British Journal of Health Psychology, 18,* 782–798.

Yoo, J., Miyamoto, Y., & Ryff, C. D. (2016). Positive affect, social connectedness, and healthy biomarkers in Japan and the US. *Emotion, 16,* 1137–1146.

4

SAVORING

A Positive Emotion Amplifier

Jaime L. Kurtz

"The most visible joy can only reveal itself to us when we've transformed it, within"

(Rilke, 1923/1950, p. 51)

In the past several decades, as positive psychology has grown in prominence and research on psychological well-being has flourished, it has become increasingly clear that people can exert a large degree of control over their own happiness (Lyubomirsky, Sheldon, & Schkade, 2005). Moreover, the sorts of activities that have proven to be effective happiness boosters are often surprisingly simple. When done regularly over several weeks or months, things like cultivating a sense of optimism, counting one's blessings, expressing gratitude to others, and prioritizing interpersonal relationships are shown to reliably increase happiness (Emmons & McCullough, 2003; King, 2001; Myers, 2000; Toepfer & Walker, 2009). A lingering question, however, relates to the process underlying many of these activities. Why, exactly, do simple activities such as these bring such an emotional benefit?

One likely reason is that they encourage the act of *savoring*, an internal process through which people up-regulate their positive feelings by directing attention to emotionally relevant events (Bryant, 1989, 2003; Bryant, Chadwick, & Kluwe, 2011; Bryant & Veroff, 2007; Quoidbach et al., 2015). If a person is genuinely feeling gratitude, for instance, it is because her attention has been drawn to something positive that has been bestowed upon her. When a person derives joy from the company of other people, it is because he is noting the important role these people play in his life. Perhaps when the French writer de la Rochefoucauld (1694/1930) stated that "happiness does not consist in things themselves but in the relish we have of them" (p. 51), he was actually describing the vitally important process of savoring.

Conceptual Background

Savoring is undoubtedly a broad concept. It can be directed inwardly toward one's inner states of calm, of pride, of joy, of love, and more. It can also be directed outwardly, toward other people, toward nature, toward beauty, or toward a warm bath, a fine wine, or a brand-new car. Sometimes it occurs spontaneously, and other times it requires much effort and concentration, and among its many synonyms include basking, marveling, reveling, luxuriating, and reflecting. Perhaps due to its complexity, until recently, the concept of savoring lacked an overarching theoretical framework with which to guide research and application (Bryant & Veroff, 2007; Quoidbach et al., 2015).

Savoring as Emotion Regulation

Although they do not describe it as savoring directly, Quoidbach, Mikolajczak, and Gross (2015) recently proposed a model of positive emotion regulation that is both synonymous with the concept of savoring and helpful in understanding how and why it occurs. Based on an emotion regulation perspective (Gross, 1998), up-regulating positive emotions requires choosing the right kind of situation ("situation selection"). For example, simply opting for a hotel room with an ocean view, versus a view of a parking lot, might make savoring a hotel stay easier. Situations can also be modified to make savoring even more likely. For example, upon arrival, a hotel guest could ask to be moved out of a room adjacent to the noisy elevator, or he might move a comfortable chair to the window, so he might better enjoy the ocean view.

Being in a relaxing and pleasant physical location is not sufficient, however. A certain degree of mindful attention is also required. Naturally, a hotel guest is unlikely to savor his ocean view when rushing off to a work meeting, while caring for a crying child, or while also trying to watch a movie.

Next, the experience needs to be imbued with some sort of value; essentially, cognitively designated as special ("cognitive change"). If the hotel guest shrugs off the beauty of the ocean view, perhaps thinking "I've seen better" or "That docked cruise ship is blocking my view and is really hideous," enjoyment will be impaired. But if he takes a minute, stops and looks, and notices the reflection of the light on the water, listens to the crashing waves, and notes how very different this is from life at home, he is savoring.

Finally, Quoidbach, Dunn, and colleagues (2015) emphasize the importance of actively enhancing positive emotions by enthusiastically sharing them with others, laughing, journaling, or any other physiological, emotional, or behavioral act that may further amplify enjoyment ("response modulation"). In sum, according to this model, savoring occurs via five specific emotion regulation processes: situation selection, situation modification, attentional deployment, cognitive change, and response modulation.

Of course, savoring need not be restricted to what is occurring in the present (Bryant & Veroff, 2007; Quoidbach et al., 2015). One can look ahead to future positive experiences and savor it via anticipation. If a fancy hotel visit is coming up, be it hours or weeks away, attention can be deployed to all of the positive qualities of the hotel and how it will feel to relax and enjoy it completely. One can also savor memories of *past* positive experiences, via reminiscence. Thinking back to that past hotel visit, trying to conjure up the sensory pleasures that took place while having cocktails on the balcony as the sun set, for instance, would qualify as past-oriented savoring. Interestingly, when asked to rate their savoring capacities, people typically report being most capable of savoring through reminiscence, moderately capable of savoring the present moment, and least capable of savoring through anticipation (Bryant, 2003), possibly because anticipating an upcoming event is more mentally taxing and physiologically arousing than is calmly reflecting back on it later (Van Boven & Ashworth, 2007).

Related States

While a decidedly positive state, savoring is distinct from pleasure or enjoyment in the sense that savoring is an effortful process of attending to pleasurable feelings and either amplifying or dampening them, prolonging, or curtailing them. Savoring is also different from mindfulness. While they share some similarities (Beaumont, 2011; Quoidbach et al., 2015; see also Langer & Ngnoumen, this volume), particularly related to the effortful direction of attention, mindfulness is generally thought of as unvalenced: one can be mindful of the good, the bad, and the neutral. Savoring, on the other hand, is decidedly positive.

Savoring can also be thought of as similar to but distinct from gratitude. Gratitude is generally thought of as having a clear object, the benefactor to whom a person feels grateful. Savoring is more general; it encompasses gratitude, since feeling grateful can certainly up-regulate one's positive feelings, but savoring can exist without gratitude. While eating a delicious piece of chocolate, for example, one can savor the sensory experience without feeling grateful to the chocolatier.

Outcomes and Correlates of Savoring

Savoring is closely linked to many desirable outcomes, including higher rates of subjective well-being or happiness (Bryant, 1989, 2003; Bryant, Smart, & King, 2005; Meehan, Durlak, & Bryant, 1993; Quoidbach, Berry et al., 2010), a tendency that seems to be especially true for those high in self-esteem (Wood, Heimpel, & Michela, 2003). In one experience-sampling study, those who used savoring strategies in their everyday lives showed a correlation between positive daily events and momentary positive mood (Jose, Lim, & Bryant, 2012). This finding suggests that savoring really is the key process that translates the objective, external conditions of one's life into the subjective, internal experience of happiness.

Savoring has been also proposed as a mechanism through which positive affect broadens awareness, encourages exploration, and expands behavioral skills (Tugade & Fredrickson, 2007). Because pleasurable experiences are typically reinforced more than neutral ones, savoring may also promote learning (Frijda & Sundararajan, 2007). In addition, savoring may facilitate the formation and strengthening of social interconnections as well as the discovery of meaning in life. As noted by Bryant and Veroff (2007) certain types of savoring, such as thanksgiving and marveling, encourage engagement with potential sources of meaning, particularly in a spiritual context.

Individual Differences in Savoring

A number of studies have identified some interesting individual differences in the ability to savor. Females report a greater tendency to savor, a difference that emerges around age ten and persists throughout the lifespan (Bryant & Veroff, 2007). Higher levels of trait mindfulness (Beaumont, 2011), extraversion, optimism, and affect intensity, and lower levels of neuroticism, guilt, and hopelessness, are associated with a greater perceived capacity to savor the moment (Bryant, 2003). Also, those in more individualistic cultures tend to savor more frequently than those in collectivistic cultures (Lindberg, 2004; Miyamoto & Ma, 2011), perhaps in accordance with cultural norms.

Operationalizating and Assessing Savoring

Self-Report Measures

The Savoring Beliefs Inventory (SBI; Bryant, 2003) is comprised of 24 items that tap into people's sense of their own ability to savor. Sample items include, "It's easy for me to rekindle the joy from pleasant memories," "When something good happens, I can make my enjoyment of it last longer by thinking or doing certain things," and "For me, once a fun time is over and gone, it's best not to think about it" (reverse-scored). Confirmatory factor analysis revealed three subscales: savoring the past through reminiscence, savoring the present moment, and savoring the future through anticipation. Scores on these subscales were predictive of how much participants savored a Christmas holiday before, during, and after, respectively.

Geared toward one's ability to savor a *specific* experience, the Ways of Savoring Checklist (Bryant & Veroff, 2007) is a 60-item assessment of the thoughts and feelings that promote savoring. It is modeled on the Ways of Coping Checklist (Folkman & Lazarus, 1980), in which respondents think about a recent difficult or stressful experience and report on the extent to which they used a number of distinct coping strategies to get through it. In the Ways of Savoring Checklist, respondents reflect on a specific, recent positive experience, and indicate the extent to which each one applied to that experience.

Ten specific savoring strategies are assessed: sharing with others ("I looked for other people to share it with"), memory-building ("I consciously reflected on the situation—took in details, tried to remember them, made comparisons"), self-congratulation ("I told myself how proud I was"), comparing ("I focused on the future, on a time when this good event would be over"), sensory-perceptual sharpening ("I tried to slow down and move more slowly, in an effort to stop or slow time"), absorption ("I closed my eyes, relaxed, and took in the moment"), behavioral expression ("I laughed or giggled"), temporal awareness ("I thought about how I wished this moment could last—reminded myself how I must enjoy it now because it would be over soon"), counting blessings ("I reminded myself how lucky I was to have this good thing happen to me"), and kill-joy thinking ("I thought about ways in which it could have been better;" reverse-scored). Each subscale shows relatively high internal consistency ($\alpha > 0.70$).

Bryant and Veroff (2007) also describe the 24-item Children's Savoring Beliefs Inventory, a modification suitable for young adolescents. It includes statements like, "I know how to have a good time," "I enjoy looking back on happy times that have already happened," and "I am not able to feel joy at happy times" (reverse-scored).

In contrast to the measures above, the Emotion Regulation Profile-Revised (ERP-R in Nelis, Quoidbach, Hansenne, & Mikolajczak, 2011) uses vignettes of hypothetical situations that could potentially elicit positive emotions. For example, one vignette reads,

> You have taken part in the latest draw of the national lottery, because there was a major jackpot at stake. You are at a friend's house and you ask them if you can watch the results of the draw on TV, even though you are not very optimistic about the result. Excitement starts to rise when you notice, with amazement, that 4 out of 6 of your numbers have been drawn! You have won about $1500.
>
> *(Nelis et al., 2011, p. 82)*

Responses options include four savoring responses, such as,

> During the next few days, you consider what you are going to do with this money. You think about spending 10 days in a sunny place for your next holiday, going to an expensive restaurant, treating yourself to a day at a spa, etc.
>
> *(Nelis et al., 2011, p. 82)*

and "You jump for joy; you express your excitement by repeatedly saying how lucky you are." Dampening responses include, "You think it's too good to be true. Today's luck cannot last forever. You already start to anticipate possible problems in the future" and "You try not to show your emotions; you keep it to yourself because it looks bad to get carried away in front of people. Besides, you don't want your friends to be jealous of you." Participants are asked to select the emotion regulation strategies that describe their most likely reaction. Exploratory factor analyses yielded two factors: Up-regulation (i.e. savoring) of positive emotions and down-regulation (i.e. dampening) of negative emotions.

Behavioral Measures

While the majority of savoring research relies on some sort of self-report, more subtle behavioral measures have also been created. In one study, the ability to savor a piece of chocolate was used as an outcome variable (Quoidbach, Dunn, Petrides, & Mikolajczak, 2010). In addition to asking participants to report on how much they enjoyed the chocolate, blind coders also rated participants' apparent enjoyment of it, using criteria such as the amount of time they took to eat it and the extent to which they displayed overt signs of enjoyment. Interrater reliability was high and ratings were consistent with researchers' hypotheses (priming the concept of money, for example, leads to less savoring, as described below).

Environmental Predictors of Savoring

Although some people may be naturally better at savoring than others (e.g. those with a "grateful disposition," McCullough, Emmons, & Tsang, 2002), environmental factors certainly play a large role as well. In keeping with Quoidbach, Mikolajczak, and Gross' (2015) model of positive emotion regulation, simply choosing to engage in suboptimal activities, being distracted in the midst of a positive experience, or lacking the skills to emotionally capitalize on the experience will inhibit savoring.

More specifically, and certainly more counterintuitively, a sense of abundance also detracts from the ability to enjoy the ordinary. One series of studies demonstrated that priming the concept of money can inhibit one's ability to savor simple pleasures (Quoidbach et al., 2010). In two studies, participant income and a money prime (a picture of money versus a neutral, blurred picture) both independently and negatively predicted savoring (as measured by the Emotion Regulation Profile-Revised; Nelis et al., 2011). Meanwhile, accounting for savoring attenuated the positive correlation between income and happiness. In a second study, subtly priming money with a photograph of cash (versus an indistinguishable, blurred photo) predicted reduced savoring of a piece of chocolate, as rated by blind coders.

Outside of the lab, reminding people of the extraordinary things they've previously experienced can further impede the ability to savor a pleasant but comparatively ordinary experience (Quoidbach, Dunn, Hansenne, & Bustin, 2015). Specifically, tourists who reported having visited more countries, subsequently reported less savoring of a trip to Boston's historical Old North Church, a landmark that holds historical appeal but can feel quite dull in comparison to Paris, Hawaii, and so on. This effect can also be experimentally manipulated: participants who were primed to feel well traveled (versus poorly traveled) spent less time in the Old North Church and also savored it less. This research suggests that there is an unforeseen downside to having extraordinary life experiences: it makes more ordinary pleasures harder to savor.

Conversely, previous life challenges actually relate to an enhanced ability to savor (Croft, Dunn, & Quoidbach, 2014). A sample of almost 15,000 adults reported the extent to which they had experienced difficulties and adversity in their lives (e.g. losing a job, death of a loved one, divorce), as well as their capacity to savor, their current mood, and their Big Five personality traits. Past experiences of adversity—*if* the respondents said they had successfully coped with them—predicted their current ability to savor (as measured by the ERP-R; Nelis et al., 2011). Those who reported struggling with current adversities, however, demonstrated an impaired ability to savor. Therefore, it seems that recent findings on the link between past adversity, resilience, and well-being (Seery, 2011) can be partially explained by the enhanced capacity to savor.

Techniques to Enhance Savoring

Savoring is thought to be a key process that underlies the experience of happiness (Bryant, 1989, 2003; Bryant et al., 2005; Meehan et al., 1993; Quoidbach, Berry et al., 2010). As such, many of the recent happiness-increasing positive intervention studies are designed to increase people's ability to better savor and derive more enjoyment from their everyday lives. (*Positive intervention* refers to a structured and fairly standardized activity "aimed at cultivating positive feelings, positive behaviors, or positive cognitions" (Sin & Lyubomirsky, 2009, p. 467), in which participants engage for an extended period of time—from several days to several months—during the course of their everyday lives.)

Past-Focused Interventions

These studies experimentally manipulate the extent to which people reminisce over a positive experience from their pasts. In one week-long study, Bryant et al. (2005) offered two 10-minute sessions each day, which were designed to teach participants how to use cognitive imagery and memorabilia (e.g. souvenirs, photographs) to reminisce about past positive events. Participants were taught one of three strategies that promote reminiscence. Some were asked to think back to a positive experience and allow the mental images associated with it to come into mind; some were asked to look at a physical memento of the event and allow associated thoughts to come into mind; and some were in a control condition, thinking about their current concerns. Participants in the first two conditions reported significantly greater feelings of happiness over the previous week, relative to controls, with those in the mental imagery condition showing the biggest gains. These findings suggest that positive reminiscing, especially when it involves cognitive imagery, can boost happiness over the course of a week.

It is also possible to reflect on and savor the good things we have done for others. Otake, Shimai, Tanaka-Matsumi, Otsui, and Frederickson (2006) encouraged individuals to keep track of acts of kindness (e.g. holding a door open, comforting a distraught friend) and to compute a daily count of these acts for 1 week. Compared to a no-treatment control group, individuals who recorded the positive things they had done for others exhibited greater increases in happiness over the course of the week, presumably because they were able to draw from and build upon their feelings of pride and social connectedness. These findings suggest that savoring the positive effects of our own actions on others may improve our levels of happiness.

Perhaps more counterintuitively, married adult participants were asked to think about a hypothetical *negative* event: how they might not have met their spouse, and what their present lives might be like without this person (Koo et al., 2008). Compared to a control group, these participants were happier and more satisfied with their marriages following this 20-minute reflection. Mentally subtracting a cherished person out of one's life seems to encourage a renewed sense of appreciation for what may normally feel quite ordinary. This finding was contrary to people's intuitions; they expected to feel sad as a result of this exercise.

The modes in which these past reflections take place also seem to play an important role. In a study that examined different ways to reminisce (Lyubomirsky, Sousa, & Dickerhoof, 2006), participants were asked to reflect on an experience that they considered joyful or happy, and then spent 15 minutes per day for 3 days either writing, talking, or thinking about the experience. Of these three, thinking about the experience was most effective in promoting happiness and well-being 4 weeks after the study began, suggesting that playing through a past positive event facilitates savoring, while writing it down may demystify it or "explain it away" (Wilson, Centerbar, Kermer, & Gilbert, 2005).

Present-Focused Interventions

These activities aim to increase people's awareness and enjoyment of positive experiences as the events unfold, by offering techniques to enhance and extend these positive experiences. One simple laboratory study (O'Brien & Ellsworth,

2012) used a framing technique to manipulate the scarcity of a very common, positive experience: tasting chocolates. While sampling a series of chocolates, some were presented with the fifth chocolate in the series, framed as "the last chocolate." Others were told it was "the next chocolate" (suggesting more were still to come). Those presented with the "last chocolate" rated it as more enjoyable than those told it was the "next chocolate." They were more likely to say it was their favorite and also rated the entire experiment as more pleasant. This suggests that one's enjoyment of something quite ordinary can be enhanced by focusing on how quickly the experience may soon be over.

In a similar study, Quoidbach and Dunn (2013) randomly assigned participants to one of three experimental conditions: some were told to eat as much chocolate as they wanted over the course of the next week, some were told to abstain from eating chocolate over the next week, and some were given no instructions regarding their chocolate consumption. When they returned one week later, those who had been abstaining from eating chocolate savored a piece of chocolate more and reported greater positive affect than the other two groups. Clearly, scarcity and strategic deprivation can transform the ordinary into something worthy of savoring.

Hurley and Kwon (2012) examined the effectiveness of several different savoring strategies, which included sharing positive experiences with others, taking mental snapshots, and counting their blessings. To better savor their daily lives, they were instructed to use the strategies that most appealed to them, as positive interventions are most effective when they "fit" with each person's unique tastes, personality, and lifestyle (Layous, Nelson, & Lyubomirsky, 2013). Participants were given a log to record how often they savored positive events, and they also received daily reminders to savor. After controlling for baseline levels of positive affect, those taught these strategies (compared to a control group) displayed a drop in negative affect over two weeks (but no gains in positive affect).

In a further attempt to encourage savoring in the present, participants were instructed to take a daily 20-minute savoring walk. While walking, they should

> try to notice as many positive things around them as they could (e.g. flowers, sunshine, music), to acknowledge each of these things in their mind when they noticed it, and to identify what it was about each thing that made it pleasurable.
>
> (Bryant & Veroff, 2007, pp. 184–185)

Relative to those instructed to take a daily walk and notice negative things, and also those told to just take a walk without instruction, savoring-walk participants reported an increase in happiness. These findings suggest that it is the mindset one brings to an experience, rather than the objective nature of an experience itself, that promotes happiness.

In another field experiment, Kurtz (2015) further unpacked the cognitive and affective effects of taking photographs of one's everyday surroundings. Participants were instructed to either take photographs in a mindful, creative way, or to take photographs in a neutral, factual way, or to do a count-your-blessings writing exercise (an activity that is known to reliably increase mood; Emmons & McCullough, 2003). Those taking mindful, creative photographs were in a significantly better mood and were significantly more appreciative and motivated than those taking neutral photographs. There were no significant differences between the photography condition and the writing activity. Again, this suggests that one can derive more appreciation from daily life, if regarding it from a perspective conducive to savoring.

Future-Focused Interventions

Much of the enjoyment of a positive experience actually lies in anticipation, thinking in advance of how pleasurable, exciting, or meaningful some future event might be. In fact, across a wide range of life experiences, anticipation is more emotionally potent than retrospection, and anticipating the future is considered to be even more emotionally intense and impactful than retrospection (Nawijn, Marchand, Veenhoven, & Vingerhoets, 2010; Van Boven & Ashworth, 2007). Several interventions have capitalized on the power of anticipation to foster savoring and enhanced enjoyment.

In one study (Quoidbach et al., 2009), participants were randomly assigned to "please try to imagine, in the most precise way, four positive events that could reasonably happen to you tomorrow. You can imagine all kinds of positive events, from simple everyday pleasures to very important positive events" (p. 351). Others were asked to imagine negative or neutral events that could reasonably happen to them the following day. After 15 consecutive days of the activity, those imagining specific good things that were going to happen increased in happiness from pre-test to post-test, relative to the other two conditions.

In another study (Kurtz, 2008), 6 weeks before college graduation, college seniors were asked to write about their college experience, with some reminded of the fact that graduation was very soon, and others reminded that it was still somewhat far off. After 2 weeks of adopting this mindset, those asked to think of graduation being soon were significantly happier than they were at the start of the study. They were also more appreciative and more motivated to make the most of their remaining time, suggesting that thinking about the ending of a cherished life experience can motivate one to fully enjoy it while it lasts. Applying to phases of life rather than to life itself, this work is consistent with socio-emotional selectivity theory (Carstensen, Isaacowitz, & Charles, 1999), which finds that people choose to pursue immediately rewarding and emotionally relevant goals when they feel their lives drawing to an end.

Curious as to whether this future-focused savoring could be enhanced well in advance of an ending, a group of freshmen and sophomores were asked to imagine moving away from their college town in 30 days, to see if this would spark savoring and motivate them to make the most of their time (Layous, Kurtz, Chancellor, & Lyubomirsky, 2017). Compared to a neutral control group who simply kept track of their daily activities, those living the month like it was their last showed a significant increase in happiness. Interestingly, this effect was driven by fulfillment of the core psychological needs—autonomy, competence, and interpersonal relatedness—that are related to well-being (Deci & Ryan, 2000). Perhaps these students felt like more active agents in their daily decision making, as time's scarcity helped to clarify their priorities. They were choosing activities they felt skilled at and were also allowing themselves to socialize with meaningful others. This study suggests that just *imagining* time running out may motivate people to mindfully attend, value, and savor.

Conclusions and Looking Ahead

While inroads have been made in the understanding of savoring, many questions remain. In the realm of interventions, future researchers should more carefully isolate savoring as a process underlying happiness-intervention research. In many cases, it is assumed to be a key mediator, but is seldom definitively pinpointed as such.

Further, the boundary conditions of savoring efforts need to be studied further. It is, apparently, possible to do happiness-boosting strategies too often, such that they become mundane or feel like a chore (Layous et al., 2013). Does this also apply to savoring? In keeping with the idea of "everything in moderation," there may be a theoretically optimal range of savoring, in which people are aware of the good things in life, but not so excessively that they are consumed by the need to reflect upon them constantly. Doing so may actually be counterproductive. For example, recent work on happiness indicates that people who are told about the many benefits of happiness actually experience less of it in response to a positive experience, such as watching a pleasant film clip, largely because they feel disappointed in their inability to cultivate the all-important happiness they seek (Mauss, Tamir, Anderson, & Savino, 2011). Those who dispositionally value happiness, agreeing with survey items such as "Feeling happy is extremely important to me" and "If I don't feel happy, maybe there is something wrong with me" tend to be less happy, more lonely, and more likely to suffer from depression (Ford, Shallcross, Mauss, Floerke, & Gruber, 2014; Mauss et al., 2011, p. 3). Whether savoring in excess could backfire in a similar way is an interesting research question.

Along these lines, not every positive experience is made better by savoring. Those activities that are absorbing and require dedicated concentration may be better experienced in the state of flow (Csikszentmihalyi, 1990). In flow, attention is not being directed to the experience of pleasure; there is no attention to spare, as it is all being devoted to the task at hand. Perhaps taking a moment *after* the flow experience to reflect on it and mark it as extraordinary (essentially, savoring it) could help enhance it. However, the fit between certain activities and certain positive states of consciousness could be an interesting avenue for future research.

Savoring has received its share of attention in the public sphere as well. The popular "slow food" movement, which encourages education and appreciation of local and sustainable cuisine, has the idea of savoring—taking one's time and attending to the sensory experience of eating—at its foundation (Petrini, 2003). This idea has been extended to a new philosophy of travel, where slowness involves choosing to be fully present in one location, rather than sprinting through as many cities and countries as possible (Kurtz, in press). In general, the quest for slowness has taken on a new urgency as the demands to connect and multitask have rapidly increased (Honore, 2009).

The ability to savor—to strategically up-regulate our positive emotions—is a critical determinant of well-being. After all, if we are unable to convert positive experiences into positive feelings, the objective conditions of our lives will never lead to happiness. The upsides of having good health, an engaging career, or supportive social relationships need to be acknowledged and appreciated in order to make us happy. The field of positive psychology should continue to build understanding of exactly how this process of savoring unfolds, to gain a more complete understanding of happiness.

References

Beaumont, S. L. (2011). Identity styles and wisdom during emerging adulthood: Relationships with mindfulness and savoring. *Identity, 11,* 155–180.

Bryant, F. B. (1989). A four-factor model of perceived control: Avoiding, coping, obtaining, and savoring. *Journal of Personality, 57,* 773–797.

Bryant, F. B. (2003). Savoring beliefs inventory (SBI): A scale for measuring beliefs about savouring. *Journal of Mental Health, 12,* 175–196.

Bryant, F. B., Chadwick, E. D., & Kluwe, K. (2011). Understanding the processes that regulate positive emotional experience: Unsolved problems and future directions for theory and research on savoring. *International Journal of Wellbeing, 1,* 107–126.

Bryant, F. B., Smart, C. M., & King, S. P. (2005). Using the past to enhance the present: Boosting happiness through positive reminiscence. *Journal of Happiness Studies, 6,* 227–260.

Bryant, F. B., & Veroff, J. (2007). *Savoring: A new model of positive experience* (pp. 184–185). Mahwah, NJ: Erlbaum Associates.

Carstensen, L. L., Isaacowitz, D. M., & Charles, S. T. (1999). Taking time seriously: A theory of socioemotional selectivity. *American Psychologist, 54,* 165–181.

Croft, A., Dunn, E. W., & Quoidbach, J. (2014). From tribulations to appreciation: Experiencing adversity in the past predicts greater savoring in the present. *Social Psychological and Personality Science, 5,* 511–516.

Csikszentmihalyi, M. (1990). *Flow: The psychology of optimal experience.* New York: HarperCollins.

de la Rochefoucauld, F. (1930). *Moral maxims and reflections.* London, England: M. Gillyflower & J. Everingham. (Original work published 1694).

Deci, E. L., & Ryan, R. M. (2000). The "what" and "why" of goal pursuits: Human needs and the self-determination of behavior. *Psychological Inquiry, 11,* 227–268.

Emmons, R. A., & McCullough, M. E. (2003). Counting blessings versus burdens: An experimental investigation of gratitude and subjective well-being in daily life. *Journal of Personality and Social Psychology, 84,* 377–389.

Folkman, S. & Lazarus, R. S. (1980). An analysis of coping in a middle-aged community sample. *Journal of Health and Social Behavior, 21,* 219–239.

Ford, B. Q., Shallcross, A. J., Mauss, I. B., Floerke, V. A., & Gruber, J. (2014). Desperately seeking happiness: Valuing happiness is associated with symptoms and diagnosis of depression. *Journal of Social and Clinical Psychology, 33,* 890–905.

Frijda, N. H., & Sundararajan, L. (2007). Emotion refinement: A theory inspired by Chinese poetics. *Perspectives on Psychological Science, 2,* 227–241.

Gross, J. J. (1998). The emerging field of emotion regulation: An integrative review. *Review of General Psychology, 2,* 271–299.

Honore, C. (2009). *In praise of slowness.* New York: HarperCollins.

Hurley, D., & Kwon, P. (2012). Results of a study to increase savoring the moment: Differential impact on positive and negative outcomes. *Journal of Happiness Studies, 13,* 579–588.

Jose, P. E., Lim, B. T., & Bryant, F. B. (2012). Does savoring increase happiness? A daily diary study. *The Journal of Positive Psychology, 7,* 176–187.

King, L. A. (2001). The health benefits of writing about life goals. *Personality and Social Psychology Bulletin, 27,* 798–807.

Koo, M., Algoe, S. B., Wilson, T. D., & Gilbert, D. T. (2008). It's a wonderful life: Mentally subtracting positive events improves people's affective states, contrary to their affective forecasts. *Journal of Personality and Social Psychology, 95,* 1217–1224.

Kurtz, J. L. (2008). Looking to the future to appreciate the present: The benefits of perceived temporal scarcity. *Psychological Science, 19,* 1238–1241.

Kurtz, J. L. (2015). Seeing through new eyes: An experimental investigation of the benefits of photography. *Journal of Basic and Applied Sciences, 11,* 354–358.

Kurtz, J. L. (in press). *The happy traveler: Unpacking the secrets of better vacations.* New York: Oxford University Press.

Layous, K., Kurtz, J. L., Chancellor, J., & Lyubomirsky, S. (2017). Reframing the ordinary: Imagining time as scarce increases well-being. *The Journal of Positive Psychology,* 1-8.

Layous, K., Nelson, S. K., & Lyubomirsky, S. (2013). What is the optimal way to deliver a positive activity intervention? The case of writing about one's best possible selves. *Journal of Happiness Studies, 14,* 635–654.

Lindberg, T. L. (2004). *Culture and savoring of positive experiences.* Unpublished doctoral dissertation. University of British Columbia, Vancouver, Canada.

Lyubomirsky, S., Sheldon, K. M., & Schkade, D. (2005). Pursuing happiness: The architecture of sustainable change. *Review of General Psychology, 9,* 111–131.

Lyubomirsky, S., Sousa, L., Dickerhoof, R. (2006). The costs and benefits of writing, talking, and thinking about triumphs and defeats. *Journal of Personality and Social Psychology, 90,* 692–708.

Mauss, I. B., Tamir, M., Anderson, C. L., & Savino, N. S. (2011). Can seeking happiness make people unhappy? Paradoxical effects of valuing happiness. *Emotion, 11*, 807–815.

McCullough, M. E., Emmons, R. A., & Tsang, J. A. (2002). The grateful disposition: A conceptual and empirical topography. *Journal of Personality and Social Psychology, 82*, 112–127.

Meehan, M., Durlak, J., & Bryant, F. B. (1993). The relationship of social support to positive life events and subjective mental health in adolescents. *Journal of Community Psychology, 21*, 49–55.

Miyamoto, Y., & Ma, X. (2011). Dampening and savoring positive emotions: A dialectical cultural script guides emotion regulation. *Emotion, 11*, 1346–1357.

Myers, D. G. (2000). The funds, friends, and faith of happy people. *American Psychologist, 55*, 56–67.

Nawijn, J., Marchand, M., Veenhoven, R., & Vingerhoets, A. (2010). Vacationers happier, but most not happier after a holiday. *Applied Research in Quality of Life, 5*, 35–47.

Nelis, D., Quoidbach, J., Hansenne, M., & Mikolajczak, M. (2011). Measuring individual differences in emotion regulation: The Emotion Regulation Profile-Revised (ERP-R). *Psychologica Belgica, 51*, 49–91.

O'Brien, E., & Ellsworth, P. (2012). Saving the last for best: A positivity bias for end experiences. *Psychological Science, 23*, 163–165.

Otake, K., Shimai, S., Tanaka-Matsumi, J., Otsui, K., & Frederickson, B. L. (2006). Happy people become happier through kindness: A counting kindness intervention. *Journal of Happiness Studies, 7*, 361–375.

Petrini, C. (2003) *Slow food: The case for taste*. New York: Columbia University Press.

Quoidbach, J., Berry, E. V., Hansenne, M., & Mikolajczak, M. (2010). Positive emotion regulation and well-being: Comparing the impact of eight savoring and dampening strategies. *Personality and Individual Differences, 49*, 368–373.

Quoidbach, J., & Dunn, E. W. (2013). Give it up: A strategy for combatting hedonic adaptation. *Social Psychological and Personality Science, 4*, 563–568.

Quoidbach, J. Dunn, E. W., Hansenne, M., & Bustin, G. (2015). The price of abundance: How a wealth of experiences impoverishes savoring. *Personality and Social Psychology Bulletin, 41*, 393–404.

Quoidbach, J., Dunn, E. W., Petrides, K. V., & Mikolajczak, M. (2010). Money giveth, money taketh away: The dual effect of wealth on happiness. *Psychological Science, 21*, 759–763.

Quoidbach, J., Mikolajczak, M., & Gross, J. J. (2015). Positive interventions: An emotion regulation perspective. *Psychological Bulletin, 141*, 655–693.

Quoidbach, J., Wood, A. M., & Hansenne, M. (2009). Back to the future: The effect of daily practice of mental time travel into the future on happiness and anxiety. *The Journal of Positive Psychology, 4*, 349–355.

Rilke, R. M. (2005). *Duino elegies* (G. Miranda, Trans.). Falls Church, VA: Azul Editions. (Original work published 1923).

Seery, M. D. (2011). Resilience: A silver lining to experiencing adverse life events? *Current Directions in Psychological Science, 20*, 390–394.

Sin, N. L., & Lyubomirsky, S. (2009). Enhancing well-being and alleviating depressive symptoms with positive psychology interventions: A practice-friendly meta-analysis. *Journal of Clinical Psychology: In Session, 65*, 467–487.

Toepfer, S. M., & Walker, K. (2009). Letters of gratitude: Improving well-being through Expressive Writing. *Journal of Writing Research, 1,* 181–198.

Tugade, M. M., & Fredrickson, B. L. (2007). Regulation of positive emotions: Emotion regulation strategies that promote resilience. *Journal of Happiness Studies, 8,* 311–333.

Van Boven, L., & Ashworth, L. (2007). Looking forward, looking back: Anticipation is more evocative than retrospection. *Journal of Experimental Psychology: General, 136,* 289–300.

Wilson, T. D., Centerbar, D. B., Kermer, D. A., & Gilbert, D. T. (2005). The pleasures of uncertainty: Prolonging positive moods in ways people do not anticipate. *Journal of Personality and Social Psychology, 88,* 5–21.

Wood, J. V., Heimpel, S. A., & Michela, J. L. (2003). Savoring and dampening: Self-esteem differences in regulating positive affect. *Journal of Personality and Social Psychology, 85,* 566–580.

5

SPENDING MONEY WELL

*Katherine B. Hanniball, Lara B. Aknin,
and Dylan Wiwad*

Many people devote a substantial portion of their waking lives to earning more money, presumably motivated by the belief that having more money will make them happier (Aknin, Norton, & Dunn, 2009; Kahneman, Krueger, Schkade, Schwarz, & Stone, 2006). While this belief may be widespread, it is not necessarily accurate; money does not always bring happiness. Indeed, a large body of research has revealed a positive but modest relationship between wealth and well-being, especially within First World nations (e.g. Diener & Biswas-Diener, 2002; Diener, Ng, Harter, & Arora, 2010; Diener & Oishi, 2000). The modest association does not mean that money *cannot* buy happiness, but instead suggests that one reason money may not always lead to well-being is because people are not informed of research-supported routes to happier spending choices. In the current chapter we aim to encourage happier spending by reviewing new evidence demonstrating that spending money in certain ways can promote well-being. We begin by summarizing the relationship between income and happiness and then discuss how having money (or even simply being exposed to reminders of money) can hinder engagement in well-known happiness-enhancing strategies. Finally, we spend the bulk of the chapter presenting strategies to overcome these hurdles and promote happier spending.

Overview of the Relationship Between Income and Happiness

Hundreds of studies have probed the relationship between income and subjective well-being (SWB; e.g. Easterlin, 1995), typically defined as the presence of high positive affect, low negative affect, and positive evaluation of one's life (Diener, 1984). While the strength of this relationship varies depending on what form of well-being is measured (e.g. daily happiness or life satisfaction), whether one looks within or across nations, and whether cross-sectional or longitudinal data are examined, the general pattern of results reveals that the association is positive, modest, and complex (Diener & Biswas-Diener, 2002; Diener et al., 2010; Diener & Oishi, 2000). In general, the strongest relationships tend to emerge when looking at the association between income and life satisfaction across countries using correlational data. For instance, at the national level, income and SWB are strongly correlated, with citizens in wealthier countries reporting higher well-being (Diener & Biswas-Diener, 2002). In one investigation, people living in richer nations were 1.25 times more likely to be satisfied with their lives than people living in poorer nations (Diener & Biswas-Diener, 2002). However, the relationship between income and SWB is weaker within nations, especially wealthy ones (Diener et al., 2010). For example, one study of 6,000 Swiss adults found a positive but small relationship between individual income and well-being—compared with the poorest Swiss citizens, only a slightly higher percentage of the wealthiest Swiss adults report being completely satisfied with their lives (Frey & Stutzer, 2000). In other work, researchers have found that income is associated with greater life satisfaction up to $75,000 a year, at which point more money does little to increase well-being (Kahneman & Deaton, 2010). Importantly, the association is weaker when income is correlated with day-to-day happiness than with overall life satisfaction (Kahneman & Deaton, 2010).

Given that money can provide the means to aid the pursuit of most goals in daily life, money should be able to effectively increase happiness. So why is the relationship between money and happiness weaker than expected? Below we consider how money can open the door to materialism, thwart the promotion of social connection and prosociality, as well as introduce time strain and an overabundance of choice.

Materialism

Materialism is defined as the belief that the acquisition of material goods leads to life satisfaction (Richins & Dawson, 1992). Research suggests that as people earn more money, they tend to consume more, which may lead to increases in materialism (Headey, Muffels, & Wooden, 2008; Keynes, 1936). Indeed in many places, one's status within society is strongly determined by the acquisition of material possessions, which function as markers of financial success (Dittmar & Pepper, 1994; Kasser & Sheldon, 2000). While possession of material goods may function as a meaningful status signal for others, materialism can also be bad news for happiness. Indeed, individuals who are more materialistic also report a series of negative psychological and emotional outcomes, such as increased likelihood of severe psychological disorders (Cohen & Cohen, 1996), increased anxiety (Kasser & Ahuvia, 2002), less positive affect, greater depression, and increased substance abuse (Kasser & Ryan, 1993, 1996, 2001). Beyond correlational results, recent longitudinal evidence provides some insight into the direction of causality by demonstrating that increases in materialism are associated with decreases in subjective well-being over time, while decreases in materialism are associated with increases in well-being (Kasser et al., 2014).

Materialism may be associated with, and lead to, lower well-being for several reasons. First, materialistic individuals hold more favorable attitudes toward taking on debt (Watson, 2003), which can result in compulsive buying and increased financial concerns (Gardarsdóttir & Dittmar, 2012). Second, because people more readily adapt to newly purchased material goods, the happiness one experiences from even the most thrilling of material purchases, such as a new sports car, can quickly fade, leaving the spender looking for the next exciting item to buy. This cycle—the thrilling purchase, excitement fade, and subsequent desire for new material possessions—grows the gap between wanting and having, which lends itself to materialism and decreased well-being (Norris & Larsen, 2011). Thus, one reason more money may not bring as much happiness as most people suspect is because increased income may lead to materialism and materialistic consumption, which has been shown to have negative psychological consequences.

Prosociality and Social Connection

Another reason why having more money may not make people happier is that money can impede prosocial behavior (Côté, House, & Willer, 2015; Piff, Kraus, Côté, Cheng, & Keltner, 2010) and increase attention to oneself as opposed to others (Vohs, Meade, & Goode, 2006, 2008), both behaviors which undermine well-known predictors of happiness: social connection and prosociality (see Helliwell & Huang, 2011; Lyubomirsky, King, & Diener, 2005). Evidence supporting these claims comes from both correlational and experimental investigations. For instance, national survey data in the United States revealed that high earning households ($100,000+ year) donate a smaller percentage of income to charity each year than low earning households (under $25,000 per year; Piff et al., 2010). Moreover, simply being led to feel that one enjoys a higher socioeconomic status (SES) than others has a causal impact on charitable behavior. For example, in one study, participants were asked to think about a ladder as representing where people stand with respect to social class in the United States. Those in the high social class condition were asked to imagine themselves close to the top of the ladder and think about the differences between themselves and those at the bottom of the ladder, whereas those in the low social class condition were asked to imagine themselves as close to the bottom, and asked to think about the differences between themselves and those near the top. Results revealed that participants made to feel that they occupied a higher relative social class provided less to charity than those led to feel that they inhabited a lower social class (Piff et al., 2010).

One reason that greater personal wealth may have a negative impact on generosity is because higher income people tend to be less likely to espouse egalitarian attitudes and exhibit empathy toward strangers (Kraus & Keltner, 2009; Piff et al., 2010). And indeed, several studies have shown that simply reminding people of money makes them more likely to turn their focus inward, and less likely to help others—even romantic partners—given the opportunity to do so (Savani, Mead, Stillman, & Vohs, 2016; Vohs et al., 2006). Taken together, these results suggest that having more money or simply being reminded of money can increase autonomous behavior and decrease prosocial action, thereby reducing happiness.

Time Use

More often than not, financial success is accompanied by demands on personal time. Indeed, top quintile earners in the United States are twice as likely as those in the bottom quintile to work more than 48 hours per week (Kuhn & Lozano, 2008). Given that there are a fixed number of hours in a day, more time spent working means less time available for other interests and emotionally rewarding activities. Supporting this logic, a time use survey of almost 9,000 Americans revealed that people who earn more than $100,000 per year spent a greater portion of their time engaging in activities that are often rated as some of the least enjoyable (e.g. commuting and compulsory non-work activities, such as grocery shopping or childcare) and less time engaging in passive leisure than those who earn less than $20,000 per year (Kahneman et al., 2006).

Beyond shaping one's daily activities, income may also influence one's daily activity partners. Results from a recent study demonstrate that wealthier Americans not only spend less time socializing than poorer Americans, but when they do socialize, higher income earners spend less time socializing with close relational ties, such as family members, and more time socializing with friends (Bianchi & Vohs, 2016). This difference in socializing patterns is hypothesized to occur because lower income individuals invest in relationships that provide instrumental support, such as money and child care, during times of need, while the wealthy need not do so because they are financially secure (Bianchi & Vohs, 2016). Thus, while financial success may be alluring, higher incomes are accompanied with time use price tags, often requiring one to spend *more* time working and engaging in mandatory non-work activities and *less* time seeking out activities shown to actively boost happiness, such as socializing with friends and family members.

The Paradox of Choice

More money brings the luxury of choice because expensive vehicles, prime real estate, and artisanal, dairy-free smoked gouda are all within reach! Meanwhile, someone who earns little money has little choice in pursuing these options and is relegated to purchasing only what is within their budget. While it may seem that having more options to choose from is more enjoyable, research has demonstrated that a plethora of choice may actually *undermine* happiness or satisfaction. Coined "the paradox of choice," findings demonstrate that having too many options can result in negative psychological consequences, such as decreased intrinsic motivation, task performance, and post-decision satisfaction (Iyengar & Lepper, 2000). In a series of three studies Iyengar and Lepper (2000) showed that people were less likely to engage in desirable behavior, described in these contexts as making a purchase or writing a college essay for extra credit, when they were given many options to choose from as opposed to only a few. In addition, while being presented with too many options did not make the selection process less pleasant, it did undermine satisfaction with one's choice after selection. Indeed, participants randomly assigned to select a chocolate from a relatively large set of 30 chocolates reported greater happiness than participants assigned to select a chocolate from a relatively small set of six chocolates, yet those selecting from the larger set were less satisfied with their choice (Iyengar & Lepper, 2000). Thus, while people often belief having a large array of choice will make them happier, it appears that having too many choices can be detrimental for well-being.

Summary

The relationship between income and well-being is positive but complicated, differing in strength as a result of numerous factors. Given that money can provide the means to achieve many desirable things, why does it not lead to greater happiness? One intriguing possibility is that money introduces challenges by promoting materialism, reducing social connection and prosocial behavior, increasing time strain, and introducing too much choice—all of which have detrimental consequences for happiness. That said, money need not be a counteracting force for happiness and, if anything, should be seen as an opportunity for increasing happiness if it is spent wisely. As such, we dedicate the remainder of the chapter to outlining several research-supported routes to happier spending.

Happier Spending

The choices an individual makes in *how* to use their finances can impact their happiness. The following section of the chapter explores how smarter spending decisions can provide an effective avenue for increasing one's happiness.

Our suggestions for happier spending are grounded in models of human well-being and psychological flourishing, which suggest that once basic physiological demands have been met (e.g. stable access to housing, food, medical care, etc.; see Diener & Biswas-Diener, 2002; Kahneman & Deaton, 2010, for reviews), financial decisions and spending choices that fulfill core psychological needs are the most likely to result in happiness. To this end, Self-Determination Theory (Ryan & Deci, 2000) explains that humans have three basic psychological needs: (1) *autonomy* defined as the need to see one's actions as self-determined, (2) *competence* defined as the need to see oneself as an effective and capable agent, and (3) *relatedness* defined as a sense of belonging or connection to others (see also Bandura, 1977; Baumeister & Leary, 1995; DeCharms, 1968; Patrick, Knee, Canevello, & Lonsbary, 2007; White, 1963). Together these three needs are crucial for experiencing physical and psychological well-being (Howell, Chenot, Hill, & Howell, 2011; Reis, Sheldon, Gable, Roscoe, & Ryan, 2000; Ryan & Deci, 2000; Sheldon, Ryan, & Reis, 1996). Spending decisions that fulfill one or more of these needs, and aid in personal growth and goal attainment, are more likely to result in greater well-being than those driven by other motives, such as wealth, fame, personal glory, or physical beauty.

Do More, Accumulate Less

While it is common to think about the benefits of money in terms of the material objects it affords, a large body of research demonstrates that one of the safest bets to make with one's money is to buy experiences, not things (Carter & Gilovich, 2010; Dunn, Gilbert & Wilson, 2011; Van Boven & Gilovich, 2003). In line with research cited earlier in this chapter demonstrating that materialistic individuals tend to report lower subjective well-being than non-materialistic individuals (Belk, 1985; Richins & Dawson, 1992), a national survey of over 1,200 Americans revealed that experiential purchases (defined as purchases made with the primary intention of acquiring a life experience, such as a vacation or fancy dinner out) were associated with greater happiness than material purchases (defined as purchases made with the primary intention of acquiring a material good, such as an article of clothing or iPhone; Van Boven & Gilovich, 2003). This association remains (albeit to differing degrees) across age, ethnicity, gender, geographic region, and political affiliation, suggesting that the hedonic value of experiential over material purchases is a robust and common phenomenon.

The relative benefit of experiential over material purchases appears to extend beyond the present moment and is detectable for recalled spending choices as well. Indeed, numerous experiments demonstrate that individuals randomly assigned to recall and describe an experiential purchase report higher happiness after the fact than individuals assigned to recall and describe a material purchase, suggesting that simply *remembering* an experiential purchase (that trip to Paris) can have mood benefits (Van Boven & Gilovich, 2003). Further, a survey of Cornell University students revealed that individuals are also more likely to "mentally revisit" their experiential purchases than their material ones (Van Boven & Gilovich, 2003), perhaps because material objects reside within our possession, whereas experiences can only be accessed via memory. In sum, it seems that the emotional benefits of experiential purchases are accessible not only during consumption, but can have far-reaching future consequences as well.

Of course, not all material purchases are disappointing and not all experiential purchases are delightful. Recent research provides insight into what types of experiential purchases are the most rewarding, when, and for whom. For instance, one recent study examining the effect of experiential versus material purchases on momentary happiness revealed that while experiential purchases provide more *intense* momentary happiness at specific occasions, such as the thrill of attending a rock concert with your best friend, material purchases lead to more *frequent* momentary happiness over a two-week period, like the satisfaction one feels using their new fitbit (Weidman & Dunn, 2016). Further, the relationship between materialistic versus experiential purchases and well-being is influenced by demographic variables, such as income and education. National survey data reveal that individuals with low income and low education report that material and experiential purchases make them equally happy (Van Boven & Gilovich, 2003). This finding is not particularly surprising in light of the fact that individuals with little discretionary income devote a larger proportion of their money to basic needs, which must be met. As such, the relative happiness benefits of experiences over possessions may only be of concern, and accessible, to those who earn enough to set aside funds for discretionary use.

Why do experiential purchases lead to greater subjective well-being than material purchases? At least four key reasons may exist. First, experiences are more likely to be shared with other people and are therefore more likely to foster social connection than material items (Caprariello & Reis, 2013; Kumar, Mann, & Gilovich, 2014). For example, when one invests in a vacation or a nice meal out on the town, it is likely that the experience will be enjoyed with friends and family. Given that positive social connections and interpersonal relationships are one of the strongest predictors of happiness (e.g. Bradburn, 1969; Diener, 1984; Fordyce, 1983; Larson, 1978; Lyubomirsky et al., 2005), one reason experiential purchases promote greater happiness than materialistic purchases are because they promote time spent with others, satisfying the basic human need for relatedness and connection.

Second, while excitement generally accompanies the acquisition of new material objects, the "joy of new toys" tends to lessen with time as buyers adapt to their presence. Therefore, another reason why experiential purchases tend to lead to greater well-being than material ones is because experiential purchases are less susceptible to adaptation. Additionally, because experiential purchases are more mutable compared to material ones, they are also open to increasingly favorable reinterpretations through retrospection, again making them more difficult to adapt to (Mitchell, Thompson, Peterson, & Cronk, 1997).

Third, material purchases are more susceptible to comparative evaluations than experiential ones, and as a number of studies have demonstrated, social comparisons can diminish the subjective value of positive events and objects (Brickman & Campbell, 1971; Easterlin, 1995; Frank, 1985, 1999). A series of studies conducted by Carter and Gilovich (2010) revealed that people experience greater indecision when making material purchases than experiential ones, in part because they were more likely to make evaluative comparisons when faced with a material purchase decision. In addition, when making a material purchase people are more likely to try and *maximize*, or compare all possible options and select the best alternative (a decision-making strategy that has been linked to negative psychological consequences; see Carmon, Wertenbroch, & Zeelenberg, 2003; Shwartz et al., 2002). In contrast, when making experiential purchases people are more likely to *satisfice* or select a minimum standard for overall quality and select the first option that meets this standard (Carter & Gilovich, 2010).

Finally, experiences lead to greater happiness than material purchase because they are more central to one's identity. Indeed, relative to material purchases, people believe experiences are more representative of their personalities and are more likely to be mentioned as part of their life stories (Carter & Gilovich, 2012). Similarly, people believe that learning about others' experiences are more revealing of their personality than material purchases (Carter & Gilovich, 2012). Thus, if you find yourself deciding between a new outfit or a weekend getaway, several converging lines of research suggest that the latter option will yield greater happiness both in the moment and in the long run.

Make Time a Priority Over Money

Time and money are two concepts that, while distinct, are inextricably linked in day-to-day life because working individuals sell their time in exchange for money. As such, people may be faced with an important decision: should they choose a higher-paying career that demands longer hours or should they work fewer hours to enjoy more free time?

When making this decision, consumers may find it helpful to know that prioritizing time or money may have well-being consequences. Indeed, data from several large surveys indicates that while the majority of Americans report a preference for having more money over more free time, those who prefer more free time report greater happiness (Hershfield, Mogilner, & Barnea, 2016; Whillans, Weidman, & Dunn, 2015). As such, it is possible that finding ways to have more time may promote happiness, and indeed, preliminary findings support this possibility. For example, in one study, participants randomly assigned to write about why having more time is preferable to having more money reported marginally higher happiness than those assigned to write about how having more money is preferable to having more time. Interestingly, additional work supports the opposite causal relationship as well; participants who underwent a happiness mood induction reported a greater preference for time over money than participants who underwent a negative affect induction (Hershfield et al., 2016).

If time and happiness are reliably linked, one intriguing possibility is to use one's financial resources to buy time and, in turn, happiness. Doing so allows individuals to outsource their unpleasant, time-consuming tasks that reduce free time and well-being, such as cooking, cleaning, and family care, for those they find more enjoyable (Whillans, Dunn, & Norton, 2016). For example, if you particularly dislike cleaning, use available funds to hire a housekeeper or if cooking dinner at the end of a long day is a particularly distasteful task, invest in a gourmet meal delivery service. Doing so not only reduces annoyances but also may promote need fulfillment by providing time with friends and family (relatedness), or opportunity to learn a new skill (competence).

Spend on Others

Another route to happier spending involves using money to benefit others. In fact, a growing body of research suggests that giving may be a reliable route to happiness. Supporting this claim, correlational data indicate that spending more money on others in an average month predicts higher levels of happiness while spending more money on oneself is not associated with well-being (Dunn, Aknin, & Norton, 2008). Moreover, the relationship between generous spending and happiness is causal. When students were randomly assigned to spend a $5 or $20 windfall on either themselves or others, those told to spend on others were significantly happier at the end of the day (Dunn et al., 2008). The emotional rewards of generous spending can be detected in brain activity (e.g. Harbaugh, Mayr, & Burghart, 2007) and in rich and poor countries around the globe (Aknin, Barrington-Leigh et al., 2013; Aknin, Broesch, Hamlin, & Van de Vondervoort, 2015). Even children under two years of age display larger smiles when sharing edible treats with others than when receiving treats themselves (Aknin, Hamlin, & Dunn, 2012).

When are the emotional rewards of generosity most likely to emerge? Givers experience the greatest happiness benefits when their gift meets at least one of three criteria. First, givers are happiest when their gift is impactful—when they can see how their generous action will benefit others. Indeed, experimental evidence indicates that individuals who elected to donate to charity were happier giving larger donations when they gave to a charity that explained how their gift would be used to assist those in need than when giving to a similar charity that did not provide this information (Aknin, Dunn, Whillans, Grant, & Norton, 2013). Therefore, understanding how one's gift will benefit others is an important catalyst for turning good deeds into good feelings. Second, the target of generosity also matters. All else being equal, spending money on strong social ties, such as friends, family, and close others leads to greater emotional rewards than spending on weak social ties, such as strangers or acquaintances (Aknin, Sandstrom, Dunn, & Norton, 2011). Third, giving is more likely to lead to happiness when generosity allows for social contact and fosters a sense of social connection, which can be achieved by selecting gifts that encourage time spent together (Aknin, Dunn, Sandstrom, & Norton, 2013). Another way to increase social connection or feelings of closeness is to give gifts that represent the giver (as opposed to the recipient). In fact, research has shown that people randomly assigned to recall a time when they gave a gift that was reflective of their "true self" and displayed their own interests, passions, or personality, reported feeling closer to the gift recipient than people assigned to recall a time they gave a gift that reflected their knowledge of the recipient's interests, passions, and personality (Aknin & Human, 2015).

In sum, there are several reasons why spending money on others is more rewarding than spending on yourself. Perhaps most importantly, using personal resources to benefit others fosters social relationships, which satisfies the fundamental human need for social connection (Aknin, Dunn, Sandstrom, & Norton, 2013). Additionally, prosocial spending provides an avenue for satisfying competence needs when it is possible to directly witness the positive impact spending decisions have on recipients (Dunn et al., 2008). Finally, behaving generously, whether by donating money to charity or spending money on a romantic partner, provides the opportunity for positive self-presentation, which itself has been shown to have a positive impact on mood (Dunn, Biesanz, Human, & Finn, 2007).

The previous sections have discussed how purchasing experiences instead of material objects, using money to buy yourself more free time, and spending money on others as opposed to oneself can lead to greater happiness. In the following sections we shift focus away from the content of spending (or *what* to spend on), and turn attention toward broader spending strategies (or *how* to spend more generally) with the aim of increasing well-being.

Avoiding Adaptation

Adaptation refers to the process of habituation or becoming accustomed to something that was once new (e.g. Frank, 1999; Frederick & Lowenstein, 1999). As humans, we adapt to both good things and bad, and this process of adaptation, coined "the hedonic treadmill" (Brickman & Campbell, 1971; Frederick & Lowenstein, 1999) applies to our purchases as well. Luckily, there is one easy and inexpensive way to forestall adaptation to pleasurable experiences, including purchases, and that is to break up larger experiences into smaller episodes (Dunn et al., 2011; Kahneman, 1999; Mellers, 2000). Not only is this strategy easier on one's pocket book, but also several small pleasures tend to bring more happiness than one large one because happiness is more strongly associated with the frequency of positive experiences than the intensity of those experiences (Diener, Sandvik, & Pavot, 1991). For instance, students given the option to get news about receiving an excellent grade on an assignment twice in one day, or on two separate days, vastly preferred the latter option (Linville & Fischer, 1991). Similarly, participants who received two 80-second massages with a 20-second break in between found the experience more pleasurable than participants who received a continuous 180-second massage (Nelson & Meyvis, 2008), even though the former group spent 20 seconds without the glorious deep tissue relaxation!

In addition, when investing in these small pleasures, be aware of the pitfalls of overconsumption. As it turns out, *it is* possible to have too much of a good thing and this truth holds for the big purchases as well as the small. Just as that chocolate cake becomes less enjoyable with each mouthful, if you end every night with a trip to your neighborhood ice cream parlor for a scoop of Dulce de Leche, the experience begins to feel routine. To avoid adapting to one's favorite items and experiences, heed advice offered by Dunn and Norton (2013) and "make it a treat." By limiting access to the things we enjoy we actually invigorate our appreciation of them, ensuring that when we *do* indulge in these pleasures, they bring us the happiness we are aiming for.

Happiness, Thrift, and Saving

After receiving a windfall of cash it is common to hear "don't let it burn a hole in your pocket." This quip serves as a reminder that just because money is accessible, money does not need to be spent. Extolling the virtues of thrift, recent work by Chancellor and Lyubomirsky (2011) illustrates how efficient (as opposed to opulent) use of one's finances can bring happiness in and of itself. These authors offer several principles to help consumers spend less and enjoy more. First, take the time to appreciate what you have by directing attention to purchases past and "savoring" what is already owned. This process, which is similar to that of counting one's blessings in a gratitude intervention, has been shown to bring about significant increases in well-being when performed on a regular basis (Emmons & McCullough, 2003; Froh, Sefick, & Emmons, 2008). Second, discover new uses for old things. As opposed to simply letting past purchases fade into the background, outsmart adaptation, and save money by discovering new uses for old items. Consider taking your old car on a new adventure, or repurposing your side-table as a bar-cart to host friends and family at a cocktail party. Strategies such as these transform material purchases into new experiences (thereby capitalizing on the emotional benefits of experiences) as well as reignite excitement about old possessions. Third, rent instead of buy. Sometimes it is not necessary to own something to experience it, and renting is often a cheaper option. The strong desire to be at the wheel of a Ferrari, or ride a sailboat around the harbor can be equally satisfied by renting the car or boat for an afternoon as it can by buying the same item (Chancellor & Lyubomirsky, 2011). In addition to saving your money, renting also allows the consumer to outsmart adaptation. Because, by necessity, one must return what has been rented, the consumer can reap all the benefits of the first "thrill" of a new purchase, but skip out on the inevitable adaptation that accompanies ownership.

Fourth, do it yourself. Recent work by Norton and colleagues (2012) has revealed that labor can lead to love. Coined the "IKEA effect," items such as IKEA furniture and paper cranes tend to be more highly valued when self-assembly was required (and successful! Many of my attempts at assembly have taken much longer than they should have done!) than when the products arrived complete. As such, when contemplating purchasing a new table or chest of drawers, a DIY approach will likely simultaneously save you money and increase your fondness for the object. Further, opting to build or assemble an object yourself has the added value potential for learning a new skill, which brings us to our final suggestion: facilitate intrinsic goals. Intrinsic goals refer to activities that are personally rewarding, provide deeper meaning, and satisfy the human needs for competence, autonomy, and relatedness (Ryan & Deci, 2000). Therefore instead of spending money on items related to externally driven goals, such as wealth, fame, or physical beauty, focus instead on pursuits that allow personal growth—for example, learning a new language, having coffee with a friend, or donating to a personally meaningful cause. Activities such as these tend to come with a lower price tag and greater emotional rewards.

While an abundance of money may not necessarily buy happiness, an abundance of debt can bring about pain. As several studies have now demonstrated, debt is associated with a range of psychological burdens such as stress, depression, and suicidal ideation/behaviors (Bridges & Disney, 2010; Brown, Taylor, & Price, 2005; Meltzer et al., 2011), as well as negative health outcomes (Sweet, Nandi, Adam, & McDade, 2013). Given that subjective well-being is just as much about infrequently feeling bad as it is about frequently feeling good (Diener et al., 1999), changing one's life to decrease negative affect can greatly alter one's well-being. Therefore individuals living with debt should focus on relieving their financial strain to bring about changes in subjective well-being (Chancellor & Lyubomirsky, 2011).

But what about saving? There is surprisingly little literature directly exploring the emotional benefits of a healthy piggy bank, however related research suggests that financial security could promote well-being. In particular, having money available for emergencies buffers against unpredictable troubles and therefore provides a sense of control, which has been linked to overall life satisfaction (Klonowicz, 2001; Lang & Heckhausen, 2001; Reis et al., 2000). Indeed, to the extent that savings permit predictable life patterns, such as consistent and reliable childcare or automobile checkups that prevent car failure, savings may contribute to a sense of well-being and purpose in life (Hicks & King, 2009; King, Hicks, Krull, & Del-Gasio, 2006).

Finally, saving money represents potential for the future, and anticipating future positive events is one way to tap into happiness at no cost. Just as many children lay awake on the evening of December 24th, imagining what delightful surprises await them under the tree, consumers can reap more benefit from their purchases by capitalizing on uncertainty and anticipation. Supporting this logic, research has shown that people often view upcoming vacations in a more positive light before the experience than during it (Mitchell et al., 1997). Greater enjoyment before experiences than during them may be a result of the fact that idyllic forecasts are rarely tarnished by the daily hassles that plague real experiences. As such, the happiness one experiences when anticipating future expenditures that could be made with one's savings may be an underappreciated source of joy that comes free of charge.

Concluding Remarks

Overall, the relationship between money and happiness is nuanced and complex. While having, or being exposed to, money may preclude some sources of happiness, intuitively it seems as though money should afford opportunities for increasing personal well-being—and the good news is that it can. Indeed, this chapter offers several suggestions for how to use money to effectively increase personal well-being. Whether by investing in positive experiences to be shared, spending on loved ones, bankrolling the pursuit of intrinsic goals, or even setting funds aside in anticipation of future desires, there are a handful of ways of turning wealth into well-being, leaving the choice of which (or all) strategies to employ up to you.

While research has uncovered numerous ways to make smarter and happier spending choices, several intriguing questions remain ripe for investigation. In particular, future work could probe the association between savings and subjective well-being. One reason people may hesitate to save money for the future may be *temporal discounting*, the tendency to place decreased value on something available in the distant future. However, if savings can be conceptualized as a "betterment" of one's current situation, an investment in one's future self, or reframed as a down payment on a new car or vacation home, consumers may be able to capitalize on the excitement of future consumption and translate tucked-away funds into an untapped source of happiness.

Along similar lines, another interesting avenue for exploration is whether we can use our funds to incentivize our own long term-goals, helping us overcome short-term weaknesses and commit to behaviors that are likely to bring happiness in the long run. For example, if running a half marathon is your fitness goal, set aside a sum of money by giving it to a friend or family member for safe-keeping to act as a reward for reaching your goal or a penalty for failing.

Then, use the funds to treat yourself for the accomplishment (e.g. buying a new running outfit) or lose out but help others (e.g. have your friend donate the funds to a charity of *her* choice). Using money to commit to beneficial behaviors that may otherwise be avoided might incentivize these actions and make it more likely that we reap the mood benefits associated with goal attainment and personal expansion.

References

Aknin, L. B., & Human, L. J. (2015). Give a piece of you: Gifts that reflect givers promote closeness. *Journal of Experimental Social Psychology, 60*, 8–16.

Aknin, L. B., Barrington-Leigh, C. P., Dunn, E. W., Helliwell, J. F., Burns, J., Biswas-Diener, R., ... Norton. M. I. (2013). Prosocial spending and well-being: Cross cultural evidence for a psychological universal. *Journal of Personality and Social Psychology, 104*, 635–652.

Aknin, L. B., Broesch, T., Hamlin, J. K., & Van de Vondervoot, J. (2015). Prosocial behavior leads to happiness in a small-scale rural society. *Journal of Experimental Psychology: General, 144*, 788–795.

Aknin, L. B., Dunn, E. W., Sandstrom, G. M., & Norton, M. I. (2013). Does social connection turn good deeds into good feelings? On the value of putting the "social" in prosocial spending. *International Journal of Happiness and Development, 1*(2), 155–171.

Aknin, L. B., Dunn, E. W., Whillans, A. V., Grant, A. M., & Norton, M. I. (2013). Making a difference matters: Impact unlocks the emotional benefits of prosocial spending. *Journal of Economic Behavior and Organization, 88*, 90–95.

Aknin, L. B., Hamlin, K. J., & Dunn, E. W. (2012). Giving leads to happiness in young children. *PLoS ONE, 7*(6), e39211.

Aknin, L. B., Norton, M. I., & Dunn E. W. (2009). From wealth to well-being? Money matters, but less than people think. *The Journal of Positive Psychology, 4*, 523–527. doi:10.1080/17439760903271421.

Aknin, L. B., Sandstrom, G. M., Dunn, E. W., & Norton, M. I. (2011). It's the recipient that counts: Spending money on strong social ties leads to greater happiness than spending on weak ties. *PLoS ONE, 6*(2), e1708.

Bandura, A. (1977). *Social learning theory.* Englewood Cliffs, NJ: Prentice Hall.

Baumeister, R. F., & Leary, M. R. (1995). The need to belong: Desire for interpersonal attachments as a fundamental human motivation. *Psychological Bulletin, 117*, 497–529.

Belk, R. W. (1985). Materialism: Trait aspects of living in the material world. *Journal of Consumer Research, 14*, 113–127.

Bianchi, E. C., & Vohs, K. D. (2016). Social class and social worlds: Income predicts frequency and nature of social contact. *Social Psychology and Personality Science, 7*(5), 479–486.

Bradburn, N. M. (1969). *The structure of psychological well-being.* Chicago: Aldine.

Brickman, P., & Campbell, D. (1971). Hedonic relativism and planning in the good society. In M. H. Appley (Ed.), *Adaptation-level theory: A symposium* (pp. 287–304). New York: Academic Press.

Bridges, S., & Disney, R. (2010). Debt and depression. *Journal of Health Economics, 29*, 388–403.

Brown, S., Taylor, K., & Price, S. W. (2005). Debt and distress: Evaluating the psychological cost of credit. *Journal of Economic Psychology, 26*, 642–663.

Carmon, Z., Wertenbroch, K., & Zeelenberg, M. (2003). Option attachment: When deliberating makes choosing feel like losing. *Journal of Consumer Research, 30*, 15–29.

Caprariello, P. A., & Reis, H. T. (2013). To do or to have, or to share? Valuing experiences over material possessions depends on the involvement of others. *Journal of Personality and Social Psychology, 104*(2), 199–215.

Carter, T. J., & Gilovich, T. (2010). The relative relativity of material and experiential purchases. *Journal of Personality and Social Psychology, 98*(1), 146–159.

Carter, T. J., & Gilovich, T. (2012). I am what I do, not what I have: The differential centrality of experiential and material purchases to the self. *Journal of Personality and Social Psychology, 102*(6), 1304–1317.

Chancellor, J., & Lyubomirsky, S. (2011). Happiness and thrift: When spending (less) is (hedonically) more. *Journal of Consumer Psychology, 21*, 131–138.

Cohen, P., & Cohen, J. (1996). *Life values and adolescent mental health*. Mahwah, NJ: Erlbaum.

Côté, S., House, J., & Willer, R. (2015). High economic inequality leads higher-income individuals to be less generous. *PNAS, 112*, 15838–15843. doi:10.1073/pnas.1511536112.

DeCharms, R. (1968). *Personal causation*. New York: Academic Press.

Diener, E. (1984). Subjective well-being. *Psychological Bulletin, 95*(3), 542–575.

Diener, E., & Biswas-Diener, R. (2002). Will money increase subjective well-being? *Social Indicators Research, 57*(2), 119–169.

Diener, E., & Oishi, S. (2000). Money and happiness: Income and subjective well-being across nations. In E. Diener & E. M. Suh (Eds.), *Culture and subjective well-being* (pp. 185–218). Cambridge, MA: MIT Press.

Diener, E., Ng, W., Harter, J., & Arora, R. (2010). Wealth and happiness across the world: Material prosperity predicts life evaluation, whereas psychosocial prosperity predicts positive feeling. *Journal of Personality and Social Psychology, 99*, 52–61. doi:10.1037/a0018066.

Diener, E., Sandvik, E., & Pavot, W. (1991). Happiness is the frequency, not the intensity, of positive versus negative affect. In F. Strack, M. Argyle, & N. Schwarz (Eds.), *Subjective well-being: An interdisciplinary perspective* (pp. 119–140). Oxford: Pergamon.

Diener, E., Suh, E. M., Lucas, R. E., & Smith, H. L. (1999). Subjective well-being: Three decades of progress. *Psychological Bulletin, 125*(2), 276–302.

Dittmar, H., & Pepper, L. (1994). To have is to be: Materialism and person perception in working-class and middle-class British adolescents. *Journal of Economic Psychology, 15*, 233–251. doi:10.1016/0167-4870(94)90002-7.

Dunn, E. W., Aknin, L. B., & Notron, M. I. (2008). Spending money on others promotes happiness. *Science, 319*, 1687–1688.

Dunn, E. W., Biesanz, J. C., Human, L. J., & Finn, S. (2007). Misunderstanding the affective consequences of everyday social interactions: The hidden benefits of putting one's best face forward. *Journal of Personality and Social Psychology, 92*, 990–1005.

Dunn, E. W., Gilbert, D. T., & Wilson, T. D. (2011). If money doesn't make you happy, then you probably aren't spending it right. *Journal of Consumer Psychology, 21*, 115–125.

Dunn, E. W., & Norton, M. I. (2013). *Happy money: The science of smarter spending*. New York: Simon & Schuster.

Easterlin, R. A. (1995). Will raising the incomes of all increase the happiness of all? *Journal of Economic Behavior and Organization, 27*, 35–47.

Emmons, R. A., & McCullough, M. E. (2003). Counting blessings versus burdens: An experimental investigation of gratitude and subjective well-being in daily life. *Journal of Personality and Social Psychology, 84*, 377–389.

Fordyce, M. W. (1983). A program to increase happiness: Further studies. *Journal of Counseling Psychology, 30*, 483–498.

Frank, R. H. (1985). *Choosing the right pond: Human behavior and the quest for status.* New York: Oxford University Press.

Frank, R. H. (1999). *Luxury fever: Why money fails to satisfy in an era of excess.* New York: Free Press.

Frederick, S., & Lowenstein, G. (1999). Hedonic adaptation. In D. Kahneman, E. Diener, & N. Schwarz (Eds.), *Well-being: The foundations of hedonic psychology* (pp. 302–329). New York: Russel Sage Foundation.

Frey, B. S., & Stutzer, A. (2000). Happiness, economy, and institutions. *Economic Journal, 110*, 918–938. doi:10.1111/1468-0297.00570.

Froh, J. J., Sefick, W. J., & Emmons, R. A., (2008). Counting blessings in early adolescents: An experimental study of gratitude and subjective well-being. *Journal of School Psychology, 46*, 213–233.

Gardarsdóttir, R. B., & Dittmar, H. (2012). The relationship of materialism to debt and financial well-being: The case of Iceland's perceived prosperity. *Journal of Economic Psychology, 33*, 471–481. doi:10.1016/j.joep2011.12.008.

Harbaugh, W. T., Mayr, U., & Burghart, D. R. (2007). Neural responses to taxation and voluntary giving reveal motives for charitable donations. *Science, 36*, 1622–1625.

Headey, B., Muffels, R., & Wooden, M. (2008). Money does not buy happiness: Or does it? A reassessment based on the combined effects of wealth, income and consumption. *Social Indicators Research, 87*(1), 65–82.

Helliwell, J. F., & Huang, H. (2011). Well-being and trust in the workplace. *Journal of Happiness Studies, 12*, 747–767. doi:10.1007/s10902-010-9225-7.

Hershfield, H. E., Mogilner, C., & Barnea, U. (2016). People who choose time over money are happier. *Social Psychological and Personality Science, 7*, 697–706. doi:10.1177/1948550616649239.

Hicks, J. A., & King, L. A. (2009). Meaning in life as a judgment and lived experience. *Social and Personality Psychology Compass, 3*, 638–653.

Howell, R. T., Chenot, D., Hill, G., & Howell, C. J. (2011). Momentary happiness: The role of psychological need satisfaction. *Journal of Happiness Studies, 12*, 1–15.

Iyengar, S. S., & Lepper, M. R. (2000). When choice is demotivating: Can one desire too much of a good thing? *Journal of Personality and Social Psychology, 79*, 995–1006. doi:10.1037/0022-3514.79.6.995.

Kahneman, D. (1999). Objective happiness. In D. Khaneman, E. Diener, & N. Schwarz (Eds.), *Well-being: Foundations of hedonic psychology* (pp. 3–25). New York: Russell Sage Foundation Press.

Kahneman, D., & Deaton, A. (2010). High income improves evaluation of life but not emotional well-being. *Proceedings of the National Academy of Sciences, 107*(38), 16489–16493.

Kahneman, D., Krueger, A. B., Schkade, D., Schwarz, N., & Stone, A. A. (2006). Would you be happier if you were richer? A focusing illusion. *Science, 312*, 1908–1910. doi:10.1126/science.1129688.

Kasser, T., & Ahuvia, A. (2002), Materialistic values and well-being in business students. *European Journal of Social Psychology, 32,* 137–146.

Kasser, T., Rosenblum, K. L., Sameroff, A. J., Deci, E. L., Niemiec, C. P., Ryan, R. M., & Hawks, S. (2014). Changes in materialism, changes in psychological well-being: Evidence from three longitudinal studies and an intervention experiment. *Motivation and Emotion, 38*(1), 1–22.

Kasser, T., & Ryan, R. M. (1993). A dark side of the American dream: Correlates of financial success as a central life aspiration. *Journal of Personality and Social Psychology, 65,* 410–422. doi:10.1037/0022-3514.65.2.410.

Kasser, T., & Ryan, R. M. (1996). Further examining the American dream: Differential correlates of intrinsic and extrinsic goals. *Personality and Social Psychology Bulletin, 22,* 280–287. doi:10.1177/0146167296223006.

Kasser, T., & Ryan, R. M. (2001). Be careful what you wish for: Optimal functioning and the relative attainment of intrinsic and extrinsic goals. In P. Schmuck & K. M. Sheldon (Eds.), *Life goals and well-being: Towards a positive psychology of human striving* (pp. 116–131). Gottingen: Hogrefe & Huber.

Kasser, T., & Sheldon, K. M. (2000). Of wealth and death: Materialism, mortality salience, and consumption behavior. *Psychological Science, 11,* 352–355. doi:10.1111/14679280.00269.

Keynes, J. M. (1936). *The general theory of employment, interest, and money.* New York: Palgrave Macmillan.

King, L. A., Hicks, J. A., Krull, J. L., & Del-Gasio, A. K. (2006). Positive affect and the experience of meaning in life. *Journal of Personality and Social Psychology, 90*(1), 179–196.

Klonowicz, T. (2001). Discontented people: Reactivity and locus of control as determinates of subjective well-being. *European Journal of Personality, 15,* 29–47.

Kraus, M. W., & Keltner, D. (2009). Signs of socioeconomic status: A thin slicing approach. *Psychological Science, 20,* 99–106. doi:10.1111/1467-9280.2008.02251.x.

Kuhn, P., & Lozano, F. (2008). The expanding workweek: Understanding trends in long work hours among U.S. men, 1979–2004. *Journal of Labour Economics, 26,* 311–343. doi:101086/533618.

Kumar, A., Mann, T. C., & Gilovich, T. D. (2014). Questioning the "I" in experience: Experiential purchases foster social connection. In J. Cotte & S. Wood (Eds.), *Advances in consumer research* (pp. 101–105). Duluth, MN: Association for Consumer Research.

Lang, F. R., & Heckhausen, J. (2001). Percieved control over development and subjective well-being: Differential benefits across adulthood. *Journal of Personality and Social Psychology, 81,* 509–523.

Larson, R. (1978). Thirty years of research on the subjective well-being of older Americans. *Journal of Gerontology, 33,* 109–125.

Linville, P. W., & Fischer, G. W. (1991). Preferences for separating or combining events. *Journal of Personality and Social Psychology, 60*(1), 2–23.

Lyubomirsky, S., King, L., & Diener, E. (2005). The benefits of frequent positive affect: Does happiness lead to success? *Psychological Bulletin, 131,* 803–855. doi:10.1037/00332909.131.6.803.

Mellers, B. A. (2000). Choice and the relative pleasure of consequences. *Psychological Bulletin, 126*(6), 910–924.

Meltzer, H., Bebbington, P., Brugha, T., Jenkins, R., McManus, S., & Dennis, M. S. (2011). Personal debt and suicidal ideation. *Psychological Medicine, 41,* 771–778.

Mitchell, T. R., Thompson, L., Peterson, E., & Cronk, R. (1997). Temporal adjustments in the evaluation of events: The "rosy view." *Journal of Experimental Social Psychology, 33*(4), 421–448.

Nelson, L. D., & Meyvis, T. (2008). Interrupted consumption: Adaptation and the disruption of hedonic experience. *Journal of Marketing Research, 45,* 654–664.

Norris, J. I., & Larsen, J. T. (2011). Wanting more than you have and it's consequences for wellbeing. *Journal of Happiness Studies, 12,* 877–885. doi:10.1007/s.10902-010-9232-8.

Norton, M. I., Mochon, D., & Ariely, D. (2012). The IKEA effect: When labor leads to love. *Journal of Consumer Psychology, 22*(3), 453–460.

Patrick, H., Knee, C. R., Canvello, A., & Lonsbary, C. (2007). The role of need fulfillment in relationship functioning and well-being: A self determination theory perspective. *Journal of Personality and Social Psychology, 92,* 434–457.

Piff, P. K., Kraus, M. W., Côté, S., Cheng, B. H., & Keltner, D. (2010). Having less, giving more: The influence of social class on prosocial behavior. *Journal of Personality and Social Psychology, 99,* 771–784. doi:10.1037/a0020092.

Reis, H. T., Sheldon, K. M., Gable, S. L., Roscoe, J., & Ryan, R. M. (2000). Daily well-being: The role of autonomy, competence, and relatedness. *Personality and Social Psychology Bulletin, 26,* 419–435.

Richins, M. L., & Dawson, S. (1992). A consumer values orientation for materialism and its measurement: Scale development and validation. *Journal of Consumer Research, 19,* 303–316.

Ryan, R. M., & Deci, E. L. (2000). Self-determination theory and the facilitation of intrinsic motivation, social development, and well being. *American Psychologist, 55*(1), 68–78.

Savani, K., Mead, N. L., Stillman, T., & Vohs, K. D. (2016). No match for money: Even in intimate relationships and collectivistic cultures, reminders of money weaken sociomoral responses. *Self and Identity, 15,* 342–355. doi:10.1080/15298868.2015.1 133451.

Sheldon, K. M., Ryan, R. M., & Reis, H. T. (1996). What makes for a good day? Competence and autonomy in the day and in the person. *Personality and Social Psychology Bulletin, 22,* 1270–1279.

Shwartz, B., Ward, A., Monterosso, J., Lyubomirsky, S., White, K., & Lehman, D. R. (2002). Maximizing versus satisficing: Happiness is a matter of choice. *Journal of Personality and Social Psychology, 83,* 1178–1197.

Sweet, E., Nandi, A., Adam, E. K., & McDade, T. W. (2013). The high price of debt: Household financial debt and its impact on mental and physical health. *Social Science and Medicine, 91,* 94–100.

Van Boven, L., & Gilovich, T. (2003). To do or to have? That is the question. *Journal of Personality and Social Psychology, 85*(6), 1193–1202.

Vohs, K. D., Mead, N. L., & Goode, M. R. (2006). The psychological consequences of money. *Science, 314,* 1154–1156. doi:10.1126/science.1132491.

Vohs, K. D., Mead, N. L., & Goode, M. R. (2008). Merely activating the concept of money changes personal and interpersonal behavior. *Current Directions in Psychological Science, 17,* 208–212. doi:10.1111/1467-8721.2008.00576.x.

Watson, J. J. (2003). The relationship of materialism to spending tendencies, savings, and debt. *Journal of Economic Psychology, 24,* 723–739. doi:10.1016/j.joep.2003.06.00.

Weidman, A. C., & Dunn, E. W. (2016). The unsung benefits of material things: Material purchases provide more frequent momentary happiness than experiential purchases. *Social Psychological and Personality Science*, 7(4), 390–399.

Whillans, A. V., Dunn, E. W., & Norton, M. I. (2016). *The benefits and barriers of buying happier time*. Data Blitz Talk, Judgment & Decision Making Preconference at the Society for Personality & Social Psychology, San Diego, CA.

Whillans, A., Weidman, A. C., & Dunn, E. W. (2015). Valuing time over money is associated with greater happiness. *Social Psychology and Personality Science*, 7(3), 213–222.

White, R. W. (1963). *Ego and reality in psychoanalytic theory*. New York: International Universities Press.

6

SIDE BY SIDE

How Merely Being with a Close Other Can Enhance Well-Being[1]

Erica J. Boothby and Margaret S. Clark

People ask close others to "just be there" as they face challenges. Many women, for instance, want a close partner and familiar medical and lay caretakers by their sides as they go through the childbirth process. Young children seek out parents during thunderstorms or when movies turn frightening, staying close to their parent until the danger has passed. It is also the case that people often want others to be with them when they experience something good. When people happen to see a beautiful sunset or taste a delicious confection, they often say things such as, "Come see this!" or "Taste this!" People making plans to go to movies or concerts typically invite others to join them despite the fact that, once there, they will for the most part simply be sitting side by side in a dimly lit venue without talking. Even when people engage in mundane pleasurable activities at home, such as watching a TV show, they often urge a partner (romantic or otherwise) to watch along with them. People seem to believe that having familiar others with them in stressful situations will buffer them from stress. They also seem to believe co-experiencing pleasurable activities will make those activities more pleasurable.

Empirical research supports these intuitions. In this brief chapter we review research demonstrating the positive effects of two types of "mere presence." Specifically: (1) Merely having a familiar partner present as a bystander as one experiences a threat attenuates the threat; and (2) Merely having a familiar partner co-experience something pleasurable enhances the experience. An example of the first type of mere presence is when a partner is present but silent, as when one is undergoing a medical examination. An example of the second type of mere presence is when a partner is sitting in the next seat over at a concert, experiencing the music simultaneously. As a whole, the extant evidence will lead us to conclude that usually, but not always, the mere presence of familiar others buffers us from momentary, day-to-day stressors and that, usually, but

not always, merely co-experiencing pleasant stimuli with f.
plifies their impact upon us.

Basic Assumptions

The idea that the mere presence of familiar by-standing part
impact of threats as people move through daily life, and the idc
periencing pleasant events simultaneously with familiar others ⌐ʊʊsts pleasure,
both rest on some theoretical assumptions that are well-grounded in research.
First, people are fundamentally social, interdependent beings (Beckes & Coan,
2011). They are motivated to connect with and become familiar to one another.
They forge social ties for many reasons, including such things as a desire to
mate and a need to engage in economic exchanges (Bugental, 2000; Clark &
Mills, 2012; Fiske, 1992), but, most importantly for the purposes of this chapter, people forge social ties with others in order to form coalitions or communal
relationships—that is, to provide one another with mutual, non-contingent
responsiveness (Bugental, 2000; Clark & Mills, 1979, 2012; Mikulincer &
Shaver, 2007; Reis & Clark, 2013). Forging such ties, in turn, affords people a
sense of security.

As attachment theorists have suggested and documented, such ties, especially
when they are strong, result in partners serving as safe havens in times of stress
and as secure bases from which to explore (Bowlby, 1962). Whereas developmental attachment theorists (Bowlby, 1962; Ainsworth, 1979) emphasized the
very strong bonds that infants ideally forge with primary and responsive caretakers, and adult attachment theorists (Hazan & Shaver, 1988; Mikulincer &
Shaver, 2007) have emphasized the strong bonds adults ideally often have with
romantic partners, the protective and beneficial bonds we discuss here are
broader. These relationships may vary in communal strength (Clark & Mills,
2012; Mills, Clark, Ford, & Johnson, 2004) and include people who are just
familiar and friendly (e.g. Coan & Maresh, 2014). What is key for us and for this
particular chapter is that people feel comfortable with one another, implicitly
trust one another, and feel that each other is beneficent.

We propose that the mere presence of familiar others activates three intrapersonal psychological processes and that these processes, in turn, result in the
"mere presence" phenomena we discuss in this chapter. First, when people are
in the presence of someone familiar, and, especially when they are in the presence of an established, caring, relational partner, they are less prone (than when
alone or with strangers) to be in a state of vigilance and to be wary of environmental threats to the self. Thus, they are less likely to be focused on protecting
themselves from potential dangers. In support of this idea are studies showing
that when partners spend time together, especially when they are satisfied with
their relationship, they show enhanced alignment in their respiratory sinus arrhythmia (RSA), a biomarker of feeling safe (Helm, Sbarra, & Ferrer, 2014).

Second, we note that the mere presence of familiar and safe partners is often characterized by a state of shared attention. That is, each person's attention to stimuli in the environment pulls the other's attention to the same stimuli (Shteynberg & Apfelbaum, 2013; Shteynberg et al., 2014). This process is likely facilitated by the fact that being in a safe relationship not only seems to heighten RSA but heightened RSA is further associated with greater cognitive flexibility and an ability to shift attention toward tasks at hand (Helm et al., 2014; Thayer & Lane, 2000). Partners can jointly be focused on one person in the relationship, as is often the case when the self has a need or desire for which the partner can provide support or the partner has a need or desire for which the person can provide support. Alternatively, they can both be focused on outside activities or stimuli when neither person has pressing individual needs or desires (Clark, Graham, Williams, & Lemay, 2008). Clark et al. (2008) have called these *relational self focus*, *relational partner focus*, and *relational activity focus* respectively, and the ability and fortitude to shift attention away from the self and to wherever it is needed most is heightened by the presence of safe, familiar partners.

Third (and not entirely separately from the relational foci of attention just discussed), the mere presence of a close relational partner triggers mentalizing and empathy with that partner (Batson, Fultz, & Schoenrade, 1987; Batson et al., 2007; Batson, Lishner, Cook, & Sawyer, 2005). This empathy can lead people to be especially aware of what their partner needs or desires, what their partner is attending to or thinking about, and how their partner may be concerned with supporting them. These three assumptions, taken together, form the basis of the mere presence effects we outline next.

A First Benefit of Partner Mere Presence: Attenuated Threat Perception

Consider first how the mere presence of familiar, close others can, and often does, buffer reactions to, and judgments of, physical threats to an individual's well-being. When a person is alone, a threat is appraised as something the person must face alone. However, based on the assumptions just outlined, when a person faces a threat or challenge and a familiar or close other is nearby, that person's appraisal will include knowledge of the partner's presence, attention, and the enhanced safety it affords. The person will still appraise the objective threat but now the person should take into account not only his or her own ability to cope with the threat (a secondary appraisal according to Lazarus) but also the partner's presence, which is a resource that can contribute to one's safety. The upshot is that appraisals of threat should, quite automatically, be attenuated when familiar or close others are present.

Research from several laboratories demonstrates that the mere presence of partners does indeed dampen people's judgments of risk, burdens, and cares (e.g. Chou & Nordgren, 2016). Coan and his colleagues (Coan, Schaefer, & Davidson, 2006) provide what is, perhaps, the best-known example of this. They recruited women and their spouses for a study in which the women would be placed in a fMRI scanner and would receive auditory signals that they might soon experience an electric shock. Women who expected to be shocked (and thus to experience pain) showed lower neural threat responses when holding a stranger's hand than when holding no one's hand, and lower neural threat responses when holding a spouse's hand compared to when holding a stranger's hand.

Similar results have been reported by Coan, Beckes, and Allen (2013), by Conner et al. (2012), and by Lougheed, Koval, and Hollenstein (2016). Coan et al. (2013), for instance, used a paradigm similar to that used by Coan et al. (2006) but with young adults rather than married women. The young adults were placed in a scanner and threatened with shock. Each participant was accompanied to the research session by a platonic friend of the other sex. While in the scanner, participants held the hand of that platonic friend, the hand of an anonymous experimenter of the other sex, or no one's hand. Controlling for maternal support and neighborhood social capital, holding hands with a friend reduced neural threat responses relative to holding a stranger's or no one's hand. Remarkably, the presence of friends interacted with participants' relational histories. Friends only reduced threat for those who had a good history of maternal support. Moreover, the nature of the communities from which participants came also made a difference. Holding hands with a stranger actually exacerbated threat responses of participants from communities generally characterized by low support, presumably because such participants have more reason than others to mistrust strangers.

Conner et al. (2012) found that anxious youths and other adolescents (with a mean age of 9.5 years) who elected to have a caregiver present during a task involving exposure to threatening words (e.g. ghost, embarrassed) as well as to non-threatening words while in a scanner showed lower neural threat responses to the threatening words in the presence of the parent than when alone. Indeed, physiological indications of threat responses for anxious participants were attenuated to levels comparable to those of healthy control participants when caregivers were merely present.

Lougheed et al. (2016) conducted a study in which adolescent girls were asked to complete a public-speaking task. Those girls allowed to hold their mothers' hands showed less physiological arousal than those not allowed to hold their mother's hand. Furthermore, and paralleling results reported by Coan et al. (2006), for those daughters reporting the highest quality relationships with their mothers, the mothers' presence reduced physiological stress relative to being alone even in the absence of hand-holding. In addition, Kamarck, Manuck, and Jennings (1990) had participants engage in mental arithmetic alone or in the presence of a friend and found that the presence of a friend resulted in reduced heart rate reactivity and attenuated rises in systolic blood pressure for one. Finally, Eden, Larkin, and Abel (1992) report evidence that when people are asked to complete stressful math tasks and mirror-tracing tasks, the presence of a friend (relative to being alone or with a stranger) was associated with lower reactivity captured in heart rate and systolic blood pressure and with a trend in the same direction for diastolic blood pressure.

The company one keeps can impact not only people's felt stress but also judgments of an environmental threat, namely how steep a hill appears to be (Schnall, Harber, Stefanucci, & Proffitt, 2008). Participants in one study estimated the steepness of a hill at which they were gazing (both by verbal report and by adjusting a physical apparatus to visually depict the slope) to be greater when they were alone than when accompanied by a friend. Participants in a second study, who had been assigned randomly to think of a supportive friend, imagining how they looked and acted and the feelings and thoughts the person elicited in them before judging the steepness of a hill, perceived the hill to be less steep than those who had randomly been assigned to think of a neutral person or of someone whom they disliked in the same situation.[2]

The results of these studies additionally show that the quality of the relationships in question matter. In the Coan et al. (2006) study, hand-holding by spouses was more effective than that of strangers, and hand-holding by spouses with whom women were satisfied was more effective than hand-holding by spouses with whom women were less satisfied. In the Schnall et al. (2008) work, feeling especially close to and experiencing warmth and happiness with the particular person imagined in the second study correlated negatively with the judged steepness of hills.

Two Caveats

Whereas the mere presence of familiar others does seem to attenuate threats for people, we hasten to add two caveats to this point. First, for these mere effects to emerge, the by-standing partner must have the ability to provide care. If the partner cannot provide such support, the effect should disappear. Moreover, if the partner does not provide support and instead one bears considerable responsibility for the partner, the effects actually may reverse in nature. The threat to us cannot be buffered by familiar others who cannot care for us, but a threat to us constitutes a threat to our ability to care for and protect them and, thus, may loom even larger. Second, whereas by-standing partners can buffer perceived threats to a person, there may be personal and/or physiological costs to the bystander.

The threat buffering effects described above obtain in peer relationships characterized by people who feel and expect mutual responsibility for one another's safety and well-being. However, sometimes we feel responsibility for the welfare of someone from whom we do not expect the same responsiveness because he or she simply does not have the ability to take responsibility for our own needs. Such is the case for parents of newborns or young children, for those taking care of a child with a disability, or for an adult taking care of elderly or disabled parents. In such cases the assumptions outlined above lead us to a different prediction. No matter how affectionate the partner is toward us, that person's mere presence or salience means that one must watch out, not only for oneself but also for the partner. Thus, one's partner's presence or salience should cause threats to be exaggerated rather than attenuated.

Indeed, that is what the empirical literature shows. Specifically, in contrast to studies showing that the mere presence of close, responsive peers reduces how threatening situations seem, research also suggests that when one has responsibility for a helpless other (who cannot reciprocate that responsiveness) the mere presence of that helpless other increases judgments of threats and challenges. Drottz-Sjoberg and Sjoberg (1990), for example, found that parents who have dependent children present in their lives judge nuclear energy to be more dangerous than do non-parents. Fitting well with this finding, Eibach and his colleagues found that parents' judgments of how dangerous the world is, spiked during the particular year their child was born (Eibach, Libby, & Gilovich, 2003). Moreover, in some experimental work Eibach and his colleagues asked (or did not ask) participants whether they were parents right before asking them to make judgments regarding the dangerousness of extreme sports, the risk of criminal victimization, and the trustworthiness of strangers. They found that reminders of parenthood resulted in greater judgments of danger and risk (Eibach & Mock, 2011; Eibach, Libby, & Ehrlinger, 2012). Finally, Fessler, Holbrook, Pollack, and Hahn-Holbrook (2014), in two different studies, found that parents who read vignettes about a potentially aggressive person (study 1) or viewed photographs of such a person (study 2), judged the person to be more formidable than did non-parents, effects that were mediated by increases in the person's judged formidability (study 1).

The second caveat is that, whereas the mere presence of a caring by-standing partner who can be responsive to one can and often does attenuate perceptions of threat, the by-standing partner may pay a price. Monin et al. (2010) recruited married couples, one of whom suffered from osteoarthritis, for a study. The spouse with osteoarthritis carried heavy logs across a room while the participant stood by and watched. The experimenters collected measures of systolic, diastolic and heart rate of the by-standing spouses during a baseline/habituation period and while watching the log-carrying task. Merely watching the partner perform the painful task increased the by-standing spouse's systolic blood pressure, diastolic blood pressure, and heart rates above baseline levels. Further, Manczak, DeLongis, and Chen (2016) recently reported having studied 247 parent–adolescent pairs. They took baseline measures of systemic inflammation (from blood samples during a laboratory visit) and obtained two weeks of daily diary reports of empathy and emotion regulation. Parental empathy was significantly associated with both better emotion regulation and less systemic inflammation (indexed by inter-leukin 1-ra, interleukin 6, and C-reactive protein) among the adolescents—results that fit well with the other buffering effects of partner presence, which we have reviewed. However, the empathic parents themselves showed higher indices of systemic inflammation.

The Mere By-Standing Presence of a Familiar Other May Enhance Pleasures

Whereas there is considerable evidence suggesting that the mere presence of a familiar other down-regulates perceptions of threat in the environment, we could find no clear evidence for another effect that we suspect exists. The effect would be that the mere presence of an observing familiar other, especially a trusted, established, caring partner, would up-regulate the pleasure a person derives from his or her good fortune. For instance, we imagine that having familiar others present and observing one's successes in athletic, artistic, or academic domains would up-regulate the pleasure the person him- or herself derives from those positive events. This might occur because, as already noted, social partners serve as resources. In the event of good fortune they are the ones who may capitalize on your success for you, feeling good for you, celebrating with you etc. (Gable & Reis, 2010). Or it may be that a person who experiences good fortune in the presence of a partner sees the good fortune through the partner's eyes as well as his or her own eyes, and that this vicarious experi-ence could magnify the positivity one feels. However, whether mere presence during a positive moment, *without communicating*, has this upregulation effect for pleasurable experiences remains to be seen.

A Second Benefit of Partner Mere Presence: Co-Experiencing Pleasant Stimuli Enhances the Pleasure of Positive Experiences

Psychologists long have known that people are driven to share experiences with those to whom they are close. Moreover, research suggests that this inclina-tion pays off. For example, when couples share novel and challenging activities (Aron, Norman, Aron, McKenna, & Heyman, 2000; Aron, Norman, Aron, & Lewandowski, 2002; Reissman, Aron, & Bergen, 1993) their relationship sat-isfaction rises. Sharing good news with a close other maximizes positive affect and life satisfaction (Gable, Gonzaga, & Strachman, 2006; Gable & Reis, 2010; Gable, Reis, Impett, & Asher, 2004; Lambert et al., 2013) and it is close oth-ers with whom we find meaning in life and establish a shared sense of reality (Przybylinski & Andersen, 2015; Rossignac-Milon, 2015). Reis, O'Keefe, and Lane (2016) also recently reported two diary studies in which people reported on their fun activities, and the researchers found that these activities involved more positive affect when others were involved.

These effects may be due, at least in part, to the mere presence of the partner but they also may be dependent upon deliberative actions, or acts of communication partners take, which heighten the pleasure derived from such experiences. Is there evidence that the *mere presence* of a familiar partner, who co-experiences stimuli, enhances how pleasurable experiences are? We recently have conducted a series of experiments ourselves (together with Leigh Smith and John Bargh) the results of which reveal the answer to be "yes."

Instead of investigating how the mere presence of observing partners (or reminders of such partners) influences perceived threat or risk, we investigated how merely *co-experiencing* stimuli with partners, that is, engaging with them simultaneously without interacting, influences people's judgments of those stimuli. In a first set of studies (Boothby, Clark, & Bargh, 2014) people performed an ice-breaker task during which they became familiar with one another and then tasted and rated a chocolate at the same time as their partner, and again tasted and rated a chocolate while their partner was engaged in a different but equally pleasant activity (looking at paintings).[3] (Unbeknown to the tasters the chocolates they tasted were identical in the two conditions.) Pleasant chocolates were better liked and more flavorful when they were co-experienced with the familiar partner than when tasted alone (while the partner sat nearby and looked at art). Boothby, Smith, Clark, and Bargh (2016) replicated this effect directly twice and also showed that it disappears if co-experiencers are complete strangers rather than people who had become familiar with one another. Providing further support for the finding that a pleasant experience improves when shared with a familiar partner, Boothby, Smith, Clark, and Bargh (in press) found that pleasant pictures were judged to be more pleasant when co-viewed with a friend than when viewed alone or with a stranger.

We suggest that amplification of sensory experiences as a function of merely co-experiencing them occurs, in part, because people's attention is drawn to the focus of familiar and safe others' attention (Friesen, Moore, & Kingstone, 2005; Samson, Apperly, Braithwaite, Andrews, & Bodley Scott, 2010; Shteynberg, 2015). In addition, we believe co-experiencing stimuli leads one to think about and empathize with familiar and liked co-experiencers (Batson et al., 2007; Beckes, Coan, & Hasselmo, 2013; Bouchard et al., 2013), to take their perspective and to automatically simulate their experiences (Miles, Griffiths, Richardson, & Macrae, 2010; Smith & Mackie, 2014; for a review see Chartrand & Lakin, 2013). Enhanced attention to external stimuli (made possible, in part, by devoting less attention to being vigilant to threat and self-protection) and empathy/mind-reading together, we believe, produces the observed amplification effects because the more one focuses on something the greater the opportunity that stimulus has to affect that person (Wilson & Gilbert, 2008).

A Caveat

There is a downside to mere co-experience effects as well. Although merely co-experiencing pleasant experiences increases the pleasantness of those experiences, a growing body of evidence demonstrates that merely co-experiencing unpleasant experiences also amplifies those experiences, making them even worse. Boothby et al. (2014) report a study in which participants co-experienced tasting unpleasant bitter chocolates either as the person, with whom they had just become familiar, did the same thing or as that person engaged in a different experience instead. The chocolate was liked less when it was eaten simultaneously compared to when it was eaten while one's partner was sitting next to them but engaged in a different activity. Shteynberg et al. (2014) likewise observed that when classmates viewed sad videos and images together they felt greater unhappiness relative to the unhappiness they felt when viewing the videos and images alone. Furthermore, Martin et al. (2015) found that people who had been randomly assigned to engage in a cold pressor task simultaneously with a friend (meaning that both people placed their hands in an ice bath simultaneously) reported it to be more painful than did people who had been randomly assigned to participate alone or alone while a friend simply watched them do so. All of this evidence tells a consistent story, which is that unpleasant experiences become worse when they are merely co-experienced with a familiar or close other. Whereas merely co-experiencing pleasant stimuli appears to amplify pleasant experiences, so too does co-experience appear to amplify unpleasant experiences.

Summary

We have explored the impact on people of merely being with a familiar partner. We have emphasized that, precisely because people are fundamentally social, easily form weak mutually supportive ties with one another, and often form stronger communal relationships as well, and because these relationships guide often people's attention and empathy, *the mere presence of others* in our day-to-day lives has the ability to systematically enhance our well-being in at least two ways. First, others "have our backs" so we can reduce vigilance to potential threats with the implicit knowledge that we have access to assistance if we need it and, therefore, judgments of just how bad stresses and threats are, are attenuated. Second, when we *co-experience* stimuli with a close other our reactions to those stimuli are amplified. Good chocolate tastes better, pleasant pictures appear more beautiful, happy videos make people happier. This, too, can enhance the positivity of our lives day-to-day.

Of course, we have pointed out some downsides to both mere presence effects as well. The mere presence of familiar others who need our support but cannot provide support to us (e.g. infants), may lead us to judge threats to be greater. Partners who are merely present when they down-regulate our negative experiences may themselves pay costs of empathy, feeling worse as we feel better. And engaging in an unpleasant or painful experience simultaneously can amplify people's negative reactions to stimuli.

Conclusions

In concluding we feel compelled to say that we believe we have only scratched the surface of understanding the mere effects of partner presence on people's well-being. There is certainly good evidence that mere partner presence can be, and often is, beneficial to people as they face the moment-to-moment stresses, challenges, and pleasures of life. Yet do these effects, in part, account for why people feel their relationships are so valuable and why being socially integrated has proven to be so closely and consistently linked to people's overall well-being (Holt-Lunstad, Smith, & Layton, 2010)? We suspect so, at least when partners are peers and each person is approximately equivalently responsive to the other. The presence of partners will blunt moment-to-moment threats, hassles, and disappointments, and partners often join a person in experiencing moments of pleasure, which together should make daily life more pleasant and less physiologically taxing. The benefits should be cumulative across days, weeks, and months.

Will the benefits of mere presence outweigh the costs of mere presence? That is, at times one will be the by-standing partner who may suffer a bit while buffering one's partner and, at times, one's negative experiences will be amplified because they are co-experienced. We suspect the benefits outweigh the costs for two reasons. First, people (and their partners) generally seek out pleasurable co-experiences (e.g. vacations, movies, good food, lovely walks, enjoyable sports activities) and will avoid unpleasant co-experiences (e.g. bad bitter food, ugly pictures, exposing one's limbs to ice water). Second, although suffering on behalf of, or with, one's partner will occur from time to time and cause one to be unhappier in the moment, in the long run, such negative experiences likely promote bonding and care-taking, strengthening the communal nature of partnerships and providing another, if perhaps longer and bumpier, route to happiness, but a route to happiness nonetheless.

Notes

1 Preparation of this chapter was supported in part by a grant from the John Templeton Foundation in support of a Hope and Optimism Collaboratory administered through Cornell University and the University of Notre Dame.
2 Related effects have been reported by Lee and Schnall (2014) who found evidence linking having a sense of power over others to reduced judgments of the weight of boxes filled with books. They found this whether they measured people's chronic sense of power over others (e.g. "In my relationships with others, I can get people

to listen to what I say" (study 1) or manipulated a sense of power over others by having people power pose (or not) (study 2) or recall (or not) a time when they had such power. Whereas in this chapter we focus on the effects of having safe, familiar peers present, it appears that other forms of ensuring that one will be socially secure (in this case safety that power affords) may have similar effects.

3 The order in which participants engaged in an activity that was shared versus not was counterbalanced across participants.

References

Ainsworth, M. S. (1979). Infant–mother attachment. *American Psychologist, 34*, 932–937.

Aron, A., Norman, C. C., Aron, E. N., & Lewandowski, G. (2002). Shared participation in self-expanding activities: Positive effects on experienced marital quality. In P. Noller & J. A. Feeney (Eds.), *Understanding marriage: Developments in the study of couple interaction* (pp. 177–194), New York: Cambridge University Press.

Aron, A., Norman, C. C., Aron, E. N., McKenna, C., & Heyman, R. E. (2000). Couples' shared participation in novel and arousing activities and experienced relationship quality. *Journal of Personality and Social Psychology, 78*(2), 273-284.

Batson, D. C., Eklund, J., Hakansson, C., Chermok, V. L., Hoyt, J., & Ortiz, B. G. (2007). An additional antecedent of empathic concern: Valuing the welfare of the person. *Journal of Personality and Social Psychology, 93*, 65–74.

Batson, C. D., Fultz, J., & Schoenrade, P. A. (1987). Distress and empathy: Two qualitatively distinct emotions with different motivational consequences. *Journal of Personality, 55*, 19–40.

Batson, C. D., Lishner, D. A., Cook, J., & Sawyer, S. (2005). Similarity and nurturance: Two possible sources of empathy for strangers. *Basic and Applied Social Psychology, 27*(1), 15-25.

Beckes, L., & Coan, J. A. (2011). Social baseline theory: The role of social proximity in emotion and economy of action. *Social and Personality Compass*, doi:10.11 1/j.1751-9004.2011.00400.

Beckes, L., Coan, J. A., & Hasselmo, K. (2013). Familiarity promotes the blurring of self and other in the neutral representation of threat. *Social, Cognitive and Affective Neuroscience, 8*, 670–677.

Boothby, E. J., Clark, M. S., & Bargh, J. A. (2014). Shared experiences are amplified. *Psychological Science, 25*, 2209–2216.

Boothby, E. J., Smith, L. K., Clark, M. S., & Bargh, J. A. (2016). Psychological distance moderates the amplification of shared experience. *Personality and Social Psychology Bulletin*, 1–14.

Boothby, E. J., Smith, L. K., Clark, M. S., & Bargh, J. A. (in press). The world looks better together: How close others enhance our visual experiences. *Personal Relationships*.

Bouchard, S., Bernier, F., Boivin, E., Dumoulin, S., Laforest, M., Guitard, T., ... Renaud, P. (2013). Empathy toward virtual humans depicting a known or unknown person expressing pain. *Cyberpsychology, Behavior, and Social Networking, 16*(1), 61–71.

Bowlby, J. (1962, 1988). *A Secure Base*. New York: Basic Books.

Bugental, D. B. (2000). Acquisition of the algorithms of social life: A domain-based approach. *Psychological Bulletin, 126*, 187–219.

Chartrand, T. L., & Lakin, J. L. (2013). The antecedents and consequences of human behavioral mimicry. *Annual Review of Psychology, 64*, 285–308.

Chou, E. Y., & Nordgren, L. F. (2016). Safety in numbers: Why the mere physical presence of others affects risk-taking behaviors. *Journal of Behavioral Decision Making.*

Clark, M. S., Graham, S. M., Williams, E., & Lemay, E. P. (2008). Understanding relational focus of attention may help us understand relational phenomena. In J. Forgas & J. Fitness (Eds.), *Social relationships: Cognitive, affective and motivational processes.* New York: Psychology Press.

Clark, M. S., & Mills, J. (1979). Interpersonal attraction in exchange and communal relationships. *Journal of Personality and Social Psychology, 37*, 12–24 (featured article). Reprinted in Reis, H.T., & Rusbult, C.E. (Eds.), *Close relationships:* Key readings. (pp. 245–256), Philadelphia, PA: Psychology Press, 2004.

Clark, M. S., & Mills, J. R. (2012). A theory of communal (and exchange) relationships. In P. A. M. Van Lange, A. W. Kruglanski, & E. T. Higgins (Eds.), *Handbook of theories of social psychology, Vol. 2* (pp. 232–250). Thousand Oaks, CA: Sage Publications Ltd.

Coan, J. A., & Maresh, E. M. (2014). Social baseline theory and the social regulation of emotion. *Handbook of Emotion Regulation, 2*, 221–236.

Coan, J. A., Beckes, L., & Allen, J. P. (2013). Childhood maternal support and social capital moderate the regulatory impact of social relationships in adulthood. *International Journal of Psychophysiology, 88*, 224–231.

Coan, J. A., Schaefer, H. S., & Davidson, R. J. (2006). Lending a hand: Social regulation of the neutral response to threat. *Psychological Science, 17*, 1032–1039.

Conner, O. L., Siegle, G. J., McFarland, A. M., Silk, J. S., Ladouceur, C. D., Dahl, R. E., ... Ryan, N. D. (2012). Mom—it helps when you're right here! Attenuation of neural stress markers in anxious youths whose caregivers are present during fMRI. *PLoS ONE, 7*(12), e50680.

Drotz-Sjoberg, B. M., & Sjoberg, K. (1990). Risk perception and worries after the Chernobyl accident. *Journal of Environmental Psychology, 10*, 135–149.

Eden, J. L., Larkin, K. T., & Abel, J. L. (1992). The effect of social support and physical touch on cardiovascular reactions to mental stress. *Journal of Psychosomatic Research, 36*, 371–382.

Eibach, R. P., Libby, L. K., & Ehrlinger, J. (2012). Unrecognized changes in the self contribute to exaggerated judgments of external decline. *Basic and Applied Social Psychology, 34*, 193–203.

Eibach, R. P., Libby, L. K., & Gilovich, T. D. (2003). When change in the self is mistaken for change in the world. *Journal of Personality and Social Psychology, 84*, 917–931.

Eibach, R. P., & Mock, S. E. (2011). The vigilant parent: Parental role salience affects parents' risk perceptions, risk-aversion, and trust in strangers. *Journal of Experimental Social Psychology, 47*, 694–697.

Fessler, D. M. T., Holbrook, C., Pollack, J. S., & Hahn-Holbrook, J. (2014). Stranger danger: Parenthood increases the envisioned bodily formidability of menacing men. *Evolution and Human Behavior, 35*, 109–117.

Fiske, A. P. (1992). The four elementary forms of sociality: Framework for a unified theory of social relations. *Psychological Review, 99*, 689–723.

Friesen, C. K., Moore, C., & Kingstone, A. (2005). Does gaze direction really trigger a reflexive shift of spatial attention? *Brain and Cognition, 57*(1), 66–69.

Gable, S. L., Gonzaga, G. C., & Strachman, A. (2006). Will you be there for me when things go right? Supportive responses to positive event disclosures. *Journal of Personality and Social Psychology, 91*, 904–917.

Gable, S. L., & Reis, H. T. (2010). Good news! Capitalizing on positive events in an interpersonal context. *Advances in Experimental Social Psychology, 42*, 195–257.

Gable, S. L., Reis, H. T., Impett, E. A., & Asher, E. R. (2004). What do you do when things go right? The intrapersonal and interpersonal benefits of sharing positive events. *Journal of Personality and Social Psychology, 87*, 228–245.

Helm, J. L., Sbarra, D. A., & Ferrer, E. (2014). Coregulation of respiratory sinus arrthythmia in adult romantic partners. *Emotion, 12*, 522–531.

Holt-Lunstad, J., Smith, T. B., & Layton, J. B. (2010). Social relationships and mortality risk: A meta-analytic review. *PLoS Med, 7*(7), e1000316.

Kamarck, T. W., Manuck, S. B., & Jennings, J. R. (1990). Social support reduces cardiovascular reactivity to psychological challenge: A laboratory model. *Psychosomatic Medicine, 52*, 42–58.

Lambert, N. M., Gwinn, A. M., Baumeister, R. F., Strachman, A., Washburn, I. J., Gable, S. L., & Fincham, F. D. (2013). A boost of positive affect: The perks of sharing positive experiences. *Journal of Social and Personal Relationships, 30*, 24–43.

Lee, E. H., & Schnall, S. (2014). The influence of social power on weight perception. *Journal of Experimental Psychology: General, 143*, 1719–1725.

Lougheed, J. P., Koval, P., & Hollenstein, T. (2016). Sharing the burden: The interpersonal regulation of emotional arousal in mother-daughter dyads. *Emotion, 16*, 83–93.

Manczak, E. M., DeLongis, A., & Chen, E. (2016). Does empathy have a cost? Diverging psychological and physiological effects within families. *Health Psychology, 35*, 211–218.

Martin, L. J., Hathaway, G., Labester, K., Mirali, S., Acland, E. L., Niederstrasser, N., … Mogil, J. S. (2015). Reducing social stress elicits emotional contagion of pain in mouse and human strangers. *Current Biology, 25*, 1–7.

Mikulincer, M., & Shaver, P. R. (2007). *Attachment in adulthood: Structure, dynamics, and change.* New York: Guilford Press.

Miles, L. K., Griffiths, J. L., Richardson, M. J., & Macrae, C. N. (2010). Too late to co-ordinate: Contextual influences on behavioral synchrony. *European Journal of Social Psychology, 40*, 52–60.

Mills, J., Clark, M. S., Ford, T., & Johnson, M. (2004). Measurement of communal strength. *Personal Relationships, 11*, 213–230.

Monin, J. K., Schultz, R., Matire, L. M., Jennings, J. R., Lingler, J. H., & Greenberg, M. (2010). Spouses' cardiovascular reactivity to their partners' suffering. *The Journals of Gerontology Series B: Psychological Sciences and Social Sciences, 65*(2), 195–201.

Przybylinski, E., & Andersen, S. M. (2015). Systems of meaning and transference: Implicit significant-other activation evokes shared reality. *Journal of Personality and Social Psychology, 109*, 636–661.

Reis, H. T., & Clark, M. S. (2013). Responsiveness. In J. A. Simpson & L. Campbell (Eds.), *The Oxford Handbook of Close Relationships* (pp. 400–423). New York: Oxford University Press.

Reis, H. T., O'Keefe, S. D., & Lane, R. D. (2016). Fun is more fun when others are involved. *The Journal of Positive Psychology*, published online before print, doi:10.108 0/17439760.2016.1221123.

Reissman, C., Aron, A., & Bergen, M. R. (1993). Shared activities and marital satisfaction: Causal direction and self-expansion versus boredom. *Journal of Social and Personal Relationships, 10*(2), 243–254.

Rossignac-Milon, M. (2015). *Fostering interpersonal closeness by manipulating shared reality.* Unpublished masters' thesis. Columbia University, New York.

Samson, D., Apperly, I. A., Braithwaite, J. J., Andrews, B. J., & Bodley Scott, S. E. (2010). Seeing it their way: Evidence for rapid and involuntary computation of what other people see. *Journal of Experimental Psychology. Human Perception and Performance, 36*(5), 1255-1266.

Schnall, S., Harber, K. D., Stefanucci, J. K., & Proffitt, D. R. (2008). Social support and the perception of geographical slant. *Journal of Experimental Social Psychology, 44*(5), 1246–1255.

Shaver, P. R., & Hazan, C. (1988). A biased overview of the study of love. *Journal of Social and Personal Relationships, 5*(4), 473-501.

Shteynberg, G. (2015). Shared attention. *Perspectives on Psychological Science, 10*(5), 579–590.

Shteynberg, G., & Apfelbaum, E. (2013). The power of shared experience: Simultaneous observation with similar others facilitates social learning. *Social Psychological and Personality Science, 4*, 738–744.

Shteynberg, G., Hirsh, J. B., Apfelbaum, E. P., Larsen, J. T., Galinsky, A. D., & Roese, N. J. (2014). Feeling more together: Group attention intensifies emotion. *Emotion, 14*, 1102–1114.

Shteynberg, G., Hirsh, J. B., Galinsky, A. D., & Knight, A. P. (2014). Shared attention increases mood infusion. *Journal of Experimental Psychology: General, 143*, 123–130.

Smith, E. R., & Mackie, D. M. (2014). Priming from others' observed or simulated responses. *Social Cognition, 32*, 184–195.

Thayer, J. F., & Lane, R. D. (2000). A model of neuro-visceral integration in emotion regulation and dysregulation. *Journal of Affective Disorders, 61*, 201–216.

Wilson, T. D., & Gilbert, D. T. (2008). Explaining away: A model of affective adaptation. *Perspectives on Psychological Science, 3*(5), 370–386.

PART II
Positive Traits and States

7

MINDFULNESS

Ellen J. Langer and Christelle T. Ngnoumen

Eastern and Western Origins of Mindfulness

Eastern approaches to mindfulness, rooted in ancient Hindu and Buddhist philosophies, make three major assumptions about human nature. First, they posit a monism between body and mind, and maintain that there is only one unified substance in terms of which human experience can be explained. A second major assumption is that consciousness (or mind) is the core of our existence. According to this view, the experiences of pleasure and pain, of good and bad, of time and space, and of life and death have no truth or objective meanings apart from our awareness (e.g. thoughts) of them. Reality therefore is a product of our conscious experience, which is itself, the product of our ever-changing sequence of thoughts. Third, because mind and body are seen as integrated units of the person, the practice of meditation is emphasized in Hindu and Buddhist philosophy as a means by which one learns to control the mind as well as bring the physical body under the control of the mind (Burns, 2013; Rao, Paranjpe, & Dalal, 2008). The Eastern concept of mindfulness has undergone numerous transformations following its introduction into Western culture and contemporary psychology.

An Eastern-derived branch of mindfulness has borrowed meditative elements from the Eastern camp and applied them to Western settings. This Eastern-derived model is exemplified by the works of Herbert Benson and Jon Kabat-Zinn. According to Benson (2001), the mind and body are one system, with the experiences of the latter capable of being regulated by the qualities of the former. Benson's work on the relaxation response showed that people can counteract the toxic effects of chronic stress by engaging in deep abdominal breathing (and other relaxation-eliciting meditative exercises), which slows down breathing rate, relaxes muscles, and reduces blood pressure.

Kabat-Zinn's work on the clinical applications of mindfulness showed that cultivating mindfulness through the practice of meditation improves health (Kabat-Zinn, 2003; Ludwig & Kabat-Zinn, 2008). Similar to Benson, Kabat-Zinn's mindfulness-based stress reduction (MBSR) program involves relaxation techniques such as yoga and breathing exercises, and has proven effective in ameliorating symptoms related to pain, stress, anxiety, depression, and other chronic conditions.

A Western conception of mindfulness, spearheaded by Langer and colleagues' work on mindlessness and choice, stands in sharp contrast to Eastern and Eastern-derived approaches in its de-emphasis of meditative practices as tools for attaining a mindful state of well-being (Ie, Ngnoumen, & Langer, 2014). Instead, this view of "mindfulness without mediation" emphasizes the cognitive processes of noticing new things, attending to variability, and of actively drawing distinctions. While Eastern and Eastern-derived approaches of mindfulness emphasize meditative practices geared toward controlling the mind by regulating and disciplining the body (e.g. breath work; sitting meditations; adherence to ritualism), Western conceptions reinforce a more flexible process of attending to novelty and variability as an avenue for increasing control over one's internal and external environments. Langer and colleagues' work on mindfulness was conducted almost entirely within a Western scientific and social psychological perspective, without any reference to Eastern spiritual thought and practice.

Western Mindfulness (by Way of Mindlessness)

During the 1970s' cognitive revolution, when social psychologists became preoccupied with understanding human thinking, Langer and colleagues observed that people were actually inattentive and disengaged (that is, *mindless*) most of the time. In one such study on mindless behavior, confederates approached unknowing participants in a printing store, asking to move ahead of them in line to make copies. Depending on the experimental condition, confederates made small (5 copies) or large (20 copies) printing requests. Furthermore, the requests were presented directly with no additional information (e.g. *"May I use the Xerox machine?"*), with nonsense information (e.g. *"May I use the Xerox machine, because I have to make copies?"*), or with real information (e.g. *"May I use the Xerox machine, because I'm in a rush?"*). They found that when the request was small (e.g. jump ahead to make fewer copies than the participant), unknowing participants defaulted to a mindless script of "a favor is being asked and a reason is given, therefore I will comply" and 93 percent of them complied when the nonsense information was given versus only 60 percent complied when no information was given. By contrast, when the request was large (e.g. jump ahead to make more copies than the participant), perhaps this more obvious cost for participants allowed them to attend to the reasons given by the confederates in a manner that made them less swayed by nonsense information (Langer, Blank, & Chanowitz, 1978).

This original exploration into human mindlessness eventually inspired the development of a more Western conception of mindfulness that was concerned with reconnecting the mind to the body. According to this introduction of mind–body monism, wherever we put the mind, we also put the body. Moreover, if the mind is in a healthy place, so will be the body, and in this way we can alter physical health and well-being by altering the mind. Across a series of experiments that exploited this mind–body connection (Park, Francesco, Reece, Phillips, & Langer, 2016; Langer, Djikic, Pirson, Madenci, & Donohue, 2010; Langer, Hatem, Joss, & Howell, 1989), Langer and colleagues were able to uncover a wide range of untapped human capabilities—that is, a "psychology of possibility"—residing in the unified space between mind and body. This "psychology of possibility" has revealed that *knowing what is* (mindlessness) versus *knowing what could be* (mindfulness) lends to strikingly different outcomes in health and well-being, and was observed by Langer and colleagues long before the positive psychology movement and its focus on happiness and human strengths emerged in the late 1990s (Seligman & Csikszentmihalyi, 2000).

From Knowing What Is (Mindlessness) to Knowing What Could Be (Mindfulness)

Chanowitz and Langer (1981) discovered that information delivered mindlessly using absolute terms tended to be taken at face value, trapping listeners into a narrowed way of thinking and behaving that was bound to the context in which the information was learned. Moreover, mindful teaching, marked by the use of conditional statements (e.g. "A could be B" rather than "A is B" or "A is a model for B"), increased students' creativity and attention, and improved memory. They concluded that the latter two presentations (e.g. "A *is* B" and "A *is a model for* B") locked listeners into seeing novel information in only one particular way, whereas the former presentation (e.g. "A *could be* B") allowed for more flexibility in thinking by opening the range of potential ways of interpreting the information. When conditional language was incorporated into instructions for assignments, for example, students demonstrated greater performance, as they were able to access their knowledge stores more flexibly as well as generate more creative responses.

In another experiment, students were given different versions of a typical examination; one version presented the information in deterministic and closed-ended terms and the other version presented the information as a set of stylized facts, whose statistical nature was apparent. They found that students who were presented with the stylized facts version were more open to criticism and generated more creative answers compared to those who were presented with the closed-ended version. Relatedly, Lieberman and Langer (1997) found that presenting information from multiple perspectives increased students' creativity and produced a better writing performance. Altogether, these experiments became the basis of Langer's theory of mindlessness. According to this theory, we become mindless when we allow distinctions and categories drawn in the past to over-determine the present by not modifying them or by not testing them against present realities.

Mindless adherence to outdated information has serious implications for health and well-being. Mindlessness locks individuals within a self-imposed view of the world that is static. This view is *static* because all incoming information is adopted at face value without challenging original categories and without consideration of the original context. Static views of the world and of the world's labels can narrow experience such as by narrowing an individual's understanding of what constitutes health and illness, the understanding of what constitutes cure, as well as their awareness of alternative therapeutic solutions. Illustrating this point, Lai, Hong, and Chee (2001) found that people who were labeled "ill" experienced a more pronounced decline in their general functioning and self-esteem than those suffering from the same symptoms, who did not receive the label. More importantly, this view is *self-imposed* because it is a function of personal choice and of the fact that we have control over our attention and over the kinds of information we decide to focus on.

In an experiment involving hotel chambermaids, Crum and Langer (2007) discovered a decrease in weight, blood pressure, body fat, waist-to-hip ratio, and body mass index among female room attendants who were informed that their "work" also qualified as "exercise" according to the Surgeon General's recommendations. This was in comparison to a control group who were not given this information. These results suggest that rigid adherence to expectations, such as what does or does not constitute "exercise," can be of disservice to us in cases where expectations are narrow. Making the chambermaids more aware—that is, more mindful—of a broader definition of exercise allowed them to reap the health benefits of significant physical activity they had previously been engaging in mindlessly. That is, increasing perceived exercise (which involves a shift in attention and focus)—independent of actual exercise—resulted in physiological benefits.

We unfortunately still live in a culture that imbues the concept of "work" with negative associations, stress being a salient one. The majority of people perceive work as a necessarily stressful experience in a manner that serves as a self-fulfilling prophecy. Perceived work contributes to higher cortisol (stress hormone) levels that have been shown to cause weight gain by creating and trapping fat deposits in the body, particularly in the abdominal area (Moyer et al., 1994). The physiological improvements experienced by the chambermaids in Crum and Langer's (2007) study could be explained by their reframing of their "work" as "exercise" in a manner that decreased cortisol stress levels and allowed for weight loss in the absence of increased actual exercise.

Carson and Langer (2006) also compared the health and well-being of breast cancer survivors who were instructed to view their cancer as either "in remission" or as "cured." Whereas "cured" primes an idea of health, "in remission" primes a notion of illness. Post-test assessments of general functioning confirmed this, revealing greater general health and emotional well-being among cancer survivors who considered themselves cured, compared to those who considered themselves in remission. These experiments show how mindful and mindless evaluations of information can directly inform happiness and well-being, as well as impact physiological functioning.

Benefits of Mindfulness on Health and Well-Being

Over 35 years of research on the topic of mindfulness reveals that the simple processes of noticing and creating variability are literally and figuratively enlivening. Classic work by Langer and Rodin (1976) found that institutionalized elderly adults who were encouraged to become more mindful by taking on more personal responsibilities and making decisions about their living environments and their daily routines (e.g. arranging furniture in their living spaces; taking care of a plant) reported greater perceived control and became more alert, active, happy, and healthy compared to a control group whose care was entirely determined by nursing home staff. This experimental group also lived longer than the control group (Rodin & Langer, 1977). Langer and colleagues realized that choice-making prompts a more mindful state by increasing one's awareness of variability and alternative results; by increasing opportunities for re-evaluation and engagement; and by creating the freedom to discover meaning in one's actions. Whereas elderly residents in the control group remained dependent on staff to make decisions for them, those in the experimental group were prompted to view the ways in which their actions had direct consequences and to perceive themselves as agentic more generally. This boost in perceived control likely became part of a larger thought pattern associated with optimism (Klein & Helweg-Larsen, 2002).

In another experiment, Langer et al. (1990) took elderly men to a retreat retrofitted 20 years earlier and instructed them to live for a week as if it were 20 years earlier. Participants in the experimental group were instructed to be psychologically where they were 20 years prior and to hold all their discussions about the past in the present tense. By comparison, control group participants were instructed to merely reminisce about the past 20 years without actively reliving them. This control group was instructed to hold all discussions about the past in the past tense. At the end of one week, the experimental group demonstrated greater dexterity, grip strength, flexibility, hearing, vision, and memory and cognition compared to controls. This experiment showed that humans have the capacity to shift discontinuously to a different—that is, earlier—context, and that such a mindset shift, or cognitive reappraisal, can also shift physical and cognitive functioning. It was the change in mindset, much the same way a placebo works, that accounted for the difference between the two groups. By priming a time when they were vital, their previously established mindsets of old age as a time of debilitation and decline became irrelevant.

Other studies have demonstrated that cognitive reappraisals provide relief from the pains of major surgery. Langer, Janis, and Wolfer (1975) instructed a group of patients undergoing surgery to replace their worries about surgery with thoughts about the positive aspects of the hospital experience and to rehearse these positive thoughts. Patients in the experimental group involving the cognitive reappraisal intervention demonstrated better post-surgery adjustment, less post-operative anxiety, less pain, and less pain medication usage compared to matched placebo control and information groups.

Since Langer et al.'s seminal finding, research continues to demonstrate that people can achieve better health by shifting their mindsets and by reorienting their attitudes toward themselves and their environments. Studies show that mindful traits such as active engagement, choice-making, orientation in the present, and cognitive reappraisal reduce negative affect and stress, cultivate creativity, heighten competence, improve psychological well-being and quality of life, and reduce burnout (Creswell, Way, Eisenberger, & Lieberman, 2007; Idler & Kasl, 1991; Kaplan & Camacho, 1983; Levy, Slade, Kunkel, & Kasl, 2002).

Mindfulness challenges assumptions and prior beliefs by generating positive potential outcomes of meaning in a manner that may be more advantageous. The mindful processes of orienting toward the present, being open to novelty, noticing distinctions, attending to differences in contexts, and managing multiple perspectives all serve to test outdated assumptions against novel circumstances. This kind of reality-testing affords individuals a chance to refine previously established expectations in a way that aligns them better within current contexts. Mindfulness also offers individuals the chance to extend beyond their perceived cognitive and physical limitations toward greater creativity and more optimal functioning.

Mindful and Mindless Evaluation

Life is the product of ongoing evaluation. The majority of our day-to-day experiences are either reactions or responses to our evaluations of events, our evaluations of other people, and our evaluations of ourselves. These unique experiences also interact with the incoming evaluations of the people around us, which are either directly or indirectly obtained during communications and the usage of labels. Events therefore are never observed as they really are; rather, they emerge already situated within our own unique viewpoints, motives, past experiences, expectations, as well as within the labels provided to us by others. All of these factors inform our subsequent observations in a manner

that automatically transforms objective events into subjective experiences. The actual objects of our observations are not inherently good or bad; rather, we evaluate objects of our observations positively or negatively. Moreover, each of these evaluations occurs mindlessly (e.g. via passive acceptance and reactance) or mindfully (e.g. via active choice and active decision making), and the documented consequences of being in either state are enormous.

While evaluations are certainly adaptive in guiding us through unpredictability, over-reliance on the evaluations, themselves, can trap us in a subjective state residing far from any objective relevance. Mindfulness involves recognizing that we are responsible for our evaluations and that evaluations do not objectively exist out in the world beyond our control. Mindfulness also helps us understand that seeming facts are merely viewpoints. When we are mindful, we become sensitive to the contexts and perspectives that outline viewpoints. This more conditional stance toward our own and others' thoughts situates us in the present, and allows us to stay responsive in our environments—by exercising choice and by choosing among alternative evaluations—in a manner that allows greater control over our environments. Increased personal control, in turn, boosts positive affect and contributes to happiness and well-being.

By contrast, mindlessness involves rigid fixation on our initial evaluations in a manner that makes us reactive to and controlled by them. When we are mindless, we are trapped in our evaluations and become prejudiced (e.g. our viewpoints become facts that are resilient to new information); are oblivious to context or perspective; are unaware that we can choose among alternative evaluations and solutions; and are consequently robbed of personal control over our environments. Decreased perceived control, in turn, increases perceived helplessness, dampens mood, and triggers unhappiness (Hiroto & Seligman, 1975).

Variability, Uncertainty, and Fear

Variability spans the terrain of life. Natural climate variability causes some days to be warmer or drier than others while genetic variation promotes a diversity of species. Within-species human variation creates individuals of differing physiques, skin tones, temperaments, and behavioral predispositions. As humans, we navigate these physical, social, and psychological variabilities by imbuing them with meaning and value; assigning positive and negative values to different things allows us to make predictions about the future and informs our future behavior. Assigning value to objects in the world allows us to know which environments, objects and people to approach ("the good") and which ones to avoid ("the bad") in the future.

Mindful and mindless evaluations of the natural variabilities found in the world can either bolster or hinder the quality of life experiences, respectively. The clearest example of this is in the phenomenon of uncertainty. For some people, uncertainty prompts anxiety and leaves them paralyzed and reliant on routine and familiarity. This form of anxiety is a product of ongoing apprehensions about not being able to predict the future, and of strongly held expectations that one *should* be able to predict the future. For other people, uncertainty prompts excitement and orients their focus toward future challenges and growth experiences. Anxiety and excitement are both rooted in fear. So how is it that two fear-based responses to uncertainty could lend to such different outcomes?

Uncertainty reflects either mindful or mindless evaluation of variability. From a young age, we are taught to value control because control holds things still and creates a sense of stability (Langer, 2009). At an implicit level, this cultural value of control suggests that natural variability is not to be accepted and tolerated. We are taught that we *should* minimize uncertainty by implementing structure and via rigid adherence to routine. When such cultural beliefs and values are adopted mindlessly (that is, at face value and as expectations), future experiences of variability trigger feelings of apprehension and anxiety. When people are mindless, moment-to-moment observations of variability in the world and in themselves (e.g. isolated reports of crime; isolated experiences of low moods) are processed unconditionally, leading to a vague and indivisible image in the mind (e.g. *crimes are happening all the time therefore the world is unsafe; I experience low moods all the time therefore I am depressed*). Uncertainty that leaves us anxious, paralyzed, and reliant on routine and familiarity reflects a mindless evaluation of variability.

By contrast, uncertainty that leaves us excited, energized, and curious about novelty reflects a mindful evaluation of variability. An examination of interviews conducted with many of the world's most successful entrepreneurs reveals a common factor: the majority are optimistic, particularly about uncertainty (Ucbasaran, Westhead, Wright, & Flores, 2010). For these individuals, uncertainty is necessary for opportunity. In some cases the two concepts are even synonymous. The business world is highly unstable and unpredictable, but a fundamentally different orientation toward variability among these individuals increases their flexibility and alertness to their environment, and enables them to extract opportunities from it. This approach to uncertainty is energy-begetting, opens up the future, and reflects a mindful evaluation of variability.

Anxiety-based and excitement-based uncertainty, therefore, reflect mindless and mindful evaluations of variability, respectively. Fear, which is the basis of both anxiety and excitement, is itself merely the body's natural way of signaling change or novelty in the environment (Öhman, 2000). However, mindlessness interprets fear as fact and as an indication that one should avoid potential unknowns by restraining future behavior. Mindfulness, on the other hand, exploits fear by allowing the individual to orient his or her attentional resources toward the changes in the environment that the body has identified, which allows for greater engagement, learning, and growth.

Applying Mindfulness

When we are mindless, we lock ourselves into a single understanding of information learned either over time or upon single exposure. Mindfulness loosens the grips of these preconceptions and expectations in a manner that exploits uncertainty and allows us to learn what things could become, rather than merely know what things are. We come to see that context and perspective matter, and by actively exercising choice to select among alternative interpretations, both actual and perceived control are increased, triggering a cascade of positive effects on health and well-being. There are many ways in which mindful evaluation can be applied in everyday scenarios to unlock potentials and promote well-being. Some of these strategies are discussed next, and they can be applied to the experience of the individual or used to frame future positive psychological research on mindfulness.

Questioning Labels

Our experience of everything is formed by the words and ideas we attach to them. Langer and Abelson (1974) had therapists evaluate the video of a person being interviewed. The same person was referred to as "patient" in a video shown to half a group of participating clinicians and was referred to as "job applicant" to the other half. Despite the fact that these were highly educated clinicians trained to be careful observers of behavior, the labels "patient" and "job applicant" primed their overall impressions of the actors. The group of clinicians presented with the "patient" judged him as needing therapy, whereas the other group of clinicians presented with the "job applicant" viewed him as well-adjusted. This research reveals the power that labels and their associated expectations have in narrowing our judgments of others' well-being. These results, alongside Carson and Langer's (2006) finding of differences in functioning among breast cancer survivors who received the labels of "cured" or "in remission," also suggest a powerful role of labels in dictating one's own experience.

Negative societal expectations about the aging process are reflected in labels and common expressions, including "senior moments," which semantically links age and forgetfulness (Bonnesen & Burgess, 2004) and "over the hill," a phrase with indicates that once a person reaches a certain (peak) age, he or she will begin to decline. These kinds of societal stereotypes of old age, driven by language and labels, have been shown to contribute to decreased perceived control and decreased sense of self-efficacy among older adults.

The more we adhere to labels and categories, the more narrowed our experiences of ourselves and of others become, and the less open we are to possibility. The use of labels should therefore be questioned and, in some cases, completely revised, particularly if the use of an alternative label could prove to be empowering and promote greater functioning and well-being.

Reevaluating Work as Play

Experiences aren't monolithic. This is to say, for example, that there isn't only one way to characterize "work" and only one way to characterize "play." Both work and play involve active engagement with the environment and determination to master a task at hand. In some cases both work and play are fiscally rewarded. In other cases, neither involve financial rewards. By simply questioning our preconceptions of what constitutes work and play, and by outlining the ways in which they are similar and different, it becomes easier to see the ways in which they are similar.

"Work" and "play" aren't necessarily orthogonal, despite the mutual exclusivity implied by their conceptions. Crum and Langer's (2007) chambermaid study once again speaks directly to this and suggests that more of our work experiences be understood more broadly (e.g. as exercise and/or as play). Not only would this allow a person to find joy in activities once experienced as drudgery, but it could also allow him to reap the positive psychological and physiological effects associated with "exercise" and/or "play" as opposed to experiencing the negative effects associated with "work."

Procrastination at work is often the result of expectations (rooted in fear) that upcoming tasks will be difficult or unpleasant. Here, too, is a case where mindful re-evaluation of work and play could be useful. Consider a high school or college basketball athlete who needs to prepare for a mathematics exam, but feels overwhelmed by cultural "dumb jock" stereotypes of student athletes being superior in athletics but scholastically inferior. The mindless adoption of such stereotypes could self-fulfill, increasing his anxiety about the test, and could reinforce his expectation that studying for the exam would involve an insurmountable amount of work or requires a "natural intelligence" that he doesn't have. Here, mindful re-evaluation of work as play could be applied to stereotype threat (Steele & Aronson, 1995) by demonstrating to the student athlete ways in which the myriad of skill sets and executive functions involved in the playing of basketball (which he *does* possess) are also involved in solving mathematics problems (e.g. working memory; cognitive flexibility; task switching; set shifting; inhibitory control). Elaborating upon the ways in which the game of basketball resembles solving mathematics, at a more underlying level, might allow him to approach the task more favorably and confidently in a manner that would improve his performance.

Reevaluating work as play also increases mindfulness by maintaining curiosity and active engagement with the environment. Continual active engagement, in turn, promotes accuracy, creativity, and productivity in work performance by keeping the individual attentive to detail, alert to novelty, mentally flexible, and optimistic (Russ & Wallace, 2013).

Letting Go of All Expectations Except Growth and Change

Expectations are anchor points. Initially, they form the basis of our experiences and provide a foundation from which to understand subsequent events. Left untested over time, however, they can trap us in the same place: the past. Some of us remain unsatisfied in relationships by continually trying to find happiness in the same places where we lost it instead of looking beyond the given context. Despite a significant inverse relationship between economic growth and levels of life satisfaction over the last 25 years (Diener & Biswas-Diener, 2002; Diener, Sandvik, Seidlitz, & Diener, 1993), many continue to believe that wealth brings happiness; we continue to collect material affluence and to chase after the jobs promising the highest salaries. Others of us become chronically unsatisfied at work and assume linearity in life. In reality, however, life is marked by change and curvilinearity, and the more our attitudes can shift to incorporate all data points (e.g. life does not necessarily have to proceed from school to work to family to retirement; sometimes people go through two or multiple stages at once or skip certain stages altogether or repeat stages), the better we'll become at adapting to future turns of events.

Attending to Variability

Alongside learning to accept growth and change comes learning to attend to variability in life. Mindfulness-based research shows that stress is the byproduct of outdated or untested (e.g. mindless) assumptions regarding the stability of illness and aging. Little attention is paid to the daily variability of our experiences. People with chronic illness assume that their illness and its associated symptoms are present all of the time. The label "chronic" in chronic illness is largely to blame for this assumption of the stability and longevity of illness. As noted earlier, people diagnosed with depression or anxiety assume they are depressed or anxious all of the time. Similarly, people who have had and have conquered cancer, and are nevertheless told they are "in remission," might assume they have an inactive form of cancer that is lurking inside them and waiting to re-emerge. We even see this in cases where, after turning a certain age deemed "older" by society, a person begins to interpret normal instances of forgetfulness or of body aches as reflecting a more ongoing process of decline. In reality, however, people diagnosed with depression and anxiety are not depressed and anxious all of the time. They also experience moments of positive mood and relaxed states that get overlooked under the hoods of their diagnoses. In a related manner, both younger and older adults experience moments of forgetfulness and pain, therefore the presence of these states among older adults should not be interpreted as necessarily reflecting a process of decline. Attention should also be placed on the absence of forgetfulness and pain.

Not attending to variability can rob "happy" people of their positive experiences. Just as depressed people are expected to be depressed all the time, happy people are expected to be happy all the time. Similar to how depression and pain are perceived, happiness is perceived as an ongoing personal quality (e.g. a trait) as opposed to discontinuous positive experiences (e.g. states). There is an expectation that happiness must occur continually in order for its experience to be valid. This expectation of happiness can mindlessly exclude and isolate someone as incapable of experiencing true happiness if he is not continuously happy. Over time, such systematic discounting of states of joy can lend to ongoing unhappiness.

Attending to the variability of our emotional states can allow us to notice, but not adopt, depressed or anxious states. By attending to variability both internally (e.g. paying attention to fluctuations in one's moods) and externally (e.g. paying attention to fluctuations in *other* people's moods) people become aware of alternative states and of the fact that they can make choices among alternatives in a manner that can significantly alter future experiences. For example, choosing to focus on positive mood states, instead of negative mood states, may yield a more positive self-evaluation of functioning overall (e.g. a person may come to think, *By focusing on my positive mood states as opposed to just my negative mood states, I realize I'm not an unhappy person after all, I've just had some bad days*). Focus on positive mood states can, in turn, self-fulfill by motivating the individual to alter his or her behavior toward being more approach-oriented (e.g. seeking out friends) as opposed to avoidant (e.g. socially withdrawing). Closer attention to the variations in our emotional experiences can also allow us to notice and fully experience happiness when it emerges in a manner that common sense expectations would not predict.

Mindful attention to sensation variability has been shown to improve expecting mothers' well-being as well as improve neonatal outcomes. Zilcha-Mano and Langer (2016) instructed a group of expecting mothers (at weeks 25–30 of pregnancy) to attend to the variability of their negative and positive physical sensations during pregnancy. The well-being of these mothers, as well as the health outcomes of their infants following delivery, were compared to a control group of expecting mothers who did not receive the mindfulness attention to variability intervention. Zilcha-Mano and Langer found that mindfully attending to sensation variability during pregnancy predicted mothers' mental health, positive and negative affect, self-esteem, and life satisfaction up to at least one month after delivery. Training can help people be more attentive to variability in their lives in ways that can promote well-being.

Embracing Mistakes and Uncertainty: On Being Versus Becoming

In a discussion on mistakes, Schwartz (2011) suggests that commonly observed anxieties about making mistakes and being uncertain are rooted in old philosophical theories about *being* versus *becoming*. Individuals espousing a *being* (and arguably mindless) mentality see themselves and the world as fixed, static, and predictable. In contrast, individuals holding a *becoming* (i.e. mindful) mentality see themselves and the world as flowing and changing and necessarily unpredictable. Whereas the former worldview suggests that there is only one ideal endpoint, the latter worldview suggests a perpetual process of unfolding not marked by an endpoint. By implying the existence of an ideal end state (e.g. perfection), the *being* perspective roots people in the fear of making mistakes. The *becoming* perspective, on the other hand, exploits mistakes and uncertainty and considers them important turning points that drive continual rediscovery, redevelopment, and redefinition of the self.

The only mistake people make is to assume that mistakes are bad and to be avoided. People mistakenly assume that challenges and work are necessarily stressful and exhausting. The overthinking and worrying involved in maintaining these assumptions—rather than actual engagement in the activities, themselves—is perhaps the only part that's actually draining.

Mindful re-evaluation of mistakes involves understanding that a mistake is merely a misalignment between expectation and outcome. The wider the gap between the two, the greater the opportunity to exercise choice. Up until the mistake occurred, the path the individual was on was just a decision. This path/decision can be changed at any moment by selecting among other alternatives that may provide more desirable outcomes. Mistakes are turning points in a larger process of becoming, not fixed endpoints of being. Furthermore, uncertainty should always breed positive emotions because what we already know is fascinating, however what we don't know is even more so.

References

Benson, H. (2001). *The relaxation response.* New York: HarperCollins.

Bonnesen, J. L., & Burgess, E. O. (2004). Senior moments: The acceptability of an ageist phrase. *Journal of Aging Studies, 18*(2), 123–142.

Burns, D. M. (2013). Buddhist meditation and depth psychology. *Access to Insight, 30.* Retrieved from www.accesstoinsight.org/lib/authors/burns/index.html.

Carson, S. H., & Langer, E. J. (2006). Mindfulness and self-acceptance. *Journal of Rational-Emotive & Cognitive Behavior Therapy, 24*(1), 29–43.

Chanowitz, B., & Langer, E. J. (1981). Premature cognitive commitment. *Journal of Personality and Social Psychology, 41*(6), 1051–1063.

Creswell, J. D., Way, B. M., Eisenberger, N. I., & Lieberman, M. D. (2007). Neural correlates of dispositional mindfulness during affect labeling. *Psychosomatic Medicine, 69*(6), 560–565.

Crum, A. J., & Langer, E. J. (2007). Mind-set matters: Exercise and the placebo effect. *Psychological Science, 18*(2), 165–171.

Diener, E., & Biswas-Diener, R. (2002). Will money increase subjective well-being? A literature review and guide to needed research. *Social Indicators Research, 57,* 119–169.

Diener, E., Sandvik, E., Seidlitz, L., & Diener, M. (1993). The relationship between income and subjective well-being: Relative or absolute? *Social Indicators Research*, *28*(3), 195–223.

Hiroto, D. S., & Seligman, M. E. P. (1975). Generality of learned helplessness in man. *Journal of Personality and Social Psychology*, *31*, 311–327.

Idler, E. L., & Kasl, S. (1991). Health perceptions and survival: Do global evaluations of health status really predict mortality? *Journal of Gerontology*, *46*, 55–65.

Ie, A., Ngnoumen, C. T., & Langer, E. J. (2014). *The Wiley Blackwell handbook of mindfulness*. Chichester: John Wiley & Sons.

Kabat-Zinn, J. (2003). Mindfulness-based interventions in context: Past, present, and future. *Clinical Psychology: Science & Practice*, *10*(2), 144–156.

Kaplan, G. A., & Camacho, T. (1983). Perceived health and mortality: A nine-year follow-up of the human population laboratory cohort. *American Journal of Epidemiology*, *117*, 292–304.

Klein, C. T. F., & Helweg-Larsen, M. (2002). Perceived control and the optimistic bias: A metaanalytic review. *Psychology and Health*, *17*, 437–446.

Lai, Y. M., Hong, C. P., & Chee, C. Y. (2001). Stigma of mental illness. *Singapore Medical Journal*, *42*(3), 111–114.

Langer, E. J. (2009). *Counter clockwise: Mindful health and the power of possibility*. New York: Ballantine Books.

Langer, E. J., & Abelson, R. F. (1974). A patient by any other name …: Clinician group difference in labeling bias. *Journal of Consulting and Clinical Psychology*, *42*, 4–9.

Langer, E. J., Blank, A., & Chanowitz, B. (1978). The mindlessness of ostensibly thoughtful action: The role of "placebic" information in interpersonal interaction. *Journal of Personality and Social Psychology*, *36*(6), 635–642.

Langer, E., Chanowitz, B., Jacobs, S., Rhodes, M., Palmerino, M., & Thayer, P. (1990). Nonsequential development and aging. In C. Alexander & E. Langer (Eds.), *Higher stages of human development*. New York: Oxford University Press.

Langer, E. J., Djikic, M., Pirson, M., Madenci, A., & Donohue, R. (2010). Believing is seeing: Using mindlessness (mindfully) to improve visual acuity. *Psychological Science*, *21*(5): 661–666.

Langer, E. J., Hatem, M., Joss, J., & Howell, M. (1989). Conditional teaching and mindful learning: The role of uncertainty in education. *Creativity Research Journal*, *2*, 139–150.

Langer, E. J., Janis, I. L., & Wolfer, J. A. (1975). Reduction of psychological stress in surgical patients. *Journal of Experimental Social Psychology*, *11*(2), 155–165.

Langer, E. J., & Rodin, J. (1976). The effects of choice and enhanced personal responsibility for the aged: A field experiment in an institutional setting. *Journal of Personality and Social Psychology*, *34*(2), 191–198.

Levy, B. R., Slade, M., Kunkel, S., & Kasl, S. (2002). Longevity increased by positive self-perceptions of aging. *Journal of Personality and Social Psychology*, *83*, 261–270.

Lieberman, M., & Langer, E. J. (1997). Mindfulness in the process of learning. In E. J. Langer (Ed.), *The power of mindful learning*. Reading, MA: Addison Wesley.

Ludwig, D. S., & J. Kabat-Zinn (2008). Mindfulness in medicine. *The Journal of the American Medical Association*, *300*(11), 1350–1352.

Moyer, A. E., Rodin, J., Grilo, C. M., Cummings, N., Larson, L. M., & Rebuffé-Scrive, M. (1994). Stress-induced cortisol response and fat distribution in women. *Obesity Research*, *2*(3), 255–262.

Öhman, A. (2000). Fear and anxiety: Evolutionary, cognitive, and clinical perspectives. In M. Lewis & J. M. Haviland-Jones (Eds.), *Handbook of emotions* (pp. 573–593). New York: The Guilford Press.

Park, C., Francesco, P., Reece, A., Phillips, D., & Langer, E. J. (2016). Blood sugar level follows perceived time rather than actual time in people with type 2 diabetes. *Proceedings of the National Academy of Sciences of the United States of America, 113*(29), 8168–8170.

Rao, R. K., Paranjpe, A. C., & Dalal, A. K. (2008). *Handbook of Indian psychology.* New Delhi: Cambridge University Press.

Rodin, J., & Langer, E. J. (1977). Long-term effects of a control-relevant intervention with the institutionalized aged. *Journal of Personality and Social Psychology, 35*(12), 897–902.

Russ, S. W., & Wallace, C. E. (2013). Pretend play and creative processes. *American Journal of Play, 6*(1), 136–148.

Schwartz, M. (2011, May, 24). *What is a mistake* [Web log post]. Retrieved from http://melschwartz.com/what-is-a-mistake-2/.

Seligman, M. E., & Csikszentmihalyi, M. (2000). Positive psychology: An introduction. *The American Psychologist, 55*, 5–14.

Steele, C. M., & Aronson, J. (1995). Stereotype threat and the intellectual test performance of African Americans. *Journal of Personality and Social Psychology, 69*(5), 797–811.

Ucbasaran, D., Westhead, P., Wright, M., & Flores, M. (2010). The nature of entrepreneurial experience, business failure, and comparative optimism. *Journal of Business Venturing, 25*, 541–555.

Zilcha-Mano, S., & Langer, E. J. (2016). Mindful attention to variability intervention and successful pregnancy outcomes. *Journal of Clinical Psychology, 72*(9), 897–907.

8

OPTIMISM, HEALTH, AND WELL-BEING

Laura C. Bouchard, Charles S. Carver,
Maria G. Mens, and Michael F. Scheier

Among the key concepts of positive psychology is the disposition to be optimistic about life. The concept of optimism has been a subject of scientific study for over 30 years. It has roots both in folk psychology and in expectancy-value models of motivation (Eccles & Wigfield, 2002). A basic assumption of expectancy-value models is that goal pursuit underlies human behavior, and that goal pursuit depends on two elements. First is a goal's value; the more important a goal is, the more likely is its pursuit (Austin & Vancouver, 1996; Carver & Scheier, 1998; Higgins, 2006). Second is expectancy, the degree of confidence one has that he or she can reach the goal. People with little confidence in their ability to reach a goal may never pursue it to begin with, or may withdraw effort from its pursuit when facing challenges. On the other hand, those with more confidence will be more likely to persist in goal pursuit, even under adversity.

People form expectancies about goal attainment with regard to many contexts in life. These range from very narrow and specific circumstances to very broad swaths of the life space. Optimism is conceptualized as a broad and generalized sense of confidence about life outcomes, as opposed to confidence about a narrow or specific set of circumstances (Scheier & Carver, 1992). From this grounding in the expectancy-value viewpoint on motivation, one could broadly anticipate that optimists are generally more persistent and assured, compared to pessimists who are more hesitant and uncertain.

Measurement

Research has taken two approaches to measuring optimism. The first approach is to directly ask people about their expectancies regarding future events. That is, do you expect outcomes in your life to generally be good or bad (Scheier & Carver, 1992)? The most widely used measure of optimism takes this approach. On the Life Orientation Test (LOT) and the LOT-Revised (LOT-R), respondents report their degree of agreement or disagreement with statements about the future, such as "In uncertain times, I usually expect the best," and "I hardly ever expect things to go my way" (reverse scored; Scheier, Carver, & Bridges, 1994). Persons who report greater agreement with positive statements about the future and disagreement with negative statements about the future are more optimistic. Persons who report greater agreement with negative statements and disagreement with positive statements are more pessimistic.

A second approach to measuring optimism involves asking respondents to make attributions, or judgments, about the causes of past events in their lives. This approach arises from the idea that expectations for future events follow from interpretations of past events (Peterson & Seligman, 1984). For example, if a person believes that past failures in a particular domain are due to causes that are stable or unchanging, then he or she will likely expect future failures in that same domain. On the other hand, if the person believes that past failures are due to unstable or variable causes, then he or she is less likely to expect future failures in the same domain, because the prior causal influence may not be present in the future. The latter, more flexible attributional style is conceptually more optimistic. Thus, assessing the stability of attributions for past events may help identify whether individuals are more optimistic or pessimistic (Peterson & Seligman, 1984).

Although these two approaches converge on the same endpoint (confidence about life outcomes), they are not interchangeable. More specifically, attributional tendencies are only modestly correlated with direct measures of expectancies (Ahrens & Haaga, 1993; Peterson & Vaidya, 2001). The reason for this relative lack of association is not well understood. However, partly because assessment and scoring of the direct measures are more straightforward than is true of the attributional measures, researchers have in more recent years largely favored assessment of direct expectancies rather than attributional style.

Regardless of the approach that is used, assessing optimism results in a continuous distribution of scores. For simplicity, we often refer to people as either optimistic or pessimistic. In reality, however, most people fall somewhere in the middle of the continuum, with an overall bias in the direction of the optimistic side. That is, most people endorse agreement with optimistic statements and disagreement with pessimistic statements, but do so to differing degrees. True pessimism is less common, with less than a quarter of most samples falling below the neutral point (Segerstrom, 2006).

One more issue about assessment bears mention, which also represents a conceptual issue. Some items of the LOT-R refer to good outcomes while others refer to bad outcomes. The intent was to assess confidence that good outcomes would occur and confidence that bad outcomes would fail to occur; these were expected to correlate strongly. However, the two item subsets do not correlate as strongly as expected. This result raises a question: Does the imperfect association derive from the fact that people semantically process good and bad items differently or because there are two traits, one pertaining to good outcomes and the other pertaining to bad outcomes?

The answer is not fully clear. Some studies have found the item subsets predicted outcomes differentially (e.g. Marshall, Wortman, Kusulas, Hervig, & Vickers, 1992; Robinson-Whelen, Kim, MacCallum, & Kiecolt-Glaser, 1997), but many other studies have not. It has also been suggested that the loss of reliability associated with reducing the scale length (by splitting it into two subsets) might yield spurious differences between the two subscales (Segerstrom, Evans, & Eisenlohr-Moul, 2011). In any event, some people hold a unidimensional view (Rauch, Schweizer, & Moosbrugger, 2007; Segerstrom et al., 2011), whereas others prefer a two-dimensional view (Herzberg, Glaesmer, & Hoyer, 2006). In this chapter we treat optimism–pessimism as one dimension.

The relationship between optimism and well-being has been studied in widely varying contexts over the past 30 years and more. Optimism has been associated with diverse aspects of human experience, including goal pursuit behavior, the developing of social networks and relationships, emotional well-being, and physical health. Some illustrative findings from each of these areas of study are reviewed in the following sections.

Goal Pursuit

As noted above, optimism is rooted in expectancy-value models of motivation. It logically follows that optimism plays a role in active goal pursuit. One could expect that greater confidence in one's ability to reach a goal (i.e. greater optimism) is related to greater goal-directed efforts. This hypothesis has been studied mostly in student samples by examining their efforts in their courses as well as other variables that seem to follow from goal-directed efforts.

In one study of college freshmen, highly optimistic students were less likely to drop out of school after their first year than were more pessimistic students (Solberg Nes, Evans, & Segerstrom, 2009). In another study, this time with law students, more optimistic first-year students had higher income 10 years later than their less optimistic classmates (Segerstrom, 2007). This finding in particular suggests a relationship between greater optimism and long-term resource growth, as well as stronger pursuit of professional goals. Another study, across an undergraduate academic semester, showed that greater optimism was related to greater goal commitment and marginally related to better goal progress throughout the semester (Segerstrom & Solberg Nes, 2006).

Not all goals are alike, of course. People often are in pursuit of many goals at once, not all of which can be actively pursued simultaneously. Sometimes the pursuit of one goal hinders the pursuit of another concurrently held goal. This state of affairs is one way of defining goal conflict. Segerstrom and Solberg Nes

(2006) assessed two types of conflict in goal pursuit. The first was *resource conflict*, which occurs when goals compete for available resources such as time and money. For example, the goal of taking a vacation may compete for monetary resources with the goal of buying Christmas gifts. The second type of conflict was *inherent conflict*, which occurs when progress toward one goal intrinsically impedes the ability to reach another goal. For example, seeking a new romantic relationship competes with the goal of avoiding rejection. This study found that optimism among students was related to greater resource conflict, but not to inherent conflict. At the same time, optimism was related to greater psychological well-being, as evidenced by lower levels of depression and less rumination.

Those authors proposed two explanations for these findings (Segerstrom & Solberg Nes, 2006). First, it may be the case that resource conflict is less distressing than inherent conflict. Thus, greater conflict over allocation of resources and greater psychological well-being are not mutually exclusive. Second, it is possible that optimism predisposes individuals to a more efficient pursuit of goals through balance between goal value and conflict. In support of this idea, goal importance seemed to guide optimists in this study. Goals that optimistic students identified as more important received more effort and were more likely to be achieved. More pessimistic students, on the other hand, did not weigh importance as strongly in their pursuit or achievement of goals.

The relationship between optimism and goal-directed efforts has also been studied among persons facing health challenges. One study of women with fibromyalgia found that women were more likely to identify barriers to goal pursuit on days in which they also reported more pain or fatigue (Affleck et al., 2001). However, on these more painful or tiring days, more optimistic women were less likely to perceive goal barriers and less likely to disengage from goal pursuit than were more pessimistic women. In another study of women with breast cancer, greater optimism was associated with less concurrent and prospective disruptions of social activities due to cancer and its treatment up to 12 months later (Carver, Lehman, & Antoni, 2003).

In some cases, goals become unattainable (e.g. three low test scores may make it impossible to get an A in a course; progression of arthritis may make it impossible to play singles tennis). This changes the nature of the challenge the person is facing. When a goal is really unattainable, it is beneficial to disengage from it and set new, more attainable goals (Wrosch, Scheier, Carver, & Schulz, 2003). Although optimists and pessimists report finding it equally challenging to disengage from unattainable goals, optimists have reported greater ease in setting new goals. Consistent with this report, in the context of illness, other research has shown that optimistic older adults were more likely to replace lost activities with alternatives, which in turn was associated with greater well-being 1 year later (Duke, Leventhal, Brownlee, & Leventhal, 2002; Rasmussen, Wrosch, Scheier, & Carver, 2006). Another recent study found that both flexibility in goal adjustment and tenacity in goal pursuit mediated the relationship between optimism and greater well-being (Hanssen et al., 2015). In particular, flexible goal adjustment emerged as the strongest mechanistic pathway.

These studies have consistently shown that greater optimism is associated with greater goal pursuit. Whether in the context of college students demonstrating more commitment to educational studies and having a better allocation of effort to more highly valued goals, or in the context of health challenges and bolstering engagement in social and goal-directed activities despite the health challenge, it appears that greater optimism has beneficial effects on goal pursuit and engagement.

Social Resources

The relationship between optimism and goal pursuit also applies to the realm of social resources. Optimism is related to the building of social networks, which have far-reaching beneficial effects through both lessening the impact of negative events and promoting positive events (Cohen & Wills, 1985).

There are several mechanisms that may explain how optimism fosters the building of social resources. First is that optimistic individuals are perceived as more desirable social partners than are pessimistic individuals. Studies of college students have shown that pessimism is associated with less social acceptance than optimism (Carver, Kus, & Scheier, 1994; Helweg-Larsen, Sadeghian, & Webb, 2002). In relationships of patients undergoing coronary artery bypass grafting (CABG) and their caregivers, greater patient pessimism was associated with greater caregiver burden (Ruiz, Matthews, Scheier, & Schulz, 2006).

Just as optimists are viewed as more desirable social partners, optimists themselves view their own social partners as more supportive than do pessimists (Srivastava, McGonigal, Richards, Butler, & Gross, 2006). Consistent with this notion, greater optimism has been associated with higher perceptions of support in general among breast cancer patients (Abend & Williamson, 2002; Trunzo & Pinto, 2003).

Finally, it appears that optimists work harder at their relationships than do pessimists, even under conditions of stress. A longitudinal study of married couples showed that greater optimism was associated with greater cooperative problem solving in response to normal disagreements between partners (Assad, Donnellan, & Conger, 2007). This in turn was associated with better perceived relationship quality concurrently and up to 2 years later, and greater likelihood of the relationship surviving during that period.

Emotional Well-Being

As stated earlier, optimism constitutes a broad and generalized sense of confidence in life outcomes. A very simple but important extension of this conceptualization is that optimists, expecting good outcomes, generally respond to challenging life events with more positive emotions. Pessimists, on the other hand, generally expect poor outcomes and subsequently respond to challenging life events with more negative emotions such as sadness, anxiety, or anger (Carver & Scheier, 1998; Scheier & Carver, 1992).

The relationship between optimism and emotional well-being has been studied extensively in multiple contexts, and greater optimism is indeed associated with better emotional well-being. This has been shown in the context of students beginning college (Aspinwall & Taylor, 1992; Brissette, Scheier, & Carver, 2002) and participating in collegiate athletics (Vealey & Perritt, 2015); among caregivers of patients with cancer (Given et al., 1993) and spousal caregivers of patients with Alzheimer's disease (Hooker, Monahan, Shifren, & Hutchinson, 1992; Shifren & Hooker, 1995); in the context of medical diagnoses such as cancer (Carver et al., 1993; Friedman et al., 1992) and the progression of AIDS (Taylor et al., 1992); among individuals undergoing medical procedures such as bone marrow transplants (Curbow, Somerfield, Baker, Wingard, & Legro, 1993), *in vitro* fertilization (Litt, Tennen, Affleck, & Klock, 1992) and coronary bypass surgery (Fitzgerald, Tennen, Affleck, & Pransky, 1993; Scheier et al., 1989); in the context of childbirth (Carver & Gaines, 1987); and among survivors of missile attacks (Zeidner & Hammer, 1992).

Most of these studies were cross-sectional in design, assessing individuals at one time in the context of a stressful event or situation. Thus, the conclusions that can be drawn from them are limited to the observation that greater optimism and better emotional well-being typically go together during adverse events. Such studies do not clarify whether optimism and emotional well-being are associated, even in the absence of an adverse event. More information on the role of adversity can be garnered from longitudinal studies, which have mostly been conducted in the context of how individuals cope with health stressors.

Many studies that have assessed the relationship between optimism and well-being have been conducted among individuals with cardiovascular disease. Studies have shown that greater optimism pre-surgery for CABG was associated with faster post-surgical physical recovery and faster return to normal life activities (Scheier et al., 1989), as well as with greater emotional well-being, 8 months post-surgery (Fitzgerald et al., 1993). In a study of individuals hospitalized with ischemic heart disease, lower levels of optimism during hospital admission for myocardial infarction or unstable angina were associated with greater depressive symptoms 1 year post-hospital discharge (Shnek, Irvine, Stewart, & Abbey, 2001).

Studies of persons with cancer have revealed similar associations. One study of patients with breast cancer showed that optimism at time of diagnosis was consistently associated with lower emotional distress at multiple time points throughout the treatment trajectory, including 1 day pre-surgery and up to 12 months post-surgery (Carver et al., 1993). Similarly, among head and neck cancer patients, greater pre-treatment optimism was associated with better global ratings of health-related quality of life before treatment initiation and up to 3-months post-treatment (Allison, Guichard, & Gilain, 2000).

Researchers and health care providers have also recognized that the effects of health stressors often reach beyond the patients (Kim, Carver, Shaffer, Gansler, & Cannady, 2015). In some cases, caregivers may even experience greater deterioration of quality of life than the patients themselves (Roach, Averill, Segerstrom, & Kasarskis, 2009). One study among cancer caregivers found that greater caregiver optimism was associated with lower reports of caregiver depression and less physical health consequences of caregiving (Given et al., 1993). Other studies have found similar results among spousal caregivers of patients with Alzheimer's disease (Hooker et al., 1992; Shifren & Hooker, 1995).

Finally, the association between greater optimism and greater emotional well-being has been shown across many developmental periods. For example, among young adults, greater optimism has been associated with less distress at the beginning and end of the first college semester (Aspinwall & Taylor, 1992; Brissette et al., 2002) and across the first semester of law school (Segerstrom, Taylor, Kemeny, & Fahey, 1998). At the other end of the developmental spectrum, the process of aging itself may produce challenges such as both minor and major illnesses, loss of mobility, and bereavement. Among elderly community-dwelling men, greater optimism was protective against the development of depressive symptoms across a 15-year follow-up (Giltay, Zitman, & Kromhout, 2006). However, recent evidence suggests that this buffering of optimism against depressive symptoms may weaken as people approach the higher end of the 65- to 90-year age range (Wrosch, Jobin, & Scheier, 2016). More study is necessary to further elucidate this relationship.

Mechanisms for Emotional Well-Being

Why does optimism lead to higher emotional well-being? One possibility is that optimists cope with adversity in ways that promote greater well-being, whereas less optimistic persons use a less effective pattern of coping.

Many different coping responses have been identified (Compas, Connor-Smith, Saltzman, Thomsen, & Wadsworth, 2001; Folkman & Moskowitz, 2004; Skinner, Edge, Altman, & Sherwood, 2003), and they have been categorized in many ways (Carver & Connor-Smith, 2010; Skinner et al., 2003). One way to categorize them is to distinguish between problem-focused coping and emotion-focused coping. Problem-focused responses emphasize doing something to change or mitigate the stressor, whereas emotion-focused responses emphasize minimizing distress caused by the stressor (Lazarus & Folkman, 1984). Another dimension distinguishes between engagement or approach coping and disengagement or avoidance coping. Engagement/approach responses emphasize facing a stressor or emotion caused by the stressor and trying to do something about it, whereas disengagement/avoidance responses emphasize escaping the stressor or associated emotion (e.g. Roth & Cohen, 1986; Skinner et al., 2003).

These two distinctions are relatively independent. When crossed, they create four categories of coping: problem-focused engagement coping, emotion-focused engagement coping, problem-focused avoidant coping, and emotion-focused avoidant coping. A meta-analysis has revealed that optimism was associated with greater engagement coping generally, through both problem-focused and emotion-focused pathways (Solberg Nes & Segerstrom, 2006). Further, optimists were more likely to display a good match between the particular stressor and the coping response invoked. For stressors that were controllable or changeable (e.g. academic stress) optimists used more problem-focused coping responses. For stressors that were uncontrollable or unchangeable (e.g. past trauma) optimists used more emotion-focused responses. This pattern resulted in efforts to alter manageable situations and relieve distress in uncontrollable situations. Often seen as optimal matching of coping strategy to particular stressor, this pattern of coping reflects flexible engagement.

Many of the studies reviewed earlier under optimism and emotional well-being also assessed the role of coping. For example, in a study of individuals with cardiovascular disease, patients who reported greater optimism pre-CABG surgery also reported greater planning and goal-setting for recovery (Scheier et al., 1989). These same persons also focused less on negative aspects of the recovery experience. When patients were followed post-surgery, more optimistic ones reported more problem-focused coping, such as information seeking about recovery, and less use of avoidant coping responses, such as suppression of thoughts related to their symptoms. A different study of students' adjustment to college found that greater optimism was associated with more positive adjustment, and this relationship was mediated by coping responses (Aspinwall & Taylor, 1992). Specifically, greater optimism was associated with less use of avoidant coping responses and greater use of active coping responses, which were in turn associated with more positive adjustment to college.

Among women with suspected breast cancer, greater pessimism pre-biopsy was associated with greater cognitive avoidance approaching the biopsy (Stanton & Snider, 1993). In turn, greater cognitive avoidance was associated with greater post-biopsy and post-surgery distress. In another study of women with confirmed breast cancer, greater optimism was associated with less distress over time (Carver et al., 1993). This relationship was largely mediated by coping responses such as acceptance of the present situation and use of humor, and less use of responses such as denial and disengagement. In yet another study, more optimistic women with breast cancer reported greater quality of life at diagnosis and 12-month follow-up compared to more pessimistic women (Schou, Ekeberg, & Ruland, 2005). This relationship was driven by the relationship between optimism and greater fighting spirit. That is, optimists were more likely to report confronting cancer with a commitment to beating it.

Taken together, the differing use of coping responses seems to be a key distinction between optimists and pessimists. The use of acceptance versus denial may be particularly crucial. Acceptance is an optimistic response and is often misconstrued. Acceptance is not "giving up" or "getting over it." Rather, acceptance is a restructuring of one's goals in light of changing circumstances. Rather than promoting disengagement from goals, acceptance may actually keep people engaged in their goals and thus engaged in their lives (Scheier & Carver, 2001). Denial, on the other hand, is an overt refusal to accept a given situation's reality.

Physical Health

Considerable research has also focused on the relationship between optimism and physical well-being. Early research on optimism and physical health focused on optimism's relation to short-term health outcomes. The main motivation behind this work was simply to test, as efficiently as possible, whether such relationships exist. These studies consistently found that optimists have better physical health than pessimists. For example, optimism was found to predict a lower likelihood of re-hospitalization after coronary artery bypass surgery (Scheier et al., 1999), as well as faster wound healing (Ebrecht et al., 2004).

More recently, a number of epidemiological studies have substantially extended the research linking optimism and physical health. Typically, these studies enroll samples of initially healthy participants and measure the incidence (number of new cases) of disease over many years. Long periods of follow-up time are necessary, as many diseases, such as cardiovascular disease and cancer, take years and even decades to develop. Furthermore, because many people do not develop these diseases, studies have to recruit large numbers of participants in order to have adequate statistical power to detect associations. Participant numbers in these studies have ranged from the 1000s to upwards of 100,000.

One of the largest epidemiological studies to investigate the effects of optimism on physical health was conducted by Tindle et al. (2009). They administered a measure of optimism to over 95,000 initially healthy Caucasian and African American women. Eight years later, they found that optimists were less likely to have developed coronary heart disease (CHD) and were less likely to have died from any cause, as compared to pessimists. Consistent with these findings, a number of other epidemiological studies have shown that optimism predicts a lower incidence of stroke and CHD (Kim, Park, & Peterson, 2011; Nabi et al., 2010), as well as lower overall mortality rates (Engberg et al., 2013; Giltay, Kamphuis, Kalmijn, Zitman, & Kromhout, 2006).

Overall, this epidemiological research strongly suggests that individual differences in optimism are associated with susceptibility to and mortality from cardiovascular diseases, such as CHD and stroke. Evidence linking optimism to other diseases, however, is more equivocal. In regards to cancer and HIV, findings have been contradictory, with some studies finding positive effects of optimism on these outcomes, and others finding no effects of optimism. In recent years, researchers have begun to explore other health domains, such as diabetes management, pregnancy, and *in vitro* fertilization in relation to optimism (e.g. Bleil et al., 2012; Brody, Kogan, Murry, Chen, & Brown, 2008; Lobel, DeVincent, Kaminer, & Meyer, 2000). These studies suggest that optimism may play a role in other health domains, but more research obviously is needed.

Physiological Mechanisms for Physical Well-Being

Given the evidence linking optimism to disease, research has begun to investigate physiological pathways by which individual differences in optimism might influence the development of specific diseases. For example, research has found that optimism predicts several biomarkers that are implicated in the development of cardiovascular diseases such as atherosclerosis (Matthews, Räikkönen, Sutton-Tyrrell, & Kuller, 2004), hypertension (Räikkönen & Matthews, 2008), obesity, cholesterol levels, triglyceride levels (Boehm, Williams, Rimm, Ryff, & Kubzansky, 2013), and indicators of systemic inflammation (Roy et al., 2010). However, research has yet to document whether these biomarkers mediate the association between optimism and the development of specific cardiovascular diseases.

In contrast to other biomarkers, optimism has shown a more qualified relationship with indicators of cell-mediated immunity. Research suggests that optimism may be related to better cell-mediated immunity under some conditions (e.g. during brief or controllable stressors), but worse cell-mediated immunity under other conditions (e.g. during prolonged or uncontrollable stressors; for a review see Segerstrom, 2005). As cell-mediated immunity is important for combating viruses and removing cancerous cells, this qualified relationship may partially explain the inconsistent findings linking optimism to cancer and HIV outcomes.

Behavioral Mechanisms for Physical Well-Being

The preceding section discussed physiological pathways that might underlie the relationship between optimism and specific disease outcomes. What these physiological pathways do not explain is how optimism exerts physiological effects in the first place. In this regard, optimism has a number of effects on behavioral and psychological factors, which may account for the relationship between optimism and health.

One of the most likely reasons optimists experience better health is that they engage in more positive health behaviors, while pessimists tend to engage in health-damaging behaviors. A number of studies have shown that optimists have a better diet (e.g. consuming more fruits and vegetables), are more physically active, and are more likely to consume alcohol in moderation (Steptoe et al., 2010). Optimists are also more educated when it comes to their health (Radcliffe & Klein, 2002) and are more likely to engage in and benefit from rehabilitative programs after major health challenges (Shepperd, Maroto, & Pbert, 1996). In contrast, pessimists are more likely to be smokers (Giltay, Geleijnse, Zitman, Buijsse, & Kromhout, 2007) and are more likely to suffer from substance abuse problems (Carvajal, Clair, Nash, & Evans, 1998). Future research is needed to test formally whether these health behaviors mediate the relationship between optimism and physical health.

Is There a Downside to Optimism?

Extensive evidence indicates that optimism is generally associated with positive life outcomes. Overall, it's good to be an optimist. Compared to pessimists, optimists generally experience less distress when faced with adversity. They address stress by coping more effectively, and they accomplish their goals and garner social resources to a greater degree than do pessimists. Taking all this evidence together, one may be left wondering if there is any downside to optimism. Perhaps.

One context in which optimism may not be expected to be beneficial is gambling. Recall that optimism is closely tied to goal engagement and persistence. Usually these behavioral properties are advantageous, but there is reason to suspect that they may work against a person in the context of gambling. In real-life circumstances, gambling ultimately always ends in losses. Gibson and Sanbonmatsu (2004) found that optimists report being more confident than pessimists at being able to win at gambling. When put into a lab situation, optimists were less likely than pessimists to reduce their bets after a loss. The meaning of that difference is hard to interpret, however, because the tendency to reduce bets after a loss and increase them after a win is superstitious behavior, earning the label "gambler's fallacy." In the same survey in which optimists reported greater confidence, they also failed to report more frequent gambling or any tendency to gamble longer than intended. This pattern raises questions about whether higher confidence actually translates into problematic behavior. Clearly more information is needed before any strong conclusion can be drawn.

Another study that raises questions about whether optimism can be problematic examined business entrepreneurs over time (Hmieleski & Baron, 2009). In this study, lower levels of optimism were associated with better performance in new ventures, in terms of revenue and employment growth. However, the authors pointed out that entrepreneurs as a group are highly optimistic to begin with. Thus, these results may suggest a curvilinear effect of optimism under specific conditions, such that there is a threshold for optimism, above which it

may stop being helpful and may even become detrimental. This possibility also warrants further study.

Applications and Future Directions

Applications

It is apparent from the preceding review that optimism is associated with many beneficial life outcomes. It is reasonable to wonder at this point how one may become more optimistic, and perhaps gain some of those beneficial outcomes. At this point there is not a great deal of systematic evidence on this question. One approach has been to guide individuals to make more optimistic explanations for events throughout their lives, or at least fewer pessimistic explanations (Seligman, 1991). Another recent study tested whether optimism can be increased through a very simple intervention in which individuals imagined their best possible self for five minutes each day (Meevissen, Peters, & Alberts, 2011). Compared to a control condition, those in the intervention group reported greater increases in optimism during the intervention period (2 weeks). However, the longer-term effects of that intervention are unknown.

One might argue, however, that many traditional approaches to psychotherapy aim in part to increase optimism among clients, despite generally having more specific focuses. For example, cognitive-behavioral therapies almost universally involve aiding people in approaching life in broadly more optimistic ways (Beck, 1976).

Nonetheless, it remains true that optimism is a personality trait, and personality traits are generally relatively stable over time, in the absence of strong intervention or a major life transition (Carver, Scheier, & Segerstrom, 2010). It is unclear whether relatively short mental simulations, such as imagining your best self, may have lasting effects. This same question could be applied to the effectiveness of traditional psychotherapies as well. Of course, the longevity of therapy effects is an important question more generally.

Future Directions

Over the past 30 years, a sizable collection of research has been accumulated to understand how optimism can affect various aspects of life, from goal pursuit to emotional well-being, to physical health. However, there are still many questions about optimism that remain unanswered. Future research has many potential paths to explore.

One of them is to gain further information on whether optimism is unidimensional. As noted in the section on measurement, current tools commonly used to assess optimism produce a distribution of scores along one dimension.

However, it is possible that optimism and pessimism are two distinct properties. This question needs further attention.

Another avenue for future research is mechanisms underlying the relationship between optimism and health. Since optimism has been reliably linked to both better physical health and health behaviors, it will be beneficial to pursue an understanding of the mechanisms of action among these relationships. Future research may also focus on the neural processes that underlie optimism, to better understand the biopsychosocial mechanisms driving relationships between optimism and physical health.

Finally, of great interest to many is the human ability to enhance optimism. Future research will likely continue to address ways to increase optimism through intervention. Another critical goal will be to determine whether therapy-induced optimism functions in the same way as does naturally occurring optimism.

Positive psychology, which represents an effort to identify and examine qualities that represent human strengths, incorporates a great many topics. These topics include a substantial number of personality traits. Surely one of the most broadly relevant of those traits is the disposition to face life with positive expectations for the future, despite the many challenges that will be confronted along the way.

References

Abend, T. A., & Williamson, G. M. (2002). Feeling attractive in the wake of breast cancer: Optimism matters, and so do interpersonal relationships. *Personality and Social Psychology Bulletin, 28*, 427–436.

Affleck, G., Tennen, H., Zautra, A., Urrows, S., Abeles, M., & Karoly, P. (2001). Women's pursuit of personal goals in daily life with fibromyalgia: A value-expectancy analysis. *Journal of Consulting and Clinical Psychology, 69*, 587–596. doi:10.1037/0022-006X.69.4.587.

Ahrens, A. H., & Haaga, D. A. F. (1993). The specificity of attributional style and expectations to positive and negative affectivity, depression, and anxiety. *Cognitive Therapy and Research, 17*, 83–98. doi:10.1007/BF01172742.

Allison, P. J., Guichard, C., & Gilain, L. (2000). A prospective investigation of dispositional optimism as a predictor of health-related quality of life in head and neck cancer patients. *Quality of Life Research, 9*, 951–960. doi:10.1023/A:1008931906253.

Aspinwall, L. G., & Taylor, S. E. (1992). Modeling cognitive adaptation: A longitudinal investigation of the impact of individual differences and coping on college adjustment and performance. *Journal of Personality and Social Psychology, 63*(6), 989–1003. doi:10.1037/0022-3514.63.6.989.

Assad, K. K., Donnellan, M. B., & Conger, R. D. (2007). Optimism: An enduring resource for romantic relationships. *Journal of Personality and Social Psychology, 93*, 285–297. doi:10.1037/0022-3514.93.2.285.

Austin, J. T., & Vancouver, J. B. (1996). Goal constructs in psychology: Structure, process, and content. *Psychological Bulletin, 120*, 338–375. doi:10.1037/0033-2909.120.3.338.

Beck, A. T. (1976). *Cognitive therapy and the emotional disorders.* New York: International Universities Press.

Bleil, M. E., Pasch, L. A., Gregorich, S. E., Millstein, S. G., Katz, P. P., & Adler, N. E. (2012). Fertility treatment response: Is it better to be more optimistic or less pessimistic? *Psychosomatic Medicine, 74*(2), 193–199. doi:10.1097/PSY.0b013e318242096b.

Boehm, J. K., Williams, D. R., Rimm, E. B., Ryff, C., & Kubzansky, L. D. (2013). Relation between optimism and lipids in midlife. *The American Journal of Cardiology, 111*(10), 1425–1431. doi:10.1016/j.amjcard.2013.01.292.

Brissette, I., Scheier, M. F., & Carver, C. S. (2002). The role of optimism in social network development, coping, and psychological adjustment during a life transition. *Journal of Personality and Social Psychology, 82*, 102–111. doi:10.1037/0022-3514.82.1.102.

Brody, G. H., Kogan, S. M., Murry, V. M., Chen, Y. F., & Brown, A. C. (2008). Psychological functioning, support for self-management, and glycemic control among rural African American adults with diabetes mellitus type 2. *Health Psychology, 27*(1S), S83–S90. doi:10.1037.0278-6133.27.1.S83.

Carvajal, S. C., Clair, S. D., Nash, S. G., & Evans, R. I. (1998). Relating optimism, hope, and self-esteem to social influences in deterring substance use in adolescents. *Journal of Social and Clinical Psychology, 17*(4), 443–465. doi:10.1521/jscp.1998.17.4.443.

Carver, C. S., & Connor-Smith, J. (2010). Personality and coping. *Annual Review of Psychology, 61*, 679–704. doi:10.1146/annurev.psych.093008.100352.

Carver, C. S., & Gaines, J. G. (1987). Optimism, pessimism, and postpartum depression. *Cognitive Therapy and Research, 11*, 449–462. doi:10.1007/BF01175355.

Carver, C. S., Kus, L. A., & Scheier, M. F. (1994). Effects of good versus bad mood and optimistic versus pessimistic outlook on social acceptance versus rejection. *Journal of Social and Clinical Psychology, 13*, 138–151. doi:10.1521/jscp.1994.13.2.138.

Carver, C. S., Lehman, J. M., & Antoni, M. H. (2003). Dispositional pessimism predicts illness-related disruption of social and recreational activities among breast cancer patients. *Journal of Personality and Social Psychology, 84*, 813–821. doi:10.1037/0022-3514.84.4.813.

Carver, C. S., Pozo, C., Harris, S. D., Noriega, V., Scheier, M. F., Robinson, D. S., … Clark, K. C. (1993). How coping mediates the effect of optimism on distress: A study of women with early stage breast cancer. *Journal of Personality and Social Psychology, 65*, 375–390. doi:10.1037/0022–3514.65.2.375.

Carver, C. S., & Scheier, M. F. (1998). *On the self-regulation of behavior.* New York: Cambridge University Press.

Carver, C. S., Scheier, M. F., & Segerstrom, S. C. (2010). Optimism. *Clinical Psychology Review, 30*, 879–889. doi:10.1016/j.cpr.2010.01.006.

Cohen, S., & Wills, T. A. (1985). Stress, social support and the buffering hypothesis. *Psychological Bulletin, 98*, 310–357. doi:10.1037/0033–2909.98.2.310.

Compas, B. E., Connor-Smith, J. K., Saltzman, H., Thomsen, A. H., & Wadsworth, M. E. (2001). Coping with stress during childhood and adolescence: Problems, progress, and potential in theory and research. *Psychological Bulletin, 127*, 87–127. doi:10.1037/0033–2909.127.1.87.

Curbow, B., Somerfield, M. R., Baker, F., Wingard, J. R., & Legro, M. W. (1993). Personal changes, dispositional optimism, and psychological adjustment to bone marrow transplantation. *Journal of Behavioral Medicine, 16*, 423–443. doi:10.1007/BF00844815.

Duke, J., Leventhal, H., Brownlee, S., & Leventhal, E. A. (2002). Giving up and replacing activities in response to illness. *Journal of Gerontology: Psychological Sciences, 57B*, 367–376.

Ebrecht, M., Hextall, J., Kirtley, L.-G., Taylor, A. M., Dyson, M., & Weinman, J. (2004). Perceived stress and cortisol levels predict speed of wound healing in healthy male adults. *Psychoneuroendocrinology, 29*(6), 798–809. doi:10.1016/S0306(03)00144-6.

Eccles, J. S., & Wigfield, A. (2002). Motivational beliefs, values, and goals. *Annual Review of Psychology, 53*, 109–132. doi:10.1146/annurev.psych.53.100901.135153.

Engberg, H., Jeune, B., Andersen-Ranberg, K., Martinussen, T., Vaupel, J. W., & Christensen, K. (2013). Optimism and survival: Does an optimistic outlook predict better survival at advanced ages? A twelve-year follow-up of Danish nonagenarians. *Aging Clinical and Experimental Research, 25*(5), 517–525. doi:10.1007/s40520-013-0122-x.

Fitzgerald, T. E., Tennen, H., Affleck, G., & Pransky, G. S. (1993). The relative importance of dispositional optimism and control appraisals in quality of life after coronary artery bypass surgery. *Journal of Behavioral Medicine, 16*, 25–43. doi:10.1007/BF00844753.

Folkman, S., & Moskowitz, J. T. (2004). Coping: Pitfalls and promise. *Annual Review of Psychology, 55*, 745–774. doi:10.1146/annurev.psych.55.090902.141456.

Friedman, L. C., Nelson, D. V., Baer, P. E., Lane, M., Smith, F. E., & Dworkin, R. J. (1992). The relationship of dispositional optimism, daily life stress, and domestic environment to coping methods used by cancer patients. *Journal of Behavioral Medicine, 15*, 127–141. doi:10.1007/BF00848321.

Gibson, B., & Sanbonmatsu, D. M. (2004). Optimism, pessimism, and gambling: The downside of optimism. *Personality and Social Psychology Bulletin, 30*, 149–160.

Giltay, E. J., Geleijnse, J. M., Zitman, F. G., Buijsse, B., & Kromhout, D. (2007). Lifestyle and dietary correlates of dispositional optimism in men: The Zutphen elderly study. *Journal of Psychosomatic Research, 63*(5), 483–490. doi:10.1016/j.psychores.2007.07.014.

Giltay, E. J., Kamphuis, M. H., Kalmijn, S., Zitman, F. G., & Kromhout, D. (2006). Dispositional optimism and the risk of cardiovascular death: The Zutphen elderly study. *Archives of Internal Medicine, 166*(4), 431–436. doi:10.1001/archinte.166.4.431.

Giltay, E. J., Zitman, F. G., & Kromhout, D. (2006). Dispositional optimism and the risk of depressive symptoms during 15 years of follow-up: The Zutphen elderly study. *Journal of Affective Disorders, 91*, 45–52. doi:10.1016/j.jpsychores.2007.07.014.

Given, C. W., Stommel, M., Given, B., Osuch, J., Kurtz, M. E., & Kurtz, J. C. (1993). The influence of cancer patients' symptoms and functional states on patients' depression and family caregivers' reaction and depression. *Health Psychology, 12*, 277–285. doi:10.1037/0278-6133.12.4.277.

Hanssen, M. M., Vancleef, L. M. G., Vlaeyen, J. W. S., Hayes, A. F., Schouten, E. G. W., & Peters, M. L. (2015). Optimism, motivational coping, and well-being: Evidence supporting the importance of flexible goal adjustment. *Journal of Happiness Studies, 16*, 1525–1537. doi:10.1007/s10902-014-9572-x.

Helweg-Larsen, M., Sadeghian, P., & Webb, M. S. (2002). The stigma of being pessimistically biased. *Journal of Social and Clinical Psychology, 21*, 92–107.

Herzberg, P. Y., Glaesmer, H., & Hoyer, J. (2006). Separating optimism and pessimism: A robust psychometric analysis of the revised life orientation test (LOT-R). *Psychological Assessment, 18*, 433–438. doi:1 0.1037/1040-3590.18.4.433.

Higgins, E. T. (2006). Value from hedonic experience and engagement. *Psychological Review, 113*, 439–460.

Hmieleski, K. M., & Baron, R. A. (2009). Entrepreneurs' optimism and new venture performance: A social cognitive perspective. *Academy of Management Journal, 52*, 473–488. doi:10.5465/AMJ.2009.41330755.

Hooker, K., Monahan, D., Shifren, K., & Hutchinson, C. (1992). Mental and physical health of spouse caregivers: The role of personality. *Psychology and Aging, 7,* 367–375. doi:10.1037/0882-7974.7.3.367.

Kim, Y., Carver, C. S., Shaffer, K. M., Gansler, T., & Cannady, R. S. (2015). Cancer caregiving predicts physical impairments: Roles of earlier caregiving stress and being a spousal caregiver. *Cancer, 121,* 302–310. doi:10.1002/cncr.29040.

Kim, E. S., Park, N., & Peterson, C. (2011). Dispositional optimism protects older adults from stroke: The health and retirement study. *Stroke, 42*(10), 2855–2859. doi:10.1161/STROKEAHA.111.613448.

Lazarus, R. S., & Folkman, S. (1984). *Stress, appraisal, and coping.* New York: Springer.

Litt, M. D., Tennen, H., Affleck, G., & Klock, S. (1992). Coping and cognitive factors in adaptation to *in vitro* fertilization failure. *Journal of Behavioral Medicine, 15,* 171–187. doi:10.1007/BF00848324.

Lobel, M., DeVincent, C. J., Kaminer, A., & Meyer, B. A. (2000). The impact of prenatal maternal stress and optimistic disposition on birth outcomes in medically high-risk women. *Health Psychology, 19*(6), 544–553. doi:10.1037/0278-6133.19.6.544.

Marshall, G. N., Wortman, C. B., Kusulas, J. W., Hervig, L. K., & Vickers, Jr., R. R. (1992). Distinguishing optimism from pessimism: Relations to fundamental dimensions of mood and personality. *Journal of Personality and Social Psychology, 62,* 1067–1074.

Matthews, K. A., Räikkönen, K., Sutton-Tyrrell, K., & Kuller, L. H. (2004). Optimistic attitudes protect against progression of carotid atherosclerosis in healthy middle-aged women. *Psychosomatic Medicine, 66*(5), 640–644. doi:10.1097/01.psy.0000139999.99756.a5.

Meevissen, Y. M. C., Peters, M. L., & Alberts, H. J. E. M. (2011). Become more optimistic by imagining a best possible self: Effects of a two week intervention. *Journal of Behavior Therapy and Experimental Psychiatry, 42,* 371–378. doi:10.1016/j.jbtep.2011.02.012.

Nabi, H., Koskenvuo, M., Singh-Manoux, A., Korkeila, J., Suominen, S., Korkeila, K., Kivimäki, M. (2010). Low pessimism protects against stroke: The health and social support (HeSSup) prospective cohort study. *Stroke, 41*(1), 187–190. doi:10.1161/STROKEAHA.109.565440.

Peterson, C., & Seligman, M. E. P. (1984). Causal explanations as a risk factor for depression: Theory and evidence. *Psychological Review, 91,* 347–374. doi:10.1037/0033-295X.91.3.347.

Peterson, C., & Vaidya, R. S. (2001). Explanatory style, expectations, and depressive symptoms. *Personality and Individual Differences, 31,* 1217–1223. doi:8869(00)00221-X.

Radcliffe, N. M., & Klein, W. M. P. (2002). Dispositional, unrealistic, and comparative optimism: Differential relations with the knowledge and processing of risk information and beliefs about personal risk. *Personality and Social Psychology Bulletin, 28*(6), 836–846. doi:10.1177/0146167202289012.

Räikkönen, K., & Matthews, K. A. (2008). Do dispositional pessimism and optimism predict ambulatory blood pressure during schooldays and nights in adolescents? *Journal of Personality, 76*(3), 605–630. doi:10.1111/j.1467-6494.2008.00498.x.

Rasmussen, H. N., Wrosch, C., Scheier, M. F., & Carver, C. S. (2006). Self-regulation processes and health: The importance of optimism and goal adjustment. *Journal of Personality, 74,* 1721–1747. doi:10.1111/j.1467-6494.2006.00426.x.

Rauch, W. A., Schweizer, K., & Moosbrugger, H. (2007). Method effects due to social desirability as a parsimonious explanation of the deviation from unidimensionality in LOT-R scores. *Personality and Individual Differences, 42,* 1597–1607. doi:10.1016/j.paid.2006.10.035.

Roach, A. R., Averill, A. J., Segerstrom, S. C., & Kasarskis, E. J. (2009). The dynamics of quality of life in ALS patients and caregivers. *Annals of Behavioral Medicine, 37,* 197–206. doi:10.1007/s12160-009-9092-9.

Robinson-Whelen, S., Kim, C., MacCallum, R. C., & Kiecolt-Glaser, J. K. (1997). Distinguishing optimism from pessimism in older adults: Is it more important to be optimistic or not to be pessimistic? *Journal of Personality and Social Psychology, 73,* 1345–1353.

Roth, S., & Cohen, L. J. (1986). Approach, avoidance, and coping with stress. *American Psychologist, 41,* 813–819. doi:10.1037/0003-066X.41.7.813.

Roy, B., Diez-Roux, A. V., Seeman, T., Ranjit, N., Shea, S., & Cushman, M. (2010). The association of optimism and pessimism with inflammation and hemostasis in the Multi-Ethnic Study of Atherosclerosis (MESA). *Psychosomatic Medicine, 72*(2), 134–140. doi:10.1097/PSY.0b013e3181cb981b.

Ruiz, J. M., Matthews, K. A., Scheier, M. F., & Schulz, R. (2006). Does who you marry matter for your health? Influence of patients' and spouses' personality on their partners' psychological well-being following coronary artery bypass surgery. *Journal of Personality and Social Psychology, 91,* 255–267. doi:10.1037/0022-3514.91.2.255.

Scheier, M. F., & Carver, C. S. (1992). Effects of optimism on psychological and physical well-being: Theoretical overview and empirical update. *Cognitive Therapy and Research, 16,* 201–228. doi:10.1007/BF01173489.

Scheier, M. F., & Carver, C. S. (2001). Adapting to cancer: The importance of hope and purpose. In A. Baum & B. L. Andersen (Eds.), *Psychosocial interventions for cancer* (pp. 15–36). Washington, DC: American Psychological Association.

Scheier, M. F., Carver, C. S., & Bridges, M. W. (1994). Distinguishing optimism from neuroticism (and trait anxiety, self-mastery, and self-esteem): A reevaluation of the life orientation test. *Journal of Personality and Social Psychology, 67,* 1063–1078. doi:10.1037/0022-3514.67.6.1063.

Scheier, M. F., Matthews, K. A., Owens, J. F., Magovern, G. J., Lefebvre, R. C., Abbott, R. A., … Carver, C. S. (1989). Dispositional optimism and recovery from coronary artery bypass surgery: The beneficial effects on physical and psychological well-being. *Journal of Personality and Social Psychology, 57,* 1024–1040. doi:10.1037/0022-3514.57.6.1024.

Scheier, M. F., Matthews, K. A., Owens, J. F., Schulz, R., Bridges, M. W., Magovern, G. J., Sr., & Carver, C. S. (1999). Optimism and rehospitalization following coronary artery bypass graft surgery. *Archives of Internal Medicine, 159,* 829–835.

Schou, I., Ekeberg, O., & Ruland, C. M. (2005). The mediating role of appraisal and coping in the relationship between optimism-pessimism and quality of life. *Psycho-Oncology, 14,* 718–727. doi:10.1002/pon.896.

Segerstrom, S. C. (2005). Optimism and immunity: Do positive thoughts always lead to positive effects? *Brain, Behavior, and Immunity, 19*(3), 195–200. doi:10.1016/j.bbi.2004.08.003.

Segerstrom, S. C. (2006). *Breaking Murphy's Law.* New York: Guilford Press.

Segerstrom, S. C. (2007). Optimism and resources: Effects on each other and on health over 10 years. *Journal of Research in Personality, 41,* 772–786. doi:10.1016/j.jrp.2006.09.004.

Segerstrom, S. C., Evans, D. R., & Eisenlohr-Moul, T. A. (2011). Optimism and pessimism dimensions in the life orientation test-revised: Method and meaning. *Journal of Research in Personality, 45,* 126–129. doi:10.1016/j.jrp.2010.11.007.

Segerstrom, S. C., & Solberg Nes, L. (2006). When goals conflict but people prosper: The case of dispositional optimism. *Journal of Research in Personality, 40*, 675–693. doi:10.1016/j.jrp.2005.08.001.

Segerstrom, S. C., Taylor, S. E., Kemeny, M. E., & Fahey, J. L. (1998). Optimism is associated with mood, coping, and immune change in response to stress. *Journal of Personality and Social Psychology, 74*, 1646–1655. doi:10.1037/0022-3514.74.6.1646.

Seligman, M. E. P. (1991). *Learned optimism.* New York: Knopf.

Shepperd, J. A., Maroto, J. J., & Pbert, L. A. (1996). Dispositional optimism as a predictor of health changes among cardiac patients. *Journal of Research in Personality, 30*(4), 517–534.

Shifren, K., & Hooker, K. (1995). Stability and change in optimism: A study among spouse caregivers. *Experimental Aging Research, 21*, 59–76.

Shnek, Z. M., Irvine, J., Stewart, D., & Abbey, S. (2001). Psychological factors and depressive symptoms in ischemic heart disease. *Health Psychology, 20*, 141–145. doi:10.1037/0278-6133.20.2.141.

Skinner, E. A., Edge, K., Altman, J., & Sherwood, H. (2003). Searching for the structure of coping: A review and critique of category systems for classifying ways of coping. *Psychological Bulletin, 129*, 216–269. doi:10.1037/0033-2909.129.2.216.

Solberg Nes, L., Evans, D. R., & Segerstrom, S. C. (2009). Optimism and college retention: Mediation by motivation, performance, and adjustment. *Journal of Applied Social Psychology, 39*, 1887–1912. doi:10.1111/j.1559-1816.2009.00508.x.

Solberg Nes, L., & Segerstrom, S. C. (2006). Dispositional optimism and coping: A meta-analytic review. *Personality and Social Psychology Review, 10*, 235–251. doi:10.1111/j.1559-1816.2009.00508.x.

Srivastava, S., McGonigal, K. M., Richards, J. M., Butler, E. A., & Gross, J. J. (2006). Optimism in close relationships: How seeing things in a positive light makes them so. *Journal of Personality and Social Psychology, 91*, 143–153. doi:10.1037/0022-3514.91.1.143.

Stanton, A. L., & Snider, P. R. (1993). Coping with breast cancer diagnosis: A prospective study. *Health Psychology, 12*, 16–23. doi:10.1037/0278-6133.12.1.16.

Steptoe, A., Wright, C., Kunz-Ebrecht, S. R., & Iliffe, S. (2010). Dispositional optimism and health behaviour in community-dwelling older people: Associations with healthy aging. *British Journal of Health Psychology, 11*(1), 71–84. doi:10.1348/135910705X42850.

Taylor, S. E., Kemeny, M. E., Aspinwall, L. G., Schneider, S. G., Rodriguez, R., & Herbert, M. (1992). Optimism, coping, psychological distress, and high-risk sexual behavior among men at risk for acquired immunodeficiency syndrome (AIDS). *Journal of Personality and Social Psychology, 63*, 460–473. doi:10.1037/0022-3514.63.3.460.

Tindle, H. A., Chang, Y. F., Kuller, L. H., Manson, J. E., Robinson, J. G., Rosal, M. C., … Matthews, K. A. (2009). Optimism, cynical hostility, and incident coronary heart disease and mortality in the Women's Health Initiative. *Circulation, 120*(8), 656–662. doi:10.1161/CIRCULATIONAHA.108.827642.

Trunzo, J. J., & Pinto, B. M. (2003). Social support as a mediator of optimism and distress in breast cancer survivors. *Journal of Consulting and Clinical Psychology, 4*, 805–811. doi:10.1037/0022-006X.71.4.805.

Vealey, R. S., & Perritt, N. C. (2015). Hardiness and optimism as predictors of the frequency of flow in collegiate athletes. *Journal of Sport Behavior, 38*, 321–388.

Wrosch, C., Jobin, J., & Scheier, M. F. (2016). Do the emotional benefits of optimism vary across older adulthood? A life span perspective. *Journal of Personality*. Advance online publication. doi:10.1111/jopy.12247.

Wrosch, C., Scheier, M. F., Carver, C. S., & Schulz, R. (2003). The importance of goal disengagement in adaptive self-regulation: When giving up is beneficial. *Self and Identity, 2*, 1–20. doi:10.1080/15298860309021.

Zeidner, M., & Hammer, A. L. (1992). Coping with missile attack: Resources, strategies, and outcomes. *Journal of Personality, 60*, 709–746. doi:10.1111/j.1467-6494.1992. tb00271.x.

9

FORGIVENESS AND WELL-BEING

Charlotte vanOyen Witvliet and Lindsey Root Luna

Forgiveness: What Is It?

Forgiveness is one of the virtues addressed in this volume that can arise only in the context of an interpersonal injustice. The possibility of forgiveness emerges when a transgressor acts, or fails to act, in a way that is unjust and wounds a victim. The victim's perception of the injustice and the wound may differ considerably from how the transgressor or witnesses perceive it. Yet, the victim must contend with his or her encounter with, and perception of, the violation and its repercussions. Depending on the relational context and the nature of the transgression, the affective wounds may include sadness, fear, anger, and their variations. Ideally, the transgressor will recognize the wrongdoing, experience remorse, and own responsibility for the violation and its implications. This internal experience would then motivate the offender to confess, apologize, make amends, and demonstrate a repentant change in behavior that honors the humanity of the victim, community, and self. In forgiving, a victim responds to the transgressor in prosocial ways that recognize the humanity of the offender, while still holding him or her accountable for the offense and genuinely desiring that person's good.

Granting forgiveness is reserved for those times when we hold someone accountable for a moral and relational breach that caused damage and hurt us (e.g. through betrayal, maligning our reputation, mockery, theft of a valued possession, murder of a loved one). In considering the breach and its attendant emotions, an important theoretical construct is the injustice gap (Davis et al., 2016; Exline, Worthington, Hill, & McCullough, 2003), which describes the degree to which a victim perceives distance between the ideal justice and the actual post-offense experience of justice. We contend that when a transgression occurs, there is also a gap between how things were in a relationship before the transgression and how they are now. Both gaps—pre-transgression versus post-transgression and actual versus ideal justice—are inextricably connected to one's relational and moral perceptions, including one's emotions. Depending on the nature of the wrongdoing, the victim may tend to totalize the offender in terms of the offense (e.g. the offender is a liar, a cheat, a thief, a murderer) in such a way that the offender is infrahumanized (i.e. seen as comparatively less human) or dehumanized (e.g. demonized, viewed as a monster). The emotional implications of the injustice gap and one's view of the offender can fuel motivations of avoidance and revenge, while diminishing benevolence (e.g. McCullough, Root, & Cohen, 2006). Emotions of sadness and fear can motivate avoidance of the offender. Alternatively, fear and anger can motivate revenge-seeking behavior, thereby seeking vindication through vindictiveness. Merely adjusting the victim's emotions does not constitute forgiveness, because there are many ways to reduce one's perception of sadness, fear, anxiety, and anger that are unrelated to forgiveness, including positive behaviors (e.g. engaging in an irrelevant but uplifting or pleasurable activity), and negative activities (e.g. exacting revenge; Wade & Worthington, 2003). Hence, forgiveness publications time after time provide lists of what forgiveness *is not*. Forgiveness is not denying, excusing, minimizing, or tolerating an offense (see Enright & Fitzgibbons, 2000; Witvliet & McCullough, 2007; Worthington, 2001, 2009). We believe that forgiveness ought to take seriously the safety of the victim (e.g. physically, emotionally, spiritually) and justice-oriented responses to the transgressor (see Worthington, 2009). Forgiveness is not the same thing as restoring an offender to a prior position, nor does it imply reconciliation (Smedes, 1996). Forgiveness involves a transformation within the victim toward the offender that can be genuine even if the words, "I forgive you" are not explicitly stated, whereas reconciliation requires trust-building, reciprocity and fair mindedness from both parties (Worthington, 2003).

Forgiveness theory and research point to the importance of focusing on the humanity of the offender (e.g. Witvliet, Hofelich Mohr, Hinman, & Knoll, 2015), which resists totalizing him or her in terms of the offense (e.g. merely a liar, cheat, thief, or murderer). This approach first tells the truth about the offender and the offense. It emphasizes the offender's humanity by saying this is a *person* who lied, a *person* who cheated, a *person* who stole, or a *person* who murdered. Telling the truth about the offense requires seeing the offense behavior for what it is, an injustice that carries with it painful, disruptive, and damaging implications. Responding morally places a special burden on the victim at the very same time he or she is worn down. Nevertheless, the victim has particular insights about the offender because of his or her role and experience in facing the offense. These insights can allow the victim to take a second step: reappraising the offender and offense, for example, by viewing the perpetrator's lie as evidence that shows his or her need to develop the moral capacity to tell the truth, or to bite one's tongue. A third element of granting forgiveness is to desire that transformation for the offender, to hope for that good change in the transgressor (whether or not the relationship can be reconciled). Granting forgiveness involves holding the perpetrator responsible for the wrongdoing, and forgiveness can be genuine even if reconciliation is not safe, possible, or wise.

Thus, a research-tested practice that facilitates forgiveness involves (1) emphasizing the humanity of the offender while holding him or her responsible for the transgression, (2) seeing the transgression as evidence that the offender needs to be transformed by learning, growing, or changing, and (3) desiring that good change for the offender (see Witvliet, DeYoung, Hofelich, & DeYoung, 2011; Witvliet, Knoll, Hinman, & DeYoung, 2010; Witvliet, Hofelich Mohr et al., 2015). We propose that these elements of granting forgiveness also have corollaries for transgressor responses. Transgressors can (1) resist totalizing themselves in terms of the offense and recognize their own humanity, (2) see the wrongdoing as evidence of the need to be transformed through learning, growing, and repentant change, and (3) desire that good change for themselves to prevent committing that injustice again and cultivate positive behavior changes toward others. Humble repentance sees the injustice clearly and does not let oneself off the moral hook, but neither does it confuse appropriate guilt and regret with unrelenting shame and self-condemnation—which work against genuine change in perpetrators (see Witvliet, Hinman, Exline, & Brandt, 2011). Rather, humble repentance sees the wrong as evidence of the need to change in ways that prompt confession, restitution, and behavior changes that prevent repetition of the wrongdoing. Furthermore, repentance and receiving forgiveness can be authentic even when the interpersonal relationship cannot be restored.

These forgiveness-oriented responses, which are inherently relational, have demonstrated beneficial side effects for the forgiver (and for the transgressor as well). These well-being side effects, specifically for the victim, have garnered substantial research attention in positive psychology for a variety of reasons (e.g. clinically minded researchers first attend to those who recognize they are hurt and desire help; people more readily identify their own hurts than the times they cause hurts to others; and research is easier to conduct on individuals than dyads and groups). Nevertheless, it is important for psychological scientists and practitioners—along with philosophers and theologians who study forgiveness—to retain a focus on the relational and moral dimensions of forgiveness for both victims and offenders, even as we attend to its implications for relational and emotional well-being.

The Science of Forgiveness and Well-Being

Within the social sciences, the measurement of forgiveness has received substantial attention (see Worthington et al., 2014, for state and trait instruments; and Witvliet, Van Tongeren, & Root Luna, 2015, on measurement within healthcare). Because there are many different ways to reduce unforgiving responses in the short term (e.g. distraction, minimizing), researchers increasingly measure both reductions in unforgiveness (e.g. avoidance and revenge; McCullough et al., 1998) and the presence of benevolent forgiveness motivations (McCullough et al., 2006). Just as interpersonal forgiveness is inextricably relational, forgiveness is a time-bound process (McCullough & Root, 2005). The injustice gap results in negative emotions and responses that change over time; these changes constitute forgiveness (in contrast, simply abstaining from negative reactions to a wrong has been dubbed "forbearance"; McCullough, Fincham, & Tsang, 2003). Overall, the steepest change in victims' emotions and motivations tend to occur near to the incident, with the rate of change slowing to an asymptote as time progresses (McCullough, Root Luna, Berry, Tabak, & Bono, 2010). These changes over time carry with them ramifications for victims, transgressors, and the relationships in which offenses occur.

Relational Well-Being and Forgiveness

Following the relationship breach of an interpersonal transgression, the response of the victim—whether it is avoidant, vengeful, benevolent, or neutral—has the potential to impact ongoing relationships. That is, granting forgiveness impacts subsequent interactions and relationship health. Using an experimental methodology, Karremans and Van Lange (2004) found that when participants recalled forgiven offenses, they endorsed more prosocial orientations (e.g. accommodation, sacrifice intentions) than when recalling unforgiven offenses and relationship partners. Specifically, participants were asked to list several important activities in their lives; participants who recalled a forgiven offender were more likely to report they would sacrifice that activity to maintain a relationship with their partner. Karremans and Van Lange also compared prosocial intentions toward a forgiven partner with intentions toward a neutral partner (no offense recalled), which indicated that a forgiving response restored intentions to baseline, rather than increasing prosociality *per se*. Similarly, when people were asked to remember a time they had forgiven a relationship partner (compared to a time when he or she had not forgiven), participants used more prosocial language (e.g. we, us), reported greater closeness with their partner, and engaged in more general prosocial behavior (i.e. donated more money to an unrelated charity). Longitudinally, among individuals who had been harmed by a relationship partner, levels of forgiveness predicted participants' subsequent ratings of closeness and commitment over a nine-week period (Tsang, McCullough, & Fincham, 2006).

Among romantic relationship partners specifically, relationship satisfaction and forgiveness appear to be bidirectional, with relationship quality predicting subsequent forgiveness (e.g. Paleari, Regalia, & Fincham, 2005) and forgiveness predicting later marital satisfaction (e.g. Fincham & Beach, 2007).

Physiologically, victims' attempts at reconciliation have been associated with reduced blood pressure in both victims and transgressors (Hannon, Finkel, Kumashiro, & Rusbult, 2012). Forgiveness has also been evaluated as a predictor of relationship outcomes; Hall and Fincham (2006), for example, found that forgiveness mediated the relationship between partner attributions and relationship dissolution following a partner's infidelity.

In practice settings, therapists are incorporating forgiveness interventions with individuals, couples, families, and groups (Enright & Fitzgibbons, 2000; Worthington & Sandage, 2016). Research studies have addressed the role of forgiveness in marriages (Olson, Marshall, Goddard, & Schramm, 2015) and families (Fincham, 2015). In couples, Braithwaite, Selby, and Fincham (2011) found that forgiveness predicted relationship-oriented self-regulation (e.g. actively looking for ways to improve the relationship) and low levels of negative interpersonal behaviors (e.g. withdrawal, avoidance, aggressive acts), and these in turn predicted the level of relationship satisfaction.

Among offenders, conciliatory transgressor behaviors—such as apologies or attempts to repair the damaged relationship—can facilitate forgiveness. Both longitudinally and experimentally, transgressor behaviors have been shown to influence forgiveness and perceptions of friendship (Tabak, McCullough, Root Luna, Bono, & Berry, 2012). Apologies that are well-timed and perceived as sincere lead to increased forgiveness (Carlisle et al., 2012; Pansera & La Guardia, 2012), which then facilitate positive relationship outcomes.

An important question arises in relational contexts: What factors predict whether victims are more or less likely to forgive their offenders? Fehr, Gelfand, and Nag (2010) conducted a meta-analysis to understand the state and trait characteristics of cognition and affect, as well as constraints that predict whether one person forgives another (measured as reduced unforgiveness and/or increased forgiveness). They found that the strongest predictor of forgiveness was the victim's state empathy for the offender, accounting for 26 percent of the variance in forgiveness scores. A close second was the victim's state anger, which accounted for 17 percent of the variance. Moderate predictors included the victim's rumination and perceptions of the transgressor's intent to harm, responsibility, and apology. Although this study did not find that gender significantly impacted these findings, Miller and colleagues specifically focused on studies designed to test gender effects and found a small yet meaningful effect indicating that females were more forgiving than males (Miller, Worthington, & McDaniel, 2008); it is possible that gender differences on trait empathy may play a role here, though the mechanism(s) driving this effect have yet to be systematically evaluated.

Among transgressors, guilt (but not shame) is associated with forgiveness-seeking (Riek, Root Luna, & Schnabelrauch, 2013). By studying the personality characteristics of transgressors, McNulty and Russell (2016) discovered an important factor in the dyadic context in which the transgression occurs, noting that transgressors' trait agreeableness is an important predictor of whether or not more transgressions will occur after being forgiven. Disagreeable transgressors committed more transgressions after being forgiven, perceiving that their forgiving partners were less likely to become angry. By contrast, agreeable transgressors committed fewer transgressions after being forgiven, feeling obligated not to transgress again.

The possibility of reoffending following the repair of an offense-damaged relationship highlights the important question of whether forgiveness always facilitates healthy outcomes for the forgiver. Although we have noted that forgiveness need not involve reconciliation (see Smedes, 1996), in the lived experience, these concepts are not always separated (Kearns & Fincham, 2004). Among women in domestic violence shelters, state forgiveness was associated with greater intentions to return to an abusive spouse (Gordon, Burton, & Porter, 2004). Similarly, McNulty (2008, 2010) found that both dispositional and state forgiveness were associated with increased offenses and negative spousal behavior among participants with high levels of negative behaviors in their marriages. McNulty and Fincham (2012) underscored that the outcomes of forgiveness may depend on context. Although forgiveness has the potential to promote closeness and relationship satisfaction among well-intentioned relationship partners, it can also facilitate continued offenses and abuse within unhealthy relationships, especially if the perpetrator's personality is disagreeable (McNulty & Russell, 2016).

The Impact of Granting Forgiveness on Psychological and Physical Well-Being

The science and practice of forgiveness are combined in research on the affective implications of granting forgiveness. Wade, Hoyt, Kidwell, & Worthington (2014) conducted a meta-analysis of the efficacy of forgiveness therapy interventions for individuals, couples, and groups. Results highlighted that theoretically grounded, explicit forgiveness interventions, which focused on helping people grant forgiveness, were more effective than alternative therapies (e.g. supportive/placebo, treatment as usual, incomplete forgiveness interventions) for significantly increasing forgiveness, while also increasing hope and mental health. Furthermore, longer doses of time spent cultivating forgiveness increased effects. Once treatment length and modality (individual, group) were controlled, treatment models were equally effective. More severe transgressions were harder to forgive and benefited from more targeted forgiveness treatments. Overall, the pre- to post-intervention effect size on forgiveness was 0.78, and the effects persisted after treatment concluded. In another meta-analysis of group interventions, empathy emerged as the key predictor of granting forgiveness (Wade, Worthington, & Meyer, 2005). Empathy is a central feature in Worthington's (2001) REACH model of forgiveness, used primarily in groups

(*Recall* the hurt, *Empathize* with the offender, *Altruistically* grant forgiveness, *Commit* to forgive, *Hold on* to forgiveness), and compassion is a key component in Enright's treatment model of forgiveness used primarily with individuals.

The relationship between forgiveness and well-being also has been assessed using longitudinal designs. Fluctuations in forgiveness were related to subsequent increases in self-reported hedonic well-being (i.e. satisfaction with life, positive and negative mood, physical symptoms; Bono, McCullough, & Root, 2008). Cross-lagged analyses supported the authors' hypothesis that forgiveness led to increased feelings of closeness with the transgressor and relationship partner, which then facilitated hedonic well-being.

Shorter paradigms have tested the emotional and physiological implications of having a more or less forgiving personality. Lawler et al. (2003) found that both trait forgivingness and state forgiveness levels during interviews about a betrayal by a parent and by a partner/friend were associated with lower blood pressure. Conversely, participants who were low in both trait and state forgiveness had the highest rate pressure product scores indicative of cardiac stress. During interviews, forgiveness was positively associated with empathy and positive emotion, and inversely related to unforgiving motivations, brow muscle tension, and blood pressure (for parent betrayals). In subsequent research, Lawler-Row, Karremans, Scott, Edlis-Matityahou, and Edwards (2008) again found that trait and state forgiveness were inversely associated with cardiac reactivity, as well as other health indicators. For example, people higher in trait forgivingness also used less alcohol and medication, and they had lower blood pressure and rate pressure product scores. State levels of forgiveness were associated with fewer physical symptoms and lower heart rate. Lawler-Row et al. (2008) further discovered that the tendency to express anger outwardly mediated relationships between trait forgivingness and heart rate, and between state forgiveness and rate pressure product effects.

Experimental paradigms have induced and tested forgiving and unforgiving responses, plus alternatives, to determine concomitant effects on well-being emotionally and physiologically. Early experimental research tested the well-being side effects of rumination, grudge-holding, empathy and forgiveness (Witvliet, Ludwig, & Vander Laan, 2001). The emotional and physiological side effects of empathy and forgiveness differed significantly from those of rumination and grudge-holding. During the two unforgiving conditions, participants demonstrated significantly more potent negative (anger, fear, and sadness) and aroused emotions, as well as greater muscle tension at the brow and under the eye, with stress reactivity in blood pressure, heart rate, and skin conductance. By contrast, during the empathic and forgiving conditions, participants demonstrated greater perceived control, positive emotion, and calmer physiological profiles.

To date, four tests of compassion inductions in relation to forgiveness have been conducted. In two of these, compassionate reappraisal was contrasted with rumination and suppression (Witvliet, DeYoung et al., 2011; Witvliet, Hofelich Mohr et al., 2015). When people developed compassion, they focused on the person's humanity, moving toward wishing the person a positive future despite the hurtful behavior; when engaged in emotional suppression, people thought about the offender and the offense, while trying not to experience or express any negative emotions associated with the offender and offense.

Witvliet, DeYoung et al. (2011) found that compared to offense ruminations, both approaches—compassion and suppression—diminished intense negative emotion (in ratings and written description of what it was like to respond in these ways) and muscle tension under the eye, while maintaining the cardiac parasympathetic response at baseline levels (whereas offense rumination impaired this cardiac response). Suppression also calmed heart rate and tension at the brow muscle. However, only compassionate reappraisal significantly increased forgiveness, along with positive emotions, smiling (zygomatic EMG), and social language.

In a subsequent experiment (Witvliet, Hofelich Mohr et al., 2015), participants learned and practiced just one of these coping responses—either compassion or suppression—launching the response immediately after rumination (on half of the trials). In this investigation, only the compassion learners had significantly higher empathy and emotional forgiveness ratings right away, after the first trial of using the strategy. This study also found that learning compassionate reappraisal prompted changes in the way participants ruminated; even though participants were not even being asked to re-evaluate the transgression or transgressor, when compassion learners ruminated at the end of the study, they did so with empathy for their offenders. Again, although both compassion and suppression coping diminished negative emotions associated with the offense (measured with ratings, language use, and brow muscle tension), only compassion increased empathy and forgiveness—along with positive emotion and calmed sympathetic nervous system activation (measured by the pre-ejection period). Cognitively, results showed that while compassion was not easy (i.e. it had subtle cognitive demands, reducing Stroop test accuracy and speed), participants were still able to perform a cognitive task within normal limits.

Two additional experiments tested compassion, but this time in contrast to benefit-focused reappraisal and offense rumination (Baker, Williams, Witvliet, Hill, 2017; Witvliet et al., 2010). The peripheral physiology study by Witvliet et al. (2010) found that both of these approaches were associated with significantly greater empathy and forgiveness, positive emotion (happiness, joy), reduced anger, reduced arousal, and greater control than rumination. They also calmed muscle tension above the brow (corrugator) and had cardiac parasympathetic response (high frequency heart rate variability; HF HRV) scores at relaxation baseline levels, whereas rumination had significantly impaired HF HRV. When compassion and benefit-focused reappraisal effects were contrasted, compassion outperformed benefit-focus reappraisal for prompting empathy, forgiveness, and social language use, as well as slower heart rates. By contrast, benefit-finding was associated with significantly more joy and gratitude language, along with the greatest increase in HF HRV, associated with parasympathetic control and emotion regulation.

Building on this approach, Baker et al. (2017) asked participants to recall a recent interpersonal offense and apply each emotion regulation strategy. Both reappraisals increased decisional and emotional forgiveness. Nevertheless, compassion-focused reappraisal prompted the greatest increases in both types of forgiveness. Both reappraisal strategies also increased positively oriented well-being measures (e.g. joy, gratitude) compared to offense rumination, and compassion-focused reappraisal prompted the largest effect on empathy. Late positive potential (LPP) amplitudes measured in response to unpleasant affect words were larger after the benefit-focused reappraisal strategy, which supported the interpretation that the unpleasant stimuli were strongly incongruent with the positive orientation of the benefit-focused reappraisal emotion regulation strategy. Compassionate reappraisal likely maintained a combination of negative and positive emotional processing, whereas benefit-focused reappraisal was more uniformly focused on finding for oneself the treasure (i.e. benefits) in the dirt of the offense.

The Impact of Seeking Forgiveness on Psychological and Physical Well-Being

The emerging literature on seeking forgiveness is showing that it can have positive side effects similar to forgiveness granting. A key point in the literature emphasizes the importance of transgressor change with responsibility for relational repair toward the victim. With this in mind, Witvliet, Hinman et al. (2011) developed a repentance-writing induction. They contrasted repentance with rumination (focused on self-condemnation) and with self-justification (which minimized the participant's agency and impact), assessing how these conditions influenced responses in relation to the victim and to the divine. Repentance involved owning responsibility for the wrongdoing while transforming negative behaviors and habits to develop a positive new response that will prevent offending again. Repentance-writing significantly decreased self-condemnation and regret while increasing conciliatory motivations toward the victim (i.e. of apology, restitution, and forgiveness-seeking). By contrast, participants who wrote with offense rumination showed more self-condemning isolation from the victim and God. When self-justifying, participants reported reduced remorse and self-condemnation, while exaggerating perceptions of divine forgiveness; this suggested that merely letting oneself off the hook may have been less aversive, but it lacked the transformative power of repentance. Another discovery was that merely ruminating about one's wrongdoing did not facilitate repentance. Offense rumination not only produced greater self-condemnation, but also less motivation to apologize, make restitution, and seek forgiveness than did repentance.

Further imagery research has considered the importance of repentance in studying forgiveness-oriented responses from the transgressor's perspective. In the first psychophysiology paradigm, Witvliet, Ludwig, and Bauer (2002) found that imagery of seeking and receiving forgiveness from one's victim prompted perceptions of being more forgiven by the victim, along with more positive emotion, less negative and aroused emotion, and less tension at the brow muscle. The repentant response of forgiveness-seeking also activated increased self-forgiveness (Witvliet et al., 2002).

A more recent investigation of the transgressor's perspective compared offense rumination to responses rooted in humble repentance: imagery of repentant forgiveness-seeking (with a begrudged or forgiven response from one's victim) as well as self-forgiveness (da Silva, Witvliet, & Riek, 2017). Self-forgiveness and receiving other-forgiveness prompted the same cardiac and affective response patterns. Specifically, self-forgiveness and imagining receiving forgiveness from one's victim decreased guilt, negative emotion, and heart rate, while they increased perceived control and positive emotion. Ruminating about one's own wrongdoing impaired participants' cardiac parasympathetic response, important in self-regulation. Thus, the cardiac emotion regulation response has been found to be impaired both by ruminating about one's own wrongdoing (da Silva et al., 2017) and by ruminating about being the victim of someone else's transgression (Witvliet et al., 2010, Witvliet, Hinman et al. 2011). Consistent with da Silva et al. (2017), an independent research group's study of romantic partners found that imagining being granted forgiveness resulted in greater empathy whereas imagining being denied forgiveness led to more anger (Jennings et al., 2016).

Applications

The psychological research literature addressing unforgiveness emerged out of a keen awareness that interpersonal wrongs hurt relationships and emotions. Because psychology has long focused on alleviating suffering, psychologists paid therapeutic and research attention to understanding and addressing these relational wrongs and emotional hurts. Although individuals may already be relatively high or low regarding the tendency to forgive (trait forgivingness), the state of granting forgiveness can be cultivated. Particular conditions that have been found to foster forgiveness—along with a more prosocial orientation, up-regulated positive emotions, down-regulated negative emotions, and less stress reactivity compared to ruminating about transgression—can be applied by clinicians and by individuals beyond the controlled research environment.

Application: Forgiving Within Therapy

Enright and Fitzgibbons (2000) equipped therapists to use the process model of forgiveness with clients who desire to overcome their anger through forgiving their offender. The authors observe that people are often motivated to forgive for many different reasons, ranging from forgiveness only after the offender is punished or makes appropriate restitution, to granting forgiveness unconditionally as a way to give moral love.

The Enright and Fitzgibbons (2000) model for applied forgiveness work in therapy has 20 specific elements that are grouped within four therapy phases. In the *uncovering phase*, clients go through many steps to become aware, understand, and develop insights about the offense and how it is connected to their psychological responses. Next is the *decision phase* in which the client undergoes change and becomes willing and committed to grant forgiveness to the offender. During the *work phase*, the client reappraises the wrongdoer and cultivates empathy and compassion toward the offender. This is the pivot point at which the client extends moral love to the transgressor. Finally, in the *deepening phase*, the client develops a sense of meaning, insight, and realization that connects one's own need for forgiveness to the process of granting forgiveness; experiences a sense of purpose and connection; and moves away from negative and toward positive affect. Clinicians are encouraged to consult Enright and Fitzgibbons' (2000) book on how forgiveness can be pursued within therapy with people who have depressive, bipolar, anxiety, substance, eating, and other disorders. The authors also specifically address forgiveness applications in marriage and family relationships, and with children and adolescents.

Application: Granting Forgiveness Through the REACH Model

Research studies and clinical applications undergird Worthington's (2001, 2003) REACH model of granting forgiveness, which has been tested in groups and is also used by individuals on their own. Worthington guides people who want to forgive, noting that those who forgive to *give* (i.e. pursuing a moral response) have been found to benefit even more than those who pursue forgiveness with the goal of getting those benefits (i.e. pursuing side effects). Thus, his model accentuates the cultivation of empathy and altruistic giving of forgiveness. Beyond the overview of Worthington's approach provided here, we recommend his books to interested readers (see Worthington, 2001 for a broad readership, and Worthington, 2003 for readers with a worldview shaped by Christianity).

R *Recall the hurt.* Worthington noted that how we recall the offense matters. Insofar as our recollections seek to understand, it is possible to remember the offense and its implications in a way that does not fuel revenge but rather moves in the direction of empathic perspective-taking.

E *Empathize.* Worthington observed that minimally, having empathy means seeking to understand the perspective of the other person, in this case the offender. A further degree of empathy may involve identifying emotionally with the person responsible for the offense. Worthington described that forgiveness is facilitated by an even deeper level of empathy in which the wounded person develops compassion for the wrongdoer. In this way the moral love emphasized by Enright and Fitzgibbons (2000) also resonates with the empathy and compassion in Worthington's (2001) model and through the empirical tests of empathy and compassion practices described above (Witvliet et al., 2001, 2010; Witvliet, DeYoung et al., 2011; Witvliet, Hofelich Mohr et al., 2015).

A *Altruistic gift of forgiveness.* Worthington (2001) observed empirically that people who developed empathy for the offender more likely forgave the offender, but not always. Another element was needed: taking the step to give forgiveness. Such generosity, Worthington (2001) noted, emerged more naturally when people were humbly aware of their own need for forgiveness and grateful for receiving forgiveness from God and from others. Both humility and gratitude facilitate giving to others out of the abundance of received forgiveness.

C *Commit publicly to forgive.* Worthington (2001) advocated telling another trustworthy person about the decision to grant forgiveness as a way of holding oneself accountable. In situations where it is not possible to identify a safe witness, it is important to memorably declare—in writing or aloud to oneself— the commitment to grant forgiveness to the person responsible for the transgression.

H *Hold on to forgiveness.* With a keen awareness of how memories are triggered, Worthington (2001) identified the importance of developing individually tailored strategies to actively resist the return of unforgiving ruminations. Specific insights can facilitate holding onto forgiveness. For example, Worthington noted that experiencing pain when remembering a hurtful offense is not the same as unforgiveness. Further, it is important to acknowledge, but not dwell on, one's negative emotions. If the forgiver has committed to forgive alone or with a witness, remembering that commitment and seeking support are helpful strategies. Finally, working through the REACH steps again can strengthen the moral muscles used to grant forgiveness.

Application: Empathy and Granting Forgiveness

As summarized above, Witvliet et al.'s (2001) brief, repeated inductions of empathy and granting forgiveness (versus transgression rumination and grudge-holding) prompted the intended increases in empathy and forgiveness, with broad effects of down-regulating negative and aroused emotion with associated stress responses. Simultaneously, empathy and forgiving imagery up-regulated positive emotion and perceptions of control. What did participants do to prompt empathy and forgiveness? To activate empathy, they focused on the human qualities of the person who hurt them and recognized their own capacity to hurt others (even unintentionally). To engage in a response of letting go and forgiving, participants focused on *releasing* their negative feelings of hurt and revenge. They considered giving a gift of mercy to the offender and wishing that person well, even in a very small way. For both imagery conditions, participants actively engaged their thoughts, feelings, and physical responses. The brief scripts used in this study (see Appendix) may help facilitate the empathy and decisional forgiveness emphasized by both Enright and Fitzgibbons (2000) and Worthington (2001, 2003).

Application: Cultivating Compassion and Forgiving

One way to cultivate compassion is to prompt people to re-think their response to the offender (Baker et al., 2017; Witvliet et al., 2010; Witvliet, DeYoung et al., 2011; Witvliet, Hofelich Mohr et al., 2015). As noted above, this necessitates telling the truth about the offender's humanity and the transgression. The offender is a human being who behaved badly, which resulted in a wound. Next, recognizing an offender's humanity helps the victim see the offender's behavior as evidence that he or she needs to experience a positive transformation. The victim then can be invited to try to genuinely wish that this person will undergo a positive or healing experience or change, even if the relationship cannot or should not be restored. Even if it is difficult, it is possible to see the humanity of the offender, the blameworthiness of the offense, and the change that one can desire for the offender—focusing one's thoughts and feelings on giving a genuine gift of mercy or compassion (see Appendix for specific directions).

Application: Benefit-Focused Reappraisal to Find Treasure in the Dirt

Some people who want to forgive may have difficulty cultivating compassion for a wrongdoer while their emotions are running hot; it may seem objectionable to generate generosity toward the wrongdoer. Yet, for those who desire to begin moving in the direction of forgiveness, identifying benefits even in the hardship is also associated with increases in forgiveness and positive effects on well-being (Baker et al., 2017; McCullough et al., 2006; Witvliet et al., 2010). This approach emphasizes what one has personally gained through facing the painful offense (see specific prompts to facilitate benefit-finding in the Appendix).

At the outset, we wish to make clear that benefit-focused reappraisal does not diminish the wrongdoing or its harmful effects (nor does it restore a person to his or her prior role). Far from being a saccharine or masochistic response, a benefit-focused response holds in tension the truth about the offense and its effects and the valuable lessons one has learned through facing the offense (e.g. recognizing personal strengths and relational supports). Benefit-finding can equip and empower the victim to tell more of the truth, not less—to see the good in addition to the bad in the transgression or post-transgression situation. In doing so, we suggest that benefit-focused reappraisal may begin to build a forgiving bridge across the injustice gap from the perspective of the victim, whereas compassion-focused reappraisal reaches across the gap to begin bridge-building from the perspective of the offender.

McCullough et al. (2006) tested the first benefit-finding writing intervention in response to an interpersonal offense. They prompted participants to write about *positive* aspects of facing the interpersonal offense. These included awareness of positive outcomes, awareness of personal strengths, the strengthening of a relationship, or becoming a stronger or wiser person. McCullough et al. (2006) discovered that participants who devoted 20 minutes to writing about benefits they had experienced through facing the transgression became significantly more forgiving of the offender compared to participants who either wrote about the transgression's traumatic features or a control condition. Based on this writing intervention, Witvliet et al. (2010) developed an imagery practice for benefit-focused reappraisal, and Baker et al. (2017) further tested this induction. Both studies specifically compared the effects of benefit-focused to compassion-focused reappraisal, while contrasting them to offense rumination. Strikingly, both the benefit-focused and compassion-focused reappraisal approaches increased forgiveness and gratitude, as well as positive emotion compared to offense rumination. However, compassion-focused reappraisal was more potent in increasing empathy and forgiveness.

Application: Repentance After an Offense

We are not only victims of wrongdoing; we also commit transgressions against others and fail to act in ways that treat others with justice and kindness. Witvliet, Hinman et al.'s (2011) repentance-writing induction was designed to help people to tell the truth and own responsibility for one's wrongdoing (confessing, apologizing, making amends), while emphasizing positive transformation through change (see Appendix for instructions). Indeed, the repentance-writing results dovetail with work by Worthington (2013), in that repentance-writing significantly decreased self-condemnation and regret while increasing conciliatory motivations toward the victim (i.e. apology, restitution, and forgiveness-seeking).

Application: Humble Repentance with Forgiveness-Seeking and Self-Forgiveness

Both forgiveness-seeking and self-forgiveness can be rooted in the transgressor's humble repentance (da Silva et al., 2017). Here, we will focus on self-forgiveness. This is in part because, as transgressors, we can pursue repentance and take steps to embrace forgiveness, but we cannot control whether the victim's response will be to forgive us or hold a grudge. For a more thorough treatment of the process of overcoming self-condemnation, we direct readers to Worthington (2013).

In da Silva et al.'s (2017) repentant self-forgiveness approach, participants focused on their responsibility for, and regret about, their role in committing the offense. As they looked at their own responsibility for causing hurt and humbly repented, they were invited to embrace mercy and forgiveness for themselves. They imagined embracing this kindness and compassion for themselves as they committed to do what they believe is right. Compared to ruminating about their wrongdoing, this approach to self-forgiveness was associated with down-regulated anger, anxiety, sadness, guilt, and heart rate, along with up-regulated positive emotion and a buffered cardiac regulatory measure (see Appendix for imagery instructions).

Summary and Future Directions

To date, most research attention has been devoted to the topic of forgiving others. An emerging literature has begun to study seeking forgiveness and self-forgiving contingent on repentance. Initial research suggests that seeking forgiveness (rather than ruminating about one's guilt) and receiving forgiveness or reconciling with one's victim (rather than being begrudged) stimulates gratitude, joy, happiness, and associated facial physiology (Witvliet et al., 2002, 2015). When it comes to forgiveness and cardiovascular and stress physiology, people who ruminate about the wrongdoing of others (Witvliet et al., 2010, Witvliet, Hinman et al., 2011) and their own wrongdoing (Witvliet et al., 2015) experience significant impairment in the cardiac vagal response, which is an important regulatory response.

While forgiveness research has largely focused on emotional and physical well-being, the field of positive psychology will benefit by directing increased attention to the effect of forgiveness on relational well-being. We recommend targeted approaches to track the impact of forgiveness as it unfolds within the dyad, both including and beyond married couples. Forgiveness may have implications that extend beyond the relationship in which the offense occurred, and which are culturally contextualized. Expanded attention to cultural factors is warranted. Forgiveness may relieve negative spillover from unresolved hurts that can burden one's other relationships with loved ones, friends, colleagues, and the divine. Such relational outcomes warrant study given that social support is an important buffer protecting mental and physical health.

Another direction for forgiveness research is to target explicitly its relationship to other virtues such as love, humility, courage, gratitude, and hope. Finer distinctions in understanding and measuring happiness, joy, and meaning will illuminate the particular ways in which forgiveness can foster not only episodes of positive emotion, but enduring and substantive transformations that promote positive growth and flourishing through virtue, with relational, spiritual, psychological, and physical implications.

Forgiveness research has made substantial strides in a short time. As this work continues, we anticipate and invite growing interdisciplinary and cross-cultural awareness in the trait and state questions studied. Given the widespread harm of interpersonal offenses at individual, dyadic, group, and societal levels, a sustained focus on repentant change and forgiveness holds great promise. Continuing to understand and develop interventions to promote relational repair and forgiveness has the potential to equip people involved in relational injustices to respond in ways that promote genuine flourishing for victims, offenders, relationships, and community.

APPENDIX

Prompts to Facilitate Empathy and Forgiveness (Witvliet et al., 2001)

Empathy

Please focus on the human qualities of the person who hurt you. Consider the hurts that person may have experienced at some time, any good qualities that person has, and what it would be like to be in that person's shoes. Remember times when you may have hurt someone, even unintentionally. During your imagery of this situation, actively imagine the thoughts, feelings, and physical responses you had or would have as you think about the human qualities of that person.

Forgiveness

Please focus on releasing your negative feelings of hurt and revenge. Consider giving a gift of mercy and wishing that person well, even in a very small way. During your imagery of this situation, actively imagine the thoughts, feelings, and physical responses you had or would have as you release the hurt and revenge, and grant forgiveness to this person.

Compassionate Reappraisal

Imagery Script A (Witvliet, Hofelich Mohr et al., 2015)

Now your job is to re-think your response to the offender. For the next 2 minutes, think of the offender as a human being who behaved badly. Even if the relationship cannot be restored, try to genuinely wish that this person experiences something positive or healing. Even though it may be hard, focus your thoughts and feelings on giving a gift of mercy or compassion.

Imagery Script B (Baker et al., 2017; Witvliet et al., 2010)

For the next 2 minutes, try to think of the offender as a human being whose behavior shows that person's need to experience a positive transformation or healing. Try to give a gift of mercy and genuinely wish that person well. During your imagery, actively focus on the thoughts, feelings, and physical responses you have as you cultivate compassion, kindness, and mercy for this person.

Benefit-Focused Reappraisal

Writing Prompt (McCullough et al., 2006)

As you write, we would like for you to write about positive aspects of the experience. In which ways did the thing that this person did to you lead to positive consequences for you? Perhaps you became aware of personal strengths that you did not realize you had, perhaps a relationship became better or stronger as a result, or perhaps you grew or became a stronger or wiser person. Explore these issues as you write. In particular, please try to address the following points: (a) In what ways did the hurtful event that happened to you lead to positive outcomes for you? That is, what personal benefits came out of this experience for you? (b) In what ways has your life become better as a result of the harmful thing that occurred to you? In what ways is your life or the kind of person that you have become better today as a result of the harmful thing that occurred to you? (c) Are there any other additional benefits that you envision coming out of this experience for you—perhaps some time in the future? As you write, really try to "let go" and think deeply about possible benefits that you have gained from this negative event, and possible benefits you might receive in the future. Try not to hold anything back. Be as honest and candid as possible about this event and its positive effects, or potential effects, on your life.

Imagery Script (Baker et al., 2017; Witvliet et al., 2010)

For the next 2 minutes, try to think of your offense as an opportunity to grow, learn, or become stronger. Think of benefits you may have gained from your experience such as self-understanding, insight, or improvement in a relationship. During your imagery, actively focus on the thoughts, feelings, and physical responses you have as you think about positive ways you benefited from your experience.

Facilitating Repentance

Writing Prompts (Witvliet, Hinman et al., 2011)

For the next 20 minutes, we would like for you to write an essay about that event, focusing on ways you can acknowledge your role in the offense and develop positive responses to it. As you write, really try to write freely and express your feelings. Try not to hold anything back. Be honest and candid about this event, your humble regret, your desire to make things better, and your intentions to develop positive behaviors that will help cultivate good habits of interacting with others. As you write, please try to address the following points:

- What happened in the instance you identified on the questionnaire? What were its consequences?
- Write in a way that takes responsibility for your actions. What are you responsible for? To whom are you responsible?
- Give an honest expression of being sorry for your actions and how they affected the other person.
- In what ways have you, or could you, realistically make amends for your actions? If it is not possible to make things right for the past situation, then write about what you could do differently next time.
- Write about your commitment to not commit that transgression again and to develop positive habits or behaviors for interacting with others in the future.

Self-Forgiveness

Imagery Prompt (da Silva et al., 2017)

For the next 2 minutes, try to imagine that you felt responsible for, and regret about, your role in committing the offense. Imagine that you felt so humbled and repentant that you wanted to be forgiven, confessed, repented, and committed to do what is right. Imagine that as you look at your own actions of causing hurt and of humbly repenting, that you embrace mercy and forgiveness for yourself. Imagine that you embrace this kindness and compassion for yourself as you commit to do what you believe is right. During your imagery, actively focus on the thoughts, feelings, and physical responses you have as you think about fully embracing forgiveness of yourself.

References

Baker, J. C., Williams, J. K., Witvliet, C. V. O., & Hill, P. C. (2017). Positive reappraisals after an offense: Event-related potentials and emotional effects of benefit-finding and compassion. *The Journal of Positive Psychology*, *12*(4), 373–384. doi:10.1080/17439760.2016.1209540.

Bono, G., McCullough, M. E., & Root, L. M. (2008). Forgiveness, feeling connected to others, and well-being: Two longitudinal studies. *Personality and Social Psychology Bulletin, 34*, 182–195.

Braithwaite, S. R., Selby, E. A., & Fincham, F. D. (2011). Forgiveness and relationship satisfaction: Mediating mechanism. *Journal of Family Psychology, 25*, 551–559.

Carlisle, R. D., Tsang, J.-A., Ahmad, N. Y., Worthington, Jr., E. L., Witvliet, C. V. O., & Wade, N. (2012). Do actions speak louder than words? Differential effects of apology and restitution on behavioral and self-report measures of forgiveness. *The Journal of Positive Psychology, 7*(4), 294–305. doi:10.1080/17439760.2012.690444.

da Silva, S. P., vanOyen Witvliet, C., & Riek, B. (2017). Self-forgiveness and forgiveness-seeking in response to rumination: Cardiac and emotional responses of transgressors. *The Journal of Positive Psychology, 12*(4), 362–372. doi:10.1080/17439760.2016.1187200.

Davis, D. E., Yang, X., DeBlaere, C., McElroy, S. E., Van Tongeren, D. R., Hook, J. N., & Worthington, Jr., E. L. (2016). The injustice gap. *Psychology of Religion and Spirituality, 8*(3), 175–184.

Enright, R. D., & Fitzgibbons, R. P. (2000). *Helping clients forgive: An empirical guide for resolving anger and restoring hope.* Washington, DC: American Psychological Association. doi:10.1037/ 10381-000.

Exline, J. J., Worthington, Jr., E. L., Hill, P., & McCullough, M. E. (2003). Forgiveness and justice: A research agenda for social and personality psychology. *Personality and Social Psychology Review, 7*(4), 337–348.

Fehr, R., Gelfand, M. J., & Nag, M. (2010). The road to forgiveness: A meta-analytic synthesis of its situational and dispositional correlates. *Psychological Bulletin, 136*(5), 894–914. doi:10.1037/a0019993.

Fincham, F. D. (2015). Forgiveness, family relationships and health. In L. Toussaint, E. Worthington, Jr., & D. Williams (Eds.), *Forgiveness and health: Scientific evidence and theories relating forgiveness to better health* (pp. 255–270). New York: Springer. doi:10.1007/978-94-017-9993-5_17.

Fincham, F. D., & Beach, S. H. (2007). Forgiveness and marital quality: Precursor or consequence in well-established relationships? *The Journal of Positive Psychology, 2*, 260–268. doi:10.1080/ 17439760701552360.

Gordon, K. C., Burton, S., & Porter, L. (2004). Predicting the intentions of women in domestic violence shelters to return to partners: Does forgiveness play a role? *Journal of Family Psychology, 18*(2), 331–338.

Hall, J. H., & Fincham, F. D. (2006). Relationship dissolution following infidelity: The roles of attributions and forgiveness. *Journal of Social and Clinical Psychology, 25*, 508–522.

Hannon, P. A., Finkel, E. J., Kumashiro, M., & Rusbult, C. E. (2012). The soothing effects of forgiveness on victims' and perpetrators' blood pressure. *Personal Relationships, 19*, 279–289. doi:10.1111/ j.1475-6811.2011.01356.x.

Jennings, D., Worthington, E. L. J., Van Tongeren, D. R., Hook, J. N., Davis, D. E., Gartner, A. L., … Mosher, D. K. (2016). The transgressor's response to a rejected request for forgiveness. *Journal of Psychology and Theology, 44*, 16–28.

Karremans, J. C., & Van Lange, P. A. M. (2004). Back to caring after being hurt: The role of forgiveness. *European Journal of Social Psychology, 34*, 207–227. doi:10.1002/ejsp.192.

Kearns, J. N., & Fincham, F. D. (2004). A prototype analysis of forgiveness. *Personality and Social Psychology Bulletin, 30*(7), 838–855.

Lawler-Row, K., Karremans, J. C., Scott, C., Edlis-Matityahou, M., & Edwards, L. (2008). Forgiveness, physiological reactivity and health: The role of anger. *International Journal of Psychophysiology, 68*(1), 51–58.

Lawler, K. A., Younger, J. W., Piferi, R. L., Billington, E., Jobe, R., Edmondson, K., & Jones, W. H. (2003). A change of heart: Cardiovascular correlates of forgiveness in response to interpersonal conflict. *Journal of Behavioral Medicine, 26*(5), 373–93.

McCullough, M. E., Fincham, F. D., & Tsang, J.-A. (2003). Forgiveness, forbearance, and time: The temporal unfolding of transgression-related interpersonal motivations. *Journal of Personality and Social Psychology, 84*(3), 540–557.

McCullough, M. E., Rachal, K. C., Sandage, S. J., Worthington, Jr., E. L., Brown, S. W., & Hight, T. L. (1998). Interpersonal forgiving in close relationships: II. Theoretical elaboration and measurement. *Journal of Personality and Social Psychology, 76*, 1586–1603.

McCullough, M. E., & Root, L. M. (2005). Forgiveness as change. In E. L. Worthington (Ed.), *Handbook of forgiveness* (pp. 91–107). New York: Routledge.

McCullough, M. E., Root Luna, L. M., Berry, J. W., Tabak, B. A., & Bono, G. (2010). On the form and function of forgiving: Modeling the time-forgiveness relationship and testing the valuable relationships hypothesis. *Emotion, 10*, 358–376.

McCullough, M. E., Root, L. M., & Cohen, A. D. (2006). Writing about the benefits of an interpersonal transgression facilitates forgiveness. *Journal of Consulting and Clinical Psychology, 74*(5), 887–897. doi:10.1037/0022-006X.74.5.887.

McNulty, J. K. (2008). Forgiveness in marriage: Putting the benefits into context. *Journal of Family Psychology, 22*(1), 171–175.

McNulty, J. K. (2010). Forgiveness increases the likelihood of subsequent partner transgressions in marriage. *Journal of Family Psychology, 24*(6), 787–790.

McNulty, J. K., & Fincham, F. D. (2012). Beyond positive psychology? Toward a contextual view of psychological processes and well-being. *American Psychologist, 67*(2), 101–110.

McNulty, J. K., & Russell, V. M. (2016). Forgive and forget, or forgive and regret? Whether forgiveness leads to less or more offending depends on offender agreeableness. *Personality and Social Psychology Bulletin, 42*(5), 616–631. doi:10.1177/0146167216637841.

Miller, A. J., Worthington, Jr., E. L., & McDaniel, M. A. (2008). Gender and forgiveness: A meta-analytic review and research agenda. *Journal of Social and Clinical Psychology, 27*(8), 843–876. doi:10.1521/jscp.2008.27.8.843.

Olson, J. R., Marshall, J. P., Goddard, H. W., & Schramm, D. G. (2015). Shared religious beliefs, prayer, and forgiveness as predictors of marital satisfaction. *Family Relations: An Interdisciplinary Journal of Applied Family Studies, 64*(4), 519–533. doi:10.1111/fare.12129.

Paleari, F. G., Regalia, C., & Fincham, F. D. (2005). Marital quality, forgiveness, empathy, and rumination: A longitudinal analysis. *Personality and Social Psychology Bulletin, 31*, 368–378. doi:10.1177/0146167204271597.

Pansera, C., & La Guardia, J. (2012). The role of sincere amends and perceived partner responsiveness in forgiveness. *Personal Relationships, 19*(4), 696–711.

Riek, B. M., Root Luna, L. M. & Schnabelrauch, C. (2013). Transgressors' guilt and shame: A longitudinal examination of forgiveness-seeking. *Journal of Social and Personal Relationships, 31*, 751–772. doi:10.1177/0265407513503595.

Smedes, L. (1996). *The art of forgiving.* New York: Random House, Inc.

Tabak, B. A., McCullough, M. E., Root Luna, L. M., Bono, G., & Berry J. W. (2012). Conciliatory gestures facilitate forgiveness by making transgressors appear more agreeable. *Journal of Personality, 80*, 503–536. doi:10.111/j.1467-6494.2011.00728.

Tsang, J.-A., McCullough, M. E., & Fincham, F. D. (2006). The longitudinal association between forgiveness and relationship closeness and commitment. *Journal of Social and Clinical Psychology, 25*, 448–472.

Wade, N. G., Hoyt, W. T., Kidwell, J. E. M., & Worthington, Jr., E. L. (2014). Efficacy of psychotherapeutic interventions to promote forgiveness: A meta-analysis. *Journal of Consulting and Clinical Psychology, 82*(1), 154–170. doi:10.1037/a0035268.

Wade, N. G., & Worthington, Jr., E. L. (2003). Overcoming interpersonal offenses: Is forgiveness the only way to deal with unforgiveness? *Journal of Counseling and Development, 81*(3), 343–353.

Wade, N. G., Worthington, E. L., Jr., & Meyer, J. E. (2005). But do they work? A meta-analysis of group interventions to promote forgiveness. In E. L. Worthington, Jr. (Ed.), *Handbook of forgiveness* (pp. 423–440). New York: Brunner/Routledge.

Witvliet, C. V. O., DeYoung, N. J., Hofelich, A. J., & DeYoung, P. A. (2011). Compassionate reappraisal and emotion suppression as alternatives to offense-focused rumination: Implications for forgiveness and psychophysiological well-being. *The Journal of Positive Psychology, 6*, 286–299.

Witvliet, C. V. O., Hinman, N. G., Exline, J. J., & Brandt, T. (2011). Responding to our own transgressions: An experimental writing study of repentance, offense rumination, self-justification, and distraction. *Journal of Psychology and Christianity, 30*, 223–238.

Witvliet, C. V. O., Hofelich Mohr, A. J., Hinman, N. G., & Knoll, R. W. (2015). Transforming or restraining rumination: The impact of compassionate reappraisal versus emotion suppression on empathy, forgiveness, and affective psychophysiology. *The Journal of Positive Psychology, 10*, 248–261.

Witvliet, C. V. O., Knoll, R. W., Hinman, N. G., & DeYoung, P. A. (2010). Compassion-focused reappraisal, benefit-focused reappraisal, and rumination after an interpersonal offense: Emotion regulation implications for subjective emotion, linguistic responses, and physiology. *The Journal of Positive Psychology, 5*, 226–242.

Witvliet, C. V. O., Ludwig, T., & Bauer, D. J. (2002). Please forgive me: Transgressors' emotions and physiology during imagery of seeking forgiveness and victim responses. *Journal of Psychology and Christianity, 21*, 219-233.

Witvliet, C. V. O., Ludwig, T., & Vander Laan, K. (2001). Granting forgiveness or harboring grudges: Implications for emotions, physiology, and health. *Psychological Science, 12*, 117–123.

Witvliet, C. V. O., & McCullough, M. E. (2007). Forgiveness and health: A review and theoretical exploration of emotion pathways. In S. Post (Ed.), *Altruism and health: Perspectives from empirical research* (pp. 259–276). New York: Oxford University Press. doi:10.1093/acprof:oso/9780195182910.003.0017.

Witvliet, C. V. O., Van Tongeren, D. R., & Root Luna, L. M. (2015). Measuring forgiveness in health-related contexts. In L. Toussaint, E. Worthington, Jr., & D. Williams (Eds.), *Forgiveness and health: Scientific evidence and theories relating forgiveness to better health* (pp. 45–58). New York: Springer.

Worthington, Jr., E. L. (2001). *Five steps to forgiveness.* New York: Crown Publishers.

Worthington, Jr., E. L. (2003). *Forgiving and reconciling: Bridges to wholeness and hope.* Downers Grove, IL: Intervarsity Press.

Worthington, Jr., E. L. (2009). *A just forgiveness: Responsible healing without excusing injustice.* Downers Grove, IL: Intervarsity Press.

Worthington, Jr., E. L. (2013). *Moving forward: Six steps to forgiving yourself and breaking free from the past.* Colorado Springs, CO: WaterBrook Press.

Worthington, Jr., E.L., Lavelock, C., Witvliet, C. V. O., Rye, M. S., Tsang, J.-A., & Toussaint, L. (2014). Measures of forgiveness. In G. Boyle, D. Saklofske, & G. Matthews (Eds.), *Measures of personality and social psychological constructs* (pp. 474–502). Oxford: Academic Press.

Worthington, Jr., E. L., & Sandage, S. J. (2016). *Forgiveness and spirituality in psychotherapy: A relational approach.* Washington, DC: American Psychological Association. doi:10.1037/14712-011.

10

COURAGE, COURAGEOUS ACTS, AND POSITIVE PSYCHOLOGY

Cynthia L. S. Pury and Shawn Saylors

One day I was hunting with my dad. We had been [in] the wood for about 2 hours when I noticed that one of our dogs was missing. So I searched for the dog for a while and ended up on a highway on the other side of our hunting land. The dog was standing in the middle of the road smelling some animal that had been hit by a car previously. Then I noticed that a car was coming pretty quickly at my dog and was not slowing down and he was not moving. So I ran out in front of the car and grabbed the dog at the last second just as the car slammed on [the] brakes and landed in the ditch.

(participant from Pury, Kowalski, & Spearman, 2007)

I had a boy in my class throughout middle school that was always picking on and teasing the girls in my class as well as those in other grades. He made many of the girls upset every day. I never really had much to do with him even though he lived a few streets away from me. He carried himself in a very mean type of manner. One day he decided to lay in on me with all kinds of derogatory remarks and I stood up and gave him a piece of my mind. I defended myself as well as many other girls he'd been picking on that day. I along with many of my friends were shocked. I was always the "innocent" girl all the time. He had just taken things too far. After that he never messed with me or my friends again.

(participant from Pury et al., 2007)

I decided to stay home from my second semester of college, because I had to go to a clinic for eating disorders. I was very sick and didn't want to leave school, but I knew it was best for me. It not only takes a lot of guts to leave school and all my friends, but it takes even more to admit to everyone that I was sick with anorexia.

(participant from Pury & Kowalski, 2007)

Each of these narratives was written by United States participants asked to describe a time they acted courageously. They are representative of the types of answers people typically give: most can think of a time in their life when they did something that was courageous and those actions tend to fall into a relatively small number of categories. In this chapter, we will explore what all of these actions have in common, or the definitional features of courage; how these actions are similar to and different from other related constructs; common groupings or typologies for courageous actions; and social psychological constructs that might contribute to understanding and intervening for courage.

Defining Courage

We define courage as *taking a worthwhile risk*, although it is not always defined as such. In this section, we will briefly review three different definitional approaches to courage, and what each one implies about courage as a positive psychology construct.

Competing Sentiments

One of the earliest psychological definitions of courage is from Lord who, in 1918, defines courage occurring when the more base sentiment of fear is overwhelmed by a more noble sentiment, with "sentiment" roughly corresponding to what we would call emotion today. In Lord's definition, we see the actor experiencing conflicting sentiments—one motivating inaction, avoidance, or flight (fear) and one motivating action. Lord then proposes a rough ranking of courageous actions determined by the nobility of the non-fear sentiment. Thus, engaging in a bar fight to avenge an insult is less courageous than going to war because one is patriotic. He ends with a reassurance that the Allied forces fighting the contemporary World War (the First) against the Germans are more courageous, because Allied patriotism arises from a sentiment of kindness and justice while German patriotism arises from a sentiment of power for power's sake. Ninety-eight years later, psychologists would likely be comfortable with the juxtaposition of emotions with competing action tendencies, but less comfortable with ranking nobility of various national sentiments (Lord, 1918).

Stripped of its political connotations, the competing sentiments approach places courage as a positive psychology construct. As an expression of a more noble sentiment acting against a base sentiment, courage, by this definition, involves being moved to action by better instincts than fear. In its highest forms, Lord would probably argue today, courage involves being such a good person that fear for the self is irrelevant.

Acting Despite Fear

Following the behaviorist and then cognitive revolutions, Rachman (e.g. Rachman, 1990) defines courage solely in terms of acting despite feeling fear. Using the tripartite model of emotion (e.g. Lang, 1968), this definition proposes that courage occurs when an actor experiences the subjective and physiological changes associated with fear. However, instead of following the action tendencies associated with fear—avoidance, escape, or freezing—the individual approaches the fear-inducing stimulus. Thus, defining courage as acting despite fear translates Lord's (1918) sentiments into emotions and removes nobility from the definition completely.

But if only standing up to fear matters for courageous action, what about those who experience less fear? In a laboratory stress task designed to induce fear, decorated bomb disposal operators showed less subjective and physiological signs of fear compared to control participants (Cox, Hallam, O'Connor, & Rachman, 1983). If courage requires fear and these people are less fearful, does that make their actions less courageous?

Moreover, a measure based on Rachman's (1990) definition (Muris, 2009; Norton & Weiss, 2009) correlates .6 with sensation-seeking (Muris, Mayer, & Schubert, 2010). While sensation-seeking might be part of a person's willingness to engage in a courageous action, it seems likely that courage requires more than a desire to experience intense feelings. Imagine two people who have been equally injured in a house fire. Both felt equally fearful as they ran into the burning building, but one ran in to save a baby and the other ran in for the experience of being surrounded by flames. Our intuition is that the first seems more courageous than the second.

Unlike the competing sentiments approach, acting despite fear might or might not belong as a construct in positive psychology. While acting despite fear to save the life of another, to uphold justice, or to pursue a life-long dream would all seem to fit with the general virtue theme of being a better person; acting despite fear for a thrill or out of a general conviction that fear is bad probably does not.

Taking a Worthwhile Risk

Here we define courage as taking a worthwhile risk. We base this definition on Rate's (Rate, 2010; see also Rate, Clarke, Lindsay, & Sternberg, 2007) implicit theory research—finding that courage consists of (1) a voluntary action, (2) taken despite personal risk, (3) for a worthwhile or noble goal.

First, courageous actions must be purposefully taken by the individual, not just accidentally experienced by them. A case could be made that the sentiment definition has a particular locus of action—the sentiments of the person—rather than any choice being made. The standing-up-to-fear definition, like much of that era of emotion theory, is mute on volition.

Next, our definition is based on the experience of risk rather than fear. This is for several reasons. First, research on those who have won awards for courage finds that they experience less fear in a laboratory setting than control participants (Cox et al., 1983). Second, individuals asked to describe a past courageous action rate it as more courageous compared to their own actions if they felt fear, but not as more courageous compared to the actions of most people, with some people describing an action as courageous but not saying they felt fear at the time (Pury et al., 2007). Finally, Rate et al.'s (2007) review of definitions of courage found that they included definitions that required fear but also definitions that required its absence. Moving the defining feature of courage from the individual's emotional response of fear to the appraisal of risk that (frequently, but not always) causes fear eliminates this concern.

Similar to Lord's (1918) definition, we also add a component of a noble goal, or a worthwhile reason for choosing to take a risk. This addition, we argue, puts courage back into the realm of virtues (Dahlsgaard, Peterson, & Seligman, 2005; Peterson & Seligman, 2004a). Awards for courage are commonly made for actions taken to assist others in serious need—a fairly universal prosocial motive—and for actions that are taken in support of the organizations' specific mission (Pury & Starkey, 2010). In other words, awards for courage are not given for actions simply taken to stand up to risk (or fear), but rather for actions that mean something.

A final part of our definition focuses on another part of the worth of the action: the likelihood that it will succeed. When asked to describe courageous actions, most people commonly describe successful actions, and actions that succeed are rated as higher in courage than actions that fail (Pury & Hensel, 2010).

Although most of the research cited above has been conducted in Western cultures, a similar picture emerges from research on courage in China. Using grounded theory, Cheng and Huang (2016) found three main features of courageous action: persistence, breakthrough, and responsibility. They describe persistence as an ongoing choice to continue to act, related to volition. Breakthrough, or surmounting obstacles, indicates that there is something to be overcome. While this obstacle might be the risk of the action or might be broader than that (e.g. going beyond one's limits) is yet to be determined. Finally, they argue that responsibility is a property of courage that has not been found in Western samples to date and thus may be uniquely Chinese. Framed in the context of both collectivistic culture and Rate's (2010) tripartite model, it might indicate a particular relationship between the actor and a noble or worthwhile goal.

Courage as taking a worthwhile risk, we argue, fits well within the positive psychology domain as a path for people to do things they find valuable.

Being able to act despite risk allows individuals to enact their other virtues (e.g. Pury & Kowalski, 2007).

Related Constructs: Resilience and Values in Action (VIA) Strengths of Courage

Resilience

Resilience, or positive adaptation following significant adversity (e.g. Masten, Cutuli, Herbers, & Reed, 2009) is similar to courage in describing the transcendence of negative events. However, they have many important differences. Both involve something that is negatively evaluated, but for courage, at least before the action is taken, the negative outcome is frequently just a possibility—a risk of social derision, the chance of failure, the possibility of physical injury. For resilience, the negative circumstance has already occurred—the person has been or is a social outcast, has failed, or has been injured. Additionally, the causal relationship between the negative risk or event and the action is different. For courage, taking the action leads to the risk. Without the action, the actor would not be facing the risk. If a stand-up comedian does not go on stage, she does not risk rejection. If a possible rescuer stays on land instead of going after a drowning swimmer, he stays safe. For resilience, the negative event has already occurred, but the actor takes constructive actions despite their past history or present adversity. These constructive actions might or might not be related to the adversity itself, for example, someone who channels the personal pain of a terrible childhood into being a stand-up comic, or someone who lost a limb in an accident but now competes in triathlons. Finally, when people write about their own courageous actions, they commonly—but not always—describe actions that take place very quickly such as confronting a bully or using their bodies to shield someone else from an immediate physical threat (e.g. Cheng & Huang, 2016; Muris, 2009; Pury & Kowalski, 2007; Pury et al., 2007). Resilience, however, often can be framed as a developmental trajectory (Masten et al., 2009) and involves healthy levels of function across multiple domains (Johnston et al., 2015; Reivich & Shatté, 2002). The closest thing to resilience in the courage literature is Finfgeld's construct of *vital courage*, or the courage to transcend significant personal challenges (commonly illness) to do something greater (Finfgeld, 1995, 1999), such as a politician who rises to prominence despite a serious illness. However, even vital courage involves confronting the current illness and the risks associated with acknowledging and coping with it.

Here we propose that a multitude of courageous actions might be part of resilience. For example, a sexual assault survivor might be resilient by strengthening a romantic relationship, continuing on a chosen educational path, and volunteering at a sexual assault center. To the extent that each of those activities brings up the threat of flashbacks or other emotionally traumatic experiences, choosing to engage in them might require courage. However, drawing from the experience of the assault and its aftermath, to be better at the relationship, education, and volunteer work would be resilience.

VIA Strengths of Courage

The VIA virtue of courage, as proposed by Peterson and Seligman (2004b) is more trait-like than a single act, and thus, like resilience, a construct that necessarily describes a much longer period of time. Theoretically, VIA courage is comprised of four strengths—or more specific positive trait-like approaches to life. These are *bravery*, or not shrinking from threat or a challenge; *authenticity*, or presenting oneself in a genuine way; *persistence*, or finishing what one starts; and *zest*, or approaching life with excitement and energy. The bravery component goes along with the risk component in the definition we propose here, as well as Cheng and Huang's (2016) component of breakthrough. The persistence component, found by Cheng and Huang, likewise complements the voluntary component of the current definition. Authenticity, like Cheng and Huang's responsibility, would enhance the valued nature of the goal. Finally, zest might give one the energy to pursue the breakthrough over risk or the persistence needed for courage.

In an empirical test of the relationship of these strengths with courageous actions, Pury & Kowalski (2007) found that recalled courageous actions were most typically described by participants as enacting the VIA courage strengths of persistence, authenticity, and bravery—but not zest. Instead, *hope* (being optimistic that one can bring about a desired outcome and classified by the VIA under the virtue of transcendence) described most courageous actions listed. Examined in light of courage as taking a worthwhile risk, hope might give the individual both a pathway to reach the desired goal and the optimism that the goal would be attained, and thus, worth the risk. *Kindness* (or doing good things for others, classified by the VIA under the virtue of humanity) described courageous actions taken on behalf of another person. Kindness presumes a value in aiding others, which enhances the worth of the goal in our model.

Types of Courage: Based on Goals and Risks

Courage has commonly been divided into specific types. Plato's (1961) Socratic dialog on courage, *Laches*, has the main characters discussing courage in battle, in ships on turbulent seas, in civic life, and in a variety of other circumstances. Modern courage scholars frequently distinguish between physical courage, such as saving someone from drowning, and moral courage, such as standing up for the rights of others (Lopez, O'Byrne, & Petersen, 2003; Putman, 2010), while more recent additions include military, vital, psychological, civic, and social courage. Pury and colleagues (Pury, Britt, Zinzow, & Raymond, 2014;

Pury et al., 2007; Pury & Starkey, 2010) have proposed that the best way to understand these distinctions is to look at the specific goals and risks involved. Because these goal–risk pairs commonly co-occur in nature, we speculate, society and researchers have labeled different types of courage.

Physical Courage

Physical courage involves physical risk to the actor. Most commonly, this is to prevent the same physical risk from harming someone else. Examples include saving someone from drowning (and risking being drowned oneself in the process), joining in a physical fight to protect someone else from being injured, and—like the first example at the start of this chapter—saving an animal from being hit by a car (and risking injury to oneself).

Moral, Civil, and Social Courage

Moral courage involves standing up for someone else or for an ideal against others, thus risking social harm for challenging the opposing person or group. Examples include standing up for one's moral beliefs against popular opinion, confronting a bully (as in the chapter opening's second example), or engaging in whistleblowing on a job. In all of these instances, people risk their own social standing to do the "right" thing. Two related constructs: *civil courage* and *workplace social courage*, have been investigated in the literature as well.

Civil courage (e.g. Greitemeyer, Osswald, Fischer, & Frey, 2007) is defined as having the goal of enforcing social and ethical norms despite a range of risks to the self. Anger at the violation of those norms fuels the courageous action. Examples include intervening to prevent criminal behavior, such as a mugging or sexual assault; volunteering with a group that opposes hate speech; and other behaviors in which one might stand for society while risking harm that ranges from verbal harassment to physical injury.

In *social courage*, the individual risks damaging relationships or social image, although the goal is open. Howard, Farr, Grandey, and Gutworth (2016) first describe a type of courage based entirely on social risk, then place it in a workplace context. In Howard et al.'s (2016) Workplace Social Courage scale, individuals rate their likelihood of taking social risks to pursue goals that lead to a better organization. Examples include giving someone an honest performance evaluation even if it might damage a friendship, or telling co-workers when one has made a mistake even though one might lose social standing as a result.

Psychological and Vital Courage

Not all types of courage involve goals directed toward others or toward higher ideals, however. Cheng and Huang (2016) found that courageous actions were taken to pursue both socially oriented and individually oriented goals. Pury et al. (2007) found that physical courage might also include stunts and extreme sports—activities taken for the goal of self-fulfillment and thrills with risks of physical injury. Putman (2004, 2010) proposes a third main type of courage: *psychological courage*, or the courage to overcome risks to one's inner peace or emotional stability to pursue wholeness. Putman's prototypical act of psychological courage is seeking treatment to overcome a past traumatic event, even though doing so will be traumatic in and of itself. Other examples from the literature include attending the best college for one's educational goals even though one might be homesick there, and admitting any type of personal shortcoming to oneself (e.g. Pury et al., 2007). As discussed above under "resilience," another type of courage that can include personal goals is vital courage (Finfgeld, 1995, 1998, 1999), in which the person transcends illness or other serious limitations to do something greater.

Blended Courage

We argue elsewhere (Pury & Starkey, 2010) that these types of courage are rough descriptors at best—fundamentally, if courage involves goals and risks, there are pairs that are more likely to naturally co-occur but these are only prototypes. *Blended courage*, or the goal of one type of courage pursued despite the risk of another type, should also occur. Active duty soldiers who need mental health treatment, for example, are commonly seeking the wellness goal of psychological courage but need to stand up to others around them to get it, facing the risks of moral or social courage (Pury et al., 2012). Other examples include civil rights protesters who take on the risks of physical courage to pursue a moral courage goal, or extreme sports enthusiasts who pursue the personal growth goal of psychological courage despite the risks of physical courage.

Other Typologies of Courage

Process and Accolade Courage

A complementary typology of courage, proposed by Pury and Starkey (2010) considers that both risk to the actor and worth of the goal are subjective judgments. Furthermore, their effect on courage depends on what is being measured: are we interested in how a person decides to take or not to take a risky action, or are we interested in how courageous we see a particular action? We propose that the first be labeled *process courage*, or the mechanism by which someone takes a risk for a worthy goal. It should be enhanced by the increased worth of the goal, but by decreased perceived risk. The second, *accolade courage*, or the process by which someone decides that the action of another or a past action of the self is more or less courageous, should be enhanced by the increased worth of the goal as well as increased perceived risk. Moreover, if perception of the risks and goals are discordant for the actor and the observer, other types of not-quite courage can occur, such as *foolish courage*, or taking a risk for a goal that is not perceived as worth it by the observer. More troubling is *bad courage*, or an actor's assumption of a risk for a goal that outside observers deem highly undesirable, such as suicide, terrorism, or spree killings (Pury, Starkey, Kulik, Skjerning, & Sullivan, 2015).

General and Personal Courage

A distinction can also be made between *general courage*, or actions for which most people have a similar appreciation of the risks and a similar (high) value for the goals; and *personal courage*, or actions in which the risks or goals (or both) are of note for the actor but more invisible to everyone else. For example, rescuing a child from a burning house (general courage) is likely to be heralded as courageous by nearly all who hear about it, as protecting the lives of children is highly valued and the risks of a house fire are obvious to nearly everyone. These types of actions could be thought of as monumental courage and commonly—but not always—lead to public accolades (Pury et al., 2007). However, consider these potential acts of personal courage. Asking a librarian if a book is available is unlikely to be seen as courageous to an observer, unless the observer knows that the actor has crippling social anxiety; the risk is not apparent from the outside. Alternatively, the goal might not be apparent to the observer: running into a burning building to save a pet hamster might be seen as foolish or courageous, depending on the value you place on pet hamsters.

Previous research has found that the more personally courageous an actor rated a past action, the higher the level of fear they reported, with no relationship to confidence at the time. The more generally courageous they rated the action, the more confidence they reported, with no relationship with fear (Pury et al., 2007). Higher reported general courage and lower reported personal courage were associated with higher overall ratings on the VIA strengths demonstrated at the time of the action (Pury & Kowalski, 2007).

Constructs Related to Courage

Constructs Related to Process Courage

In our theory, process courage should be influenced by constructs that increase the individual's assessment of the value of the goal, decrease the person's assessment of risk or its attendant inhibiting emotions, and increase the person's general sense of efficacy in being able to reach the goal and/or cope with the risks. Although these propositions have not been studied extensively, there are hints of empirical support. Constructs that are related to the perceived value of goals have been studied for morally motivated acts of courage. Fagin-Jones and Midlarsky (2007) found that Holocaust rescuers are higher than matched controls on social responsibility, altruistic moral reasoning, and empathy. Brandstätter, Jonas, Koletzko, and Fisher (2016) found that participants with higher levels of benevolence and universality were more likely to perceive norm violation in written moral courage scenarios. Finally, Halmburger, Baumert, and Schmitt (2015) found that the more anger participants experienced when seeing a confederate "steal" a cell phone, the more likely they were to intervene.

Constructs that affect the subjective experience of risk have also been studied, in both physical and moral courage contexts. Rachman's original work with decorated bomb disposal operators (Cox et al., 1983; O'Connor, Hallam, & Rachman, 1985) indicates that winning an award for valor is associated with lower subjective symptoms and physiological signs of fear. Similarly, Fagin-Jones and Midlarsky (2007) found that risk-taking is more prevalent in Holocaust rescuers than in matched controls. Brandstätter and colleagues (2016) found that participants with higher behavioral inhibition and state orientation perceived higher risk in written moral courage scenarios. Additionally, the anger experienced by Halmburger et al. (2015) may reduce perceptions of risk (Lerner & Tiedens, 2006).

To our knowledge, there have not been studies conducted examining the effects of efficacy on process courage. However, popular notions of *encouragement* may be a place to start. "You can do it," a common statement of encouragement, may represent an attempt by those close to an actor to increase efficacy, and thus, to increase courage.

Constructs Related to Accolade Courage

Like process courage, accolade courage should be affected by increasing perceived value of the goal and perceived efficacy. However, the relationship between perceived risks and accolade courage should be in the opposite direction, with higher perceived risks associated with higher perceived courage. Research on accolade courage is scant, however. Rate and colleagues (e.g. Rate et al., 2007) found that, generally, all three components need to be present for accolade courage. One feature related to perceived efficacy—the retrospective success of an action—seems to increase accolade courage. An analysis of one year's worth of a major US award for courage found that it was almost always awarded when both the possible victim and the would-be rescuer lived. However, in those cases where the would-be victim died, the would-be rescuer died too (Pury & Starkey, 2010). Retrospective reports of one's own courage (turning the accolade lens on oneself) are characterized by successful actions, and higher ratings for accolade courage are made for scenarios in which the actor succeeds in their goal, rather than when they fail, even if the failure has an external attribution (Pury & Hensel, 2010).

Applications and Future Directions

Practical Applications

Research courage to date provides some important suggestions for everyday life. First, courageous acts need not be monumental (Pury et al., 2007). Instead, personal courage—a courageous act that is such because the individual overcomes a particular personal fear or pursues a personally important goal—also matters. To outside observers, however, such an action might not seem courageous unless they are able to see the risks and goals from the actor's point of view. Second, we might be prone to overlook actions that took courage for the actor, or that took courage for us in the past, if they did not ultimately succeed. Thus, the accolades of courage that we bestow on those of others and on our past selves might be undercounting some actions that should be seen as courageous.

On the other hand, our model of accolade courage also suggests that there might be instances where people do not want to be acknowledged as courageous. Calling an action courageous implies that the actor took a risk and that the goal was not only worthwhile, but also attained. There may be instances when people do not want to think about the danger that they were in, or to acknowledge that they have a particular limitation that makes an action courageous. What about actions that are at best limited in their success, for instance, if only some people were saved from the fire, if the bad behavior prompting moral courage continues, or if the person's time at a difficult college is not that great? Calling attention to the actor might in some cases draw attention to the ways in which it fell short of the goal. Finally, modesty might also prevent people from wanting to be called courageous (Biswas-Diener, 2012).

This model also suggests ways in which a courage intervention might work. Any such interventions might focus on clarifying and valuing goals, promoting self-efficacy, and reducing both actual risks and the fear response to them. We remind potential developers of such interventions, however, that such interventions could potentially aid people in carrying out acts of bad courage as well as socially desirable acts (see Pury, Starkey, Breeden, Kelley, Murphy, & Lowndes, 2014).

Future Directions for Research and Theory

As defined here, courage is a complex construct with multiple parts. As such, measurement of individual differences in process courage may be quite difficult. Existing measures either focus solely on the standing-up-to-fear model (Norton & Weiss, 2009) or else contain double-barreled items, such as *Despite appearing dumb in front of an audience, I would volunteer to give a presentation at work* (Howard et al., 2016) and *If it looked like someone would get badly hurt, I would intervene directly in a dangerous domestic dispute* (Woodard & Pury, 2007). Thus, respondents might reject or endorse an item based on their appraisal of the risk, their appraisal of the goal, or both. Additionally, the varieties of risks and goals covered by measures are either quite specific, such as the risk of social rejection to do what is best for an organization (Howard et al., 2016), or represent a sampling across multiple types of risks and goals (Woodard & Pury, 2007).

One possible alternative might be to measure specific constructs that influence the appraisals of risk, value, and self-efficacy, both in general and for particular sorts of situations. Appraisal of risk in moral courage situations has been found to be predicted by behavioral inhibition and state orientation (Brandstätter et al., 2016), and, as these constructs are related to a general tendency to respond to the world as threatening might also predict appraisal of risk in other types of potentially courageous situations. Additional constructs that might predict general appraisal of risk might be general anxiety or neuroticsm scales. Specific fears, for example, fear of negative evaluation (social risk), blood-injection-injury fears (helping out in a medical emergency), and various animal fears might predict specific risk assessments in particular circumstances, especially for personal courage.

Individual differences should also predict the valuation of the goal of a potentially courageous action, and thus the likelihood of assuming a risk to meet it. Brandstätter et al. (2016) found that benevolence and universalism predicted ratings of need to intervene in moral courage situations: they might also be expected to predict ratings of need to intervene when someone else is in physical danger from the natural world, such as about to fall off a cliff. Other values, such as a need for power, achievement, hedonism, stimulation, self-direction, tradition, conformity, security, and so on (e.g. Cieciuch & Schwartz, 2012) might predict the value or worth of other types of goals.

Finally, the estimated likelihood that one will succeed in both avoiding risk and reaching a goal might be predicted by general self-efficacy and by specific efficacies related to the specific task. Self-efficacy for avoiding injury, taking on social risks, or coping with stress might also predict assessment of risks; while self-efficacy for whatever the action required, might predict assessment of worthiness as well—if it is unlikely to be sucessful, then it may be unlikely to be worthwhile.

State changes in any or all of these constructs related to assessment of risks, goals, and efficacy might be investigated as ways to increase courage. Similarly, mindfulness, focus, and even flow could also be considered as playing a role in process courage—to what extent is someone who is taking a courageous action focused on the goal they are pursuing versus the risk that they are taking? Does a change in attention lead to a change in taking or not taking a courageous action?

Given the prevalence of awards for courage, another fruitful area for future research might be to examine the effects of receiving an award on the honoree.

Does getting an award for courage make the awardee feel more committed to the goal they were pursuing? If the goals were only partially met, does the award make the person feel better or worse about their actions? What is the effect of an award on a person who does not see what they did as extraordinary? An additional set of questions, perhaps with easier answers, is the effect of the award on observers. Does hearing about an awardee lead to increased elevation, and are awards more likely to be given in the first place for actions that lead to increased elevation (Haidt, 2000)?

Conclusions

In this chapter, we reviewed the evidence for considering courage to be, succinctly, taking a worthwhile risk. The introduction of *worth* into the study of courage moves it beyond mere risk-taking into a virtue that allows people to transcend a variety of risks to do the right thing. This definition has three main components: a noble or worthwhile goal, a risk that might or might not lead to fear, and the judgment that it is worth voluntarily assuming the risk to pursue the goal. Subjective assessments of the value of the goal, the risk assumed, and the likelihood of reaching the goal are made by the actor prior to taking action (process courage) and by observers of the action either at the time or in retrospect (accolade courage). The particular relationship between types of goals and related, typical risks to pursue them leads to the commonly described varieties of courage. While few interventions for courage currently exist, we remain optimistic that further inquiries into the nature of courage and its antecedents will aid in their development.

Acknowledgments

This chapter benefited greatly from discussions with Charles Starkey and Faezeh Zand. Research support has been provided to the first author by the Clemson University Creative Inquiry Fund.

References

Biswas-Diener, R. (2012). *The courage quotient: How science can make you braver.* San Francisco, CA: Jossey-Bass.

Brandstätter, V., Jonas, K. J., Koletzko, S. H., & Fischer, P. (2016). Self-regulatory processes in the appraisal of moral courage situations. *Social Psychology*, *47*(4), 201–213. doi:10.1027/1864-9335/a000274.

Cheng, C., & Huang, X. (2016). An exploration of courage in Chinese individuals. *The Journal of Positive Psychology*, 1–10. doi:10.1080/17439760.2016.1163406.

Cieciuch, J., & Schwartz, S. H. (2012). The number of distinct basic values and their structure assessed by PVQ-40. *Journal of Personality Assessment*, *94*(3), 321–328. doi:10.1080/00223891.2012.655817.

Cox, D., Hallam, R., O'Connor, K., & Rachman, S. (1983). An experimental analysis of fearlessness and courage. *British Journal of Psychology*, *74*(1), 107–117. doi:10.1111/j.2044-8295.1983.tb01847.x.

Dahlsgaard, K., Peterson, C., & Seligman, M. E. P. (2005). Shared virtue: The convergence of valued human strengths across culture and history. *Review of General Psychology*, *9*(3), 203–213. doi:10.1037/1089-2680.9.3.203.

Fagin-Jones, S., & Midlarsky, E. (2007). Courageous altruism: Personal and situational correlates of rescue during the Holocaust. *The Journal of Positive Psychology*, *2*(2), 136–147. doi:10.1080/17439760701228979.

Finfgeld, D. L. (1995). Becoming and being courageous in the chronically ill elderly. *Issues in Mental Health Nursing*, *16*(1), 1–11. doi:10.3109/01612849509042959.

Finfgeld, D. L. (1998). Courage in middle-aged adults with long-term health concerns. *The Canadian Journal of Nursing Research = Revue Canadienne De Recherche En Sciences Infirmières*, *30*(1), 153–169.

Finfgeld, D. L. (1999). Courage as a process of pushing beyond the struggle. *Qualitative Health Research*, *9*(6), 803–814. doi:10.1177/104973299129122298.

Greitemeyer, T., Osswald, S., Fischer, P., & Frey, D. (2007). Civil courage: Implicit theories, related concepts, and measurement. *The Journal of Positive Psychology*, *2*(2), 115–119. doi:10.1080/17439760701228789.

Haidt, J. (2000). The positive emotion of elevation. *Prevention & Treatment*, *3*(1). doi:10.1037/1522-3736.3.1.33c.

Halmburger, A., Baumert, A., & Schmitt, M. (2015). Anger as driving factor of moral courage in comparison with guilt and global mood: A multimethod approach. *European Journal of Social Psychology*, *45*(1), 39–51. doi:10.1002/ejsp.2071.

Howard, M. C., Farr, J. L., Grandey, A. A., & Gutworth, M. B. (2016). The creation of the workplace social courage scale (WSCS): An investigation of internal consistency, psychometric properties, validity, and utility. *Journal of Business and Psychology*, 1–18. doi:10.1007/s10869-016-9463-8.

Johnston, M. C., Porteous, T., Crilly, M. A., Burton, C. D., Elliott, A., Iversen, L., … Black, C. (2015). Physical disease and resilient outcomes: A systematic review of resilience definitions and study methods. *Psychosomatics: Journal of Consultation and Liaison Psychiatry*, *56*(2), 168–180. doi:10.1016/j.psym.2014.10.005.

Lang, P. J. (1968). Fear reduction and fear behavior: Problems in treating a construct. In J. M. Shlien (Ed.), *Research in Psychotherapy* (pp. 90–102). Washington, DC: American Psychological Association.

Lerner, J. S., & Tiedens, L. Z. (2006). Portrait of the angry decision maker: How appraisal tendencies shape anger's influence on cognition. *Journal of Behavioral Decision Making*, *19*(2), 115–137. doi:10.1002/bdm.515.

Lopez, S. J., O'Byrne, K. K., & Petersen, S. (2003). Profiling courage. In S. J. Lopez & C. R. Snyder (Eds.), *Positive psychological assessment: A handbook of models and measures* (pp. 185–197). Washington, DC: American Psychological Association.

Lord, H. G. (1918). *The psychology of courage*. Boston, MA: John W. Luce.

Masten, A. S., Cutuli, J. J., Herbers, J. E., & Reed, M.-G. J. (2009). Resilience in development. In C. R. Snyder & S. J. Lopez (Eds.), *Oxford Handbook of Positive Psychology* (2nd ed., pp. 117–131). New York: Oxford University Press.

Muris, P. (2009). Fear and courage in children: Two sides of the same coin? *Journal of Child and Family Studies*, *18*(4), 486–490. doi:10.1007/s10826-009-9271-0.

Muris, P., Mayer, B., & Schubert, T. (2010). "You might belong in Gryffindor": Children's courage and its relationships to anxiety symptoms, big five personality traits, and sex roles. *Child Psychiatry and Human Development, 41*(2), 204–213. doi:10.1007/s10578-009-0161-x.

Norton, P. J., & Weiss, B. J. (2009). The role of courage on behavioral approach in a fear-eliciting situation: A proof-of-concept pilot study. *Journal of Anxiety Disorders, 23*(2), 212–217. doi:10.1016/j.janxdis.2008.07.002.

O'Connor, K., Hallam, R. S., & Rachman, S. (1985). Fearlessness and courage: A replication experiment. *British Journal of Psychology, 76*(2), 187–197. doi:10.1111/j.2044-8295.1985.tb01942.x.

Peterson, C., & Seligman, M. E. P. (2004a). *Character strengths and virtues: A handbook and classification.* Washington, DC: American Psychological Association; New York: Oxford University Press.

Peterson, C., & Seligman, M. E. P. (2004b). Introduction to a 'Manual of the Sanities.' In C. Peterson & M. E. P. Seligman (Eds.), *Character strengths and virtues: A handbook and classification* (pp. 3–32). Washington, DC: American Psychological Association and New York: Oxford University Press.

Plato. (1961). *Laches* (B. Jowett, Trans.). In E. Hamilton & H. Cairns (Eds.), *The collected dialogues of Plato, including the letters* (pp. 123–144). Princeton, NJ: Princeton University Press.

Pury, C. L. S., Britt, T. W., Zinzow, H. M., & Raymond, M. A. (2014). Blended courage: Moral and psychological courage elements in mental health treatment seeking by active duty military personnel. *The Journal of Positive Psychology, 9*, 30–41. doi:10.1080/17439760.2013.831466.

Pury, C. L. S., & Hensel, A. D. (2010). Are courageous actions successful actions? *The Journal of Positive Psychology, 5*(1), 62–72. doi:10.1080/17439760903435224.

Pury, C. L. S., & Kowalski, R. M. (2007). Human strengths, courageous actions, and general and personal courage. *The Journal of Positive Psychology, 2*(2), 120–128. doi:10.1080/17439760701228813.

Pury, C. L. S., Kowalski, R. M., & Spearman, J. (2007). Distinctions between general and personal courage. *The Journal of Positive Psychology, 2*(2), 99–114. doi:10.1080/17439760701237962.

Pury, C. L. S., & Starkey, C. B. (2010). Is courage an accolade or a process? A fundamental question for courage research. In C. L. S. Pury & S. J. Lopez (Eds.), *The psychology of courage: Modern research on an ancient virtue* (pp. 67–87). Washington, DC: American Psychological Association.

Pury, C. L. S., Starkey, C. B., Breeden, C., Kelley, C., Murphy, H., & Lowndes, A. (2014). Courage interventions: Future directions and cautions. In A. C. Parks (Ed.), *Wiley-Blackwell handbook of positive psychological interventions* (pp. 168–178). Oxford: Wiley-Blackwell.

Pury, C. L. S., Starkey, C. B., Kulik, R. E., Skjerning, K. L., & Sullivan, E. A. (2015). Is courage always a virtue? Suicide, killing, and bad courage. *The Journal of Positive Psychology, 10*(5), 383–388. doi:10.1080/17439760.2015.1004552.

Pury, C. L. S., Zinzow, H., Burnette, C., McFadden, A., Gillispie, S., Raymond, M. A., & Britt, T. (2012). *Psychological (and moral) courage as a factor in treatment seeking in an active duty military sample.* Paper presented at the 120th Annual Convention of the American Psychological Association, Orlando, FL.

Putman, D. (2004). *Psychological courage.* Dallas, TX: University Press of America.

Putman, D. (2010). Philosophical roots of the concept of courage. In C. L. S. Pury & S. J. Lopez (Eds.), *The psychology of courage: Modern research on an ancient virtue* (pp. 9–22). Washington, DC: American Psychological Association.

Rachman, S. J. (1990). *Fear and courage* (2nd ed.). New York: W. H. Freeman/Times Books/Henry Holt & Co.

Rate, C. R. (2010). Defining the features of courage: A search for meaning. In C. L. S. Pury & S. J. Lopez (Eds.), *The psychology of courage: Modern research on an ancient virtue* (pp. 47–66). Washington, DC: American Psychological Association.

Rate, C. R., Clarke, J. A., Lindsay, D. R., & Sternberg, R. J. (2007). Implicit theories of courage. *The Journal of Positive Psychology, 2*(2), 80–98. doi:10.1080/17439760701228755.

Reivich, K., & Shatté, A. (2002). *The resilience factor: Seven essential skills for overcoming life's inevitable obstacles*. New York: Broadway Books.

Woodard, C. R., & Pury, C. L. S. (2007). The construct of courage: Categorization and measurement. *Consulting Psychology Journal: Practice and Research, 59*(2), 135–147. doi:10.1037/1065-9293.59.2.135.

PART III

Positive Institutional Perspectives and New Directions

11

POSITIVE PSYCHOLOGY IN THE WORKPLACE

The Important Role of Psychological Capital (PsyCap)

Fred Luthans and Regina Frey

As indicated in this volume, positive psychology is now established, recognized, and embedded in most academic and applied domains in the behavioral sciences. This chapter's purpose is to provide a current overview of positive psychology in the workplace. We present the theoretical foundation and research support for the relevance of positivity in general, and specifically the role positive psychological capital or PsyCap plays in desired employee attitudes, behaviors, and performance.

We first briefly summarize the more umbrella areas of Positive Organizational Scholarship (POS) (Cameron, Dutton, & Quinn, 2003) and Positive Organizational Behavior (POB) (Luthans, 2002a, 2002b). Then in the remainder of the chapter we provide a summary of the extensive research on the antecedents, development, and outcomes of the POB core construct of PsyCap which consists of the positive psychological resources of Hope, Efficacy, Resilience, and Optimism, or the HERO within (Luthans, Luthans, & Luthans, 2004; Luthans & Youssef, 2004; Luthans, Youssef, & Avolio, 2007; Luthans, Youssef-Morgan, & Avolio, 2015). We conclude by providing avenues for needed future research.

Positivity in Organizational Settings

Cameron (2008) observes that even though humans tend to be more attracted by what is beautiful, positive, and pleasant, negativity also has its place. He notes this is because there tend to be four prominent biases toward negativity. First, negative stimuli are perceived as being more *intense* than neutral or positive stimuli. Perhaps stemming from evolutionary roots, the negative is often perceived as a threat and therefore must be attended to more quickly and resolutely. The second bias Cameron identifies pertains to *novelty*. While neutral or positive stimuli are more common, they tend to go less noticed. The third bias refers to *adaptation*. A negative stimulus points toward a possible maladaptation of the individual, and, therefore, is in need of change. Fourth and final is *singularity*. This infers that a singular negative stimulus could be a warning sign for a defective element in the system, which could threaten the functioning or very survival of the individual.

Because of these biases toward negativity, positivity may often be overlooked. Negativity grasps more attention and provides more motivation to change. Even though the field of management and organizational behavior has undoubtedly over the years given relatively more attention and priority than psychology to positive constructs (e.g. job satisfaction, organizational commitment, organizational citizenship behavior), there has still too often been the tendency for a positive approach to be considered by both academics and practitioners as evasive or even problematic. As Wright and Quick (2009) have observed, this is because a positive perspective and accompanying constructs were often thought to be distal, vague, and under-specified. However, with the advent of positive psychology, positivity in the workplace has received renewed attention and is now seen as having major relevance and impact (Luthans & Avolio, 2009a, 2009b).

Even though positive psychology is being well received in the management and organizational behavior arena, some of the carry-over perceptions remain. For example, through positive psychologist Fredrickson's (2003) broaden-and-build research, positivity is seen as having a highly desirable broadening effect on individuals' thought-action repertoires, building up desired psychological, social, and even physical resources. Negativity, in comparison, was found to elicit undesirably narrow action tendencies toward a more instinctual fight-or-flight response to threatening situations. However, this still shows negativity does yield more clearly observable reactions, which tend to be more immediate and direct than positivity. In addition, Fredrickson's research verifies positivity's broadened responses are still more distal, vague, or uncertain (Wright & Quick, 2009). Unfortunately, this evasive nature of positivity makes it relatively more difficult to observe and measure, and therefore study and understand its outcomes.

In contrast to positivity, as indicated, the negativity signals that something is maladaptive and often induces immediate responses to avoid detrimental consequences. This makes negativity occurring in organizations an effective prompt for managers to make direct responses to avoid or minimize problems. Positivity, on the other hand, rarely entails negative consequences if attended to late or even ignored (Youssef-Morgan & Luthans, 2013). However, natural positive tendencies may be ignored or suppressed due to professional norms or time pressure. Positivity is therefore needed to counter-balance the rigidity, which will occur with too much emphasis on negativity in order to facilitate the benefits of both positivity and negativity (Baumeister, Bratslavsky, Finkenauer, & Vohs, 2001; Cameron, 2008; Youssef-Morgan & Luthans, 2013).

Finally, negativity exhibits a narrow singularity as described above. One breach of contract might result in substantial, long-run distrust among the parties. For example, being lied to shatters trust between parties, and being cheated on by a spouse very often leads to divorce. On the other hand, however, a fulfilled promise does not immediately lead to trust, either. Rather, promises need to be kept consistently and rapport must be established over time in order to build trust in relationships, that is, also on any work-related relationships.

Positive psychology supports ratios of higher positivity over negativity for optimal functioning and "flourishing" (Fredrickson, 2009). Fredrickson effectively uses the analogy of the tall mast of a sailing ship as representing the positive (i.e. channeling the wind behind the sails to power the ship) and the much smaller, but still important, keel beneath the ship representing the negative (i.e. keeping the ship from flopping over on its side and providing some direction). In more complex marital relationships, according to Gottman's (1994) studies a number of years ago, the positivity ratio needs to be higher at about 5:1 for a marriage to flourish. The need for positivity to outweigh negativity for effective functioning is explained by Baumeister and colleagues (2001) because of the stronger and more lasting impacts negative events have on memory, self-concept, information processing, and relationships. In order to counterbalance these outcomes of negativity, especially in an organizational setting, there is a need for a relatively stronger emphasis on positivity.

Positive Organizational Scholarship (POS)

POS integrates two paradigms in organizational research. While POS acknowledges competitive pressure and the quest for profitability as major goals, at least for private sector organizations, it also calls attention to the importance of the phenomena of positivity and positive deviance *per se*. POS differs from the traditional paradigm in being relatively more concerned and focused on organizations' positive outcomes, processes, and attributes of their members (Cameron, Dutton, Quinn, & Wrzesniewski, 2003, p. 4). POS encompasses an expanded positive perspective focusing on goodness, compassion, and human potential, and addressing enablers, motivations, and outcomes such as vitality, meaningfulness, exhilaration, and high-quality relationships. In a nutshell, POS seeks to understand what represents and brings out the best of the human condition. Thus, POS serves as an umbrella concept in bringing positive psychology to the workplace by incorporating a variety of positive perspectives such as positive traits, states, dynamics, and outcomes which are relevant to organizations.

Cameron and Spreitzer (2012) identify four major characteristics of POS: (1) a positive, *unique* or, at least, *alternative lens*, through which phenomena are viewed and thus problems can be interpreted as challenges or even opportunities for learning and growth; (2) a positive approach which focuses on *extraordinary outcomes*; (3) a positive approach which has an *affirmative bias* focusing more strongly on positive than on negative constructs, dynamics, and outcomes; and (4) an organization which fosters *positivity for its own sake* by aiming at a better understanding of the best of the human condition, such as flourishing, thriving, flow, and other life-giving dynamics. To date, there has been considerable conceptualization under the POS umbrella (e.g. there are 79 entries in Cameron and Spritzer's 2012 edited Handbook of POS; also see Spreitzer & Cameron, 2012), but there is a need for more basic, empirical research directly testing these concepts.

Positive Organizational Behavior (POB)

While POS has focused relatively more on the organizational level, POB to date has been more at the micro, individual level. POB is defined as "the study and application of positively-oriented human resource strengths and psychological capacities that can be measured, developed, and effectively managed for performance improvement in today's workplace" (Luthans, 2002a, p. 59). POB has emerged as a scholarly link, bridging the gap between practitioner-oriented popular books taking a positive approach to personal development, and organizational behavior scholars' theory/research-driven search for understanding, predicting, and managing positive human behavior in organizations.

In taking positive psychology to the workplace after being inspired at the inaugural Positive Psychology Summit in 1999 (Luthans & Avolio, 2009b for details on the historical background), Luthans (2002a, 2002b) founded and made the case for a proactive, positive approach that he termed Positive Organizational Behavior or POB. In order for a concept or construct to be included in POB as a positive psychological resource, four scientific criteria had to be met (Luthans, 2002a): Besides being positive, it must (1) be theory- and research- based; (2) have valid measurement; (3) be open to development or "state-like," as opposed to being relatively fixed or "trait-like"; and (4) relate to desirable employee attitudes, behaviors, and, especially, performance in the workplace. After an extensive search of the positive psychology literature (not organizational behavior), it was determined that the constructs which best met these inclusion criteria were hope, efficacy, resilience, and optimism. These four positive psychological resources were then combined into what Luthans called Psychological Capital or simply PsyCap (Luthans et al., 2004; Luthans & Youssef, 2004).

Psychological Capital

The foundation for PsyCap draws from positive psychology in general and specifically Bandura's (1997) Social Cognitive Theory (SCT). SCT posits a reciprocal triangular relationship between the individual, the environment, and behavior. It focuses on five components for agentic processing: symbolizing, forethought, observation, self-regulation, and self-reflection. It posits further, through interaction with the environment and others' behaviors, that learning and growth occur. This social learning leads to confidence and belief in the ability to intentionally (i.e. agentically) take control over one's future and eventual destiny. This triangular relationship builds the basis for efficacy. This form of agency, in turn, motivates positively-oriented (1) cognitions, such as proactivity and positive expectations, (2) self-directed behaviors, such as devoting time and effort toward goals, (3) emotions such as positive mood and affect, and (4) influences on others and the environment (Bandura, 2008; Youssef-Morgan & Luthans, 2013).

Drawing on SCT, and with the purpose of transitioning POB into the practice of human resource management, the higher-order construct of PsyCap was formulated from the four POB positive psychological resources, and then conceptually (Luthans, Youssef et al., 2007) and empirically validated (Luthans, Avolio, Avey, & Norman, 2007). PsyCap is defined as

> an individual's positive psychological state of development that is characterized by (1) having confidence (self-efficacy) to take on and put in the necessary effort to succeed at challenging tasks; (2) making a positive attribution (optimism) about succeeding now and in the future; (3) persevering toward goals and, when necessary, redirecting paths to goals (hope) in order to succeed; and (4) when beset by problems and adversity, sustaining and bouncing back, and even beyond (resilience) to attain success.
>
> *(Luthans, Youssef et al., 2007, p. 3)*

Hope is defined as "a positive motivational state based on an interactively derived sense of successful (a) agency (i.e. goal-directed energy) and (b) pathways (planning to meet goals)" (Snyder, Irving, & Anderson, 1991, p. 287). The two inherent dimensions of this definition can be described as agency, which represents the willpower to pursue goals, and pathways or "waypower," which represents the ability to proactively develop alternative plans if the original path is blocked (Luthans & Youssef-Morgan, 2017; Snyder, 2002).

Efficacy, in turn, is defined as "the individual's conviction or confidence about his or her abilities to mobilize the motivation, cognitive resources or courses of action needed to successfully execute a specific task within a given context" (Stajkovic & Luthans, 1998, p. 66). Bandura (1997) established four major ways of developing efficacy: (1) mastery, or successful experiences; (2) vicarious learning or modeling of relevant others; (3) social persuasion and positive feedback; and (4) physiological and psychological arousal.

Resilience is defined as "the capacity to rebound or bounce back from adversity, conflict, failure, or even positive events, progress, and increased responsibility" (Luthans, 2002a, p. 702). It represents the deployment of positive adaptation patterns and processes to overcome adversities or risk factors by capitalizing on personal, social, or psychological assets (Masten, Cutuli, Herbers, & Reed, 2009).

Drawing from Seligman (1998), optimism can be described as a positive attribution style (i.e. explanatory style) which links positive events to personal, permanent and pervasive causes, and attributes negative events to external, temporary, and situation-specific factors. Similarly, optimism can be described as a generalized positive outlook, which yields global positive expectancies (see, for example, Carver, Scheier, Miller, & Fulford, 2009).

As indicated, PsyCap is conceptualized (Luthans, Youssef et al., 2007; Luthans & Youssef-Morgan, 2017; Luthans et al., 2015; Youssef-Morgan & Luthans, 2013) and empirically validated (Avey, Reichard, Luthans, & Mhatre, 2011; Luthans, Avolio et al., 2007) as a higher-order, core construct as opposed to four first-order individual constructs. The common underlying mechanism linking the four dimensions is a positive, agentic, and developmental capacity toward "positive appraisal of circumstances and probability for success based on motivated effort and perseverance" (Luthans, Avolio et al., 2007, p. 550). For the most recent comprehensive review of the theory and research on PsyCap see Luthans and Youssef-Morgan (2017).

Alternative measures to capture PsyCap in individuals, and especially in relation to the workplace, have been developed. The most prevalent measure applied in empirical studies on PsyCap is the 24-item Psychological Capital Questionnaire (PCQ-24; Luthans, Youssef et al., 2007). It was originally adapted from six items each from Parker's (1998) role breadth self-efficacy scale, Snyder et al.'s (1996) state hope scale, Wagnild and Young's (1993) resilience scale, and Scheier and Carver's (1985) optimism scale. This PCQ-24 has been very widely used and has been empirically validated (e.g. Avey, Reichard et al., 2011; Dawkins, Martin, Scott, & Sanderson, 2013; Luthans, Avolio et al., 2007; Newman, Ucbasaran, Zhu, & Hirst, 2014). By statistically determining the best items from the PCQ-24, an abbreviated measure, the PCQ-12 was formulated. This PCQ-12 is being increasingly used and also has been validated in a number of studies (Avey, Avolio, & Luthans, 2011; Wernsing, 2014). Both scales (with numerous translations) can be obtained from www.mindgarden.com for research purposes at no cost.

In order to help overcome potential social desirability biases (as in all self-report measures,) an implicit measure of PsyCap was recently developed (Implicit Psychological Capital Questionnaire, I-PCQ; Harms & Luthans, 2012). Unlike the classic personality implicit, projective instruments such as the Rorschach Inkblot (Exner et al., 2008) or Thematic Apperception Test (TAT) (Bellak & Abrams, 1997), the I-PCQ is simple to administer and objectively scored. Validation with minimal social desirability and faking has been empirically demonstrated (Harms & Luthans, 2012; Krasikova, Harms,

Luthans, 2012) and a very recent adaptation for Health PsyCap has been validated (IPCQ-H, Harms, Vanhove, & Luthans, in press).

Antecedents of PsyCap

The reported research on antecedents of PsyCap is relatively less than the extensive empirical evidence on its impact on desired employee attitudes, behaviors, and performance. To date, organizational and supervisor support have been shown to be reliable predictors of PsyCap. For example, Luthans, Norman, Avolio, and Avey (2008) demonstrated in three diverse samples that a supportive climate at the workplace is positively related to PsyCap. Also, Liu (2013) found that supervisor support was a significant antecedent for PsyCap in a Taiwanese sample.

Drawing on socialization resources theory (Saks & Gruman, 2011), Nigah, Davis, and Hurrell (2012) demonstrated that successful onboarding through a "buddying" process positively contributed to employees' PsyCap. The study shows that onboarding graduates in a professional services firm were more successful if the newcomers received an experienced "buddy." This practice was shown to develop not only PsyCap, but to also increase work engagement, underlining the power of positively-oriented human resource practice. These findings contribute to the growing evidence that positively-oriented human resource management practices are related to personal resources, such as PsyCap, of newcomers within organizations.

In one of the few studies that directly tested for antecedents of PsyCap, Avey (2014) found that authentic and ethical leadership have a significantly positive effect on PsyCap, whereas abusive supervision did not. In this study, proactive personality, self-esteem, and task complexity also predicted PsyCap. However, in terms of demographics, only age showed a significant relationship with PsyCap, in that PsyCap seems to strengthen with age.

Development of PsyCap: Implications for Practice

Closely aligned to the antecedents related to PsyCap are the proactive training interventions to develop PsyCap in human resource management. Remembering the PsyCap inclusion criterion that the positive psychological resource must be open to development and "state-like," there has been considerable attention given to both the design of the PsyCap training to increase the participants' level of PsyCap (e.g. see Luthans, Avey, Avolio, Norman, & Combs, 2006) and experimental studies to demonstrate that short training interventions can cause PsyCap to increase.

An example of the developmental research would be the experimental study by Luthans, Avey, and Patera (2008). They designed and analyzed a PsyCap web-based training intervention. This intervention consisted of two 2-hour online sessions. In the first session, the participants were initially educated on what PsyCap is and how it is beneficial to work outcomes. This overview was followed by participants being asked to consider work situations, which they perceived to be challenging or difficult in terms of needing to draw from their resiliency and efficacious thoughts and processes. In relation to those work challenges, participants were asked to distinguish what was within their direct influence, and what was outside their direct influence in order to create and carry out specific courses of action in their actual work situations.

In the second session, the other two PsyCap components of optimism and hope were emphasized. Participants were first educated about the relevance of personal values and the realistic challenge of accomplishing tasks and goals. Next they were directed to write down several tasks they would like to accomplish that were realistic, important to their personal values, and applicable to their workplace. Participants were then asked to choose one of their goals and to break it down into smaller, more easily attainable goals. This stepping process made it more obvious for participants to see that smaller goals are actually relatively easily attainable and should develop their confidence (efficacy), willpower (hope) and also foster their optimism (promote making positive attributions about their success and failure and have a positive expectation about their future). Finally, they were asked to identify real and potential obstacles and alternative ways to get around them. This part of the exercise accounts for the, too often ignored, pathways part of hope and also enhances the participants' resiliency by being able to overcome adversity.

Comparing randomly assigned treatment and control groups, Luthans and colleagues (2010) found that the training intervention significantly increased within subjects' level of PsyCap from Time 1 to Time 2, whereas no significant change was observed in the control group. This pre-test, post-test, control group experiment allows for the rare but definitive conclusion that the training intervention caused the participants' PsyCap to increase. Longitudinal studies using latent growth modeling also support that PsyCap causes enhanced performance over time (Peterson, Luthans, Avolio, Walumbwa, Zhang, 2011) and there is even an ideal Solomon Four Group designed study showing that a short training intervention caused employees' PsyCap to increase (Ertosun, Erdil, Deniz, & Alpkan, 2015). Another study in a Fortune 50 firm using a face-to-face 2.5 hour PsyCap training intervention found similar results (Luthans, Avey, Avolio, & Peterson, 2010).

Moreover, using actual dollars and cents utility analysis, a 270 percent return on investment (ROI, revenue generated from the increased PsyCap minus the cost of the training, divided by the cost) was calculated for the PsyCap training of 74 engineers working on an internationally known major project in this high-tech firm (see Luthans et al., 2015, p. 263). Obviously, this very high dollars and cents return on psychological capital investment, compared to financial capital investment, can and should receive the attention of today's high-pressured business executives facing dramatic change and competitive pressures in the global economy. This key state-like developmental characteristic is why PsyCap has such visible positive implications for practice and has been so widely recognized and accepted by consultants and professional managers (see Luthans, 2012).

Outcomes of PsyCap

Besides the growing attention being given to the antecedents and the development of PsyCap, by far most of the research attention to date has been devoted to the relationship and impact that PsyCap has with a wide variety of outcomes. We first summarize the more direct impact PsyCap has on work-related outcomes, and then we present the impact PsyCap has on well-being outcomes which has more indirect implications for the workplace. Table 11.1 provides a representative summary of the empirical studies on the outcomes of PsyCap.

TABLE 11.1 Summary of Representative PsyCap Studies

Author(s)	Year	Dependent variable(s)	Key findings
Avey, Hughes, Norman, and Luthans	2008	Empowerment, intent to leave, cynicism	• Transformational leadership and positive psychological capital were significantly related to feelings of empowerment. Empowerment was significantly related to intentions to quit but not employee cynicism.
Avey, Luthans, and Jensen	2009	Stress symptoms, intent to leave, job search behaviors	• PsyCap may be key to better understanding the variation in perceived symptoms of stress, as well as intentions to quit and job search behaviors.
Avey, Luthans, Smith, and Palmer	2010	Well-being	• The status of PsyCap as a positive resource used to enhance employee psychological well-being is established using longitudinal data.
Avey, Luthans, and Youssef	2010	OCB, cynicism, intent to leave, CWB, person–organization and person–job fit	• PsyCap was positively related to extra-role OCBs and negatively to organizational cynicism, intentions to quit, and counterproductive workplace behaviors. • With one exception, PsyCap also predicted unique variance in these outcomes beyond demographics, self-evaluation, personality, and person–organization and person–job fit.

(Continued)

TABLE 11.1 (*Continued*)

Author(s)	Year	Dependent variable(s)	Key findings
Avey, Nimnicht, and Pigeon	2010	Employee deviance, organizational citizenship behavior	• Employees highest in PsyCap and most strongly identified with the organization were most likely to engage in organizational citizenship behaviors and least likely to engage in deviance behaviors.
Avey, Patera, and West	2006	Absenteeism	• PsyCap reduces the levels of voluntary and involuntary absenteeism and, as a second-order construct, has a stronger relationship with absenteeism than the four dimensions individually.
Avey, Wernsing, and Luthans	2008	Positive emotions, engagement, cynicism, OCB, deviance	• PsyCap was related to their positive emotions that in turn were related to attitudes (engagement and cynicism) and behaviors (organizational citizenship and deviance). • Positive emotions generally mediated the relationship between psychological capital and the attitudes and behaviors.
Harms and Luthans	2012	Performance	• Implicit PsyCap positively related to performance and converges with self-report measure of PsyCap.
Krasikova, Lester, and Harms	2015	Mental health and substance abuse	• A higher degree of soldiers' PsyCap before deployment lowers the rates of mental illness diagnoses and substance abuse after deployment.
Larson and Luthans	2006	Satisfaction, commitment	• PsyCap explains more of the desirable work attitudes than human and social capital alone.
Luthans, Avey, Clapp-Smith, and Li	2008	Manager-rated work performance	• Workers' PsyCap, tenure and education were significantly related to manager-rated performance.
Luthans, Avolio, Avey, and Norman	2007	Work performance and job satisfaction	• Positive relationship regarding the second-order PsyCap over each of the 4 facets with performance and satisfaction. • PsyCap more malleable than personality traits and less than emotions.
Luthans and Jensen	2005	Intent to stay, commitment	• Highly significant positive relationship between PsyCap and the "intentions to stay" and commitment to the mission, values, and goals of the hospital.

Author(s)	Year	Dependent variable(s)	Key findings
Luthans, Youssef, and Rawski	2011	Problem-solving, innovation, PsyCap development	• Both PsyCap and reinforcing feedback, especially when partially mediated through a mastery-oriented mindset, were positively related to problem-solving performance, reported innovation, and subsequent psychological capital.
Luthans, Youssef, Sweetman, and Harms	2013	Health & relationship outcomes, satisfaction, well-being	• PsyCap is an antecedent to satisfaction appraisals in all three domains (health, relationships, overall well-being).
Norman, Avey, Nimnicht, and Pigeon	2010	Deviance, OCB, identification	• Organizational identity was found to moderate the relationship between PsyCap and both employee deviance and organizational citizenship behaviors such that employees highest in PsyCap and most strongly identified with the organization were most likely to engage in organizational citizenship behaviors and least likely to engage in deviance behaviors.
Nguyen and Nguyen	2012	Quality of work life, job performance, quality of life	• PsyCap has positive impacts on both job performance and QWL of Vietnamese marketers. • In addition, quality of work life underlies both job performance and quality of life of Vietnamese marketers.
Paterson, Luthans, and Jeung	2014	Agentic work behaviors, self-development, thriving	• Supervisor support and PsyCap positively affect self-development and agentic work behaviors.
Peterson, Luthans, Avolio, Walumbwa, and Zhang	2011	PsyCap development over time, supervisor-rated performance	• Change in PsyCap is related to change in performance outcomes (latent growth modeling). • High PsyCap in t=1 leads to higher performance in t=2 (cross-lagged panel analysis).
Rego, Sousa, Marques, and Pina e Cunha	2012	Employee creativity	• PsyCap partly mediates the relationship between authentic leadership and follower's creativity

(Continued)

TABLE 11.1 (*Continued*)

Author(s)	Year	Dependent variable(s)	Key findings
Story, Youssef, Luthans, Barbuto, and Bovaird	2013	Follower PsyCap	• Contagion of leader PsyCap to follower PsyCap at a distance existed, but the quality of the relationship did mediate this effect. • The potential undesirable effects of distance seemed to be buffered by the global leaders' PsyCap.
Sun, Zhao, Yang, and Fan	2012	Job embeddedness self-reported performance	• Strong relationship between the self-reported psychological capital, job embeddedness and performance of Chinese nurses. • Findings suggest that improving the individual-accumulated psychological state of nurses will have a positive impact on their retention intention and job performance.
Sweetman, Luthans, Avey, and Luthans	2011	Creative performance	• PsyCap predicts creative performance over and above each of its four dimensions

Impact of PsyCap on Work-Related Outcomes

Employee performance, arguably the most crucial outcome in human resource management, has been clearly demonstrated to be significantly related to PsyCap. For example, in a meta-analysis of 51 studies that met the inclusion criteria, Avey and colleagues (2011) found that PsyCap is positively related ($r = 0.26$) to multiple measures of performance (self-rated, supervisor-rated, and objective performance, with no significant difference among these three).

PsyCap is also significantly, but negatively, related to turnover intentions (Avey et al., 2011; Gu, 2016). Employee turnover incurs substantial costs to organizations, both in terms of direct expenditures and indirect costs (e.g. lowered morale, outflow of knowledge). Based on the classic theory of planned behavior (Ajzen, 1991), individuals' behavioral intentions to quit their jobs are a strong and valid predictor of actual turnover. For turnover intentions, not only situational or organizational factors come into play, but also personal dispositions (Zimmerman, 2008). Thus, it can be argued that PsyCap fosters employees' focus on positivity and active coping with adversity which lowers, in turn, negative affect, increases a sense of competency and control, and therefore reduces turnover intentions. This outcome reflects the positive nature of PsyCap; if employees exhibit positive attitudes such as optimistic outlooks, and act hopeful, the likelihood of leaving their job decreases (Luthans & Jensen, 2005; Avey, Hughes, Norman, & Luthans, 2008; Avey, Wernsing, & Luthans, 2008; Avey, Luthans, & Jensen, 2009).

Besides the direct effects on performance and retention, PsyCap has also been shown to positively affect organizational citizenship behavior (OCB). Organ (1988, p. 4) defines OCB as "individual behavior that is discretionary, not directly or explicitly recognized by the formal reward system, that in the aggregate promotes the effective functioning of the organization." OCB is based on three major dimensions: (1) OCBs are conceptualized as distinct, discretionary behaviors which are not part of the job in and of itself, but are performed as a result of employees' personal choice; (2) OCBs cover only behaviors that are non-enforceable by the employer; and (3) OCBs refer to behaviors which are ultimately beneficial to the organization in its functioning and effectiveness. In their meta-analysis, Avey et al. (2011) found that OCBs and PsyCap are strongly linked ($r = 0.46$) across multiple studies and contexts. In addition to OCB, PsyCap has also been reported to be positively associated with problem-solving behavior and employee creativity (Avey, Hughes et al., 2008; Rego, Sousa, Marques, & Pina e Cunha, 2012; Sweetman, Luthans, Avey, & Luthans, 2011; Luthans, Youssef, & Rawski, 2011).

In line with the positive relationship between PsyCap and desired employee behaviors, there is also evidence of significant negative direct effects of PsyCap on counterproductive work behavior (CWB) (e.g. Avey, Hughes et al., 2008; Norman, Avey, Nimnicht, & Pigeon, 2010). CWB is defined as intentional employee behavior that is harmful to the legitimate interests of an organization (Gruys & Sackett, 2003; Martinko, Gundlach, & Douglas, 2002; Avey, Nimnicht, & Pigeon, 2010). In their meta-analysis, Avey et al. (2011) investigated the relationship between PsyCap and CWB, as well as closely related constructs such as deviance, and found a strong and significant negative effect ($r = -0.43$).

PsyCap also has been shown to be a powerful predictor for desired employee attitudes such as job satisfaction and commitment across multiple empirical studies (e.g. Luthans, Avolio et al., 2007; Larson & Luthans, 2006). Luthans, Avolio et al (2007) suggest that the hope dimension is the most crucial factor for this positive effect on satisfaction because employees exhibiting high levels of hope should be enabled by their jobs to have both the motivation and also the plan (i.e. to pursue proactive alternative pathways) to make the best of their situation. In addition, this effect on satisfaction should be reinforced if individuals exhibit high levels of optimism simultaneously in doing their job, and high levels of resilience to cope more quickly and effectively with setbacks. In their meta-analysis, Avey et al. (2011) did find a strong effect of PsyCap on both job satisfaction ($r = 0.45$) and commitment ($r = 0.40$).

PsyCap has also been studied in the context of thriving, although not as a direct antecedent. Thriving, mostly associated with POS, is defined as a two-dimensional construct consisting of learning and vitality (Spreitzer, Sutcliffe,

Dutton, Sonenshein, & Grant, 2005). Learning, in this thriving context, is characterized by the acquisition and application of new knowledge and skills (Elliott & Dweck, 1988), and vitality is characterized by positive feelings, having energy and zest. Paterson, Luthans, and Jeung (2014) tested the effect of PsyCap as an antecedent of thriving, mediated by task focus and heedful relating (agentic work behaviors). PsyCap significantly affected task focus and heedful relating, which in turn had positive effects on thriving.

Finally, Story, Youssef, Luthans, Barbuto, and Bovaird (2013) analyzed the contagion effect of leader PsyCap on followers' PsyCap, drawing on leader–member exchange (LMX) theory. The study investigated the impact of distance and quality of the relationship leaders' level of positive PsyCap contagion effect on their followers. The results indicated that contagion at a distance existed, but the quality of the relationship did mediate this effect. That is, PsyCap of leaders can become contagious to their followers, even at a distance, and this happens more often if the relationship between leader and followers is good, than if it is bad.

Impact of PsyCap on Well-Being Outcomes

Under the umbrella of POB, PsyCap has so far been mainly concerned and associated with bringing positive psychology to the workplace. However, recently PsyCap has extended beyond just its direct effects on the workplace and is giving increasing attention to its impact on well-being. Although not as direct to the workplace as PsyCap outcomes such as employee attitudes, behaviors, and performance, employee well-being is being increasingly recognized as having at least indirect importance in today's organizations. As Choi and Lee (2014, p. 126) note, "people spend a significant portion of their daily lives contributing to their organizations, (hence), workplaces have become an important source of peoples' happiness."

As shown in Table 11.1, several studies have analyzed the effects of PsyCap on employee well-being (e.g. Avey, Luthans, Smith, & Palmer, 2010; Choi & Lee, 2014; Rabenu, Yaniv, & Elizur, 2016; Roche, Harr, & Luthans, 2014). Widely recognized positive psychologist Ed Diener (2000, p. 1) defines subjective well-being as "people's cognitive and affective evaluations of their lives." Thus, people's PsyCap may contribute to an overall sense of well-being by helping them interpret their work and life experiences more positively, attain success, and overcome frustration and setbacks more easily. Studies have demonstrated such a relationship, and the PsyCap meta-analysis found $r = 0.40$ between PsyCap and commitment, and PsyCap and psychological well-being (Avey et al., 2011).

In line with the findings on well-being, Krasikova, Lester, and Harms (2015) recently found a positive effect of PsyCap on mental health. On a large military sample, they measured the pre-deployment PsyCap levels of soldiers' impact on their post-deployment mental illness and substance abuse. They found that the higher the pre-deployment PsyCap of the soldiers, the significantly lower the post-deployment rates of diagnosed mental illness and substance abuse, which of course has implications for PTSD. In other words, the soldiers' PsyCap may have helped serve as a preventative buffer to dysfunctional outcomes of the trauma and stress of their deployment experience. There is also preliminary evidence that PsyCap may help combat the growing mental depression epidemic of organizational leaders (Roche et al., 2014) and employees (Kan & Yu, 2016) in today's global workplace.

Luthans, Youssef, Sweetman, and Harms (2013) specifically extended the scope of work-related PsyCap into "Health PsyCap" and "Relationship PsyCap." Research in positive psychology has clearly shown that it positively affects both health and relationships (e.g. Layous, Sheldon, & Lyubomirsky, 2014). Luthans and colleagues (2013, p. 3) define Health PsyCap as "drawing from one's psychological resources of hope, efficacy, resiliency, and optimism in making positive appraisals of health-related success based on motivated effort and perseverance." Their research found Health PsyCap was positively related to satisfaction with one's health and negatively related to objective measures of both body-mass index (BMI, height and weight, the lower the better) and cholesterol levels. In addition, Harms et al. (2017) recently found their implicit Health PsyCap measure (IPCQ-H) related to both general health and mental health.

Luthans et al. (2013) conceptualized Relationship PsyCap as drawing from one's psychological resources of hope, efficacy, resiliency, and optimism in making positive appraisals of relationships and probability for relationship success based on motivated effort and perseverance. Similar to health, they found a positive effect of Relationship PsyCap with relationship satisfaction, and with an objective measure of time spent with family and friends. Importantly, both Health PsyCap and Relationship PsyCap contributed significantly to a time-lagged measure of overall well-being. This extension of PsyCap into the well-being domain seems to be another, more indirect, path of bringing positive psychology into the workplace.

Under- and Un-Explored Future Research Needed on PsyCap

As indicated above and shown in Table 11.1, as a vehicle of taking positive psychology to the workplace, PsyCap has been given and has received considerable attention (see Luthans & Youssef-Morgan, 2017; Luthans, Youssef-Morgan et al., 2015; Warren, Donaldson, & Luthans, 2017). Besides the numerous applications of PsyCap in the workplace covered in this chapter, there are also many other practical applications of positivity such as the US Army and Airforce investments in developing resilience (Cornum, Matthews, & Seligman, 2011). Empirical studies are beginning to show that these initiatives in building positivity and promoting well-being help buffer negativity and stress in challenging situations and mission critical roles (Krasikova et al., 2015). Although the body of research to date has provided a solid basis of knowledge on PsyCap, the time has now come for further theory-building and research to refine and better understand the underlying mechanisms, and explore further synergies with other academic theories/perspectives and practice domains.

An example of further refinements would be to examine PsyCap as a mediator and/or moderator. Such research has been initiated around the world. In China, for example, such research is starting to take off. Wang and colleagues (2014) found that the PsyCap of employees mediates the relationship between authentic Chinese business leaders and performance; as a moderator, Cheung, Tang, and Tang (2011) found that PsyCap attenuates the effect of emotional labor and burnout among Chinese school teachers; and Teo, Roche, Pick, and Newton (2014) found that PsyCap attenuates the effects of organizational change on the stress of Chinese nurses. Similar studies are also being reported in other countries (e.g. PsyCap was found to mediate the relationship between the organizational climate and organizational citizenship behaviors of Jordanian bank employees, Suifan (2016), and the relationship between authentic leadership and commitment of Portuguese employees, Rego et al., 2012).

Future research refining PsyCap might also explore it as a moderating/mediating variable in relation to other organizational behavior theoretical perspectives such as the Job Demands-Resources (JD-R) model (Bakker & Demerouti, 2007). For example, we suggest that PsyCap, as a psychological resource, may play a substantial role in coping with emotional labor, stress, and other such "job demands" by attenuating (moderating) stressful emotions. The JD-R model relies on the assumption that every job or profession has its own specific risk factors associated with stress, and that these factors can be classified in two general categories—job demands and job resources. Job demands refer to those aspects of a job or profession, which are associated with certain physiological or psychological costs. Examples include making important decisions under time pressure, dealing with emotionally demanding and draining client interactions, or coping with an unfavorable work environment. Job resources, on the other hand, refer to physical, social, psychological, or organizational aspects of a job or profession, which help attain work goals, reduce job demands and the associated costs, or stimulate learning and personal growth (Bakker & Demerouti, 2007).

When employees face high job demands, a "strain process" is initiated. This strain leads employees to seek performance protection strategies. These strategies can be executed by mobilizing sympathetic activation, and/or increased subjective effort, to actively control information processing regarding the situational strain. That is, the greater the activation and/or effort, the greater the indirect costs for the individual (Bakker & Demerouti, 2007). Job resources, in contrast, can initiate a "motivation process," assuming that job resources have motivational potential and lead to work engagement, low cynicism, and high performance. They can initiate an intrinsic motivational process for personal learning and growth, or an extrinsic motivational process to achieve work goals to fulfill needs for autonomy, competency, and relatedness.

Carrying this representative example further, we suggest that PsyCap might moderate the relationship between personality traits and job demands. Thus, individuals high in neuroticism might be more prone to stress, have more difficulties in coping with stress, and tend to exhibit more anxiety. However, with PsyCap as a positive psychological resource, it would be hypothesized that a high level of PsyCap attenuates the effect of neuroticism on stress, anxiety, and emotional labor.

Besides neuroticism, another potential application for PsyCap for future research might lie in moderating potential detrimental traits. Personality traits, such as the "dark triad" (narcissism, Machiavellianism, and psychopathy; Paulhus & Williams, 2002), have been shown to cause a multitude of deviant behaviors in the workplace (O'Boyle, Forsyth, Banks, & McDaniel, 2012). First, it might be interesting if individuals with dark personality traits can exhibit higher levels of PsyCap at all. Second, PsyCap might attenuate the detrimental outcomes of dark traits such as CWB, absenteeism, and cynicism.

In highly stressful or interactive jobs such as those in the frontline of the service industry or the so-called "dull, dirty, dangerous jobs" (e.g. roofer, window washer, animal slaughterer), employees could profit a great deal from building up PsyCap as a resource to counter-balance job demands and stress. The service profit chain (Heskett, Sasser, & Schlesinger, 1997) establishes relationships between employee satisfaction, loyalty, and productivity on the one side, and customer satisfaction, loyalty, and profitability on the other side. Thus, employee attitudes and behaviors are supposed to be "mirrored" by customers. The considerable empirical research on this service profit chain underlines the relevance of employee attitudes, states, and resources in services. It is therefore rather surprising that with some important exceptions in the restaurant industry (e.g. Gu, 2016; Mathe-Soulek, Scott-Halsell, Kim, & Krawczyk, 2014), little research to date has examined the relevance of PsyCap for service employees (e.g. Karatepe & Karadas, 2015).

Even though PsyCap has recently been introduced into the marketing field (Friend, Johnson, Luthans, & Sohi, 2016), future research might profitably examine the impact of PsyCap on customer satisfaction. As indicated, research had shown contagion effects between leader PsyCap and follower PsyCap, but it might also be interesting to study to what extent PsyCap can be transferred between clients and employees given a close collaboration over a longer period of time. Moreover, future study of client–employee dyads that are either similarly high or low on PsyCap, and dyads that have very different PsyCap levels in the dyad formation phase may yield interesting results. For example, do the individuals converge, and which dyads report higher relationship satisfaction, advance more quickly in their projects, or have better outcomes faster? In addition, PsyCap could be examined as a moderator/mediator between customer service and emotional labor, coping, and customer-induced stress.

PsyCap, as an individual psychological resource, also needs to be studied more in a multi-level context. Again, although studies have analyzed the contagion of PsyCap from leaders to followers (Story et al., 2013; Wang et al., 2014) and there has been some initial PsyCap research at the team level (e.g. see Dawkins, Martin, & O'Donoghue, 2016), substantial empirical evidence as to what extent PsyCap translates into variables on the organizational level is still generally lacking. Multi-level studies are often difficult to achieve in a field-setting, and especially in the work context, but organizational and individual-level positive constructs need to be operationalized and measured in ways that can help establish and quantify various potential interactions. Research that tests PsyCap at higher levels of analysis is just starting to emerge (e.g. Mathe-Soulek et al., 2014; McKenny, Short, & Payne, 2013; Memili, Welsch, & Luthans, 2013), but still needs more empirical validation.

Another avenue for future research is establishing the discriminant validity of PsyCap with newly emerging variables associated with positivity, such as flourishing (e.g. Diener et al., 2010), thriving (e.g. Benson & Scale, 2009), hardiness (Maddi & Khoshaba, 2001) and mental toughness (Nicholls, Polman, Levy, & Backhouse, 2008). While some initial research on PsyCap and these other positive psychological resources has recently emerged (e.g. for thriving see Paterson et al., 2014), more research is still needed. For example, flourishing is conceptualized and measured according to Diener et al. (2010) as the individual's perceived success in terms of relationships, self-esteem, purpose, and optimism. However, to date, no studies we are aware of have been reported on relating PsyCap and flourishing, although they might complement each other to some extent and potentially overlap with optimism and hope.

Similarly, little is known about PsyCap's relationship with mental toughness (e.g. measured by the Psychological Performance Inventory according to Loehr, 1986). Mental toughness is considered a higher-order construct of (1) self-confidence; (2) negative energy control; (3) attention control; (4) visualization and imagery control; (5) motivation; (6) positive energy; and (7) attitude control. Equally little is known about PsyCap's relationship with hardiness as measured by the Personal View's Survey III-R. Maddi and Khoshaba (2001, p. 160) define hardiness as a "combination of attitudes that provide the courage and motivation to do the hard and strategic work of turning stressful circumstances from potential disasters into growth opportunities." They conceptualize hardiness as a second-order construct with the three sub-constructs of commitment, control, and challenge. While the control and challenge dimensions might have some aspects in common with PsyCap, specifically resilience and hope, it might be interesting to explore to what extent the commitment dimension of hardiness supplements PsyCap when it comes to success. To date, there are preliminary findings of a significant relationship between PsyCap and at least dispositional hardiness (Van Dyk, 2015).

Finally, little is still known about PsyCap's development over time. While longitudinal research has shown within person change of PsyCap over time (Peterson et al., 2011) and Avey (2014) found a low correlation between PsyCap and age ($r = 0.13$), more longitudinal research is needed on PsyCap's development. Although Avey (2014) finds a linear relationship in his adult sample, PsyCap might actually develop a curvilinear relationship over time. Children might have an unrealistically high level of PsyCap because of their unleashed phantasy, but it may decrease through teenage and college years, when tough challenges, a more realistic sense of daily life, and potential failures are faced. After overcoming the stressful process of entering the workforce, PsyCap might build up in a linear manner again with experience and mastery. Although research on the development of PsyCap at the individual level is off to a good start (Ertosun et al., 2015; Luthans, Avey, & Patera, 2008; Luthans et al., 2010), not much is known yet about collective PsyCap (cPsyCap) training and development at the team, organizational and community/country levels (see Broad & Luthans, in press).

In conclusion, positive psychology's inclusion and acceptance in both the academic (Donaldson, Dollwet, & Rao, 2015; Warren & Donaldson, 2017) and clinical (Gander, Proyer, Ruch, & Wyss, 2013) sides of the field of psychology are now widely acknowledged. As indicated in this chapter, through both POS and, what was focused on in this review on POB and specifically psychological capital (PsyCap) consisting of the positive psychological resources of hope, efficacy, resilience, and optimism, there is now also general acceptance and considerable supporting research on the value of positive psychology in the workplace (see Luthans & Youssef-Morgan, 2017). We first summarized the derivation, meaning, and measurement of PsyCap, and then reviewed the research on its antecedents and development. However, most attention over the years and in this review was devoted to the considerable research findings on the relationship between PsyCap and many desirable work-related outcomes and the more recent extension into well-being. Finally, we closed by identifying some of the under-explored and un-explored needed future PsyCap research.

References

Ajzen, I. (1991). The theory of planned behavior. *Organizational Behavior and Human Decision Processes, 50*(2), 179–211.

Avey, J. B. (2014). The left side of psychological capital: New evidence on the antecedents of PsyCap. *Journal of Leadership & Organizational Studies, 21*(2), 141–149.

Avey, J. B., Avolio, B. J., & Luthans, F. (2011). Experimentally analyzing the impact of leader positivity on follower positivity and performance. *Leadership Quarterly, 22*, 282–294.

Avey, J. B., Hughes, L. W., Norman, S. M., & Luthans, K. W. (2008). Using positivity, transformational leadership and empowerment to combat employee negativity. *Leadership & Organization Development Journal, 29*(2), 110–126.

Avey, J. B., Luthans, F., & Jensen, S. M. (2009). Psychological capital: A positive resource for combating employee stress and turnover. *Human Resource Management, 48*(5), 677–693.

Avey, J. B., Luthans, F., Smith, R. M., & Palmer, N. F. (2010). Impact of positive psychological capital on employee well-being over time. *Journal of Occupational Health Psychology, 15*(1), 17–28.

Avey, J. B., Luthans, F., & Youssef, C. M. (2010). The additive value of positive psychological capital in predicting work attitudes and behaviors. *Journal of Management, 36*(2), 430–452.

Avey, J. B., Nimnicht, J. L., & Pigeon, N. (2010). Two field studies examining the association between positive psychological capital and employee performance. *Leadership & Organization Development Journal, 31*(5), 384–401.

Avey, J. B., Patera, J. L., & West, B. J. (2006). The implications of positive psychological capital on employee absenteeism. *Journal of Leadership & Organizational Studies, 13*(2), 42–60.

Avey, J. B., Reichard, R. J., Luthans, F., & Mhatre, K. H. (2011). Meta-analysis of the impact of positive psychological capital on employee attitudes, behaviors, and performance. *Human Resource Development Quarterly, 22*(2), 127–152.

Avey, J. B., Wernsing, T. S., & Luthans, F. (2008). Can positive employees help positive organizational change? Impact of psychological capital and emotions on relevant attitudes and behaviors. *The Journal of Applied Behavioral Science, 44*(1), 48–70.

Bakker, A. B., & Demerouti, E. (2007). The job demands-resources model: State of the art. *Journal of Managerial Psychology, 22*(3), 309–328.

Bandura, A. (1997). *Self-efficacy: The exercise of control.* New York: W. H. Freeman.

Bandura, A. (2008). An agentic perspective on positive psychology. In S. Lopez (Ed.), *Positive psychology,* (Vol. 1, pp. 167–196). Westport, CT: Greenwood Publishing Co.

Baumeister, R. F., Bratslavsky, E., Finkenauer, C., & Vohs, K. D. (2001). Bad is stronger than good. *Review of General Psychology, 5*(4), 323.

Bellak, L., & Abrams, D. M. (1997). *The thematic apperception test, the children's apperception test, and the senior apperception technique in clinical use.* Boston, MA: Allyn & Bacon.

Benson, P. L., & Scales, P. C. (2009). The definition and preliminary measurement of thriving in adolescence. *The Journal of Positive Psychology, 4*(1), 85–104.

Broad, J. D., & Luthans, F. (in press). Leading and developing health and safety through collective psychological capital. In K. Kelloway, K. Nielsen, & J. Dimoff (Eds.), *Leading to occupational health and safety.* New York: Wiley.

Cameron, K. S. (2008). Paradox in positive organizational change. *The Journal of Applied Behavioral Science, 44*(1), 7–24.

Cameron, K., Dutton, J., & Quinn, R. (Eds.). (2003). *Positive organizational scholarship: Foundations of a new discipline.* San Francisco, CA: Berrett-Koehler Publishers.

Cameron, K., Dutton, J., Quinn, R., & Wrzesniewski, A. (2003). Developing a discipline of positive organizational scholarship. In K. Cameron, J. Dutton, & R. Quinn (Eds), *Positive organizational scholarship: Foundations of a new discipline* (pp. 361–370). San Francisco, CA: Berrett-Koehler Publishers.

Cameron, K. S., & Spreitzer, G. M. (2012). Introduction: What is positive about positive organizational scholarship? In K. C. Cameron & G. Spreitzer (Eds.), *The Oxford handbook of positive organizational scholarship* (pp. 1–14). New York: Oxford University Press.

Carver, C. S., Scheier, M. F., Miller, C. J., & Fulford, D. (2009). *Oxford handbook of positive psychology* (pp. 303–312). New York: Oxford University Press.

Cheung, F., Tang, C. S. K., & Tang, S. (2011). Psychological capital as a moderator between emotional labor, burnout, and job satisfaction among school teachers in China. *International Journal of Stress Management, 18*(4), 348–373.

Choi, Y., & Lee, D. (2014). Psychological capital, big five traits, and employee outcomes. *Journal of Managerial Psychology, 29*(2), 122–140.

Cornum, R., Matthews, M. D., & Seligman, M. E. (2011). Comprehensive soldier fitness: Building resilience in a challenging institutional context. *American Psychologist, 66*(1), 4–9.

Dawkins, S., Martin, A., & O'Donoghue, W. (2016). *Evaluating the impact of a team-level psychological capital intervention.* Paper presented at Human Resources International Conference (HRIC), Sydney, Australia.

Dawkins, S., Martin, A., Scott, J., & Sanderson, K. (2013). Building on the positives: A psychometric review and critical analysis of the construct of psychological capital. *Journal of Occupational and Organizational Psychology, 86*(3), 348–370.

Diener, E. (2000). Subjective well-being: The science of happiness and a proposal for a national index. *American Psychologist, 55*(1), 34–43.

Diener, E., Wirtz, D., Tov, W., Kim-Prieto, C., Choi, D. W., Oishi, S., & Biswas-Diener, R. (2010). New well-being measures: Short scales to assess flourishing and positive and negative feelings. *Social Indicators Research, 97*(2), 143–156.

Donaldson, S. I., Dollwet, M., & Rao, M. A. (2015). Happiness, excellence, and optimal human functioning revisited: Examing the peer-reviewed literature linked to positive psychology. *The Journal of Positive Psychology, 10*(3), 185–195.

Elliott, E. S., & Dweck, C. S. (1988). Goals: An approach to motivation and achievement. *Journal of Personality and Social Psychology, 54*(1), 5–12.

Ertosun, O. G., Erdil, O., Deniz, N., & Alpkan, L. (2015). Positive psychological capital development: A field study by the Solomon four group design. *International Business Research, 8*(10), 102–111.

Exner, J., Exner, J., Levy, A., Exner, J., Groth-Marnat, G., Wood, J. M., … Garb, H. N. (2008). *The Rorschach: A comprehensive system. Volume 1: The Rorschach, basic foundations and principles of interpretation.* New York: Wiley.

Fredrickson, B. L. (2003). Positive emotions and upward spirals in organizations. In K. Cameron, J. Dutton, & R. Quinn (Eds.), *Positive organizational scholarship* (pp. 163–175). San Francisco, CA: Berrett-Koehler.

Fredrickson, B. L. (2009). *Positivity.* New York: Crown Publishers.

Friend, S. B., Johnson, J. S., Luthans, F., & Sohi, R. S. (2016). Positive psychology in sales: Integrating psychological capital. *Journal of Marketing Theory and Practice, 24*(3), 306–327.

Gander, F., Proyer, R. T., Ruch, W., & Wyss, T. (2013). Strength-based positive intervention: Further evidence for their potential in enhancing well-being and alleviating depression. *Happiness Studies, 14*, 1241–1259.

Gottman, J. M. (1994). *What predicts divorce?* Hillsdale, N.J.: Erlbaum.

Gruys, M. L., & Sackett, P. R. (2003). Investigating the dimensionality of counterproductive work behavior. *International Journal of Selection and Assessment, 11*(1), 30–42.

Gu, B. (2016). Effects of psychological capital on employee turnover intentions. *Journal of Global Tourism Research*, *1*(1), 21–28.

Harms, P. D., & Luthans, F. (2012). Measuring implicit psychological constructs in organizational behavior: An example using psychological capital. *Journal of Organizational Behavior*, *33*(4), 589–594.

Harms, P. D., Vanhove, A., & Luthans, F. (2017). Positive projections and health: An initial validation of the implicit psychological capital health measure. *Applied Psychology: An International Review*, *66*(1), 78–108.

Heskett, J. L., Sasser, W. E., & Schlesinger, L. A. (1997). *The service profit chain: How leading companies link profit and growth to loyalty, satisfaction, and value*. New York: Free Press.

Kan, D., & Yu, X. (2016). Occupational stress, work-family conflict and depressive symptoms among Chinese bank employees: The role of psychological capital. *International Journal of Environmental Research and Public Health*, *13*, 1–11.

Karatepe, O. M., & Karadas, G. (2015). Do psychological capital and work engagement foster frontline employees' satisfaction? A study in the hotel industry. *International Journal of Contemporary Hospitality Management*, *27*(6), 1254–1278.

Krasikova, D. V., Harms, P. D., & Luthans, F. (2012). *Telling stories: Validating an implicit measure of psychological capital*. Paper presented at 27th Meeting of Society for Industrial and Organizational Psychology, San Diego, CA.

Krasikova, D. V., Lester, P. B., & Harms, P. D. (2015). Effects of psychological capital on mental health and substance abuse. *Journal of Leadership and Organizational Studies*, *22*(3), 280–291.

Larson, M., & Luthans, F. (2006). Potential added value of psychological capital in predicting work attitudes. *Journal of Leadership and Organizational Studies*, *13*(2), 75–92.

Layous, K., Sheldon, K. M., & Lyubomirsky, S. (2014). The prospects, practices, and prescriptions for the pursuit of happiness. In E. Nafstad & S. Joseph (Eds), *Positive psychology in practice: Promoting human flourishing in work, health, education, and everyday life* (pp. 183–206). New York: Wiley.

Liu, Y. (2013). Mediating effect of positive psychological capital in Taiwan's life insurance industry. *Social Behavior and Personality: An International Journal*, *41*(1), 109–111.

Loehr, J. E. (1986). *Mental toughness training for sports: Achieving athletic excellence*. London: Penguin Books.

Luthans, F. (2002a). The need for and meaning of positive organizational behavior. *Journal of Organizational Behavior*, *23*(6), 695–706.

Luthans, F. (2002b). Positive organizational behavior: Developing and managing psychological strengths. *Academy of Management Executive*, *16*, 57–72.

Luthans, F. (2012). Psychological capital: Implications for HRD, retrospective analysis, and future directions. *Human Resource Development Quarterly*, *23*(1), 1–8.

Luthans, F., Avey, J. B., Avolio, B. J., Norman, S. M., & Combs, G. M. (2006). Psychological capital development: Toward a micro intervention. *Journal of Organizational Behavior*, *27*(3), 387–393.

Luthans, F., Avey, J. B., Avolio, B. J., & Peterson, S. J. (2010). The development and resulting performance impact of positive psychological capital. *Human Resource Development Quarterly*, *21*(1), 41–67.

Luthans, F., Avey, J. B., Clapp-Smith, R., & Li, W. (2008). More evidence on the value of Chinese workers' psychological capital: A potentially unlimited competitive resource? *The International Journal of Human Resource Management*, *19*(5), 818–827.

Luthans, F., Avey, J. B., & Patera, J. L. (2008). Experimental analysis of a web-based training intervention to develop positive psychological capital. *Academy of Management Learning & Education, 7*(2), 209–221.

Luthans, F., & Avolio, B. J. (2009a). Inquiry unplugged: Building on Hackman's potential perils of POB. *Journal of Organizational Behavior, 30*(2), 323–328.

Luthans, F., & Avolio, B. J. (2009b). The "point" of positive organizational behavior. *Journal of Organizational Behavior, 30*(2), 291–307.

Luthans, F., Avolio, B. J., Avey, J. B., & Norman, S. M. (2007). Positive psychological capital: Measurement and relationship with performance and satisfaction. *Personnel Psychology, 60*(3), 541–572.

Luthans, K. W., & Jensen, S. M. (2005). The linkage between psychological capital and commitment to organizational mission: A study of nurses. *Journal of Nursing Administration, 35*(6), 304–310.

Luthans, F., Luthans, K. W., & Luthans, B. C. (2004). Positive psychological capital: Beyond human and social capital. *Business Horizons, 47*, 45–50.

Luthans, F., Norman, S. M., Avolio, B. J., & Avey, J. B. (2008). The mediating role of psychological capital in the supportive organizational climate—employee performance relationship. *Journal of Organizational Behavior, 29*(2), 219–238.

Luthans, F., & Youssef, C. M. (2004). Human, social, and now positive psychological capital management: Investing in people for competitive advantage. *Organizational Dynamics, 33*(2), 143–160.

Luthans, F., Youssef, C. M., & Avolio, B. J. (2007). *Psychological capital: Developing the human competitive edge.* Oxford, UK: Oxford University Press.

Luthans, F., Youssef, C. M., & Rawski, S. L. (2011). A tale of two paradigms: The impact of psychological capital and reinforcing feedback on problem solving and innovation. *Journal of Organizational Behavior Management, 31*(4), 333–350.

Luthans, F., Youssef, C. M., Sweetman, D. S., & Harms, P. D. (2013). Meeting the leadership challenge of employee well-being through relationship PsyCap and Health PsyCap. *Journal of Leadership & Organizational Studies, 20*(1), 118–133.

Luthans, F., & Youssef-Morgan, C. M. (2017). Psychological capital: An evidence-based positive approach. In F. Morgason (Ed.), *Annual review of organizational psychology and organizational behavior*, New York: Wiley.

Luthans, F., Youssef-Morgan, C. M., & Avolio, B. J. (2015). *Psychological capital and beyond.* New York: Oxford University Press.

Maddi, S. R., & Khoshaba, D. M. (2001). *Personal views survey III-R: Internet instruction manual.* Newport Beach, CA: Hardiness Institute.

Martinko, M. J., Gundlach, M. J., & Douglas, S. C. (2002). Toward an integrative theory of counterproductive workplace behavior: A causal reasoning perspective. *International Journal of Selection and Assessment, 10*(1–2), 36–50.

Masten, A. S., Cutuli, J. J., Herbers, J. E., & Reed, M. G. (2009). Resilience in development. In S. J. Lopez & C. R. Snyder (Eds.), *The Oxford handbook of positive psychology* (2nd ed., pp. 117–131). New York: Oxford University Press.

Mathe-Soulek, K., Scott-Halsell, S., Kim, S., & Krawczyk, M. (2014). Psychological capital in the quick service restaurant industry: A study of unit-level performance. *Journal of Hospitality & Tourism Research*, DOI: 10.1177/1096348014550923.

McKenny, A. F., Short, J. C., & Payne, G. T. (2013). Using computer-aided text analysis to elevate constructs: An illustration using psychological capital. *Organizational Research Methods, 16*(1), 152–184.

Memili, E., Welsh, D. H., & Luthans, F. (2013). Going beyond research on goal setting: A proposed role for organizational psychological capital of family firms. *Entrepreneurship Theory and Practice, 37*(6), 1289–1296.

Newman, A., Ucbasaran, D., Zhu, F., & Hirst, G. (2014). Psychological capital: A review and synthesis. *Journal of Organizational Behavior, 35*, S120-S138.

Nguyen, T. D., & Nguyen, T. T. (2012). Psychological capital, quality of work life, and quality of life of marketers: Evidence from Vietnam. *Journal of Macromarketing, 32*(1), 87–95.

Nicholls, A. R., Polman, R. C., Levy, A. R., & Backhouse, S. H. (2008). Mental toughness, optimism, pessimism, and coping among athletes. *Personality and Individual Differences, 44*(5), 1182–1192.

Nigah, N., Davis, A. J., & Hurrell, S. A. (2012). The impact of buddying on psychological capital and work engagement: An empirical study of socialization in the professional services sector. *Thunderbird International Business Review, 54*(6), 891–905.

Norman, S. M., Avey, J. B., Nimnicht, J. L., & Pigeon, N. G. (2010). The interactive effects of psychological capital and organizational identity on employee citizenship and deviance behaviors. *Journal of Leadership & Organizational Studies, 17*(4), 380–391.

O'Boyle, E. H., Forsyth, D. R., Banks, G. C., & McDaniel, M. A. (2012). A meta-analysis of the dark triad and work behavior: A social exchange perspective. *Journal of Applied Psychology, 97*(3), 557–579.

Organ, D. W. (1988). *Organizational citizenship behavior: The good soldier syndrome.* Lanham, MD: Lexington Books.

Parker, S. K. (1998). Enhancing role breadth self-efficacy: The roles of job enrichment and other organizational interventions. *Journal of Applied Psychology, 83*(6), 835–852.

Paterson, T. A., Luthans, F., & Jeung, W. (2014). Thriving at work: Impact of psychological capital and supervisor support. *Journal of Organizational Behavior, 35*(3), 434–446.

Paulhus, D. L., & Williams, K. M. (2002). The dark triad of personality: Narcissism, Machiavellianism, and psychopathy. *Journal of Research in Personality, 36*(6), 556–563.

Peterson, S. J., Luthans, F., Avolio, B. J., Walumbwa, F. O., & Zhang, Z. (2011). Psychological capital and employee performance: A latent growth modeling approach. *Personnel Psychology, 64*(2), 427–450.

Rabenu, E., Yaniv, E., & Elizur, D. (2016). The relationship between psychological capital, coping with stress, well-being, and performance. *Current Psychology*, DOI: 10.1007/512144-016-9477-4.

Rego, A., Sousa, F., Marques, C., & Pina e Cunha, M. P. (2012). Authentic leadership promoting employees' psychological capital and creativity. *Journal of Business Research, 65*(3), 429–437.

Roche, M. A., Harr, J. M., & Luthans, F. (2014). The role of mindfulness and psychological capital on the well-being of leaders. *Journal of Occupational Health Psychology, 19*, 476–489.

Saks, A. M., & Gruman, J. A. (2011). Organizational socialization and positive organizational behaviour: Implications for theory, research, and practice. *Canadian Journal of Administrative Sciences, 28*(1), 14–26.

Scheier, M. F., & Carver, C. S. (1985). Optimism, coping, and health: Assessment and implications of generalized outcome expectancies. *Health Psychology*, *4*(3), 219–247.

Seligman, M. E. P. (1998). *Learned optimism*. New York: Pocket Books.

Snyder, C. R. (2002). Hope theory: Rainbows in the mind. *Psychological Inquiry*, *13*, 249–275.

Snyder, C. R., Irving, L. M., & Anderson, J. R. (1991). Hope and health. In C. R. Snyder & D. R. Forsyth (Eds.), *Handbook of social and clinical psychology* (pp. 285–305). Elmsford, NY: Pergamon.

Snyder, C. R., Sympson, S. C., Ybasco, F. C., Borders, T. F., Babyak, M. A., & Higgins, R. L. (1996). Development and validation of the state hope scale. *Journal of Personality and Social Psychology*, *70*(2), 321–335.

Spreitzer, G. M., & Cameron, K. C. (2012). Conclusion. A path forward: Assessing progress and exploring core questions for the future of positive organizational scholarship. In K. C. Cameron & G. Spreitzer (Eds.), *The Oxford handbook of positive organizational scholarship* (pp. 1034–1048). New York: Oxford University Press.

Spreitzer, G., Sutcliffe, K., Dutton, J., Sonenshein, S., & Grant, A. M. (2005). A socially embedded model of thriving at work. *Organization Science*, *16*(5), 537–549.

Stajkovic, A. D., & Luthans, F. (1998). Social cognitive theory and self-efficacy: Going beyond traditional motivational and behavioral approaches. *Organizational Dynamics*, *26*(4), 62–74.

Story, J. S., Youssef, C. M., Luthans, F., Barbuto, J. E., & Bovaird, J. (2013). Contagion effect of global leaders' positive psychological capital on followers: Does distance and quality of relationship matter? *The International Journal of Human Resource Management*, *24*(13), 2534–2553.

Suifan, T. (2016). The impact of organizational climate and psychological capital on organizational citizenship behavior. *International Journal of Business and Management*, *11*(1), 224–230.

Sun, T., Zhao, X. W., Yang, L. B., & Fan, L. H. (2012). The impact of psychological capital on job embeddedness and job performance among nurses: A structural equation approach. *Journal of Advanced Nursing*, *68*(1), 69–79.

Sweetman, D., Luthans, F., Avey, J. B., & Luthans, B. C. (2011). Relationship between positive psychological capital and creative performance. *Canadian Journal of Administrative Sciences*, *28*(1), 4–13.

Teo, S., Roche, M., Pick, D., & Newton, C. J. (2014). Psychological capital as moderator of organizational change demands on nursing stress. *Academy of Management Annual Meeting Proceedings*, Philadelphia, PA.

Van Dyk, G. (2015). Hardiness as predictor of work readiness: A preliminary exploratory study. *Journal of Psychology in Africa*, *25*(1), 80–82.

Wagnild, G., & Young, H. (1993). Development and psychometric evaluation of the resiliency scale. *Journal of Nursing Measurement*, *1*(2), 165–178.

Wang, H., Sui, Y., Luthans, F., Wang, D., & Wu, Y. (2014). Impact of authentic leadership on performance: Role of followers' positive psychological capital and relational processes. *Journal of Organizational Behavior*, *35*(1), 5–21.

Warren, M., Donaldson, S., & Luthans, F. (2017). Taking positive psychology to the workplace: Positive organizational psychology, positive organizational behavior and positive organizational scholarship. In M. Warren & S. Donaldson (Eds.), *Scientific advances in positive psychology* (pp. 195–227). Santa Barbara, CA: Praeger.

Wernsing, T. (2014). Psychological capital: A test of measurement invariance across 12 national cultures. *Journal of Leadership & Organizational Studies, 21*(2), 179–190.

Wright, T. A., & Quick, J. C. (2009). The emerging positive agenda in organizations: Greater than a trickle, but not yet a deluge. *Journal of Organizational Behavior, 30*(2), 147–159.

Youssef-Morgan, C. M., & Luthans., F. (2013). Psychological capital theory: Toward a positive holistic model. In A. B. Bakker (Ed.), *Advances in positive organizational psychology* (pp. 145–166). Bingley, UK: Emerald.

Zimmerman, B. J. (2008). Investigating self-regulation and motivation: Historical background, methodological developments, and future prospects. *American Educational Research Journal, 45*(1), 166–183.

12

APPLYING PRINCIPLES OF POSITIVE PSYCHOLOGY TO STUDENT SUCCESS AND WELL-BEING: ENABLING ALL STUDENTS TO THRIVE

Laurie A. Schreiner

Research on college student success over the past five decades has developed extensive frameworks for defining and understanding the complex nature of such success, as well as strategies for creating campus environments to cultivate it. In this chapter, I will explore the contribution of positive psychology to college student success, with a two-pronged focus on fostering success in individual students and creating environments that promote success.

Despite the concerted effort of many campuses to foster student success in the last several decades, graduation rates have changed little in that time, with 41 percent of all students who enter four-year institutions failing to graduate within 6 years (U.S. Department of Education, 2015). Of greater concern, however, is the lack of progress in closing the gap of 10 to 30 percentage points that continues to exist between the graduation rates of Black, Native American, and Latino/a students and their Asian and Caucasian counterparts (U.S. Department of Education, 2015). The income gap is even greater: among academically qualified students, 81 percent of high-income students complete a bachelor's degree, while only 36 percent of equally qualified low-income students do so (Long, 2010).

Much of the literature defines student success as an outcome, such as degree completion, a goal that aligns with the current focus of the US legislative and political environment on graduation rates and gainful employment after college. Yet this goal is not congruent with the historical purposes of higher education, nor with what positive psychologists consider "what makes life worth living" (Seligman & Csikszentmihalyi, 2000, p. 5). Viewing student success as degree completion leads to the inevitable conclusion that admissions selectivity is the most effective student success strategy, a conclusion that ignores the importance of the personal growth, intellectual development, and civic engagement that comprise the college experience (Kinzie, 2012). If a college education is to be a transformational experience that leads to not only a good job, but a good life, then student success is best viewed as an individual longitudinal process (Seifert, 2016) in which students are equipped and empowered to engage an increasingly complex and interconnected world in meaningful and productive ways. Such engagement will require more than intellectual skills and a diploma. A focus on well-being during the college years could equip students for the relational and psychological demands of a diverse and rapidly changing world (Harward, 2016).

An emphasis on well-being requires expanding the goal of higher education beyond academic success and degree completion, but it also requires a re-examination of the definition of student success. Therefore, throughout this chapter I will posit a view of student success as a holistic and malleable process toward optimal functioning. The hallmark of this process is intellectual, psychological, and social engagement that enables students to make the most of their college experiences and extends into a meaningful and productive life.

Thriving in College

Positive psychologists have empirically investigated positive emotion, positive character, and positive institutions (Seligman, Steen, Park, & Peterson, 2005), with an emphasis on the "fulfilled individual and the thriving community" (Seligman & Csikszentmihalyi, 2000, p. 5) and the goal of enabling a greater percentage of the world's population to flourish (Seligman, 2011). This foundational philosophy of studying what makes for a good life provides a framework not only for measuring college student success, but designing interventions and environments that may enable a greater percentage of students to succeed.

At the heart of this philosophical framework is *flourishing* (Keyes, 2003; Seligman, 2011). Flourishing adults have high levels of both emotional well-being and positive functioning (Keyes, 2003); they are productively and meaningfully engaged in their work and in society, connecting to others in fulfilling and healthy ways. They rise to meet the challenges of life; they also look beyond themselves and help others find purpose and satisfaction in life. Vitally engaged, they are enthusiastic about life and exhibit a level of self-awareness and acceptance of others that encourages growth (Keyes, 2003). Using this definition, Keyes (2016) found that 46 percent of a sample of over 5,000 college students who completed the Healthy Minds Study in 2007 could be labeled as flourishing.

The goal of flourishing exists within a broader theory of well-being that can frame the application of positive psychology to the higher education setting. Seligman (2011) maintained that there are five elements of well-being that enable humans to flourish: positive emotion, engagement, meaning, accomplishment, and positive relationships. The research on college student *thriving* (Schreiner, 2010a, 2012, 2015, 2016) has extended the concept of flourishing and current theories of well-being to higher education, with the goal of enabling a greater proportion of students to not only survive to graduation, but to be vitally engaged during the college experience and beyond.

Defined as being "fully engaged intellectually, socially, and emotionally in the college experience" (Schreiner, 2010a, p. 4), thriving is an integrative view of student success in college, as it incorporates not only academic and cognitive processes, but the quality of interpersonal and psychological engagement in the college experience. Thriving students are engaged in their learning, investing effort and applying their strengths to the challenges they face. They are connected to others in healthy and supportive ways, are open to differences in others, and have a desire to make a meaningful difference in the world around them. They have a positive perspective on life that is growth-oriented and that enables them to reframe negative events as learning experiences. Each of these aspects of thriving is malleable, meaning that intentional interventions can enhance levels of thriving. As a result, students' pre-college experiences and demographic characteristics are not as predictive of their success when programs and services are carefully designed to promote student thriving (Schreiner, 2015).

The Thriving Quotient

This holistic definition of student success has been reliably measured in thousands of college students by the 24-item Thriving Quotient (Schreiner, 2016). Confirmatory factor analysis with large national samples of college students indicates that thriving is a higher-order factor comprised of five latent variables: Engaged Learning, Academic Determination, Positive Perspective, Social Connectedness, and Diverse Citizenship. In contrast to relatively stable personality traits, each of the factors represents an element of academic, interpersonal, or psychological thriving that has been empirically demonstrated to be amenable to change within students (Schreiner, 2016).

In a national study of 14,067 students from 53 public and private four-year institutions, students' levels of thriving were found to account for an additional 11–23 percent of the variation in such outcomes as college grades and intent to graduate, over and above what was explained by institutional differences and students' demographic characteristics. Research has demonstrated strong internal consistency of the Thriving Quotient ($\alpha = 0.89$), excellent fit of the model to national samples of college students [$\chi^2_{(114)} = 1093.83$, $p < 0.001$, CFI = 0.954; RMSEA = 0.054 with 90 percent confidence intervals from 0.052 to 0.058], and evidence of predictive validity connecting scores on the instrument to intent to graduate, institutional fit, satisfaction, learning gains, perception of the value of tuition, and grade point average (GPA; Schreiner, 2016). Each aspect of thriving will be briefly described below and connected to the research on college student success.

Engaged Learning

Congruent with Seligman's (2011) *engagement* component in his well-being theory, Engaged Learning refers to "a positive energy invested in one's own learning, evidenced by meaningful processing, attention to what is happening in the moment, and involvement in learning activities" (Schreiner & Louis, 2011, p. 6). This mindful engagement leads to higher-order thinking, what Tagg (2003) refers to as deep learning, that meaningfully connects ideas and lasts beyond an academic course, contributing significantly to academic performance, persistence, graduation, and post-collegiate success (Bain, 2004; Schreiner & Louis, 2011). Thriving students are energized by the learning process, evidencing an intellectual vitality and curiosity that undergirds lifelong learning.

Much of the literature about student engagement in learning focuses on observable behaviors, such as classroom participation or interactions with faculty (Kuh, Kinzie, Buckley, Bridges, & Hayek, 2007). However, judging engaged learning solely by observable behaviors may not take into consideration cultural or gender differences in participation in the classroom or fully reflect a student's level of cognition. Therefore, the indirectly observable processes of focused attention, or mindfulness (Langer, 1997; see also Langer & Ngnoumen, this volume), and the meaning-making inherent in deep learning (Tagg, 2003) differentiate the concept of engaged learning from other conceptualizations of engagement in learning. Students who are engaged in learning are not only psychologically present and active in the learning process, but also make connections between what they learn in class and other aspects of their lives (Schreiner & Louis, 2011). An example of a college student who is highly engaged in the learning process is one who has questions about what he or she has read in preparation for class, dialogs with classmates about the reading, participates actively in class discussion, and continues thinking about what was learned long after class is over. This engaged student is energized by learning and sees ways of applying that learning to other areas of his or her life or to future goals.

Academic Determination

This component of academic thriving is similar to Seligman's (2011) *accomplishment* component of flourishing, but it also includes an emphasis on goal-setting, self-regulated learning (Pintrich, 2004), investment of effort (Robbins et al., 2004), time and resource management (Ryff & Keyes, 1995), and the application of one's strengths to academic tasks, which leads to higher levels of academic self-efficacy (Lopez & Louis, 2009; Louis & Schreiner, 2012). Students with high levels of Academic Determination are aware of their unique strengths, and they are intentional in deploying their strengths in academic settings in order to maximize their effort (Louis, 2015). Thriving students exhibit a powerful motivation to reach their educational goals; they also invest significant effort and implement effective self-regulatory strategies to succeed.

Hope theory (Snyder, 1995) provides key insights into students' motivation to invest effort in their academic endeavors, as this theory underscores the importance of agency and pathways to achieving one's educational goals. Snyder et al. (2002) have established that higher levels of hope in college students are predictive of timely degree completion. Investment of effort also impacts a student's academic performance and persistence (Lichtinger & Kaplan, 2011). Students who believe that hard work, focus, and effort will positively affect their success often effectively regulate their responses to the external environment. This environmental mastery (Ryff, 1989) enables students to feel a sense of control and engenders confidence when faced with academic challenges. Self-regulated learning enables college students to take ownership of the diverse demands of their education by fostering the cognition, adaptability, and behaviors necessary to set and monitor progress toward achieving meaningful goals (Lichtinger & Kaplan, 2011; Pintrich, 2004). As Pintrich and Zusho (2002) have noted, self-regulation, investment of effort, and academic motivation are often a reciprocal process. The degree to which students value educational goals influences their investment of effort, as well as the amount of planning, monitoring, controlling, and reflection they do regarding their own learning.

Positive Perspective

This psychological component of thriving represents the lens through which students view life; it is based on Carver, Scheier, Miller, and Fulford's (2009) construct of optimism (see also Bouchard et al., this volume). Students who are thriving view the world and their future with confidence; they expect positive outcomes and are able to reframe negative events into learning experiences (Schreiner, 2012). As a result, they are more likely to experience the *positive emotion* inherent in well-being (Seligman, 2011) that can expand their creativity and complex problem solving (Fredrickson, 2001; see also Le Nguyen & Fredrickson, this volume).

Students with a positive perspective are more likely to take a long-term view of events. As a result, they are less likely to overreact to negative events; they can put things in perspective and reframe these events to find some positive benefit or learning opportunity. This realistic optimism enables students to experience more positive emotions on a regular basis, which leads to higher levels of psychological well-being and greater development of social networks (Burris, Brechting, Salsman, & Carlson, 2009), as well as deeper satisfaction with the college experience (Schreiner, 2012). Students who report high levels of Positive Perspective also exhibit high levels of resilience that enable them to recover from adversity with even greater levels of functioning (Schreiner, 2015).

Social Connectedness

Healthy relationships with others who are supportive and caring is one of the elements of interpersonal thriving. The Social Connectedness factor is based on Ryff and Keyes' (1995) construct of *positive relations* and is congruent with the *positive relationships* dimension of Seligman's (2011) theory of well-being. The ability to form and maintain healthy relationships has been positively correlated to persistence in college (Allen, Robbins, Casillas, & Oh, 2008) and is an important element in college student development theory (Chickering & Reisser, 1993). A central aspect of positive psychological functioning in all humans (Diener, 2000), feeling a sense of social connectedness is especially beneficial for academic achievement and persistence among students of color (Hausmann, Ye, Schofield, & Woods, 2009; Museus & Quaye, 2009).

The Social Connectedness factor measures three aspects of healthy relationships. The first is how easily the student makes friends, particularly the extent to which they perceive it is difficult to make friends in their current institution. The second is the desire for close friendships and students' perceived loneliness; this aspect incorporates students' perceptions that others have more friends than they do and that they have as many close friends as they would like. The final aspect is the quality of the relationships: the degree to which college students perceive their friends care about them, the extent to which they can share their concerns, and the degree of contentment they feel when they are around their friends (Schreiner, 2016).

Diverse Citizenship

A second component of interpersonal thriving, Diverse Citizenship reflects an appreciation of multiple perspectives as well as the desire to make a contribution to one's community. Thriving students are open to differences in others, learn from multiple viewpoints, and want to make a difference in their community (Schreiner, 2016), a goal that reflects the *meaning* component of flourishing (Seligman, 2011) and is consistent with the civic engagement objectives that have historically characterized higher education.

Diverse Citizenship is derived from higher education research on *openness to diversity* (Miville et al., 1999) and *citizenship* as reflected in the Social Change Model of Leadership Development (Astin et al., 1996). Thriving students cultivate a sense of meaning and agency from engaging as citizens within a broader community. Higher scores on this factor are predictive of persistence in college and gains in critical thinking skills (Schreiner, 2010b).

Pathways to Thriving

Because thriving levels can explain up to 22 percent of the unique variance in such student success outcomes as college grades, learning gains, satisfaction with college, perception of tuition as a worthwhile investment, and intent to graduate (Schreiner, 2016), thriving has potential as a worthy student success outcome in and of itself. As a malleable construct, its changing nature is reflective of the student success process that Seifert (2016) posits is more congruent with the goal of higher education to empower students for meaningful, productive, and fulfilling lives of engagement in the world.

Four primary pathways to thriving have emerged in the large-scale research conducted to date; these pathways contribute most significantly to the variation in students' levels of thriving: (1) campus involvement, including peer interaction; (2) the quality and frequency of student–faculty interaction; (3) spirituality, including a sense of meaning and purpose; and (4) a psychological sense of community on campus (Schreiner, 2012). However, the contribution of each pathway to thriving among students of color in predominantly White institutions varies considerably (Schreiner, 2014a). For example, campus involvement and peer interaction play a different role in adjustment and success depending on the student's racial identification, with students of color experiencing more negative peer interactions, greater hurdles to campus involvement, and less benefits from participating in student organizations on campus (Schreiner, 2014a). Likewise, Cole (2007) has established that the interactions students of color have with faculty are qualitatively different from those of White students and contribute less to their learning gains. Our research has confirmed that frequent student–faculty interaction is a pathway to thriving that varies by race and ethnicity, advantaging the thriving of White students considerably more than students of color; however, we also have found that when the quality of these relationships is positive and validates students of color, student–faculty interaction is a powerful predictor of thriving regardless of race (Schreiner, 2014a).

Although spirituality is a pathway to thriving among all students, McIntosh (2015) found its contribution to thriving among students of color was twice as strong as that seen among White students. We have defined spirituality as students' perception of meaning and purpose in life and their reliance on this sense of meaning and purpose as both a coping mechanism and a lens through which to view the world. Thus, spirituality as defined in our research represents the transcendence beyond oneself that Astin, Astin, and Lindholm (2010) describe as religious commitment, although our items refer to both spiritual and religious beliefs. The largest effects of spirituality on thriving were among Asian and African-American students; spirituality was also a strong pathway for students of color to experience a sense of community on campus (McIntosh, 2015).

A psychological sense of community (PSC) is comprised of feelings of belonging, mattering, interdependence, and emotional connections to others in a group (McMillan & Chavis, 1986). Students with a strong sense of community on campus feel they are part of and contribute to a dependable network of people who care about them, are committed to their well-being, and are able to meet one another's needs (Lounsbury & DeNeui, 1995). Previous studies have highlighted the significant differences in the sense of community that can be attributed to campus interventions designed to reduce stereotype threat (Walton & Cohen, 2011), but also have found mixed results of interventions explicitly designed to promote a sense of belonging among African-American students (Hausmann et al., 2009). Walton and Cohen's (2011) intervention targeted African-American students over a three-year period with messages designed to normalize academic adversity so that students did not attribute academic difficulties to their race, but rather were encouraged to perceive these challenges as a normal part of college life. The authors expected the intervention to have a significant effect on student GPA, which it did, but the intervention also increased a sense of belonging among these students. In contrast, Hausmann et al.'s (2009) intervention to create a sense of belonging by sending frequent communication and university logo-bearing gifts to students only affected the sense of belonging among White students on a predominantly White campus; the African-American students in the sample demonstrated no differences in sense of belonging as a result of the intervention. The authors concluded that sense of belonging is more complex and requires a more powerful intervention for students of color. Likewise, in our research we have found each component of PSC varies by race and ethnicity, as does the relative contribution of PSC to thriving (Schreiner, 2014a).

A sense of community on campus consistently contributes the most to the variation in all students' ability to thrive, but what leads students to experience a sense of community differs significantly across racial groups. For example, interaction with faculty is the strongest contributor to a sense of community among White students, but for Latino/a students it is involvement in campus organizations, for African-American students it is spirituality, and for Asian students it is the fit within their major (Schreiner, 2014a). For all students of color, however, perceptions of *institutional integrity* are the strongest predictor of their sense of community that ultimately led to thriving (Ash & Schreiner, 2016). Institutional integrity reflects the degree to which an institution is accurately portrayed during admissions, faculty and staff embody the mission of the institution, and students' expectations are met or exceeded (Braxton et al., 2014). As was evidenced in the Ash and Schreiner (2016) study of students of color on predominantly White faith-based campuses, when institutional integrity is compromised, students are not likely to feel they are part of the campus community or that the institution is a good fit for them; ultimately, their ability to thrive and their desire to graduate from that institution is compromised, as well.

Applications: Enabling Thriving for All Students

The implications of the research on thriving and student success are that this process is amenable to intervention and that a two-pronged focus on individual student thriving as well as the campus conditions that promote or inhibit thriving are worthy of examination. One of the most beneficial perspectives positive psychology offers higher education is a focus on optimal functioning. Bloom, Hutson, He, and Konkle (2013) have labeled this approach *appreciative education* and describe it as "actively seek[ing] out the best in other people" (p. 8). By developing students' strengths and potential to help them reach their goals, educators who apply the principles of positive psychology can enable a greater percentage of students to not merely survive, but thrive in college.

The two-pronged emphasis on (a) the individual student success process and (b) the institutional environment that promotes or inhibits thriving will be reflected in the applications outlined below. The goal in each of these recommendations is to promote success and flourishing; thus, the focus is not on the deficits of either the student or the campus environment, but rather on the strengths and assets each brings to the process.

Equip All Students to Thrive

The expanded goal of higher education, from the vantage point of positive psychology, is to promote the well-being of students for a lifetime, equipping and empowering all students to make the most of their college experience and to be able to live meaningful and productive lives that contribute to the public good—in short, to thrive. Institutions are beginning to explicitly state this goal as part of their mission and vision (Dahill-Brown & Jayawickreme, 2016). Whether in the counseling center, the career development office, the learning enrichment center, the residence halls, or the classroom, a concerted effort to promote student well-being can result in significant student growth and higher levels of mental health during the college years (Robitschek & Thoen, 2015).

Provide All Students with an Advising Relationship that Helps Them Develop Their Strengths, Design Individualized Pathways to Success, and Connect to Their Calling

The advising relationship is the ideal vehicle for applying positive psychology principles to enable more students to thrive in college, as it is a pre-existing structure within every institution whereby each student has the opportunity for an ongoing individual interaction with a representative of the institution (Schreiner, 2013). Good advising is not simply course selection; it is an intentional, student-centered, and learning oriented process of helping students make meaning within their college experience. Ensuring that every student designs a clear pathway to success in consultation with his or her advisor is one of the most effective ways to help students thrive (Bloom, Hutson, & He, 2013). Particularly when the pathways to thriving differ across cultural contexts and student backgrounds, advisors who are culturally competent, knowledgeable about student development and the institution, and who see as their mission helping students find meaning and purpose in their college experience can make a significant difference in these students' lives. Partnering advising with career services, so that students encounter a seamless experience of choosing a major and exploring career options within a context of meaning and purpose, exponentially increases the impact of advising (Schreiner, 2013).

A focus on strengths development within the advising relationship is integral to thriving, as "people who have the opportunity every day to do what they do best—to act on their strengths—are far more likely to flourish" (Fredrickson, 2009, p. 189). Strengths-based advising rests on the premise that capitalizing on one's areas of greatest talent likely leads to greater success than investing comparable time and effort to remediate areas of weakness (Clifton & Harter, 2003); it also represents a paradigm shift for higher education from deficit remediation and students' past experiences to talent development and the possibilities for the future. Rather than aiming to prevent failure, the goal is transformed into promoting success and assisting students in discerning their calling. Seifert (2016) uses the word "calling" to refer to students' discernment of "what they believe, who they want to be, and who they want to be in relation to others" (p. 152).

Instead of assessing where the student is deficient, strengths-based advising assesses the personal assets or talents that the student brings into the college environment and considers how they can be multiplied by gaining the necessary knowledge and skills to develop them into strengths. As students learn how to develop their strengths and apply them to meet challenges and reach important goals, they experience a level of self-efficacy that can sustain them through difficult times. They also develop a wider repertoire of success strategies and proactive coping skills because they learn to use their strengths as pathways to their goals and as the foundation for addressing the inevitable challenges of college life (Schreiner, 2013). Students' strengths also can be perceived as clues to areas of vocation that might be fulfilling. Advisors who use a strengths development approach apply the best of empirically established positive psychology principles represented in appreciative inquiry (Bloom et al., 2008) and signature strengths interventions (Seligman et al., 2005). Advising that applies an appreciative mindset to students and their goals helps students make the most of their college experience and connect to their calling (Bloom et al., 2013).

Teach Students Coping Skills that Build Resilience, Beginning in Their First-Year Experience

College students inevitably face challenges and experience negative events, despite individualized plans for success. Because students with proactive coping skills and an ability to reframe negative events as learning opportunities have a higher likelihood of success in college (Bean & Eaton, 2000) and report higher levels of thriving, teaching students these skills early in their college experience sets them on a trajectory for success. Specific coping skills that can undergird student success include what Dweck (2006) calls a *growth mindset*, a belief that change is possible and that it is the quality of the effort that determines the level of one's success. Research has demonstrated that faculty can teach students a growth mindset using readings, brief videos, and tips from successful students (Louis, 2015).

Another key to resilience lies in students' explanatory style—the way they explain negative events that occur in their lives. Thriving students have what Seligman (2006) calls an *optimistic explanatory style*: they perceive negative events as externally caused, changeable, and specific to the situation. This perspective enables them to adapt and recover from adversity. In contrast, those who perceive negative events as "personal, permanent, and pervasive" (p. 52) have a pessimistic explanatory style that leads to passivity. Such passivity results in a decreased likelihood of exercising proactive coping skills to address the challenge; it also can result in feelings of depression or discouragement that lead to disengagement from active problem solving. As is often the case when problems are not addressed early and effectively, the situation then only deteriorates. Reivich and Shatté (2002) maintain that this pessimistic thinking is the "number-one roadblock to resilience" (p. 11).

However, there is evidence that an optimistic explanatory style can be taught to students; Seligman (2011) and colleagues have experienced considerable success with grade-school students, first-year college students, and members of the American military. Teaching students to perceive failures as temporary setbacks attributable to controllable causes, such as insufficient effort or incorrect strategies, builds resilience and hope, enabling them to approach future events with greater confidence that success is possible. Louis (2015) has suggested that these coping skills can be introduced at orientation and can be taught by peer leaders, advisors, and faculty early in the term, then reinforced as students seek help from academic support services, career counselors, and counseling center professionals.

Often overlooked as a coping resource, acknowledging and cultivating students' spirituality can also be a pathway to thriving, particularly for students of color (McIntosh, 2015). Building on this strength means expanding campus awareness of different cultural expressions of faith and spirituality and providing welcoming space for students to explore meaning and purpose in life and to struggle with existential questions (Astin et al., 2010).

Teach Students to Thrive

Explicitly teaching positive psychology principles in the classroom, whether as a stand-alone course in the psychology curriculum or woven into existing courses, affords the opportunity for students to benefit from the research and emphasis on fulfilled individuals and thriving communities. Courses on positive psychology are becoming more common, often structured around the three pillars of positive psychology: positive emotions, positive individual traits, and positive institutions.

When woven into first-year seminar courses or other classes, teaching students to thrive focuses on an application of such positive psychology principles as those outlined by Magyar-Moe (2015): strengths-based education, well-being theory, the broaden-and-build theory of positive emotions, active-constructive responding, and hope-building. The first-year seminar is the ideal place to teach students to thrive, as it sets the stage for the college experience and, when done well, is considered a "high-impact practice" (Kuh, 2008) that leads to significant gains in students' learning and development. Explicitly teaching a growth mindset (Dweck, 2006), encouraging mindfulness (Langer, 1997), and integrating attributional retraining (Perry, Hall, & Ruthig, 2005) into the first-year experience can equip students with the skills to thrive in college (Louis, 2015).

Create a Thriving Campus Culture

Equipping students to thrive is only half the equation for student success, however. Without a positive context in which to interact, students' psychological well-being is likely to decline over the college years, as Astin (2016) has noted. In our own research on thriving, we also have discovered that levels of thriving tend to decline over a semester unless there are positive interactions or interventions that occur. Creating a positive campus climate can support the thriving process in students and can sustain the efforts of advisors and faculty as they work with individual students. Park and Peterson (2003) assert that thriving organizations are those that have an articulated moral vision or goal that is embraced by members and constituents alike. These organizations have explicit and equitable reward structures and treat people as individuals, allowing them to "do what they do best" (p. 41). Collaboration and trust characterize the daily work within these institutions, feedback is valued, and there is a commitment to keeping the promises implicit within the mission of the institution. The recommendations below are aimed at creating and sustaining such a thriving culture on campus.

Cultivate a Strong Sense of Community on Campus

Research on college student thriving indicates that a sense of community on campus is the primary predictor of whether students thrive (Schreiner, 2016). Students, faculty, and staff who report a strong sense of community on campus feel they are part of and can contribute to a dependable network of people who value them, are committed to their welfare, and are able to meet their needs (Lounsbury & DeNeui, 1995). McMillan and Chavis (1986) originally defined a psychological sense of community as "a feeling that members have of belonging and being important to each other, and a shared faith that their needs will be met by their commitment to be together" (p. 9). Recent adaptations of this definition have focused on four aspects of a sense of community that provide a roadmap for creating a thriving campus. These four aspects include membership, ownership, relationship, and partnership (Schreiner, 2015).

Membership is the aspect of a sense of community that has been explored most within higher education research. Grounded in a sense of belonging, membership includes feeling that one is part of something larger than oneself and is valued by others in the community (McMillan & Chavis, 1986). The use of rituals, traditions, honor codes, and symbols of the university conveys membership. Celebrating the accomplishments of students and faculty can be a powerful way of tangibly demonstrating the value the university places on members of its community (Schreiner, 2010b). Faculty, staff, and administrators who are not only committed to the mission of the institution, but who exhibit an unwavering commitment to student learning as their primary purpose, create a climate in which students are likely to feel valued and supported in their educational goals.

Ownership refers to voice and contribution; members of the community perceive that their input matters and that they have something to offer the community (McMillan & Chavis, 1986). Including students, faculty, and staff in institutional decision making and soliciting their regular feedback bolsters their sense of community. Particularly for students of color on predominantly White campuses, when the curriculum incorporates multiple cultural perspectives and includes the history, traditions, and intellectual contributions of people from all ethnic and racial groups across the world, feelings of ownership are likely to be strengthened (Ash & Schreiner, 2016).

The *relationship* aspect of a sense of community refers to the development of emotional connections and positive interactions with other community members (McMillan & Chavis, 1986). Frequent opportunities to celebrate and to experience shared positive emotions enhance this element of a sense of community. Fredrickson (2013) has noted that higher "positivity ratios" (p. 1) signal flourishing environments. Attending to the ratio of positive to negative emotions within a university setting may provide the foundation for a flourishing campus.

Finally, *partnership* refers to working together toward common goals and experiencing the synergy that occurs when accomplishment is shared (McMillan & Chavis, 1986). Student–faculty research, interdisciplinary teaching and scholarship, and cross-departmental projects are examples of the types of partnerships that build a psychological sense of community (Schreiner, 2010b). At the faculty and staff level, collaborative engagement is one of the hallmarks of campuses whose student success rates are higher than predicted. When student success is perceived as a shared responsibility, partnerships between academic and student affairs professionals create seamless learning environments that can impact students' lives (Kuh et al., 2005). Examples of faculty–staff partnerships include care teams of faculty, academic support staff, and student life staff who respond to students in need; team approaches to learning communities; and regular cross-department collaboration on the design, implementation, and assessment of student success programs.

Because a sense of community on the campus is the single most powerful predictor of thriving across all student groups (Schreiner, 2016), focusing on the development of each aspect of a sense of community can cultivate an environment where students, faculty, staff, and administrators are likely to thrive. Attending to the ways in which students' backgrounds and prior experiences interact with the expectations and existing culture of the campus can ensure that all students feel a sense of belonging and ownership that goes beyond the "welcome" extended to guests (Strayhorn, 2012).

Strengthen Perceptions of Institutional Integrity by Delivering on Your Promises

Although the sense of community on campus is the most significant predictor of thriving, students' perceptions of institutional integrity are significantly predictive of their sense of community (Ash & Schreiner, 2016; Schreiner, 2014a), as well as of student satisfaction and persistence to graduation (Braxton et al., 2014). This perception of institutional integrity is a measure of the degree to which the institution is delivering on its promises (Braxton et al., 2014). Such promises are implicit as well as explicit and begin during the admissions process, as they are conveyed through admissions materials, websites, campus tours, and conversations with admissions counselors. When the post-enrollment campus experience is not what was portrayed during the admissions process, students may feel a sense of betrayal—and this perception is more keenly felt by students of color (Schreiner, 2014a). Examining policies and practices through the eyes of students, and particularly through the eyes of students who are not in the majority on campus, can pinpoint ways in which the institution may not be portraying itself accurately.

Students' perceptions of institutional integrity are also influenced by the extent to which their expectations are met, which implies that institutions are aware of what these expectations are. Although many expectations are created by the institution through the admissions process and institutional mission statements, students also may bring expectations of which university leaders are not aware. Surveying students at the beginning of the academic year to determine the expectations students have of their academic, residence hall, and college life experiences could help shape the academic culture and determine the kind of actions educators take. The results of such a survey would help institutional leaders clarify expectations, make adjustments to programs and activities, or build more realistic expectations within students to proactively create environments that are conducive to thriving.

Finally, perceptions of institutional integrity are often a function of whether students view the actions of faculty and staff as congruent with the mission of the institution. As Kuh et al. (2005) have noted, the mission of an institution establishes the tone of the campus, conveys its purposes, and provides direction for the future, but too often there is a gap between the espoused mission of an institution and its enacted mission—what the institution actually does on a daily basis. The enacted mission is far more important to student success and thriving than the espoused mission. In thriving institutions, there is little difference between the espoused and enacted missions; as Kuh et al. note: "their mission is 'alive.' Faculty members, administrators, staff, students, and others use it to explain their behavior and to talk about what the institution is, the direction it is heading, and how their work contributes to its goals" (2005, p. 27). This congruence between the espoused mission and the daily actions of faculty and staff influence the perceptions students hold of the institution's integrity, which then contributes to their sense of community and ability to thrive on campus.

Thomas Long, president emeritus of Elizabethtown College, asserts that "We have diminished our educational birthright by abandoning the effort to educate the whole person" (2016, p. 246) and suggests that well-being should be central to the institutional mission and "woven into the daily life of the institution" (p. 244). When thriving is viewed as a core aspect of the institutional mission, it becomes embedded in the academic program as well as the co-curricular program and student services. A thriving campus integrates principles of well-being into the curriculum, identifies specific points where flourishing can be nurtured, develops "affirmative and experiential pedagogies" (p. 245), and regularly assesses levels of thriving in students.

Equip Faculty for Effective Engagement with Diverse Learners

When students feel a sense of belonging, they are more likely to become engaged in the campus community and in their own learning experiences (DeNeui, 2003). The primary opportunity for developing a psychological sense of community on campus occurs through the classroom experiences that are common to both residential and commuter students. With more diverse learners on college campuses, the challenges of effectively engaging with students to build community in the classroom increase, but the rewards do, as well. As Ash and Schreiner (2016) discovered:

> when students of color perceived that faculty were sensitive to the needs of diverse learners, they were then more likely to engage in the learning process, to seek out faculty outside of class, to perceive the institution as

committed to their welfare and delivering on its promises, to experience a sense of community, to feel that they fit, and to report high levels of thriving and an intent to graduate from that institution. These are not trivial outcomes.

(p. 56)

Effective engagement with diverse learners begins with faculty attitudes. Bain (2004) noted that the best college teachers were those who "look for and appreciate the individual value of each student" and "had great faith in students' ability to achieve" (p. 72). This attitude is congruent with a strengths-based approach to teaching. Such an approach leverages the instructor's strengths and deliberately connects students' strengths to strategies for mastering the course content, so that students are more engaged in the learning process. Engaged learning is the desired outcome of strengths-based teaching practices (Schreiner, 2014b). Kuh et al.'s (2005) study of 20 highly engaging colleges and universities confirmed that faculty knowledge of their students—"where they came from, their preferred learning styles, their talents, and when and where they need help" (p. 301) was foundational to student success. Knowledge about one's students provides an instructor with a foundation for connecting with those students' interests and prior learning. Perceiving their strengths and potential contributions to the learning experience enables professors to connect with students not only in the classroom, but also in an advising session and in interactions outside the classroom.

Equally important are behaviors exhibited by faculty beginning on the first day of class, such as messages of validation that convey to students of color that they belong and deserve to be part of the learning community. Body language, an attitude of humility, valuing relationships with students, supporting students as they face challenges, and responding compassionately to students' ongoing struggles are vital aspects of culturally responsive pedagogy (Davis, 2006).

Using pedagogical approaches that encourage active learning builds positive emotions, as classroom learning experiences that actively engage students with the content and with each other lead to higher levels of enjoyment as well as to greater learning. Active learning demands students "do something" with the course content, which promotes persistence in all students (Braxton, Jones, Hirschy, & Hartley, 2008), but can be particularly powerful when such activities encourage interaction with those of a different culture. Intentionally creating diverse learning teams and teaching students how to work effectively together, capitalizing on the strengths each contributes to the team, helps students see beyond their own strengths to the talents of others and the synergy that occurs when the team harnesses their mutual strengths. Focusing on students' interests, qualities, and learning styles, as well as connecting new material to what students already know, creates a powerful dynamic in the classroom that fosters intrinsic motivation (Ryan & Deci, 2000).

Effective engagement with students does not just occur in the classroom, however. The type of feedback faculty provide to students and the quality of their interactions with students outside of class also influence student thriving (Schreiner, 2015). Although feedback is essential for learning to occur in all students, students from varied cultural backgrounds receive such feedback in different ways. For example, communicating high expectations and a belief in students' ability is likely to enhance academic self-concept and learning among historically underrepresented students, while students from cultures that have historically been well represented in higher education may value more direct and evaluative feedback (Cole, 2007). As faculty develop relationships with students of color outside of class, students of color begin to trust faculty more and become more open to their feedback, which then leads to increased levels of thriving (Schreiner, 2014a).

As faculty learn to provide clear expectations, optimal challenges, and timely informative feedback, students' competence levels increase, as does their engaged learning. Providing tools and strategies to help faculty design meaningful assignments within a context of choice meets students' needs for autonomy. Structuring collaborative, active learning in their classrooms can meet students' needs for relatedness and can build positive emotions that expand students' engaged learning (Fredrickson, 2001). Meeting students' needs for competence, autonomy, and relatedness in these ways then leads to intrinsic motivation and a higher likelihood of success (Ryan & Deci, 2000; Schreiner & Louis, 2011).

Future Directions for Research

As the research on college student thriving and well-being has burgeoned within the last decade, there remain some gaps in the knowledge base that could lead to more effective interventions on postsecondary campuses. Three particular recommendations for future research arise from an analysis of the current literature on student success, well-being, and thriving.

The first recommendation is to focus on intervention studies. Experimental designs are difficult to implement within higher education due to the challenge of random assignment to condition. However, small-scale interventions can be empirically tested and then, if effective, scaled-up for use in larger settings. For example, conducting a controlled experiment of the impact of a thriving curriculum or a strengths development advising approach could be piloted, refined, then implemented throughout a first-year experience on campus. Most of the current research on well-being in higher education is correlational in nature; carefully controlled experiments are now needed to determine the impact of positive psychology principles on such student success outcomes as thriving, GPA, and graduation.

Along with the need for more experimental research designs, there is also a need to determine whether interventions must be delivered directly to students or can target faculty, staff, peer mentors, resident assistants, or other campus personnel to significantly affect the student success process. For example, if resident assistants are trained to promote thriving in the programming they deliver to their residents and in the way in which they interact with them, will that have a significant effect on the levels of thriving reported by the residents themselves? A corollary question would be what effect faculty development has on student thriving; does training the faculty in effective pedagogy for well-being ultimately impact the thriving levels of the students in class with those faculty? If faculty developers are able to cultivate a growth mindset in faculty, does that have any effect on student success?

Finally, longitudinal studies of student success across the college years and beyond are needed. In particular, alumni studies would be able to document whether students who are thriving in college are more likely to thrive in life as well. *The Gallup-Purdue Index* (Gallup, 2014) is an example of a large-scale study of the impact of college on alumni, but it is a cross-sectional survey, not a longitudinal study. As such, it requires participants to respond with their retrospective opinions or attitudes about their time in college. What is needed are studies that assess the thriving levels of college student cohorts at the beginning of college and follow that same cohort throughout each year of college and at regular intervals beyond college. Although some longitudinal mixed methods studies have been conducted on student thriving across a semester (Derrico, Tharp, & Schreiner, 2015), these have tended to be studies conducted within a small number of homogeneous institutional types. A longer time frame, a broader representation of postsecondary institutions, and regular intervals of follow-up beyond graduation would enhance the understanding of the experiences that are most likely to promote or inhibit thriving in college and beyond.

Conclusion

As the principles of positive psychology continue to influence the research on student success and the practices that promote thriving, educators enhance their potential for reaching the goal of "fulfilled individuals and thriving communities" (Seligman & Csikszentmihalyi, 2000, p. 5). Equipping individual students to thrive provides an opportunity to apply principles of positive psychology to classroom pedagogy, the advising relationship, the first-year experience, the work of university counseling and career centers, and the support provided to students outside of class. Creating a campus culture that promotes flourishing for all ensures that well-being is central to the mission of the institution and that students, faculty, and staff alike experience a sense of community that enables them to thrive.

References

Allen, J., Robbins, S. B., Casillas, A., & Oh, I. S. (2008). Third-year college retention and transfer: Effects of academic performance, motivation, and social connectedness. *Research in Higher Education, 49*(7), 647–664.

Ash, A., & Schreiner, L. A. (2016). Pathways to success in students of color on Christian campuses. *Christian Higher Education, 15*(1–2), 38–61.

Astin, A. W. (2016). Why well-being is fundamental to liberal learning. In D. W. Harward (Ed.), *Well-being and higher education: A strategy for change and the realization of education's greater purposes* (pp. 91–98). Washington, DC: Bringing Theory to Practice.

Astin, A. W., Astin, H. S., Boatsman, K. C., Bonous-Hammarth, M., Chambers, T., Goldberg, L. S. … Shellog, K. M. (1996). *A social change model of leadership development: Guidebook (Version III).* College Park, MD: National Clearinghouse for Leadership Programs.

Astin, A. W., Astin, H. S., & Lindholm, J. A. (2010). *Cultivating the spirit: How college can enhance students' inner lives.* San Francisco, CA: Jossey-Bass.

Bain, K. (2004). *What the best college teachers do.* Cambridge, MA: Harvard University Press.

Bean, J. P., & Eaton, S. B. (2000). A psychological model of college student retention. In J. M. Braxton (Ed.), *Reworking the student departure puzzle* (pp. 48–61). Nashville, TN: Vanderbilt University Press.

Bloom, J., Hutson, B., & He, Y. (2008). *The appreciative advising revolution.* Champaign, IL: Stipes.

Bloom, J. L., Hutson, B. L., He, Y., & Konkle, E. (2013). Appreciative education. In P. C. Mather & E. Hulme (Eds.), *Positive psychology and appreciative inquiry in higher education* (pp. 5–18). New Directions for Student Services, no. 143.

Braxton, J. M., Doyle, W. R., Hartley III, H. V., Hirschy, A. S., Jones, W. A., & McLendon, M. K. (2014). *Rethinking college student retention.* San Francisco, CA: Jossey-Bass.

Braxton, J. M., Jones, W. A., Hirschy, A. S., & Hartley III, H. V. (2008). The role of active learning in college student persistence. *New Directions for Teaching and Learning, 2008*(115), 71–83.

Burris, J. L., Brechting, E. H., Salsman, J., & Carlson, C. R. (2009). Factors associated with psychological well-being and distress of university students. *Journal of American College Health, 57*(5), 536–544.

Carver, C. S., Scheier, M. F., Miller, C. J., & Fulford, D. (2009). Optimism. In S. J. Lopez & C. R. Snyder (Eds.), *Oxford handbook of positive psychology* (2nd ed., pp. 303–312). Oxford, England: Oxford University Press.

Chickering, A. W., & Reisser. L. (1993). *Education and identity.* San Francisco, CA: Jossey-Bass.

Clifton, D. O., & Harter, J. K. (2003). Investing in strengths. In K. S. Cameron, J. E. Dutton, & R. E. Quinn (Eds.), *Positive organizational scholarship* (pp. 111–121). San Francisco, CA: Berrett-Koehler.

Cole, D. (2007). Do interracial interactions matter? An examination of student–faculty contact and intellectual self-concept. *The Journal of Higher Education, 78*(3), 249–281. doi:10.1353/jhe.2007.0015.

Dahill-Brown, S. E., & Jayawickreme, E. (2016). What constitutes indices of well-being among college students? In D. W. Harward (Ed.), *Well-being and higher education: A strategy for change and the realization of education's greater purposes* (pp. 123–134). Washington, DC: Bringing Theory to Practice.

Davis, B. M. 2006. *How to teach students who don't look like you: Culturally relevant teaching strategies*, Thousand Oaks, CA: Corwin.

DeNeui, D. L. C. (2003). An investigation of first-year college students' psychological sense of community on campus. *College Student Journal, 37*, 224–235.

Derrico, C. M., Tharp, J. L., & Schreiner, L. A. (2015). Called to make a difference: Experiences of students who thrive on faith-based campuses. *Christian Higher Education, 14*(5), 298–321.

Diener, E. (2000). Subjective well-being: The science of happiness and a proposal for a national index. *American Psychologist, 55*, 34–43.

Dweck, C. S. (2006). *Mindset: The new psychology of success*. New York: Random House.

Fredrickson, B. L. (2001). The role of positive emotions in positive psychology: The broaden-and-build theory of positive emotions. *American Psychologist, 56*(3), 218–226. doi:10.1037/0003-066X.56.3.218.

Fredrickson, B. L. (2009). *Positivity*. New York: Crown.

Fredrickson, B. L. (2013, July 15). Updated thinking on positivity ratios. *American Psychologist*. Advance online publication. doi:10.1037/a0033584.

Gallup. (2014). *The Gallup-Purdue Index*. Retrieved from www.gallup.com/services/178496/gallup-purdue-index-inaugural-national-report.

Harward, D. W. (2016). Well-being essays and provocations: Significance and implications for higher education. In D. W. Harward (Ed.), *Well-being and higher education: A strategy for change and the realization of education's greater purposes* (pp. 3–20). Washington, DC: Bringing Theory to Practice.

Hausmann, L. R. M., Ye, F., Schofield, J. W., & Woods, R. L. (2009). Sense of belonging and persistence in White and African American first-year students. *Research in Higher Education, 50*, 649–669. doi:10.1007/s11162-009-9137-8.

Keyes, C. L. M. (2003). Complete mental health: An agenda for the 21st century. In C. L. M. Keyes & J. Haidt (Eds), *Flourishing: Positive psychology and the life well-lived* (pp. 293–309). Washington, DC: American Psychological Association.

Keyes, C. L. M. (2016). Why flourishing? In D. W. Harward (Ed.), *Well-being and higher education: A strategy for change and the realization of education's greater purposes* (pp. 99–108). Washington, DC: Bringing Theory to Practice.

Kinzie, J. (2012). Introduction: A new vision of student success. In L. A. Schreiner, M. C. Louis, & D. D. Nelson (Eds.), *Thriving in transitions* (pp. xi–xxx). Columbia: University of South Carolina, National Resource Center for The First-Year Experience and Students in Transition.

Kuh, G. D. (2008). *High-impact educational practices: What they are, who has access to them, and why they matter*. Washington, DC: Association of American Colleges & Universities.

Kuh, G. D., Kinzie, J., Buckley, J. A., Bridges, B. K., & Hayek, J. C. (2007). *Piecing together the student success puzzle: Research, propositions, and recommendations. ASHE Higher Education Report* (Vol. 35, p. 5). San Francisco, CA: Jossey-Bass.

Kuh, G. D., Kinzie, J., Schuh, J. H., & Whitt, E. J. (Eds.). (2005). *Student success in college: Creating conditions that matter*. San Francisco, CA: Jossey-Bass.

Langer, E. J. (1997). *The power of mindful learning*. Reading, MA: Addison Wesley.

Lichtinger, E., & Kaplan, A. (2011). Purpose of engagement in academic self-regulation. *New Directions for Teaching and Learning, 126*, 9–19. doi:10.1002/tl.440.

Long, B. T. (2010, December). *Grading higher education: Giving consumers the information they need* (paper jointly released by the Center for American Progress and the Hamilton Project).

Long, T. (2016). Mobilizing campus communities for well-being. In D. W. Harward (Ed.), *Well-being and higher education: A strategy for change and the realization of education's greater purposes* (pp. 243–246). Washington, DC: Bringing Theory to Practice.

Lopez, S. J., & Louis, M. C. (2009). The principles of strengths-based education. *Journal of College and Character, 10*(4), 1–8. doi:10.2202/1940-1639.1041.

Louis, M. C. (2015). Enhancing intellectual development and academic success in college: Insights and strategies from positive psychology. In J. C. Wade, L. I. Marks, and R. D. Hetzel (Eds.), *Positive psychology on the college campus* (pp. 99–132). Oxford, UK: Oxford University Press.

Louis, M. C., & Schreiner, L. A. (2012). Helping students thrive: A strengths development model. In L. A. Schreiner, M. C. Louis, & D. D. Nelson. (Eds.), *Thriving in transitions: A research-based approach to college student success* (pp. 19–40). Columbia: University of South Carolina, National Resource Center for the First-Year Experience and Students in Transition.

Lounsbury, J. W., & DeNeui, D. (1995). Psychological sense of community on campus. *College Student Journal, 29*(3), 270–277.

Magyar-Moe, J. L. (2015). Positive psychology in the classroom. In J. C. Wade, L. I. Marks, & R. D. Hetzel (Eds.), *Positive psychology on the college campus* (pp. 133–166). Oxford, UK: Oxford University Press.

McIntosh, E. J. (2015). Thriving and spirituality: Making meaning of meaning making for students of color. *About Campus, 19*(6), 16–23.

McMillan, D. W., & Chavis, D. M. (1986). Sense of community: A definition and theory. *Journal of Community Psychology, 14*, 6–23.

Miville, M. L., Gelso, C. J., Pannu, R., Liu, W., Touradji, P., Holloway, P., & Fuertes, J. (1999). Appreciating similarities and valuing differences: The Miville-Guzman University-Diversity Scale. *Journal of Counseling Psychology, 46*, 291–307.

Museus, S. D., & Quaye, S. J. (2009). Toward an intercultural perspective of racial and ethnic minority college student persistence. *The Review of Higher Education, 33*(1), 67–94.

Park, N., & Peterson, C. M. (2003). Virtues and organizations. In K. S. Cameron, J. E. Dutton, & R. E. Quinn (Eds.), *Positive organizational scholarship: Foundations of a new discipline* (pp. 33–47). San Francisco, CA: Berrett-Koehler.

Perry, R. P., Hall, N. C., & Ruthig, J. C. (2005). Perceived (academic) control and scholastic attainment in higher education. In J. C. Smart (Ed.), *Higher education: Handbook of theory and research* (Vol. 20, pp. 363–436). Norwell, MA: Springer.

Pintrich, P. R. (2004). A conceptual framework for assessing motivation and self-regulated learning in college students. *Educational Psychology Review, 16*(4), 385–407.

Pintrich, P. R., & Zusho, A. (2002). The development of academic self-regulation: The role of cognitive and motivational factors. In W. Allan & J. S. Eccles (Eds.), *Development of achievement motivation* (pp. 249–284). San Diego, CA: Academic Press.

Reivich, K., & Shatté, A. (2002). *The resilience factor: Seven keys to finding your inner strength and overcoming life's hurdles.* New York: Broadway.

Robbins, S. B., Lauver, K., Le, H., Langley, R., Davis, D., & Carlstrom, A. (2004). Do psychosocial and study skill factors predict college outcomes? A meta-analysis. *Psychological Bulletin, 130*, 261–288.

Robitschek, C., & Thoen, M. A. (2015). Personal growth and development. In J. C. Wade, L. I. Marks, & R. D. Hetzel (Eds.), *Positive psychology on the college campus* (pp. 219–238). Oxford, UK: Oxford University Press.

Ryan, R. M., & Deci, E. L. (2000). Self-determination theory and the facilitation of intrinsic motivation, social development, and well-being. *American Psychologist, 55*(1), 68–78.

Ryff, C. D. (1989). Happiness is everything, or is it? Explorations on the meaning of psychological well-being. *Journal of Personality and Social Psychology, 57*(6), 1069–1081.

Ryff, C. D., & Keyes, C. L. M. (1995). The structure of psychological well-being revisited. *Journal of Personality and Social Psychology, 69*, 719–727.

Schreiner, L. (2010a). The "Thriving Quotient": A new vision for student success. *About Campus, 15*(2), 2–10.

Schreiner, L. (2010b). Thriving in community. *About Campus, 15*(4), 2–11.

Schreiner, L. A. (2012). From surviving to thriving during transitions. In L. A. Schreiner, M. C. Louis, & D. D. Nelson (Eds.), *Thriving in transitions: A research-based approach to college student success* (pp. 1–18). Columbia: University of South Carolina, National Resource Center for The First-Year Experience and Students in Transition.

Schreiner, L. A. (2013). Strengths-based advising. In J. K. Drake, P. Jordan, & M. A. Miller (Eds.), *Academic advising approaches: Strategies that teach students to make the most of college* (pp. 105–120). San Francisco, CA: Jossey-Bass.

Schreiner, L. A. (2014a). Different pathways to thriving among students of color: An untapped opportunity for success. *About Campus, 19*(5), 10–19.

Schreiner, L. A. (2014b). Strengths-oriented teaching: Pathways to engaged learning. In B. F. Tobolowsky (Ed.), *Paths to learning: Teaching for engagement in college* (pp. 77–92). Columbia: The University of South Carolina, National Resource Center for The First-Year Experience and Students in Transition.

Schreiner, L. A. (2015). Positive psychology and higher education: The contribution of positive psychology to student success and institutional effectiveness. In J. C. Wade, L. I. Marks, & R. D. Hetzel (Eds.), *Positive psychology on the college campus* (pp. 1–26). Oxford, UK: Oxford University Press.

Schreiner, L. A. (2016). Thriving: Expanding the goal of higher education. In D. W. Harward (Ed.), *Well-being and higher education: A strategy for change and the realization of education's greater purposes* (pp. 135–148). Washington, DC: Bringing Theory to Practice.

Schreiner, L. A., & Louis, M. (2011). The engaged learning index: Implications for faculty development. *Journal on Excellence in College Teaching, 22*(1), 5–28.

Seifert, T. (2016). Well-being and student persistence: Reframing student success. In D. W. Harward (Ed.), *Well-being and higher education: A strategy for change and the realization of education's greater purposes* (pp. 149–156). Washington, DC: Bringing Theory to Practice.

Seligman, M. E. P. (2006). *Learned optimism: How to change your mind and your life.* New York: Random House.

Seligman, M. E. P. (2011). *Flourish: A visionary new understanding of happiness and well-being.* New York: Free Press.

Seligman, M. E. P., & Csikszentmihalyi, M. (2000). Positive psychology: An introduction. *American Psychologist, 55*, 51–82.

Seligman, M. E. P., Steen, T. A., Park, N., & Peterson, C. (2005). Positive psychology progress: Empirical validation of interventions. *American Psychologist, 60*(5), 410–421.

Snyder, C. R. (1995). Conceptualizing, measuring, and nurturing hope. *Journal of Counseling & Development, 73*(3), 355–360.

Snyder, C., Shorey, H., Cheavens, J., Pulvers, K., Adams, V., & Wiklund, C. (2002). Hope and academic success in college. *Journal of Educational Psychology*, *94*(4), 820–826.

Strayhorn, T. L. (2012). *College students' sense of belonging: A key to educational success for all students*. New York: Routledge.

Tagg, J. (2003). *The learning paradigm college*. Bolton, MA: Anker Publishing.

U.S. Department of Education, National Center for Education Statistics. (2015). *The condition of education 2015 (NCES 2015–144), Institutional retention and graduation rates for undergraduate students*. Retrieved from http://nces.ed.gov/fastfacts/display.asp?id=40.

Walton, G. M., & Cohen, G. L. (2011). A brief social-belonging intervention improves academic and health outcomes of minority students. *Science*, *331*(6023), 1307–1310.

13

EXISTENTIAL MEANING IN LIFE AND POSITIVE PSYCHOLOGICAL FUNCTIONING

Andrew G. Christy, Grace Rivera, Kaiyuan Chen, and Joshua A. Hicks

> "...that entity which in its Being has this very Being as an issue..."
> *(Heidegger, trans. 1927/1962, p. 68)*

The existential philosophy of Martin Heidegger, articulated most completely in *Being and Time* (1962), situates the question of the meaning of Being as the most fundamental philosophical question. On Heidegger's analysis, the situation we find ourselves in as human beings necessitates an attitude of care or concern toward our own existence. Upon the realization that we are "thrown" into being in an essentially arbitrary set of life circumstances with a finite lifespan, determining how to live our lives becomes an urgent problem. In essence, we must find some way to make sense of our existence and navigate the circumstances we find ourselves in; our own being is an issue for us.

Thus, on the Heideggerian view, meaning is the fundamental problem of human existence, and all people must resolve this problem in some way in order to function optimally. Similar views are expressed by Albert Camus (1991) in his essay "The Myth of Sisyphus." The mythical figure of Sisyphus, whose punishment in the underworld is to every day push a boulder uphill only to have it inevitably roll to the bottom again at day's end, is presented as an analogy for the human condition. Camus implies that we are all in a Sisyphean situation—our existence is objectively absurd and meaningless, but even if we acknowledge this we must nonetheless commit ourselves to some kind of purpose in order to live and be happy.

Setting aside the issue of whether human existence is objectively meaningful versus meaningless, both of these philosophical perspectives (and many more not mentioned) converge on the idea that subjectively experienced meaning is of critical importance to our lives. Some sense of meaning is necessary even to merely "get by" in life, let alone to flourish as a person. It is this subjectively experienced sort of meaning that we address in this chapter.

Psychological research on the experience of meaning in life has flourished in recent years. The growth of this research area can be seen as part of the broader positive psychology movement (e.g. Seligman & Csikszentmihalyi, 2000), which seeks to understand the psychology of positive experiences and optimal human functioning. In this arena, meaning in life is often conceptualized as a subjective judgment (e.g. King & Hicks, 2009), and is usually measured with face-valid self-report instruments in which participants answer straightforward questions about how meaningful their lives are (e.g. the Meaning in Life Questionnaire; Steger, Frazier, Oishi, & Kaler, 2006). Research using these instruments suggests that most people judge their lives to be quite meaningful (Heintzelman & King, 2014), and, contrary to the ideas of many existential philosophers, they arrive at these conclusions via intuitive rather than deliberative processes (Heintzelman & King, 2013). In considering whether our lives are meaningful, we generally do not run down a checklist of criteria and determine which ones we meet and which ones we don't. Instead, judgments of meaning are the product of intuitive "gut feelings" and holistic impressions (e.g. King, Hicks, Krull, & Del Gaiso, 2006).

While these findings illustrate that most people find their own lives meaningful, they do little to help us understand what meaning is in the first place. To some extent, this may be appropriate given the highly subjective and intuitive nature of meaning in life (e.g. Heintzelman & King, 2013). However, certain common threads seem to run through most putative definitions of meaning, and these commonalities suggest that there is at least a rough consensus among scholars on the nature of this construct.

The first, and perhaps the most basic, component commonly ascribed to meaning is a cognitive component, sometimes labeled *coherence* (King, Heintzelman, & Ward, 2016). This component of meaning refers to the subjective experience that things make sense, that the world works in more or less orderly ways, and is organized into recognizable patterns. Most of the time, our experience has this quality of coherence; we are usually able to fit the objects, people, and events we encounter in life into some kind of comprehensible cognitive framework. This is in part because the world really does work according to consistent rules (i.e. laws of nature, such as gravity), which give rise to regularities and patterns that we become familiar with. Thus, to this extent, meaning in the sense of coherence really is an objective feature of the world that our cognitive systems are sensitive to and allow us to detect, and to predict as we become increasingly familiar with these experienced regularities (see also Heintzelman & King, 2014).

The second commonly proposed component of meaning is a motivational component, which can be labeled *purpose* (King et al., 2016). This component refers to having a subjective sense of direction for one's life, whether this involves a commitment to a single specific goal (a "calling" or "mission" for one's life) or a more general commitment to a way of living or approaching life. While a case can be made that coherence is an objective feature of reality, purpose seems to be a primarily subjective construction, a "merely psychological" construct. This fact in no way diminishes the importance of a subjectively experienced purpose in life; even if there is no fact of the matter about what one's purpose in life really is, people still benefit from experiencing purpose in their lives. Victor Frankl (1984) emphasizes purpose in his classic work *Man's Search for Meaning*, elaborating on Friedrich Nietzche's famous insight that, "He who has a why to live can bear almost any how." Among other benefits, a sense of purpose in life can help us persist in the face of adversity. If we have an overarching purpose in life, we are better able to transcend the particulars of any given situation in which we find ourselves, including situations as bleak and hellish as a concentration camp. It is purpose that enables Sisyphus to happily continue his eternal task.

The third and final component of meaning commonly identified by theorists is an evaluative component, sometimes labeled *significance* (King et al., 2016). This component refers to subjective appraisals of oneself and/or one's life as somehow mattering, as being worthwhile or important. As with purpose, this component of meaning can manifest in myriad forms, ranging from a grand sense of global or universal significance to a more circumscribed sense of significance (e.g. that one matters to one's family or to one's community). Also similar to purpose, and in contrast with coherence, it is not clear that subjectively experienced significance corresponds to any objective reality; we have no way of determining whether our lives really matter in any cosmic sense. Nevertheless, the subjective experience of significance remains critically important. Believing that our lives somehow matter gives us a reason to continue living. The nihilist who views his life as utterly insignificant will find that he has no good reason to do anything. We must view ourselves as having some modicum of value or worth in order to function at all (see also Baumeister, 1991).

In sum, most attempts to characterize the construct of existential meaning have included one or more of these three components. There is thus reasonable scholarly consensus that meaning consists in things making sense (coherence), in having a sense of direction (purpose) in one's life, and in feeling that one's life matters (significance), even if there are differences of opinion about which of these components is most important or fundamental (for a discussion of the distinction between a meaningful life and a happy life, see Baumeister, Vohs, Aaker, & Garbinsky, 2013). Having introduced the concept of existential meaning, we next review theory and research examining the causes of existential meaning.

The Antecedents of Existential Meaning

In this section, we will discuss the various factors that are believed to lead to the experience of meaning in life, and how these factors might work to enhance or detract from an individual's feeling that their life is meaningful. While our list is far from exhaustive, considering meaning may arise from many idiosyncratic sources, we believe these categories represent the most widely empirically examined sources of meaning (see Baumeister, 1991; Hicks & Routledge, 2013; Markman, Proulx, & Lindberg, 2013; Wong, 2013 reviews).

Positive Affect

One robust predictor of meaning in life is the extent to which one experiences positive emotions, both in daily life and in the moment (Hicks & King 2007; King et al., 2006). Although it is easy to imagine how feeling that your life is meaningful might lead to more happiness (see below), research reveals that the opposite is also true (e.g. King et al., 2006). For example, positive affect is a strong predictor of a person's global feelings of meaning in life (MIL), daily reports of MIL, and the extent to which they find their daily activities to be meaningful (e.g. Hicks & King, 2007, 2008, 2009). Inducing positive mood similarly enhances judgments of meaning in life. In fact, positive mood predicts meaning even after accounting for many related variables including self-esteem, religiosity, autonomy, competence, and relatedness to others (e.g. Hicks & King, 2009). Moreover, people who report low levels of other basic sources of meaning (e.g. religiosity; Hicks & King, 2007) still indicate that their lives are meaningful if they routinely experience positive emotions.

Although we know that positive affect accounts for a lot of the variance in meaning in life judgments, there are still many unanswered questions about this relationship. For example, it is unclear what mechanism underlies this relationship. Perhaps happy people are able to think more broadly, enabling them to better understand the "why" of their existence (e.g. Fredrickson, 1998). Alternatively, happiness may simply serve as a heuristic people use when making abstract global judgments about the quality of their existence, or it may produce other outcomes that are directly associated with meaning (e.g. friendships). Furthermore, research has yet to demonstrate if discrete positive (or negative) emotions uniquely influence meaning in life judgments. For instance, it is possible that the experience of awe has a greater impact on the experience of meaning in life than other discrete emotions, inasmuch as awe often involves encounters with stimuli that are vast and self-transcendent (e.g. the night sky, the ocean, a forest of redwoods), and that lead people to reevaluate their place in the "big picture" of existence (e.g. Piff, Dietze, Feinberg, Stancato, & Keltner, 2015).

Social Relationships

The need to belong is arguably the most important psychological need humans aim to satisfy (Baumeister & Leary, 1995). Humans belong to complex social networks consisting of immediate family members (e.g. parents and children), more distant relations (e.g. grandparents, cousins), romantic partners, friends, workers, and community members. In order to feel that one's life is meaningful, humans as complex social beings need frequent contact, support, and feelings of connection with others. As such, it is not surprising that social relationships represent a fundamental source of meaning according to the vast majority of meaning scholars. For instance, Deci and Ryan (1985) argue that an individual's satisfaction of the human need for social relatedness is one of three (the others being a need for autonomy and a need for competence) universal requirements for psychological well-being.

Many studies have shown a robust relationship between the perception that one has satisfying social relationships and psychological well-being, including meaning (e.g. Lambert et al., 2010). Relationships with family have been shown to serve as an important source of meaning for young adults (Lambert et al., 2010), as have romantic relationships, particularly in the first half of the human lifespan (Baum & Stewart, 1990). Social relationships enhance our sense of meaning in life, via perceptions of belongingness, more so than perceptions of social support or value (Lambert et al., 2013). Cross-cultural research lends confidence to the claim that the social relationships are valuable predictors of meaning, as relatedness need satisfaction has been linked to meaning in life in various cultures (Church et al., 2013).

Similarly, research on social ostracism indicates that when people are socially threatened (e.g. not included in friends' plans), they feel that their lives have less meaning (e.g. Van Beest & Williams, 2006). Both in the moment, exclusion and ongoing loneliness have been linked to reduced perceptions of meaning in life (Stillman et al., 2009). This effect was mediated by feelings of value, efficacy, purpose, and self-worth, which are argued to be essential for leading a meaningful life (see Baumeister, 1991).

Together, these complimentary bodies of literature suggest that social relationships play a key role in our perceptions, not only by providing us with social support and feelings of belonging and connectedness with others, but by protecting us from the negative effects of loneliness and isolation. Without social relationships, people might be particularly susceptible to feeling that their life is meaningless.

True Self-Knowledge

One of the most robust predictors of meaning in life is feeling in touch with your true self. Much research has been conducted investigating the role of true self-concept in the experience of psychological well-being. The true self is believed to be the part of the self that is real and unchanging, and it can be operationalized as people's beliefs about who they "really are" inside (Gergen, 1991). The true self is thought to be distinct from other aspects of the self, such as who one is, on an everyday basis (i.e. the behavioral or actual self) and who they hope to be (i.e. the ideal or future self) (Markus & Nurius, 1986). Compared to these other selves, research suggests that people place greater value and importance on the true self (e.g. Andersen & Williams, 1985; Kernis & Goldman, 2006), likely because people use the contents of their true selves as a sort of "philosophical guide" to help inform them about which activities, goals, and relationships are particularly important and worthy pursuits (Schlegel, Hicks, Arndt, & King, 2009; see also Bellah, Madsen, Sullivan, Swindler, & Tipton, 1985). Consequently, behaviors and decisions that are seen to be in line with one's true self are deemed particularly valuable specifically *because* of their relationship to the true self (e.g. Waterman, 1984).

Recent research has illuminated the importance of knowing your true self and feeling that you live life in accordance with your true self when making judgments about existential meaning (Schlegel et al., 2009; Schlegel & Hicks, 2011). Specifically, true self-knowledge has consistently been found to predict meaning in life over and above mood, self-esteem, and actual self-knowledge (Schlegel et al., 2011). Additionally, those who can quickly and easily access knowledge about the true self report heightened levels of meaning (Schlegel et al., 2009). A theoretical explanation for the relationship between true self-knowledge and meaning is that contemplating one's true self as a guide to life (using it as a compass for decisions and living in accordance with one's core values) can imbue life with meaning (for a review, see Schlegel & Hicks, 2011). Similarly, efforts to distinguish a meaningful life from merely a happy life have identified concerns related to self-expression and identity as key factors in this difference (Baumeister et al., 2013).

Religion

Religious beliefs are often viewed as a key source of existential meaning, as they provide a framework of values and expectations about life, and couch one's individual existence within a larger cosmic context (e.g. Batson & Stocks, 2005). Religion can shape how people understand both their own self and their relation to the world by functioning as a meaning-making system or schema (McIntosh, 1995; Park, 2005), and serving as a value base that guides them to what is moral, provides a sense of purpose, and outlines a divine coherent plan that leads people to believe that everything happens for a reason (Baumeister, 1991). In a similar way, religion may help people derive deeper meaning in life by helping make sense of pain and suffering in the world, as well as the inevitability of death.

Many lines of research support the claim that religious beliefs are associated with meaning in life (e.g. Steger & Frazier, 2005). Research also suggests that the relationship between religiosity and meaning can be moderated by individual differences, such as one's cognitive capacity to take the perspectives of others (Routledge, Roylance, & Abeyta, 2016). A high capacity for this type of perspective, taken in combination with higher levels of religiosity, predicted the greatest reports of meaning in life, which Routledge and colleagues (2016) explain might likely be due to a heightened ability to envision powerful and immortal supernatural agents watching over them and imbuing their life with purpose and value.

Mortality Awareness

When thinking about the meaning of life, it is hard not to wonder about life's darker counterpart, the awareness that life eventually comes to an end. While mortality awareness may make the potential meaninglessness of one's existence salient, it might also facilitate a richer sense of meaning in life. In fact, many existential philosophers argue that the creation of a meaningful existence is contingent upon the acknowledgment of one's mortality. Supporting these claims, research on near death experiences suggests that some people report becoming more spiritual and finding more meaning in life after brushes with death (e.g. Kinnier, Tribbensee, Rose, & Vaughan, 2001). Furthermore, recent research demonstrates that the ability to vividly recall an experience that prompted individuals to contemplate their mortality was strongly associated with self-reports of meaning in life (Seto, Hicks, Vess, & Geraci, 2016).

In social psychology, terror management theory (e.g. Greenberg et al., 1990) posits that mortality awareness triggers a need to affirm that one's life is meaningful. Although some research has shown that salient thoughts of mortality increase self-reports of meaning in life (e.g. King, Hicks, & Abdelkhalik, 2009), other studies suggest that this relationship is more nuanced. For example, Vess, Routledge, Landau, and Arndt (2009) showed that people high in a dispositional desire for structured knowledge reported higher levels of meaning in life after thinking about death, whereas people low in need for structure demonstrated decreased levels of meaning. Furthermore, research also shows that reminders of death *decrease* feelings of meaning in life for those who are close to completing a long-term goal, such as graduating from a PhD program (Vess, Rogers, Routledge, & Hicks, 2016). While individual need for structure and goal progress are not the only factors that may moderate the relationship between death and meaning, they provide a clear example of how reminders of death can have a nuanced effect on people's perceptions of meaning in life (see also Cozzolino, 2006).

In this section, we discussed some of the most common sources of meaning highlighted in the literature. Of course, the experience of meaning in life is also believed to serve a function. That is, meaning in life is also viewed as a predictor of many important outcomes. In the next section, we will examine the outcomes that are theorized to derive from meaning in life.

The Consequences of Experiencing Meaning in Life

As previously mentioned, meaning in life is often viewed as a cornerstone of psychological well-being (see Hicks & Routledge, 2013; Markman et al., 2013; Steger, 2013). Research supports this idea by showing a robust and consistent link between meaning and psychological well-being across various measures and samples (e.g. Ho, Cheung, & Cheung, 2010; Krause, 2003; Noonan & Tennstedt, 1997; Reker, Peacock, & Wong, 1987; Zika & Chamberlain, 1992). For example, self-reports of meaning in life are associated with levels of life satisfaction (Krause, 2003; O'Connor & Vallerand, 1998; Steger & Kashdan, 2007), vitality (Steger et al., 2006), a higher level of global happiness (Debats, 1996; Ryff & Keyes, 1995; Steger, Kawabata, Shimai, & Otake, 2008), and less depression (e.g. Zika & Chamberlain, 1992), just to name a few of these outcomes.

In addition, existential meaning may contribute to the development of a healthy and positive self-concept. According to research on narrative theory (e.g. Bauer, McAdams, & Pals, 2008; McLean & Fournier, 2008), the self is represented by a life story articulated by both past and present experiences. This perspective implies that a psychologically healthy self would have successfully integrated life experiences into a coherent narrative (Deci & Ryan, 1985). In a real sense, meaning helps people construct a more cohesive life story by fostering stronger connections between their past and present experiences with their future-oriented desires and hopes. Therefore, existential meaning should relate to self-understanding as people derive a sense of continuity over their experiences. Indeed, several studies have documented the link of meaning to self-esteem (Debats, 1996; O'Connor & Vallerand, 1998; Reker, 1977; Ryff, 1989; Shek, 1992; Steger et al., 2006), self-actualization (Ebersole & Humphreys, 1991), self-confidence (Crumbaugh, Raphael, & Shrader, 1970), and self-empowering traits such as self-control (Garfield, 1973), internal locus of control (Reker, 1977), ego resiliency (Tryon & Radzin, 1972), self-concept clarity and self-understanding (Schlegel et al., 2009, 2011), and personal growth (Ryff, 1989; Steger, Kashdan, Sullivan, & Lorentz, 2008).

Research and theory also suggests that the experience of meaning contributes to physical health. For instance, it has been found that people with a high level of meaning are less likely to report physical illnesses (e.g. Brassai, Piko, & Steger, 2011). As a forbear in the field, Frankl (1984) famously made the personal observation that those without a purpose were most likely to perish in the Nazi concentration camps. While it is impossible to substantiate this claim, recent research (e.g. Krause, 2009) has demonstrated a link between feelings of purpose and mortality rates showing that adults with a strong sense of purpose lived longer and experienced fewer mortality risks. In fact, Hill and Turiano (2014) demonstrated how this effect persists after controlling for many relevant covariates, including age, sex, race, education level, relationship quality, and positive and negative affect.

Finally, existential meaning may also be beneficial during difficult experiences (Frankl, 1984). The trauma literature has shown that a sense of meaning can sometimes lead to more effective psychological adjustment following stressful events (e.g. Park & Folkman, 1997). Traumatic events can shatter people's basic assumptions that the world is structured with order, that they are worthwhile beings with some control over the life outcomes they experience (Janoff-Bulman, 1989), leading to negative emotions, distress, and rumination (e.g. Pennebaker, 1990). While this eventually renders people vulnerable to physical or mental health issues (e.g. Lehman, Wortman, & Williams, 1987), existential meaning may help mitigate these effects considering it is related to more effective coping, positive emotional regulation, and optimism toward the future (e.g. Mascaro & Rosen, 2006), as well as a more positive perception of the world and toward life in general (Sharpe & Viney, 1973). These mechanisms may account for why individuals with a strong sense of meaning in life are less likely to exhibit depression and post-traumatic stress disorder symptoms (e.g. Crumbaugh & Maholick, 1964).

Taken together these findings suggest that existential meaning is essential for healthy psychological functioning. Next, we address some potential applications aimed at enhancing the experience of meaning in life.

Applications

Given the potential importance between meaning in life and psychological and physical health, it is crucial to examine the efficacy of interventions aimed at enhancing perceptions of meaning. For instance, longitudinal studies (e.g. Hill & Turiano, 2014) suggest meaning in life clearly predicts health (both mental and physical) and mortality. If global meaning in life indeed has a casual influence on these important outcomes, it may be worthwhile to develop large-scale interventions aimed specifically at augmenting one's sense of meaning *before* people develop chronic illnesses. While we have noted that it may be difficult to directly intervene in meaning in life itself, interventions might be developed to target some of the precursors to meaning that we have identified previously, such as self-knowledge or feelings of belongingness. If these precursor variables can be promoted via intervention, this in turn should foster enhanced meaning in life. If meaning does indeed play a causal role in producing mental and physical health, the ultimate effect of such interventions should be to promote positive outcomes (e.g. longevity, life satisfaction) and reduce negative outcomes (e.g. mortality, illness, depression).

In addition to promoting health and well-being, meaning in life interventions might also be used to help students maintain motivation in the classroom (e.g. Kelly, Davis, Kim, Tang, & Hicks, 2016; Yeager et al., 2014). Recently, research found that asking students to think about "why" it is important to do well in school, compared to thinking about "how" one does well in school, led to increased perceptions of academic goal importance and self-reported motivation to pursue those goals (Kelly et al., 2016), suggesting that understanding the higher-order meaning behind one's actions may lead to more successful goal pursuit. As such, it may be important, for example, for more educators to develop college or high school courses aimed at helping students understand why it is important to do well in the classroom.

Future Directions

Although we believe cultivating the experience of meaning in life may lead to many positive outcomes, we acknowledge that this claim may be overstated, given the lack of experimental and longitudinal research examining the outcomes of meaning. As such, understanding if and why meaning in life directly contributes the aforementioned outcomes should be a central aim of future research. In this vein, we next turn to some possible explanations for the relationship between meaning in life and well-being.

Meaning in Life Revisited: A Component of, Contributor to, or Mere Indicator of Well-Being?

There are a few primary ways of understanding where meaning fits in the context of well-being. First, we may understand meaning in and of itself as (at least partially) constitutive of well-being. Alternatively, we may view meaning as a precursor or contributor to well-being, but not as a part of well-being *per se*. Finally, it may be that meaning is simply an indicator of well-being, but is itself neither a component of well-being nor a contributor to well-being. In the following, we elaborate on each of these views and their implications.

Meaning as Constitutive of Well-Being

The view that meaning is part of well-being is widespread among psychologists and laypeople alike. Positive psychologists commonly distinguish between hedonic and eudaimonic well-being (e.g. Ryan & Deci, 2001). Hedonic well-being entails experiencing pleasure or positive affect, the absence of pain or negative affect, and being generally satisfied with one's life. Eudaimonic well-being, on the other hand, entails personal growth toward the realization of one's potential and engagement in purpose-driven, personally meaningful activities. Psychologists who accept the hedonic/eudaimonic binary, thus regard meaning as its own special type of well-being, something distinct from simply feeling good and being satisfied. This mirrors the intuitions of laypeople, who see subjective happiness (i.e. hedonic well-being) and meaning, as making independent contributions to an overall "good life" (King & Napa, 1998).

Meaning as a Precursor to Well-Being

If meaning is not itself a kind of, or a part of, well-being, perhaps meaning is at least conducive to well-being. That is, people who experience meaning in their lives may have an easier time achieving well-being for a variety of reasons. Perhaps the experience of meaning signals the presence of predictability and regularity in one's environment (Heintzelman & King, 2014), indicating that all is well and that one's pre-existing sense-making frameworks are functioning adequately and can continue to be relied upon. Interruptions in this experience may, in turn, signal either a breakdown in environmental regularity or that one's sense-making frameworks are inadequate and in need of revision. In this way, the experience of meaning may be adaptive, facilitating our ability to successfully navigate the environment and achieve our needs and goals, thereby fostering well-being.

Meaning as an Epiphenomenal Indicator of Well-Being

A final possibility is that meaning is merely a non-functional correlate of well-being, and is neither a constituent of, nor a contributor to, well-being. We do not expect this to be a popular view among psychologists, particularly those who study meaning themselves, but it is nonetheless a view worth presenting briefly. On this view, meaning is an epiphenomenon, a byproduct of real well-being that has no causal or explanatory power unto itself. If this is the case, measures of meaning may be reliable indicators of well-being, but they are not measuring a construct that is meaningfully distinct from general well-being. In other words, we may experience meaning when we are in a good mood, when we are generally satisfied with our lives, when we feel close to others, and so on, but the experience of meaning doesn't do anything for us over and above these more basic experiences. On this view, whatever functional roles we might be tempted to ascribe to meaning can be explained away, reduced down to the functions of some more basic process(es).

Conclusion

Considerable progress has been made in the psychology of existential meaning. We have learned a great deal about the experiences, beliefs, and actions that give rise to meaning, as well as the many benefits to health, well-being, and motivation that seem to accrue when people experience meaning in their lives. The available evidence suggests that meaning is an important psychological variable, whether we consider it to be a kind of well-being itself or a stepping-stone to well-being. We eagerly anticipate the next generation of research on meaning, which promises to clarify our understanding of this construct and its role in our psychology and apply this understanding in ways that are broadly beneficial to human well-being.

References

Andersen, S. M., & Williams, M. (1985). Cognitive/affective reactions in the improvement of self-esteem: When thoughts and feelings make a difference. *Journal of Personality and Social Psychology, 49*(4), 1086.

Batson, C. D., and Stocks, E. L. (2005) Religion and Prejudice. In *On the Nature of Prejudice: Fifty Years after Allport* (eds J. F. Dovidio, P. Glick, and L. A. Rudman), Oxford: Blackwell Publishing Ltd.

Bauer, J. J., McAdams, D. P., & Pals, J. L. (2008). Narrative identity and eudaimonic well-being. *Journal of Happiness Studies, 9*(1), 81–104.

Baum, S. K., & Stewart Jr., R. B. (1990). Sources of meaning through the lifespan. *Psychological Reports, 67*(1), 3–14.

Baumeister, R. F. (1991). *Meanings of life.* New York: Guilford.

Baumeister, R. F., & Leary, M. R. (1995). The need to belong: Desire for interpersonal attachments as a fundamental human motivation. *Psychological Bulletin, 117*(3), 497.

Baumeister, R. F., Vohs, K. D., Aaker, J. L., & Garbinsky, E. N. (2013). Some key differences between a happy life and a meaningful life. *The Journal of Positive Psychology, 8*(6), 505–516.

Bellah, R. N., Madsen, R., Sullivan, W. M., Swindler, A., & Tipton, S. M. (1985). *Habits of the heart: Individualism and commitment in American life.* Berkeley, CA: University of California Press.

Brassai, L., Piko, B. F., & Steger, M. F. (2011). Meaning in life: Is it a protective factor for adolescents' psychological health? *International Journal of Behavioral Medicine, 18*(1), 44–51.

Camus, A. (1991). *The myth of Sisyphus and other essays.* (J. O'Brien, Trans.). New York: Vintage Books. (Original work published in 1942).

Church, A. T., Katigbak, M. S., Locke, K. D., Zhang, H., Shen, J., de Jesús Vargas-Flores, J., ... & Mastor, K. A. (2013). Need satisfaction and well-being: Testing self-determination theory in eight cultures. *Journal of Cross-Cultural Psychology, 44*(4), 507–534.

Cozzolino, P. J. (2006). Death contemplation, growth, and defense: Converging evidence of dual-existential systems? *Psychological Inquiry, 17*(4), 278–287.

Crumbaugh, J. C., & Maholick, L. T. (1964). An experimental study in existentialism: The psychometric approach to Frankl's concept of noogenic neurosis. *Journal of Clinical Psychology, 20*(2), 200–207.

Crumbaugh, J., Raphael, M., & Shrader, R. R. (1970). Frankl's will to meaning in a religious order. *Journal of Clinical Psychology, 26*, 206–207.

Debats, D. L. (1996). Meaning in life: Clinical relevance and predictive power. *British Journal of Clinical Psychology, 35*(4), 503–516.

Deci, E. L., & Ryan, R. M. (1985). The general causality orientations scale: Self-determination in personality. *Journal of Research in Personality, 19*(2), 109–134.

Ebersole, P., & Humphreys, P. (1991). The short index of self-actualization and purpose in life. *Psychological Reports, 69*(2), 550–550.

Frankl, V. E. (1984). *Man's search for meaning: An introduction to logotherapy.* (I. Lasch Trans.) New York: Touchstone.

Fredrickson, B. L. (1998). What good are positive emotions? *Review of General Psychology, 2*(3), 300–319.

Garfield, C. A. (1973). A psychometric and clinical investigation of Frankl's concept of existential vacuum and of anomia. *Psychiatry, 36*(4), 396–408.

Gergen, K. J. (1991). *The saturated self: Dilemmas of identity in contemporary life*. New York: Basic Books.

Greenberg, J., Pyszczynski, T., Solomon, S., Rosenblatt, A., Veeder, M., Kirkland, S., & Lyon, D. (1990). Evidence for terror management theory II: The effects of mortality salience on reactions to those who threaten or bolster the cultural worldview. *Journal of Personality and Social Psychology, 58*(2), 308–318.

Heidegger, M. (1962). *Being and time* (J. Macquarrie & E. Robinson, Trans.). New York: Harper & Row. (Original work published in 1927).

Heintzelman, S. J., & King, L. A. (2013). On knowing more than we can tell: Intuitive processes and the experience of meaning. *The Journal of Positive Psychology, 8*(6), 471–482.

Heintzelman, S. J., & King, L. A. (2014). Life is pretty meaningful. *American Psychologist, 69*, 561–574.

Hicks, J. A., & King, L. A. (2007). Meaning in life and seeing the big picture: Positive affect and global focus. *Cognition and Emotion, 21*(7), 1577–1584.

Hicks, J. A., & King, L. A. (2008). Religious commitment and positive mood as information about meaning in life. *Journal of Research in Personality, 42*(1), 43–57.

Hicks, J. A., & King, L. A. (2009). Positive mood and social relatedness as information about meaning in life. *The Journal of Positive Psychology, 4*(6), 471–482.

Hicks, J. A., & Routledge, C. (Eds.). (2013). *The experience of meaning in life: Classical perspectives, emerging themes, and controversies*. New York: Springer Press.

Hill, P. L., & Turiano, N. A. (2014). Purpose in life as a predictor of mortality across adulthood. *Psychological Science, 25*(7), 1482–1486.

Ho, M. Y., Cheung, F. M., & Cheung, S. F. (2010). The role of meaning in life and optimism in promoting well-being. *Personality and Individual Differences, 48*(5), 658–663.

Janoff-Bulman, R. (1989). Assumptive worlds and the stress of traumatic events: Applications of the schema construct. *Social Cognition, 7*(2), 113–136.

Kelly, N. J., Davis, W. E., Kim, J., Tang, D., & Hicks, J. A. (2016). Motivating the academic mind: Abstract construal of academic goals enhances motivation. *Motivation and Emotion, 42*, 193–202.

Kernis, M. H., & Goldman, B. M. (2006). A multicomponent conceptualization of authenticity: Theory and research. *Advances in Experimental Social Psychology, 38*, 283–357.

King, L. A., Heintzelman, S. J., & Ward, S. J. (2016). Beyond the search for meaning: A contemporary science of the experience of meaning in life. *Current Directions in Psychological Science, 25*(4), 211–216.

King, L. A., & Hicks, J. A. (2009). Detecting and constructing meaning in life events. *The Journal of Positive Psychology, 4*(5), 317–330.

King, L. A., Hicks, J. A., & Abdelkhalik, J. (2009). Death, life, scarcity, and value: An alternative perspective on the meaning of death. *Psychological Science, 20*(12), 1459–1462.

King, L. A., Hicks, J. A., Krull, J. L., & Del Gaiso, A. K. (2006). Positive affect and the experience of meaning in life. *Journal of Personality and Social Psychology, 90*(1), 179.

King, L. A., & Napa, C. K. (1998). What makes a life good? *Journal of Personality and Social Psychology, 75*(1), 156.

Kinnier, R. T., Tribbensee, N. E., Rose, C. A., & Vaughan, S. M. (2001). In the final analysis: More wisdom from people who have faced death. *Journal of Counseling & Development, 79*(2), 171–177.

Krause, N. (2003). Religious meaning and subjective well-being in late life. *The Journals of Gerontology Series B: Psychological Sciences and Social Sciences, 58*(3), S160–S170.

Krause, N. (2009). Meaning in life and mortality. *The Journals of Gerontology Series B: Psychological Sciences and Social Sciences, 64*(4), 517–527.

Lambert, N. M., Stillman, T. F., Baumeister, R. F., Fincham, F. D., Hicks, J. A., & Graham, S. M. (2010). Family as a salient source of meaning in young adulthood. *The Journal of Positive Psychology, 5*(5), 367–376.

Lambert, N. M., Stillman, T. F., Hicks, J. A., Kamble, S., Baumeister, R. F., & Fincham, F. D. (2013). To belong is to matter: Sense of belonging enhances meaning in life. *Personality and Social Psychology Bulletin, 39*(11), 1418–1427.

Lehman, D. R., Wortman, C. B., & Williams, A. F. (1987). Long-term effects of losing a spouse or child in a motor vehicle crash. *Journal of Personality and Social Psychology, 52*(1), 218–231.

Markman, K. D., Proulx, T. E., & Lindberg, M. J. (2013). *The psychology of meaning.* Washington, DC: American Psychological Association.

Markus, H., & Nurius, P. (1986). Possible selves. *American Psychologist, 41*(9), 954.

Mascaro, N., & Rosen, D. H. (2006). The role of existential meaning as a buffer against stress. *Journal of Humanistic Psychology, 46*(2), 168–190.

McIntosh, D. N. (1995). Religion-as-schema, with implications for the relation between religion and coping. *The International Journal for the Psychology of Religion, 5*(1), 1–16.

McLean, K. C., & Fournier, M. A. (2008). The content and processes of autobiographical reasoning in narrative identity. *Journal of Research in Personality, 42*(3), 527–545.

Noonan, A. E., & Tennstedt, S. L. (1997). Meaning in caregiving and its contribution to caregiver well-being. *The Gerontologist, 37*(6), 785–794.

O'Connor, B. P., & Vallerand, R. J. (1998). Psychological adjustment variables as predictors of mortality among nursing home residents. *Psychology and Aging, 13*(3), 368.

Park, C. L. (2005). Religion as a meaning-making framework in coping with life stress. *Journal of Social Issues, 61*(4), 707–729.

Park, C. L., & Folkman, S. (1997). Meaning in the context of stress and coping. *Review of General Psychology, 1*(2), 115.

Pennebaker, J. W. (1990). *Opening up: The healing power of confiding in others.* New York: Guilford Press.

Piff, P. K., Dietze, P., Feinberg, M., Stancato, D. M., & Keltner, D. (2015). Awe, the small self, and prosocial behavior. *Journal of Personality and Social Psychology, 108,* 883–899.

Reker, G. T. (1977). The purpose-in-life test in an inmate population: An empirical investigation. *Journal of Clinical Psychology, 33*(3), 688–693.

Reker, G. T., Peacock, E. J., & Wong, P. T. (1987). Meaning and purpose in life and well-being: A life-span perspective. *Journal of Gerontology, 42*(1), 44–49.

Routledge, C., Roylance, C., & Abeyta, A. A. (2016). Further exploring the link between religion and existential health: The effects of religiosity and trait differences in mentalizing on indicators of meaning in life. *Journal of Religion and Health, 56*(2), 604–613.

Ryan, R. M., & Deci, E. L. (2001). On happiness and human potentials: A review of research on hedonic and eudaimonic well-being. *Annual Review of Psychology, 52*(1), 141–166.

Ryff, C. D. (1989). Happiness is everything, or is it? Explorations on the meaning of psychological well-being. *Journal of Personality and Social Psychology, 57*(6), 1069.

Ryff, C. D., & Keyes, C. L. M. (1995). The structure of psychological well-being revisited. *Journal of Personality and Social Psychology, 69*(4), 719.

Schlegel, R. J., & Hicks, J. A. (2011). The true self and psychological health: Emerging evidence and future directions. *Social and Personality Psychology Compass, 5*(12), 989–1003.

Schlegel, R. J., Hicks, J. A., Arndt, J., & King, L. A. (2009). Thine own self: True self-concept accessibility and meaning in life. *Journal of Personality and Social Psychology, 96*(2), 473.

Seligman, M. E., & Csikszentmihalyi, M. (2000). Special issue: Positive psychology. *American Psychologist, 55*(1), 5–14.

Seto, E., Hicks, J. A., Vess, M. & Geraci, L. (2016). The association between vivid thoughts of death and authenticity. *Motivation and Emotion, 40*(4), 520–540.

Sharpe, D., & Viney, L. L. (1973). Weltanschauung and the purpose-in-life test. *Journal of Clinical Psychology, 29*(4), 489–491.

Shek, D. T. (1992). Meaning in life and psychological well-being: An empirical study using the Chinese version of the purpose in life questionnaire. *The Journal of Genetic Psychology, 153*(2), 185–200.

Steger, M. F. (2013). *Wrestling with our better selves: The search for meaning in life.* Washington, DC: American Psychological Association.

Steger, M. F., & Frazier, P. (2005). Meaning in life: One link in the chain from religiousness to well-being. *Journal of Counseling Psychology, 52*(4), 574.

Steger, M. F., Frazier, P., Oishi, S., & Kaler, M. (2006). The meaning in life questionnaire: Assessing the presence of and search for meaning in life. *Journal of Counseling Psychology, 53*(1), 80.

Steger, M. F., & Kashdan, T. B. (2007). Stability and specificity of meaning in life and life satisfaction over one year. *Journal of Happiness Studies, 8*(2), 161–179.

Steger, M. F., Kashdan, T. B., Sullivan, B. A., & Lorentz, D. (2008). Understanding the search for meaning in life: Personality, cognitive style, and the dynamic between seeking and experiencing meaning. *Journal of Personality, 76*(2), 199–228.

Steger, M. F., Kawabata, Y., Shimai, S., & Otake, K. (2008). The meaningful life in Japan and the United States: Levels and correlates of meaning in life. *Journal of Research in Personality, 42*(3), 660–678.

Stillman, T. F., Baumeister, R. F., Lambert, N. M., Crescioni, A. W., DeWall, C. N., & Fincham, F. D. (2009). Alone and without purpose: Life loses meaning following social exclusion. *Journal of Experimental Social Psychology, 45*(4), 686–694.

Tryon, W. W., & Radzin, A. B. (1972). Purpose-in-life as a function of ego resiliency, dogmatism and biographical variables. *Journal of Clinical Psychology, 28*(4), 544–545.

Van Beest, I., & Williams, K. D. (2006). When inclusion costs and ostracism pays, ostracism still hurts. *Journal of Personality and Social Psychology, 91*(5), 918.

Vess, M., Rogers, R., Routledge, C., & Hicks, J. A. (2016). When being far away is good: Exploring how mortality salience, regulatory mode, and goal progress affect judgments of meaning in life. *European Journal of Social Psychology, 47*(1), 82–91.

Vess, M., Routledge, C., Landau, M. J., & Arndt, J. (2009). The dynamics of death and meaning: The effects of death-relevant cognitions and personal need for structure on perceptions of meaning in life. *Journal of Personality and Social Psychology*, *97*(4), 728.

Waterman, A. S. (1984). Identity formation: Discovery or creation? *The Journal of Early Adolescence*, *4*(4), 329–341.

Wong, P. T. P. (2013). *The human quest for meaning: Theories, research, and applications* (2nd ed.). New York: Routledge.

Yeager, D. S., Henderson, M. D., Paunesku, D., Walton, G. M., D'Mello, S., Spitzer, B. J., & Duckworth, A. L. (2014). Boring but important: A self-transcendent purpose for learning fosters academic self-regulation. *Journal of Personality and Social Psychology*, *107*(4), 559.

Zika, S., & Chamberlain, K. (1992). On the relation between meaning in life and psychological well-being. *British Journal of Psychology*, *83*(1), 133–145.

14

A POSITIVE PSYCHOLOGY FOR DISABILITY AND REHABILITATION

Some Recent Advances

Dana S. Dunn

> A person's healthy, physical and mental attributes can become a basis for alleviating difficulties as well as providing a source of gratification and enrichment of life. Special care must be taken to avoid overemphasis on the pathologic that leaves one inadequately sensitized to stabilizing and maturity inducing factors. Those attributes of the person that are healthy and promising must be supported and developed.
>
> *(Beatrice A. Wright, 1972, p. 39)*

Unlike many subfields of psychology, rehabilitation psychology has always relied on positive perspectives for theory and practice. Although a declared and articulated positive psychology of disability and rehabilitation may be new (e.g. Dunn & Brody, 2008; Dunn & Dougherty, 2005; Ehde, 2010; Wehmeyer, 2013), the concepts and constructs underlying much of it are not (Shogren, 2013). Rehabilitation professionals historically assumed that disabled clients' mental and physical attributes—including personality characteristics and individual strengths—can and should be identified and used to promote health, welfare, choice, independence, life satisfaction, functional abilities, and social role participation during and after the rehabilitation process.

Beatrice A. Wright, a Lewinian social psychologist and one of the founders of rehabilitation psychology, avoided emphasizing pathology by focusing on existing or potential positive qualities found among people with disabilities (e.g. Wright, 1983). Following Lewin (1935), Wright also argued that disability is a person x situation interaction, the result of social, psychological, and physical forces found in the perceived and experienced environment (e.g. attitudes, lack of accessible entries) and not solely a characteristic of people with disabilities themselves (see also Dunn, 2011).

Indeed, rehabilitation psychology's positive perspectives on both congenital and acquired disability have recently been codified (see Table 14.1). These foundational principles are designed to help professionals and laypersons better understand the experience of disability and how to meaningfully engage with people with disabilities (PWDs; Dunn, Ehde, & Wegener, 2016). These principles also inform much of the research reviewed in this chapter. To begin, we outline positive psychology's three levels of analysis in terms of disability and rehabilitation. Research related to each level is then discussed in some detail, followed by a closing section on the importance of intentional activities.

TABLE 14.1 Foundational Principles of Rehabilitation Psychology

The person–environment relation	Attributions about people with disabilities tend to focus on presumed dispositional rather than available situational characteristics. Environmental constraints usually matter more than personality factors to living with a disability.
The insider–outsider distinction	People with disabilities (insiders) know what life with a chronic condition is like (e.g. sometimes challenging but usually manageable) whereas casual observers (outsiders) who lack relevant experience presume that disability is defining, all encompassing, and decidedly negative.
Adjustment to disability	Coping with a disability or chronic illness is an ongoing dynamic process, one dependent on making constructive changes to the social and the physical environment.
Psychosocial assets	People with disabilities possess or can acquire personal or psychological qualities that can ameliorate challenges posed by disability and also enrich daily living.
Self-perception of bodily states	Experience of bodily states (e.g. pain, fatigue, distress) is based on people's perceptions of the phenomena, not exclusively the actual sensations. Changing attitudes, expectations, or environmental conditions can constructively alter perceptions.
Human dignity	Regardless of the source or severity of a disability or chronic health condition, all people deserve respect, encouragement, and to be treated with dignity.

Source: Table 1 in Dunn, Ehde, & Wegener (2016, p. 2).

Positive Psychology and Disability

As originally formulated, positive psychology relied on three levels of analysis for advancing prevention and treatment, and enhancing daily life—positive subjective states, positive individual traits, and positive groups and institutions (e.g. Seligman & Csikszentmihalyi, 2000). *Positive subjective states* are comprised of people's personal construals of their lives, including future perspectives (e.g. hope, optimism), present experiences (e.g. positive emotions, flow), and past reflections (e.g. life satisfaction, well-being). Such personal appraisals are presumed to be relatively steady and consistent across time; however, they can be disrupted by significant life events or critical incidents, including the onset of disability (Lucas, 2007a, 2007b). Following a disabling event, a person with a disability's subjective perspective is frequently a significant influence on his or her capacity to respond favorably, regain strength, display resilience, and adjust to the situation (Dunn, Uswatte, & Elliott, in press; Elliott, Kurylo, & Rivera, 2002).

In turn, *positive individual traits* represent a role for personality variables linked to responding adaptively to disability. Such traits include character strengths and virtues (Peterson & Seligman, 2004) such as persistence, courage, self-regulation, and transcendence. PWDs should be encouraged to identify, maintain, and rely on existing strengths (Wright & Lopez, 2009) or to cultivate new ones that encourage psychological or physical recovery. Dunn and Dougherty (2005) suggested that self- or other assessments of strengths and abilities could be examined in concert with standard coping and depression measures, as a means for attaining a detailed and comprehensive view of a person with a disability's personality and emotional responses.

Positive groups and institutions constitute the third level of analysis, one that has generated less scholarly inquiry than the other two areas in positive psychology generally and that focused on disability and rehabilitation issues specifically. In effect, what group factors or organizational qualities afford PWDs the chance to thrive in the workplace, schools, the community, and related venues? How can the good works performed by local institutions, charities, and public works, among others, help citizens, including disabled ones, to flourish? Naturally, a group level of analysis linked to disability should consider the beneficial impact of legislation aimed at PWDs (e.g. the Americans with Disabilities Act), as well as the socio-political activism of the disability rights movement (e.g. Charlton, 1998; Johnson, 2005).

We now review recent, selected research related to the three levels of analysis, beginning with positive subjective states.

Positive Subjective States

One of the key issues regarding positive subjective states and disability is the degree to which the latter affects the former; for example, how the onset of disability due to accident or other trauma affects levels of subjective well-being (SWB) and their accustomed set point. There is clear evidence that the usual "hedonic adaptation" to events (Brickman & Campbell, 1971)—whether good or bad—may not happen with disability (Anusic, Yap, & Lucas, 2014; Diener, 2008; Diener, Lucas, & Scollon, 2006). Research involving people with spinal cord injuries, for example, finds that, compared to the general population, they have lower levels of self-reported happiness that tends to mirror the severity of their acquired disabilities (e.g. Dijkers, 2005; Lucas, 2007a, 2007b). It is likely that depression or depressive symptoms, common secondary complications associated with a spinal cord injury, influence this particular outcome (Elliott & Kennedy, 2004).

Low levels of SWB among people with disabilities are well documented in European nations. Using data from the European Social Survey, van Campen and van Santvoort (2013) observed that PWDs from 21 European countries reported lower SWB than their non-disabled counterparts; however, gaps between these groups were lower among citizens of Eastern European nations. What factors seem to be associated with lower SWB among PWDs in these data? The researchers found that level (severity) of disability, socio-economic status, and work participation had little impact. Instead, personal resources (or the lack thereof) were associated with lower SWB. Personal resources include supportive relationships, social cohesion, vitality, and a variety of self-reported items (e.g. optimism, resilience, autonomy, engagement, meaning, and purpose, among others). As this research was cross-sectional rather than longitudinal, causality could not be determined. Still, as the researchers suggest, ideas for policy and practice might be obtained if targeted qualitative interviews were linked to the study's quantitative findings.

Recently, Smedema (2014) applied the concept of core self-evaluations (CSEs) to understanding the state of well-being among persons with disabilities. CSEs are comprised of those overarching perceptions people hold regarding their self-worth and capabilities as people (Judge, Locke, Durham, & Kluger, 1998). Linked to self-concept, CSEs represent a higher order construct that entails familiar personality traits and processes, including general self-efficacy, self-esteem, emotional stability, and locus of control. In effect, people who view themselves as inherently competent and good will respond more effectively to life challenges (disability onset) than those who feel they are incompetent or lack a strong sense of self-worth. The presence of a positive or a negative "frame," then, can influence how much effort a person puts into the rehabilitative process.

According to Smedema (2014), disabled persons with a higher level of CSE should be able to better navigate the demands and aftermath of a disabling experience than those with lower levels of CSE. Although no specific research linking CSEs to disability appears in the published literature, Smedema cites the four CSE traits noted above (self-esteem, self-efficacy, locus of control, and emotional stability—i.e. low neuroticism), as being related to well-being in PWDs. In fact, one theoretical advantage of examining CSE among persons with disabilities may be to more clearly operationalize personal factors (e.g. individual characteristics, competencies) as predictors of well-being linked to disability (see also Chan, Tarvydas, Blalock, Strauser, & Atkins, 2009). At present, empirical efforts should be directed toward understanding whether and how CSEs are linked to positive subjective states among PWDs.

Traits: Individual Levels of Analysis

In contrast to positive subjective states, the individual level of analysis explores how the presence of positive traits can ameliorate the experience of disability. Resilience, which is an increasingly popular trait within positive psychology (and the discipline more generally) and within rehabilitation psychology, can also be seen as a psychosocial asset (see Table 14.1). Resilience refers to people's abilities to persist when confronted with stressors or other obstacles, to recover from setbacks, and to flourish when facing challenges (Bonanno, 2004). What makes resilience intriguing is that it is not necessarily a fixed quality that a person possesses; rather, it entails processes that reside within both the person and the environment (Murray & Doren, 2013). Thus, resilience is quite Lewinian, so that how people make use of the resources available to them may be a major determinant of how and whether they rally when coping with the consequences of disability.

One recent study examined how resilience, aging, and perceived symptoms affect living with a long-term medically-related disability (Terrill et al., 2016). Resilience could reduce the influence of secondary factors (e.g. fatigue, pain) on quality of life among people who are aging with a disability. Furthermore, resilience might promote successful aging by bolstering older people's beliefs about their lives, encouraging them to see their health as acceptable despite the presence of age-related diseases or disability. In other words, physical disability may be perceived as a normative part of aging, but when it is an "off-time" event—when it happens to younger people—it is seen as pathological and therefore problematic. In a large sample of individuals aging with long-term physical disabilities linked to spinal cord injury (SCI), muscular dystrophy (MD), multiple sclerosis (MS), and post-polio syndrome (PPS), Terrill and colleagues found that levels of resilience were lowest among younger and middle-aged participants (i.e. under 64 years of age), as well as those who were depressed. Among older participants (i.e. over 65 years of age), however, resilience was found to mediate associations between secondary symptoms and quality of life, despite the fact that greater age was associated with higher levels of pain and fatigue.

Alschuler, Kratz, and Ehde (2016) examined how vulnerability and resilience influence the experience of chronic pain and disability. Vulnerability involves factors that promote suffering, including catastrophic thinking, depressive moods, and maladaptive beliefs regarding pain. Alschuler and colleagues wanted to determine whether and how vulnerability and resilience affect pain interference, self-efficacy linked to managing pain, and global mental and physical health. To do so, they performed a secondary analysis on extensive batteries of data collected from a previous study involving people who experienced chronic pain due to SCI, MS, or an amputation. When combined, both vulnerability and resilience factors accounted for substantial variance in physical outcomes, but neither one independently made a greater predictive contribution than the other. However, where mental health outcomes were concerned, resilience factors proved superior, making a more meaningful contribution than vulnerability factors. Researchers and practitioners should consider the important contribution that resilience can make toward understanding and reducing the psychosocial experience of chronic pain. Alschuler and colleagues recommend that investigators make certain to include measures of both resilience and vulnerability in research efforts examining chronic pain and disability.

Some recent research efforts have explored a new construct that is trait-like: disability identity. *Disability identity* encompasses favorable and beneficial self-beliefs possessed by some PWDs, as well as a sense of close, positive ties to members of the disability community (e.g. Dunn, 2015; Dunn & Burcaw, 2013; Gill, 1997). Disability identity varies along a broad continuum, one that ranges from no or low disability identity (e.g. an individual has a disability in an objective sense but remains unaware of it, as in mild hearing loss) or denies it (as can occur following stroke to certain areas of the brain) to high disability identity (e.g. disabled activists who seek social, educational, political, and economic equality for PWDs) (Dunn, 2015; see also Nario-Redmond & Oleson, 2016). As Siebers (2011) wrote, "To call disability an identity is to recognize that it is not a biological or a natural property, but an elastic social category both subject to social control and capable of effecting social change" (p. 4). One author argues that the formation of disability identity follows a stage process, one aligned with the psychosocial experiences of other minority groups who have experienced marginalization in society (Gill, 1997).

Dunn and Burcaw (2013) suggested that one way to examine disability identity is to explore narratives written by PWDs, as these can reveal important aspects of people's personalities or what personality psychologist Dan McAdams (2006; McAdams & McLean, 2013) calls *narrative identity*. To McAdams, our personal narratives are ways to explain how we shape our unfolding stories by both intentionally and unconsciously merging various aspects of ourselves. These identity stories are inherently subjective, so the truth *per se* is less important than the supporting beliefs people use to make sense out of their lives (McAdams, 1993).

Where disability identity is concerned, narratives link autobiography to favorable as well as unfavorable aspects of the social lives of PWDs. Dunn and

Burcaw (2013) studied PWDs' published narratives in order to highlight key themes previously identified as important by disability and rehabilitation investigators. Table 14.2 lists six key themes found in the autobiographies used in Dunn and Burcaw's sample.

Communal attachment and *affirmation of disability*, the first two entries in the table, emphasize the point that part of disability identity emerges from active associations with disability culture and affiliation with other PWDs. In turn, *self-worth*, *pride*, and *discrimination* are linked to research on disability politics and the disability community's hope and struggle for greater civil rights. These particular themes also support PWDs by helping them to cope with, and respond constructively to, stereotypes, daily hassles, and the often negative attitudes held by non-disabled people about disability. Table 14.2's final entry, *personal meaning*, refers to reflecting on and managing the onset and consequences of disability, as well as a person's acceptance of disability.

Moving beyond the theoretical potential of disability identity, Bogart (2014) examined the role that possessing a disability self-concept can play where adaptation to congenital versus acquired disability is concerned. The social psychology of disability posits that individuals with congenital as opposed to acquired disabilities adapt better to their lives and situations; however, few investigations explore this hypothesis or point to potential mechanisms underlying it. Using a cross-sectional online survey, Bogart invited PWDs with congenital and acquired mobility disabilities to complete measures of disability identity, disability self-efficacy, satisfaction with life, self-esteem, and demographics. Results indicated that self-esteem, disability identity, disability self-efficacy, and income predicted participants' reported satisfaction with life. However, congenital onset of disability predicted higher satisfaction with life, and both disability identity and disability self-efficacy (not self-esteem) mediated this

TABLE 14.2 Six Key Themes of Disability Identity

Communal attachment	Wishes to affiliate with other PWDs
Affirmation of disability	Holds thoughts and feelings of being part of society and of enjoying the same rights and responsibilities of other citizens
Self-worth	Values the self with disability; feels equal to non-disabled people
Pride	Feels proud of identity despite recognizing that disabled is often viewed by non-disabled people to be a devalued quality
Discrimination	Aware that being a person with a disability means being a recipient of prejudicial behavior in daily life
Personal meaning	Finds significance in, identifies benefits with, and makes sense of disability

Source: Adapted from Dunn & Burcaw (2013, p. 151).

relation. In a subsequent study of people with multiple sclerosis, Bogart (2015) found that the presence of an affirming disability identity served as a unique predictor of lower levels of depression and anxiety. In addition, being an older adult (as opposed to a younger or middle-aged person) and being able to carry out more daily activities were also predictive of lower depression and anxiety.

Cultivating positive disability identities among PWDs may be a constructive way to help people adapt to disability, particularly acquired disabilities. Bogart (2014) observes that instead of trying to "normalize" clients' experiences, which can reduce disability identity (Olkin, 2009), health care professionals should focus on helping patients form disability self-concepts, which can be achieved by promoting disability pride and encouraging involvement in advocacy groups and the greater disability community. Disability support groups could also shape disability identities in beneficial ways. These sorts of psychosocial interventions should be studied in future research efforts. In addition, researchers should also consider how families and friends of PWDs might serve as supportive resources for developing disability identities. Having examined positive states and traits linked to disability, we now consider the group level of analysis and positive institutions.

Positive Groups and Institutions

To date, in both positive psychology proper and rehabilitation psychology, the arena of positive groups and institutions has received little empirical attention. Instead, researchers have focused more on subjective experiences and traits in critically examining the impact of institutions (e.g. schools, businesses, organizations, clubs) on people's well-being. Positive institutions are construed as organizations that cultivate civic virtues by encouraging people to behave like good and productive citizens while contributing to the collective good. One explanation for the paucity of work dealing with positive institutions is that by their very nature, most institutions are inherently complex; as the late Christopher Peterson (2006) put it, they are "invariably a mix of the good and the bad" (p. 277). Thus, positive institutions may not be completely positive or, put another way, their good qualities are often circumscribed.

The role of positive institutions and organizations in the lives of PWDs has received little attention from rehabilitation psychologists. Primarily non-profit institutions can be local, that is, community-based, national, or even international in scope. Some may be affiliated with rehabilitation or veterans hospitals, others may not. Some institutions may provide vocational training or job opportunities for PWDs, while others may be dedicated to social or recreational purposes. Still others may have a legal or political agenda that involves lobbying or organized protests. The common thread among these groups is simply that their primary purpose is to advance the welfare and well-being of PWDs as defined by their respective institutional missions.

Where the study and possible development of positive institutions is concerned, PWDs are likely to be attracted to organizations that display the same qualities that involve non-disabled persons. One difference, of course, is that interested institutions or organizations should necessarily consider how the experience of disability informs the nature of their espoused virtues or values. Peterson (2006) identified five institutional-level virtues that should characterize a positive institution's conduct; these are listed and defined in Table 14.3. Two of these virtues—*humanity* and *dignity*—echo the value-laden beliefs and principles advanced by Wright (1972, 1983), suggesting that rehabilitation psychology could be an effective field of service as well as research (see Table 14.3). Three other virtues (*purpose, fairness, safety*) outline appropriate conduct for a positive organization and how it connects with its members (see Table 14.3).

A sixth virtue, *expertise*, has been added as a reminder that PWDs must be recognized as the primary experts regarding their conditions and particular needs (see the last entry in Table 14.3). This last virtue is linked with Wright's (1983, p. xvii) principle 19, which indicates that, given their direct experience with rehabilitation issues, members should serve as "coplanners, coevaluators, and consultants," that is, as experts, as in participant action research. As a virtue, expertise is also promoted by the disability movement (Hagen-Foley, Rosenthal, & Thomas, 2005; National Institute on Consumer-Directed Long-Term Services, 1996).

Although the presence of such virtues in an institution could promote happiness among its members, Peterson (2006) suggested the better use of virtues is to contribute to fulfillment. The term *fulfillment* is more complex than mere happiness as it involves active engagement, direct choice, and following morally

TABLE 14.3 Six Virtues Linked to Positive Institutions and Organizations

Purpose	An articulated, shared vision of the organization's moral goals; members are reminded of the goals through remembrances and celebrations
Fairness	The organization relies on equitable rules for governance; rewards and punishments are consistently enforced
Humanity	The organization and its members express mutual care and concern for one another
Dignity	Regardless of role or positions, all persons in the organization are treated as individuals
Safety	Members are protected from threat, danger, and exploitation
Expertise	The organization operates under the assumption that its members are experts regarding their disabilities and any related needs or services

Source: Adapted from Peterson (2006, p. 298) and National Institute on Consumer-Directed Long-Term Services (1996).

admirable actions that benefit the institution and its members (Peterson, 2006). A fulfilling institution is one that satisfies its members' needs and gratifies them in the process. Besides benefiting members, fulfilling institutions are also likely to contribute to the life of the communities in which they reside. Such contributions can be social (e.g. volunteer opportunities), economic (e.g. employment opportunities), or educational (e.g. workshop or continuing education opportunities). Fulfillment for the members of an institution can also be derived from positive psychological capital (PsyCap; see Luthans & Frey, this volume).

A recent clinical review paper advocates positive changes in an essential organizational setting linked to acquired disability—the intensive care unit (ICU)—as preparations for helping clients make the often-challenging transition to in-patient rehabilitation facilities (IRFs; Merbitz, Westie, Dammeyer, Butt, & Schneider, 2016). In particular, the authors highlight the fact that many ICU patients display a *post-intensive care syndrome* (PICS) or *ICU delirium*, where new-onset cognitive or emotional impairments (or both) develop and persist beyond the critical illness and acute care hospitalization. Merbitz and colleagues call for a re-evaluation and revision of what happens to clients in the ICU and afterwards. The researchers' goal is to encourage hospital and rehabilitation professionals, including psychologists, to adopt a multilevel perspective on clients' experiences in and after critical care. This perspective entails concentrating on the clients and their families as well as considering the biopsychosocial context linked to disability and any cognitive and emotional impairments, and the impact of compromised role identities and the influence of environmental factors (in both the Lewinian and ICF Model senses; World Health Organization, 2001). According to Merbitz and colleagues, in-patient rehabilitation psychologists can educate clients and families about typical and predictable psychosocial and physical barriers that may affect post-ICU life while helping all concerned—including the medical team—to create interventions for overcoming such barriers. In order for positive institutions in community settings to be maximally beneficial for PWDs, making significant changes to the ICU and post-ICU experiences would seem to be a necessary beginning.

Conclusion: The Promise of Intentional Actions

Clearly, positive psychology is a proven complement to established perspectives in rehabilitation psychology, but what does the future hold? One of the most promising aspects of positive psychology is what can be changed where people's behavior and feelings of happiness or well-being are concerned. Lyubomirsky, Sheldon, and Schkade (2005) argued that ongoing happiness is influenced by *intentional actions* or particular concrete behaviors people make (or can make) in the course of daily living (e.g. exercise, recreational activities). In contrast, the respective contributions from genetic factors and a person's life circumstances (e.g. age, gender, life history) are not malleable, which means the behavioral and emotional choices people enact are really the only way to enhance happiness and well-being. As noted earlier in this chapter, happiness may be changed—often decreased—by the onset of disability (Lucas, 2007a, 2007b). With effective rehabilitation counseling, clients can seek out intentional actions that foster positive subjective states and traits, and perhaps identify positive organizations in their communities where they can benefit from services or even contribute their time and efforts to aid others. By making intentional choices, then, persons with disabilities can pursue the good life (see Dunn & Brody, 2008, for broader discussion of these and related issues). Rehabilitation psychologists interested in promoting positive states and traits in PWDs should consider pursuing these and related research leads.

Recently, Nierenberg et al. (2016) encouraged rehabilitation psychologists to consider how the foundational principles (see Table 14.1) can be constructively linked to well-being therapy (e.g. Fava & Ruini, 2003; Ruini & Fava, 2012; Ryff, 1989) to combat the development of psychological disorders (e.g. depression, anxiety, post-traumatic stress disorder) following acquired disability. In essence, well-being therapy relies on a structured, directive, and problem-oriented approach based on an educational model. Ryff (1989), for example, argued that well-being is comprised of six factors that are reflective of the foundational principles (see Table 14.1): self-acceptance, purpose in life, personal growth, positive relations with others, environmental mastery, and autonomy. Self-observation is key; clients use a structured diary and meet several times with a therapist. A more detailed explication of well-being therapy is beyond the scope of this chapter; however, Nierenberg and colleagues make the case that the approach might be a helpful tool when applied to people with acquired disabilities such as individuals with SCI. As Nierenberg and colleagues put it:

> ... the route to more positive and enduring adaptation lies not entirely in eliminating the negative but instead building the positive. From another standpoint, this can be understood as a logical extension of certain foundational RP [Rehabilitation Psychology] principles: (1) no amount of physical disability erases a person's assets and (2) individuals able to cope tend to balance a focus on their old and newly found strengths, whereas those who mostly succumb tend to mainly be aware of their losses (Treischmann, 1988).
>
> *(p. 38)*

Practitioners, then, should discern how the intentional aspects of well-being therapeutic approaches, coupled with the foundational principles, could be used to promote positive well-being among PWDs and other chronic illnesses, and not simply focus on alleviating negative affective states. Positive psychological interventions (e.g. Parks & Schueller, 2014) hold great promise for further development of a positive psychology of disability and rehabilitation.

Acknowledgment

I am grateful to Bruce Caplan for providing thoughtful comments on an earlier version of this chapter.

References

Alschuler, K. N., Kratz, A. L., & Ehde, D. M. (2016). Resilience and vulnerability in individuals with chronic pain and disability. *Rehabilitation Psychology, 61,* 7–18.

Anusic, I., Yap, S. C., & Lucas, R. E. (2014). Testing set-point theory in a Swiss national sample: Reaction and adaptation to major life events. *Social Indicators Research, 119,* 1265–1288.

Bogart, K. R. (2014). The role of disability self-concept in adaptation to congenital or acquired disability. *Rehabilitation Psychology, 59,* 107–115. doi:10.1037/a0035800.

Bogart, K. R. (2015). Disability identity predicts lower anxiety and depression in multiple sclerosis. *Rehabilitation Psychology, 60,* 105–109. doi:10.1037/rep0000029.

Bonanno, G. A. (2004). Loss, trauma, and human resilience: Have we underestimated the human capacity to thrive after extremely aversive events? *American Psychologist, 59,* 20–28.

Brickman, P., & Campbell, D. T. (1971). Hedonic relativism and planning the good society. In M. H. Appley (Ed.), *Adaptation level theory: A symposium* (pp. 287–302). New York: Academic Press.

Chan, F., Tarvydas, V. M., Blalock, K., Strauser, D., & Atkins, B. (2009). Unifying and elevating rehabilitation counseling through model-driven, diversity-sensitive evidence-based practice. *Rehabilitation Counseling Bulletin, 52,* 114–119. doi:10.1177/0034355208323947.

Charlton, J. I. (1998). *Nothing about us without us: Disability oppression and empowerment.* Berkeley, CA: University of California Press. doi:10.1525/california/9780520207950.001.0001.

Diener, E. (2008). Myths in the science of happiness, and directions for future research. In M. Eid & R. J. Larsen (Eds.), *The science of subjective well-being* (pp. 493–514). New York: Guilford Press.

Diener, E., Lucas, R. E., & Scollon, C. N. (2006). Beyond the hedonic treadmill: Revising the adaptation theory of well-being. *American Psychologist, 61,* 305–314. doi:10.1037/0003-066X.61.4.305.

Dijkers, M. P. J. M. (2005). Quality of life of individuals with a spinal cord injury: A review of conceptualization, measurement, and research findings. *Journal of Rehabilitation Research and Development, 42,* 87–110. doi:10.1682/JRRD.2004.08.0100.

Dunn, D. S. (2011). Situations matter: Teaching the Lewinian link between social psychology and rehabilitation psychology. *History of Psychology, 14*(4), 405–411. doi:10.1037/a0023919.

Dunn, D. S. (2015). *The social psychology of disability.* New York: Oxford University Press.

Dunn, D. S., & Brody, C. (2008). Defining the good life following acquired physical disability. *Rehabilitation Psychology, 53,* 413–425.

Dunn, D. S., & Burcaw, S. (2013). Disability identity: Exploring narrative accounts of disability. *Rehabilitation Psychology, 58*(2), 148–157. doi:10.1037/a0031691.

Dunn, D. S., & Dougherty, S. B. (2005). Prospects for a positive psychology of rehabilitation. *Rehabilitation Psychology, 50,* 305–311.

Dunn, D. S., Ehde, D., & Wegener, S. T. (2016). The foundational principles as psychological lodestars: Theoretical inspiration and empirical direction in rehabilitation psychology. *Rehabilitation Psychology, 61*(1), 1–6.

Dunn, D. S., Uswatte, G., & Elliott, T. R. (in press). Happiness and resilience following physical disability. In S. J. Lopez, L. Edwards, & S. Marques (Eds.), *Oxford handbook of positive psychology* (3rd ed.). New York: Oxford University Press.

Ehde, D. M. (2010). Application of positive psychology to rehabilitation psychology. In R. G. Frank, M. Rosenthal, & B. Caplan (Eds.), *Handbook of rehabilitation psychology* (2nd ed., pp. 417–424). Washington, DC: American Psychological Association.

Elliott, T. R., & Kennedy, P. (2004). Treatment of depression following spinal cord injury: An evidence-based review. *Rehabilitation Psychology, 49,* 134–139. doi:10.1037/0090-5550.49.2.134.

Elliott, T. R., Kurylo, M. & Rivera, P. (2002). Positive growth following acquired physical disability. In C. R. Snyder & S. J. Lopez (Eds.), *Handbook of positive psychology* (pp. 687–699). New York: Oxford University Press.

Fava, G. A., & Ruini, C. (2003). Development and characteristics of well-being enhanced psychotherapeutic strategy: Well-being therapy. *Journal of Behavior Therapy and Experimental Psychiatry, 34,* 45–63. doi:10.1016/S0005-7916(03)00019-3.

Gill, C. J. (1997). Four types of integration in disability identity development. *Journal of Vocational Rehabilitation, 9,* 39–46. doi:10.1016/S1052-2263(97)00020-2.

Hagen-Foley, D. L., Rosenthal, D. A., & Thomas, D. F. (2005). Informed consumer choice in community rehabilitation programs. *Rehabilitation Counseling Bulletin, 48,* 110–117.

Johnson, H. M. (2005). *Too late to die young: Nearly true tales from a life.* New York: Henry Holt.

Judge, T. A., Locke, E. A., Durham, C. C., & Kluger, A. N. (1998). Dispositional effects in job and life satisfaction: The role of core evaluations. *Journal of Applied Psychology, 83,* 17–34. doi:10.1037/0021-9010.83.1.17.

Lewin, K. A. (1935). *A dynamic theory of personality.* New York: McGraw-Hill.

Lucas, R. (2007a). Adaptation and the set-point model of subjective well-being: Does happiness change after major life events? *Current Directions in Psychological Science, 16,* 75–79. doi:10.1111/j.1467-8721.2007.00479.x.

Lucas, R. (2007b). Long-term disability is associated with lasting changes in subjective well being: Evidence from two nationally representative longitudinal studies. *Journal of Personality and Social Psychology, 92,* 717–730. doi:10.1037/0022-3514. 92.4.717.

Lyubomirsky, S., Sheldon, K. M., & Schkade, D. (2005). Pursuing happiness: The architecture of sustainable change. *Review of General Psychology, 9,* 111–131. doi:10.1037/1089-2680.9.2.111.

McAdams, D. P. (1993). *The stories we live by: Personal myths and the making of the self.* New York: Morrow.

McAdams, D. P. (2006). *The person: A new introduction to personality psychology.* Hoboken, NJ: Wiley.

McAdams, D. P., & McLean, K. C. (2013). Narrative identity. *Current Directions in Psychological Science, 22,* 233–238. doi:10.1177/0034355210386971.

Merbitz, N. H., Westie, K., Dammeyer, J. A., Butt, L., & Schneider, J. (2016). After critical care: Challenges in the transition to inpatient rehabilitation. *Rehabilitation Psychology, 61,* 186–200. doi:10.1037/rep0000072.

Murray, C., & Doren, B. (2013). Resilience and disability: Concepts, examples, cautions, and prospects. In M. L. Wehmeyer (Ed.), *Oxford handbook of positive psychology and disability* (pp. 182–197). New York: Oxford University Press.

Nario-Redmond, M. R., & Oleson, K. C. (2016). Disability group identification and disability-rights advocacy: Contingencies among emerging and other adults. *Emerging Adulthood, 4,* 207–218. doi:10.1177/2167696815579830.

National Institute on Consumer-Directed Long-Term Services. (1996). *Principles of consumer-directed home and community-based services.* Washington, DC: Author.

Nierenberg, B., Mayersohn, G., Serpa, S., Holovatyk, A., Smith, E., & Cooper, S. (2016). Application of well-being therapy to people with disability and chronic illness. *Rehabilitation Psychology, 61,* 32–43.

Olkin, R. (2009). Disability-affirmative therapy. In I. Marini & M. Stebnicki (Eds.), *The professional counselor's desk reference* (pp. 355–370). New York: Springer.

Parks, A. C., & Schueller, S. M. (Eds.). (2014). *The Wiley-Blackwell handbook of positive psychological interventions.* Malden, MA. Wiley-Blackwell.

Peterson, C. (2006). *A primer in positive psychology.* New York: Oxford University Press.

Peterson, C., & Seligman, M. E. P. (2004). *Character strengths and virtues: A handbook and classification.* Washington, DC: APA Press.

Ruini, C., & Fava, G. A. (2012). Role of well-being therapy in achieving a balanced and individualized path to optimal functioning. *Clinical Psychology & Psychotherapy, 19,* 291–304.

Ryff, C. D. (1989). Happiness is everything, or is it? Explorations on the meaning of psychological well-being. *Journal of Personality and Social Psychology, 57,* 1069–1081. doi:10.1037/0022-3514.57.6.1069.

Seligman, M. E. P., & Csikszentmihalyi, M. (2000). Positive psychology: An introduction. *American Psychologist, 55,* 5–14. doi:10.1037/0003-066X.55.1.5.

Shogren, K. A. (2013). Positive psychology and disability: A historical analysis. In M. L. Wehmeyer (Ed.), *The Oxford handbook of positive psychology and disability* (pp. 19–33). New York: Oxford University Press.

Siebers, T. (2011). *Disability theory.* Ann Arbor: University of Michigan Press.

Smedema, S. M. (2014). Core self-evaluations and well-being in persons with disabilities. *Rehabilitation Psychology, 59,* 407–414. doi:10.1037/rep0000013.

Terrill, A. L., Molton, I. R., Ehde, D. M., Amtmann, D., Bombardier, C. H., Smith, A. E., & Jensen, M. P. (2016). Resilience, age, and perceived symptoms in persons with long-term physical disabilities. *Journal of Health Psychology, 21,* 640–649. doi:10.1177/1359105314532973.

Treischmann, R. (1988). *Spinal cord injuries: The psychological, social, and vocational rehabilitation* (2nd ed.). New York: Demos.

van Campen, C., & van Santvoort, M. (2013). Explaining low subjective well-being of persons with disabilities in Europe: The impact of disability, personal resources, participation and socio-economic status. *Social Indicators Research, 111,* 839–854. doi:10.1007/s11205-012-0036-6.

Wehmeyer, M. L. (Ed.). (2013). *Oxford handbook of positive psychology and disability.* New York: Oxford University Press.

World Health Organization. (2001). *International classifications of functioning, disability, and health.* Geneva, Switzerland: WHO.

Wright, B. A. (1972). Value-laden beliefs and principles for rehabilitation psychology. *Rehabilitation Psychology, 19*, 38–45. doi:10.1037/h0090837.

Wright, B. A. (1983). *Physical disability: A psychosocial approach.* New York: Harper & Row. doi:10.1037/10589-000.

Wright, B. A., & Lopez, S. J. (2009). Widening the diagnostic focus: A case for including human strengths and environmental resources. In C. R. Snyder & S. J. Lopez (Eds.), *Handbook of positive psychology* (2nd ed., pp. 71–88). New York: Oxford University Press. doi:10.1093/oxfordhb/9780195187243.013.008.

15

TOWARD A POSITIVE PSYCHOLOGY OF SINGLE LIFE

Bella DePaulo

For the first few decades of my adult life, I did not study single life; I just practiced it. I'm 63. I have always been single and always will be. I never fantasized about the color of my bridesmaids' dresses or drew up lists of optimal qualities in a mate. Marrying never interested me. There was a time during my early adult years when I thought that maybe I was just slow in getting bitten by the marriage bug, but that eventually, I, too, would want to marry. I wish I could remember how old I was when I finally realized, "No, self, you are never going to want to marry. Single is who you are. It suits you." I now call people like me "single at heart." We are people who live our best, most authentic, and most meaningful and fulfilling lives as single people.

I used to keep a secret file of notes about ways in which I thought I was treated differently just because I was single. When my married colleagues from work included me in lunch outings during the week but socialized only with other couples on the weekends, was that an example of what I would later call singlism? What about when every faculty member was required to contribute the same flat fee toward the department picnic, and on that same dime, my department chair brought his wife and four kids, and I brought me? The examples were all small stuff. At the time, I still had no idea of the big, systematic ways in which married people were benefited and protected and single people were not, including ways written right into the laws of the land.

Tentatively at first, I approached other single people and asked if they ever felt that they were viewed more judgmentally or treated less fairly just because they were single. The responses were overwhelming. If I did this at a social event, one person after another would join the conversation, and share their own experiences. After the first such event, I wrote notes for two hours afterwards. The next day, when I logged into my email, I found messages from people from the night before saying, "Oh, and another thing…"

It was clear that I was hitting a nerve. I was also feeling deeply engaged with the topic. Soon I would commit to putting the study of single people at the center of my research life. But I also wanted to reach far beyond the hallowed halls of academe, initially by writing a book about singles (DePaulo, 2006) based on research but readable to smart people with no scientific training.

I knew that such a book would need to address the voluminous research on the implications of getting married for health and well-being. At the time, I was familiar with media headlines proclaiming that people who marry become happier and healthier and all the rest. Even though I did not think I would be happier if I got married, I thought I was the exception. I had no reason to doubt the underlying message.

I approached my deep dive into the original research reports with the hope that I would find some wrinkle in the data—maybe some demographic subgroup for whom getting married wasn't such a great thing. I was stunned by what I discovered. The design and analyses of the relevant studies could never support the kinds of claims that were being made. What's more, even when I focused only on the very best studies, I found that getting married did not result in the uniformly beneficial outcomes that have become part of our conventional wisdom. In fact, in some ways, it was the lifelong single people who were doing the best.

So I was wrong when I believed the prevailing cultural narrative about the superiority of people who marry, but I was more on target than I could have ever imagined when I first started wondering whether single people were stereotyped and stigmatized just because they were single. Juxtaposing single people's status as inferiors with their many positive actual life outcomes raises an important question: How is this possible? Or paraphrasing the subtitle of my book, *Singled Out*, how is it that single people are stereotyped, stigmatized, and ignored, and still live happily ever after? The answer to that question offers the beginnings of a positive psychology of single life.

In the rest of this chapter, I will discuss each of these points in greater detail, marshaling the most relevant research when it is available. First, though, I'll address the question of who counts as single.

Who Counts as Single?

The most straightforward definition of single, often used by the Census Bureau, is a legal one: People are single if they are not legally married. Legally single people include people who are divorced and widowed as well as those who have always been single.

The legal definition is enormously consequential because a vast array of benefits and protections are accorded solely to people who are legally married. At the federal level alone, more than 1,000 laws advantage only people who are legally married (Government Accountability Office, 2004). The countless people who worked so hard for the legalization of same-sex marriage had many motivations; one of them was desire for access to all those perks and protections.

In everyday life, though, what often matters more is a person's social status. Are you seen as part of a committed couple? If so, you are socially coupled. If not, you are socially single. If you are married, you count as not just legally coupled but socially coupled, too. If you are cohabiting with a romantic partner, you are also seen as socially coupled even if you are not legally married. Beyond that, the criteria are less clear: Do you seem to be in a serious romantic relationship? How long have you been in that relationship? Do others expect you to stay in that relationship?

Personal status could also be distinguished from social status. Personal status is self-defined: Do you consider yourself single? It is a category that acknowledges that our own view of things does not always accord with other people's.

In almost all of the social science research on marital status and life outcomes, married people are those who are legally married. When the prestigious *Journal of Marriage and Family* was first launched in 1938, cohabitation was rare. Now that it is more commonplace, studies sometimes include the socially coupled cohabiters either as a separate group or in with the legally married group.

Actual Differences Between Single and Married People: Exaggerations, Misrepresentations, and Unwarranted Claims About Causality

Egregious Flaws in the Research and Arguments About the Purportedly Beneficial Effects of Getting Married

Studies of the implications of getting married, or the way the results are interpreted, are too often deeply flawed. There are four problems that are particularly troublesome.

First, we can never do the kinds of studies that would allow us to make definitive causal claims about the implications of getting married. People cannot be randomly assigned to marital status. The people who get married, get divorced, get remarried, or stay single are different people. Attempts to control for possible differences statistically do not fully resolve this problem. We can never know what unmeasured factors may remain significant. If the kinds of people who choose to marry enjoy certain benefits (and the claims that they do are often greatly exaggerated), that does not necessarily mean that the people who choose to be single would reap the same benefits if they were pressured into marrying. We simply cannot make causal claims about the implications of getting married, such as "Getting married makes people happier" or "Getting married benefits people," and we should challenge any such claims that appear in the media.

Second, many studies of marital status are cross-sectional. Again, we cannot make causal claims based on cross-sectional data.

The third problem is pervasive and highly consequential. Yet it is one of the least recognized and least understood issues, despite the fact that methodologically, it is very straightforward. The problem is that the vast majority of claims about the implications of getting married are based on comparisons of people who are currently married to people who are not currently married. But the people who are currently married do not include all the people who got married and then got divorced (or became widowed). The percentage of married people who divorce is substantial, probably more than 40 percent (Amato, 2010), and those people are not divorcing because they found their marriages fulfilling. Yet researchers take this very big chunk of people who got married and set them aside, and look only at the people who have remained married. Then they compare them to lifelong single people. Or worse still, they include divorced and widowed people in with the lifelong single people (because they are all unmarried). Then they compare just the currently married to everyone else, and if the currently married seem to be doing better, they say, "Look, getting married makes people do better!"

Imagine if a pharmaceutical company, in testing a new drug, found that more than 40 percent of the people in the new drug condition hated the drug so much that they refused to continue taking it. Yet, when the company reported on the results of their research, they compared only the people who continued to take the drug with everyone else. They then conclude that the drug was beneficial. No respectable medical journal would allow that, and no respectable journal in the social sciences should allow the same when it comes to claims about the implications of getting married (DePaulo, 2006).

Or imagine that when analyzing your own research, you could remove from the key group more than 40 percent of the participants who did not behave in the way you predicted. How much would that improve your chances of making the claims you want to make? That's what has been happening for decades in the research on the implications of getting married.

Longitudinal studies are far superior to cross-sectional ones for elucidating the implications of getting married. They allow us to see how happiness or health or other outcomes change as the same people go from living single to getting married. The fourth problem, though, is that even longitudinal research is still only suggestive with regard to causal claims. Most analyses of longitudinal research are marred by the problem I just described. They focus on only those people who get married and stay married. The implications of getting married might be very different if everyone who ever got married were compared to lifelong single people. However, even if all the people who ever got married were compared to the lifelong single people and the married people did better, we would still be left with the first and most fundamental problem. The people who choose to marry are different people than the people who stay single—and they are probably especially different from those who *choose* to live single. Just because people who choose to marry do better than those who stay single (*if* they do) does not mean that single people would do better, too, if only they got married.

Actual Differences between Single and Married People: The Evidence

There are hundreds of studies comparing the life outcomes of people of different marital statuses. My review cannot possibly be comprehensive (see DePaulo, 2015b, for a more extensive review). In deciding which studies to mention, I looked for the strongest research, methodologically. So, for example, I favored longitudinal studies over cross-sectional ones. I also looked for meta-analyses (Luhmann, Hofmann, Eid, & Lucas, 2012). When I did include cross-sectional studies, I tried to find large, nationally representative samples—or better still, representative samples from multiple nations (Greitemeyer, 2009). I will also highlight an example in which the conclusions drawn from a study (as described in the abstract) exaggerate the extent to which the data support the advantages of getting married.

Getting Married and Not Getting Happier

Research on happiness is so popular that when Luhmann and her colleagues (2012) set out to do a meta-analysis of some of the most sophisticated studies available—prospective studies in which subjective well-being was measured before and after the marriage, multiple times—they found 18 studies that qualified. They looked separately at three different varieties of well-being: "affective well-being," including ratings of happiness and depressed mood; "cognitive well-being," ratings of life satisfaction; and "relationship satisfaction," participants' ratings of satisfaction with their partner.

Results for affective well-being showed that participants were not any happier after the wedding than they were before, and over time, their happiness did not change. The only hint of an increase in well-being was for cognitive well-being, but it was short-lived. Participants became a bit more satisfied with their lives just after the wedding than they were before, but then their satisfaction continually decreased over time. The implications of getting married were especially dim for relationship satisfaction: Participants reported less satisfaction with their partners after they got married than they had before, and their satisfaction continued to decline over time.

Strikingly, here is what did *not* happen: Except for the brief honeymoon effect for life satisfaction, getting married did not result in improvements in well-being. Those findings are especially remarkable because for at least nine of the 18 studies, only those people who got married and stayed married were included in the research. That means the studies were already biased to produce results favoring marriage. Other reports of individual studies (for example, Lucas, Clark, Georgellis, & Diener, 2003) show that people who get married and then divorce do not even enjoy the brief honeymoon effect in life satisfaction around the time of the wedding; they are already becoming less satisfied.

A 16-year longitudinal study of life satisfaction published after the Luhmann et al. (2012) meta-analysis (Kalmijn, 2017) found a very small increase in satisfaction for people who got married; satisfaction then decreased over the subsequent years of the marriage (but did not return to the level of satisfaction before the participants got married). The people who divorced became significantly less satisfied than they were when they were married—an effect that was more than three times larger than the increase in satisfaction from getting married. Over the course of their single lives after divorcing, participants' life satisfaction increased, returning nearly to what it was when they were married.

Many cross-sectional studies of happiness have also been conducted. Of course, such studies cannot support causal inferences. They are especially biased to produce results that favor marriage when only those people who are currently married (and not everyone who ever got married) are compared to single people. Yet, even with such a methodologically indefensible advantage, married people do not always report greater well-being than single people. In one of the most compelling examples, Greitemeyer (2009) analyzed data from the European Social Survey, which includes representative samples from more than 30 nations. When participants were asked to indicate how satisfied they were with their lives on a 0–10 scale (with 10 indicating the greatest satisfaction), the mean ratings of the currently married people were nearly identical to those of the lifelong single people, 7.10 and 7.12, respectively.

Getting Married and Not Getting Healthier

In a 16-year longitudinal study of more than 11,000 Swiss adults between 18 and 65 years of age (Kalmijn, 2017), participants were asked every year about their general health (overall health, satisfaction with health, and health impediments to everyday activities) and illness (suffering from illnesses, number of doctor visits, and reliance on medication in order to function). People who got married became significantly *less* healthy (on the general health index) than they were when they were single—though the effect was very small. Over the course of their marriages, they continued to become significantly less healthy—though again, the effect was very small. People who got divorced became slightly, though significantly, less healthy than they were when they were married. Their general health did not change in the subsequent years of their single life after their divorce.

On the illness index, people who got married were no less ill than they were when they were single, and their illness did not change over the course of their marriage. People who divorced became slightly, though significantly, more ill, but their level of illness did not change in the subsequent years of their single life after their divorce.

Kalmijn (2017) concluded that marriage is not protective of health. People who get married do not become any healthier, and there are no benefits to health that accrue over the course of a marriage. People who get divorced become less healthy than they were when they were married, but there is no accumulation of illness over the course of their single lives after divorce.

Getting Married and Not Living Longer

Studying the implications of getting married for mortality is more challenging than studying something like health or happiness. Whereas well-being can be assessed repeatedly in longitudinal studies, potentially revealing changes over time, death occurs just once.

In an example of one approach to the study of mortality, nearly 300,000 Americans, who were at least 45 years old at the onset of the study, were tracked for up to 11 years (Johnson, Backlund, Sorlie, & Loveless, 2000). Who was still living at the end of the study? People who were currently married at the start of the study were compared to those who were divorced or widowed or had always been single. In the abstract, the authors suggested that their results were straightforward and spelled doom for everyone who was not married. With regard to their measure of relative risk of dying (RR), they said: "Each of the non-married categories showed elevated RR of death compared to married persons." The actual details of their findings, however, were considerably more complex.

For each of the marital statuses, the authors computed mortality risks for eight different subgroups: men and women, who were Black or White, and who, when the study began, were either between 45 and 64 or 65, and older. Were the lifelong single people more likely to die young than the people who were currently married at the start of the study? Not among the Blacks: for three of the four subgroups, there was no difference in mortality. For whites, the lifelong singles did have higher mortality rates than those who started out married. But getting married did not increase people's lifespans. The people who started the study divorced were people who *had* gotten married—they just didn't stay married. In seven of the eight comparisons, the divorced people had higher mortality rates than the people who started out married. But did they live longer than they might have if they just stayed single? No, just the opposite. In seven of eight comparisons, the divorced people had the same or higher mortality rates than the lifelong single people.

Another approach to studying the link between marital status and mortality is to follow people over the entire course of their lives. The Terman Life-Cycle Study, which began in 1921 with 1,528 11-year-olds and is probably the longest-running study on record, found that the people who lived the longest were those who stayed single, along with those who married and stayed married (Tucker, Friedman, Wingard, & Schwartz, 1996). People who divorced, whether or not they remarried, had shorter lives. Consistency (staying single or staying married) was what mattered, not marriage.

Getting Married and Not Getting any Less Lonely

I know of no longitudinal studies that assess loneliness as people transition from single life into marriage. There is, though, longitudinal research on marital status in later life, in which lifelong single people are not included. Those studies show that people who became widowed experienced greater loneliness than they did when they were married (Victor & Bowling, 2012; Wenger & Burholt, 2004). Such studies do not speak to any risk to staying single; they show that there may be a risk to getting married and then becoming unmarried.

The important distinction between staying single and becoming single after having been married is often missed. For example, the authors of a large nationally representative study of Germans compared the loneliness of people who were single and not living with a partner to people who were married or had a partner (Luhmann & Hawkley, 2016). The single group included all unmarried people regardless of whether they had married in the past or were lifelong single people. They found that the unmarried people had higher levels of loneliness, but never presented results separately for the lifelong single people. Even after giving that unfair advantage to the married group, the authors still found no differences whatsoever in levels of loneliness when they looked at the results only for those adults under the age of 30. Differences only showed up among the older groups, likely to include greater proportions of divorced and widowed people among the unmarried.

There was one type of relationship that was consistently linked with lower loneliness for every age group. It wasn't the spousal or romantic relationship, but friendship. Across the lifespan, people with more friends were less likely to be lonely.

In a cross-sectional study of Americans aged 57 and older, Wright and Brown (2016) predicted that married people would have the greatest psychological well-being, followed by cohabiting people. Single people who are dating would be next. Unpartnered single people were expected to have the worst outcomes. Instead, for the women, there were no differences. Women higher on the romantic partnership hierarchy were not any less lonely, less stressed, or less depressed. For the men, there were some differences but not as many as the authors predicted. The married men did no better than the cohabiting men (and sometimes did worse) and the single men who were dating did no better than those who were not. What *did* matter was social support from family and friends. Men and women who had friends and family they could open up to, and rely on when they had a problem, were the ones who were less lonely, less stressed, and less depressed.

Getting Married and Becoming More Insular

The belief that single people are alone is so strong that the word "alone" is not just a stereotype, it is a synonym. Single people are described as "alone" and lifelong single people are labeled as "alone forever." By marrying, it is assumed, people become more socially integrated.

Results of a stack of studies turn this assumption on its head. Large, nationally representative studies show that it is the lifelong single people who are more likely than the currently married or previously married to socialize with, support, and exchange help with neighbors, friends, siblings, and parents (Gerstel & Sarkisian, 2006; Sarkisian & Gerstel, 2008, 2016). This is true for men and women, rich and poor, Blacks and Whites, and people with children as well as people without children (Gerstel, 2011). Research also suggests that single people have more friends than do married people (Gillespie, Lever, Frederick, & Royce, 2015). Longitudinal studies show that people who get married become more insular. They have less contact with their siblings than they did when they were single (White, 2001), and they also have less contact with their parents and spend less time with their friends (Musick & Bumpass, 2012).

Research on people who live alone is also relevant to the social integration of single people, although single people who live alone are a minority of all single people. Solo dwellers, it has been found, are more engaged in the life of the towns and cities where they live (Klinenberg, 2012). For example, they participate in more civic groups and public events, pursue more informal social activities, go out to dinner more often, and take more art and music classes. Counterintuitively, results of the large German study of loneliness (Luhmann & Hawkley, 2016) showed that once income was controlled, people who lived alone were significantly *less* lonely than people who lived with others.

Getting Married and Becoming More Self-Centered

One of the stickiest stereotypes of single people is that they are selfish and self-centered. But research documenting a variety of ways of giving and caring suggests just the opposite.

For example, a study of adults in their fifties and sixties showed that those who had always been single were more likely than married people to help friends, neighbors, and co-workers in a variety of ways such as doing errands, shopping, housework, yard work and repairs, and providing rides. They were also more helpful in psychological ways, offering more encouragement, advice, and moral and emotional support (Kahn, McGill, & Bianchi, 2011). Another study of Australian women in their seventies showed that women who had always been single and had no children did more volunteering than married women with or without children (Cwikel, Gramotnev, & Lee, 2006).

In cities and towns, people who live alone are more involved in civic groups than are people who live with others (Klinenberg, 2012). A study that included only men (Nock, 1998) found that men who marry spend no more time in service clubs or political groups than they did when they were single, but they do participate less often in workplace-related service groups such as farm organizations, unions, and professional societies. Men who marry are no more generous in the money they give to relatives than they were when they were single. They are, though, less generous with their friends (DePaulo, 2006; Nock, 1998).

When aging parents need help, it is their single adult children (whether men or women, Black or White), more so than their married children, who are there for them (Laditka & Laditka, 2001). When other people, whether kin or non-kin, are ill or disabled or elderly and need help for three months or longer, again it is the people who are single who are more likely than those who are married to provide that assistance (Henz, 2006).

Adults who have always been single are less likely to have children than those who are married. Yet they are just as likely to express concern with the next generation (McAdams & de St. Aubin, 1992).

Even More Ways in Which Getting Married Does not Result in Better Outcomes

In a longitudinal study with a variety of outcome measures, Musick and Bumpass (2012) included people who had gotten married (or transitioned into a cohabiting union) within the past 3 years, people who had been married (or cohabiting) between 4 and 6 years, and unmarried people (including previously married people who were not cohabiting). Consistent with previous research, the authors did find some honeymoon effects. Those who became coupled within the past 3 years were happier, healthier, less depressed, and had higher self-esteem than the unmarried people. However, for people who had been married (or cohabiting) for more than 3 years, none of those advantages persisted. They were no happier, no healthier, no less depressed, and had no higher self-esteem than the unmarried people (a group disadvantaged by the inclusion of some previously married people). There were also ways in which the unmarried people always did better than the married (or cohabiting) people, both in the short term and the long term: They spent more time with their friends and had more contact with their parents.

Data on self-esteem were also reported in the 30-nation study that Greitemeyer (2009) analyzed. Only those who were currently married were compared to lifelong single people. Even with that advantage accorded to the married group (because of the omission of those who got married and then got divorced), the lifelong single people and the currently married people reported identical levels of self-esteem.

In the literature on marital status, many of the outcome measures are based on participants' own judgments—for example, their self-reports of their happiness or health. In an example of a different approach, Greitemeyer (2009) recruited people (average age of 33) to interact in small groups, without any knowledge of anyone's relationship status. They then rated the other group members. The coupled participants did not differ significantly from the single people in any way. They were not rated as any more attractive, agreeable, extroverted, conscientious, open to new experiences, or satisfied with their lives than the single people. They were not seen as any less neurotic or as enjoying any higher self-esteem.

Singlism and Matrimania

Although the actual differences in health and well-being between people who marry and those who stay single are not what we have been led to believe, the perceived differences are something else entirely. Single people are routinely judged more harshly than married or coupled people. That stereotyping of single people is one component of singlism (the stereotyping, stigmatizing, and discrimination against single people). The flip side of singlism is matrimania— the over-the-top hyping of weddings and coupling and marriage. Both sets of processes contribute to the same outcome: The lives of single people are less valued and less respected than those of married people.

Singlism

Perceived Differences between Single and Married People: Pervasive Stereotypes

Studies of stereotyping have been conducted in several countries and they involve a variety of methodologies, but the results are always the same: Single people are viewed more negatively than married people on almost every characteristic (Conley & Collins, 2002; Etaugh & Malstrom, 1981; Greitemeyer, 2009; Hertel, Schütz, DePaulo, Morris, & Stucke, 2007; Morris, DePaulo, Hertel, & Taylor, 2008; Morris & Osburn, 2016). In a series of studies my colleagues and I conducted (Morris et al., 2008), we created brief biographical sketches of people that were identical in every way except for the key dimensions that we manipulated, such as the marital status of the person profiled. The people in the sketches who were described as single were rated more harshly than the identical people described as married. They were viewed as less well adjusted (e.g. less happy and secure), more socially immature (e.g. more immature, lonely, and fearful of rejection), and more self-centered and envious. They were, though, also perceived as more independent and career-oriented.

In some of our studies, we manipulated the age of the person in the sketch, describing them as either 25 or 40. The single people were judged more harshly than the married people at both ages, but the difference was greater for the 40-year-olds.

In all our studies, we manipulated whether the person in the sketch was a man or a woman, but that made little difference. Single women and single men were viewed equally negatively, relative to their married counterparts. The gender of the participants did not matter, either, and neither did their relationship status. Men and women, single people and coupled people, all judged single people more harshly than married people.

In another set of studies, all the people in the sketches were described as college students, and we manipulated whether they were currently in a romantic relationship and whether they had ever been in a romantic relationship. The bias against single people persisted. College students who were not currently in a romantic relationship, and those who had never been in a romantic relationship, were judged more harshly than their coupled counterparts.

A series of studies conducted in Germany used the same biographical sketch methodology, except that the profiles described people who were single and people who were coupled (regardless of whether they were married), rather than just married people (Greitemeyer, 2009). The single people were again negatively stereotyped. For example, they were viewed as less satisfied with their lives, less agreeable, less conscientious, less attractive, less socially skilled, lower in self-esteem, more interested in changing their relationship status, and more neurotic. They were, though, also seen as more open to new experiences. Again, single people (both single men and single women) were stereotyped by both men and women, and by fellow single people as well as coupled people.

Taking a different, open-ended approach, my colleagues and I (Morris et al., 2008) also asked 950 undergraduates to write down what comes to mind when they think of people who are married (for about half of the participants) or people who are single (for the others). Among those who were describing married people, nearly every other participant (49 percent) spontaneously came up with the qualities of kind, caring, or giving. In contrast, only 2 percent of the participants describing single people mentioned those characteristics. Nearly a third of the participants describing married people (32 percent) said they were loving. Not even one person (0 percent) said the same thing about single people. Married people were also more often described as happy, loyal, compromising, secure, and reliable, and less often described as lonely. Single people, though, were more often described as independent.

Discrimination against Single People

People who are single are excluded from many significant perks and protections available only to people who are legally married. For example, when married people die, their Social Security benefits go to their spouse. When lifelong single people die, their money goes back into the system. They cannot designate a recipient and no one else can designate them as a recipient of their benefits. Married people also get many tax breaks that single people do not get, including, for example, on estate taxes, retirement accounts, and income taxes (Kahng, 2010).

The Family and Medical Leave Act (FMLA) is more protective of married people than single people. Anyone, regardless of marital status, can take time off under the Act to care for a parent or child if they are in an eligible workplace and meet the requirements. Married people can also take time off to care for a spouse. Single people, in contrast, cannot take time off to care for a comparable person in their life, such as a sibling or close friend, nor can any such person take time off to care for the single person.

In a series of studies, my colleagues and I (Morris, Sinclair, & DePaulo, 2007) documented housing discrimination against people who are single. Other research shows that single men are paid less than married men (Bellas, 1992; Toutkoushian, 1998), even when they have the same seniority and re-cord of accomplishments, and even, in fact, when the single and married men are identical twins (Antonovics & Town, 2004). In the marketplace, married couples often pay less per person than single people for the same goods or ser-vices, such as insurance, health club memberships, professional memberships, and travel packages (see DePaulo, 2006, 2011 for many more examples of dis-crimination against single people).

Matrimania

Prevailing norms and practices do not just stereotype and stigmatize single people, they also relentlessly celebrate and value married people, weddings, and couples (DePaulo, 2006). Such matrimania is evident in the endless books, movies, and television shows that lean on romantic plots, in advertising that incorporates imagery of brides and weddings (even for products with no obvi-ous relevance to newlyweds), and in extravagant weddings and sensationalized wedding proposals and all the attention they attract.

There is little systematic research on matrimania. The available evidence, though, does suggest that the effects can be pernicious, perhaps especially for women. For example, women who associate the word "boyfriend" with mat-rimaniacal descriptors such as "hero" or "Prince Charming" instead of more mundane descriptors such as "Average Joe," express less interest in high status jobs or the commitment to higher education that they require (Rudman & Heppen, 2003). Other research (Park, Young, Troisi, & Pinkus, 2011) shows that women's interest in math and science can be undermined by matrimania-cal cues, such as exposure to stereotypical romantic imagery or a conversation about a great date, and that women pay less attention in math class and spend less time on math homework on days when they are paying attention to a romantic partner.

Bridging the Gap between Real and Perceived Experiences of Single People: Ideology and Resilience

Why do people continue to believe that married people are superior to single people in so many ways, when the actual differences between people who stay single and those who marry are far smaller or more qualified than we have been led to believe, and sometimes actually favor single people? And how is it possible that lifelong single people do as well as they do, when singlism and matrimania are rampant? The answer to the first question, I believe, is that beliefs about marriage and single life are not just any ordinary set of beliefs; they instead comprise an ideology, a worldview in which people are invested. My tentative answer to the second question is that single people may in some ways be more resilient than married people.

The Ideology of Marriage

In a target article for *Psychological Inquiry*, Wendy Morris and I described a set of beliefs that constitute an ideology of marriage (or committed romantic coupling): (1) Just about everyone wants to marry and just about everyone does marry. (2) The marital relationship is the one truly important peer relationship. (3) Those who marry are better people—more valuable, worthy, and important. Compared to people who do not marry, the ideology maintains, they are happier, more mature, and less lonely, and their lives are more meaningful and more complete (DePaulo & Morris, 2005).

We characterized the beliefs as an ideology because they seem to constitute a worldview that is accepted uncritically as part of the conventional wisdom of our time. People seem to be invested in these beliefs about marriage and defend them against threats. Social scientists, too, are influenced by the ideology of marriage, perhaps unwittingly. The ideology plays a role in determining the questions they ask, the questions they never think to ask, and the way they analyze and interpret their data. Researchers studying marital status, for example, seek overwhelmingly to advance our understanding of marriage and its purported benefits; only rarely are their studies designed to illuminate single life. Many of the social scientists studying marriage are quite accomplished, and yet they sometimes make claims about the benefits of marrying based on dubious comparisons (for example, comparing just the currently married to people who are not married). When they do find differences that seem to favor married people, they reach for flattering portrayals of marriage (for example, as sites of companionship and social support) while rarely acknowledging the unfair advantages accorded to married people that have nothing to do with the quality of their marital relationships (for example, the federal laws that benefit them).

Research has demonstrated some of the reasons people cling to their ideological beliefs about marriage (Day, 2016; Day, Kay, Holmes, & Napier, 2011). For example, those beliefs can offer a sense of predictability and control: Get married, and you will be happier and healthier and all the pieces of your life will fall into place. Ideological beliefs can also be personal, as, for example, when valuing committed romantic relationships is part of a person's self-concept. Belief in the tenets of the marriage ideology can also be part of a broader defense of the status quo, a way of justifying the prevailing social system.

If people are invested in their ideological beliefs about marriage, then it should follow that they will be particularly critical of people who flout those beliefs—people, for example, who *choose* to be single. In research from Israel (Slonim, Gur-Yaish, & Katz, 2010) and the United States (Morris & Osburn, 2016), participants read brief biographical sketches of people who were married (or coupled), people who were single but wanted to be married (or coupled), and people who were single and wanted to stay that way. As usual, the single people were judged more harshly than the married or coupled people, regardless of whether or not they wanted to be single. Even more tellingly, the single people who chose to be single were criticized more than those who were single but wished they weren't. They were judged as less well adjusted (e.g. less happy and less secure), more self-centered, and as leading less exciting lives (Morris & Osburn, 2016). They were also seen as more miserable and lonely, while the single people who wanted to be partnered were viewed as warmer and more sociable (Slonim et al., 2015). Perhaps most significantly, the single people who chose to be single made people mad; more anger was expressed toward them than toward the single people who were pining for a partner (Slonim et al., 2015).

It may seem ironic that the single people who had just the life they wanted (those who chose to be single) were rated as less happy than those who did not have their preferred lives, but that's just what should happen if judgments are ideologically driven. The anger those single people elicited also demonstrates the emotional force behind the ideology.

People who want to believe that getting married makes people happy are going to be resistant to single people's claims that they are already happy. That's what Morris and I found (DePaulo & Morris, 2005). We created pairs of biographical sketches that were identical except that half the time, the people in the sketches were described as single, and the other half, married. We constructed profiles that highlighted different kinds of skills and accomplishments, such as great career accomplishments, remarkable altruism, or laudable interpersonal ties. We asked participants to indicate how happy they thought the person in the profile would claim to be, and how happy the person really was.

The participants thought that everyone exaggerated their happiness, but that the single people did so even more than the married people.

Consistent with my argument about the power, pervasiveness, and uncritical acceptance of the ideology of marriage were the findings (reviewed above) that stereotypes of single people are widely embraced—by men and women, people in different countries, and single people as well as coupled people. Even though single people are demeaned by the ideological view of their lives as less valuable and fulfilling, they may also be attracted by what the ideology offers, such as a clear path to a more respected and predictable life. And, of course, the uncritical acceptance of the ideology is self-perpetuating; single people, like everyone else, are unlikely to challenge the tenets of the ideology because they have so rarely heard them challenged.

The prevailing and largely unquestioned belief that just about everyone wants to marry and just about everyone does marry makes it difficult to know how many single people actually want to stay single. With few narratives about happy and fulfilled single people in the media, popular culture, or even scholarly writings, single people would need to take it upon themselves to proclaim something they are rarely hearing anywhere else. Even so, a non-trivial number of single people do so. For example, when a national sample of single people was asked whether they want to get married, 25 percent said no and another 29 percent said they were not sure (Taylor, 2010).

Some research suggests that more single than coupled people want to change their relationship status (Greitemeyer, 2009). But that comparison is problematic. Coupled people who want to change their relationship status can simply walk away, leaving disproportionate numbers of contented couples in the group that is currently coupled. In contrast, single people who want to change their relationship status cannot do so single-handedly; they need to find a partner.

Is it Possible that Single People are Actually More Resilient than Married People?

In untold numbers of ways, single people are perceived and treated as less worthy than married people. Some single people claim that they have never experienced singlism, but that reflects a lack of awareness rather than a lack of actual prejudice or discrimination; preferential treatment of married people is written right into American laws. Compared to other more familiar isms such as racism, sexism, and heterosexism, singlism is more often practiced without apology or even awareness (Morris et al., 2007).

Because single people are stereotyped, stigmatized, marginalized, and discriminated against, and because they are also devalued by the pervasive matrimania that celebrates people who have escaped their status, it would be entirely understandable if single people really were worse off than people who marry in all sorts of physical, emotional, and interpersonal ways. But they aren't. Sure, there are differences, especially when methodologies and analyses give married people huge unwarranted advantages, but even then, the differences are sometimes small or complicated by important qualifications (DePaulo, 2015b), and sometimes it is the lifelong single people who do better than everyone else (e.g. Cwikel et al., 2006; Krull & Haugseth, 2012; White, 1992).

Scholars who write about the purported benefits of marrying like to point to "social causation" as an explanation of why married people (supposedly) do better than single people. Lamb and his colleagues (Lamb, Lee, & DeMaris, 2003), for example, explained it this way: "...married persons benefit directly from their relationships with their spouses, in terms of support, intimacy, caring, companionship..." They also added that marriage can have a buffering effect "by moderating the effects of events or circumstances that would result in lower well-being for unmarried persons." But if people who marry get all that support and buffering, and all the matrimaniacal valuing of their status, and single people instead get stereotyped, stigmatized, and marginalized, then again, how is it possible that lifelong single people are doing as well as they are?

Perhaps, then, it is single people, more so than married people, who are especially resilient. That's just a hypothesis. What seems clear is that there are single people who choose to live single and that many single people—including even some who would prefer to be partnered—thrive while living single, despite all the singlism and matrimania. But why? A robust positive psychology of single people would provide answers to that question. We don't have that yet. Next, I will offer an outline of what those answers might include.

Why Some People are Drawn to Single Life and Thrive There

There are many reasons why some people are drawn to single life and thrive there. I will describe what I believe to be five of the most important ones.

1. *Single people invest in "the ones" instead of "The One."*
    The dominance of the ideology of marriage has focused our attention on what single people do not have—a spouse—and left us oblivious to what they *do* have. Single people are more involved in the life of their communities, they have more friends, and they do more to maintain their ties with siblings, parents, neighbors, friends, and co-workers. Single people, it seems, maintain a more diverse relationship portfolio. They may also use a different relationship investment strategy; whereas people who marry let their non-marital relationships slide, single people hold onto the relationships in which they have invested.

    In the social science literature on interpersonal relationships as well as in the conversations of everyday life, the word "relationship" is often used as a shorthand for "romantic relationship." Single people, though, may have bigger and broader views of relationships and love.

Of course, relationship quality and not just quantity is important and one measure of quality is whether a relationship qualifies as a "full-blown attachment." Research on adult attachment focuses primarily on romantic relationships. In one of the few studies of other adult relationships (Doherty & Feeney, 2004), all four components of an attachment relationship were measured (providing a secure base, a safe haven, a target for seeking proximity, and a source of separation protest when contact cannot be maintained) and the kinds of relationships important to single people were assessed. Single people, it was found, often have relationships with siblings, parents, friends, or children that fulfill all four functions and therefore qualify as full-blown attachment relationships.

Research suggests that married people who invest primarily in their relationship with their spouse, to the exclusion of other relationships, may be vulnerable in ways that single people with more diversified relationship portfolios are not. For example, for some married people, their spouse is "the focal point of the person's social world, acting as confidant, provider of emotional and practical support, and constant companion" (Spencer & Pahl, 2006). They score lower on mental health than people whose personal communities include more friends or family or neighbors in the inner circles.

Looking to just one person to deal with the regulation of most emotions also appears to be risky. People who turn to different people for different emotional needs (e.g. cheering them up when they are sad, calming them down when they are anxious or angry) report better well-being than those who got most of their emotion-regulation needs met by just one person or a few people (Cheung, Gardner, & Anderson, 2014).

2. *Rather than fearing loneliness, many single people savor solitude.*
Although single people, on average, do more to maintain their ties to other people than do married people, they are not especially likely to be extroverted (Marks, 1996).

All people seem to want some combination of time with other people and time alone (DePaulo, 2015a). People who are drawn to single life probably favor a greater than average proportion of time to themselves. In preliminary research, I found that when people who are single at heart think about spending time alone, they are highly likely to expect to savor their solitude, and very unlikely to worry about being lonely.

Social scientists have conducted thousands of studies of the perils of loneliness. The less extensive research on the potential benefits of spending time alone suggests that solitude offers opportunities for creativity, self-discovery, inner peace, freedom from social constraints, relaxation, contemplation, and spirituality (Averill & Sundararajan, 2014; Long & Averill, 2003; Long, Seburn, Averill, & More, 2003).

People who spend a lot of time alone have not fared well in popular culture. They are portrayed as the weirdos, the outcasts, and the violent criminals. Perhaps, as *Party of One* author Anneli Rufus (2003) suggests, the people at risk for poor outcomes are those who spend a lot of time alone when they don't want to, especially if they have been rejected by other people. It's a different story for those who like their time alone (Hagemeyer, Neyer, Neberich, & Asendorpf, 2013). They have several positive personality traits, including greater open-mindedness and less neuroticism. They are also less likely to be lonely.

3. *Single people contribute in meaningful ways.*
    Single people provide help and support and care to many different people and groups, in many different domains, in ways large and small. Single people's contributions matter to others; that's one of the ways their lives are purposeful and meaningful. Research has yet to be conducted on the ways in which single people make contributions beyond what they give to other individuals and groups. For example, a philosopher has made the case, unscientifically, that many of the most influential philosophers in history were single (Wolff, 2016). We need to know more about the marks that singles have made on science, medicine, the humanities, the arts, and every other domain.

4. *Single people value opportunities to pursue their interests and passions, and to do the kind of work they find meaningful.*
    Single people seem to prioritize meaningfulness and authentic values. Living their lives in pursuit of what matters most to them may also help to explain why many people are drawn to single life and thrive there.

    A study of what people wanted from their work lives found that among high school students, those who would marry within the next nine years said that they cared more about extrinsic factors such as pay and job security, whereas the students who would stay single cared more about intrinsic considerations, such as the meaningfulness of their work (Johnson, 2005). By age 27, those who stayed single still cared more about intrinsic factors than those who got married.

    Longitudinal research also underscores the special value to single people of autonomy and self-determination (Marks & Lambert, 1998). Over a five-year period, people who had been single all their lives were more likely than those who were married the whole time to describe growing autonomy, as indicated by their agreement with items such as "I judge myself by the values of what I think is important, not by the values of what others think is important."

5. *Single people experience more personal growth and development.*
    The experience of personal growth is often part of a meaningful life, and single people do well on that dimension, too. In the same longitudinal study (Marks & Lambert, 1998), the lifelong single people were more

likely than the continuously married people to endorse items of a personal growth scale such as "For me, life has been a continuous process of learning, change, and growth." In contrast, over the five-year period, the married people were more likely to agree with items such as, "I gave up trying to make big improvements in my life a long time ago."

Conclusions, Applications, and Future Directions

The belief in the transformative power of getting married is so strong, so enduring, and so resistant to change that it is not just any ordinary belief—it is an ideology. The Ideology of Marriage insists that just about everyone wants to marry, that people who marry become happier, healthier, and better off in many other ways, too, and that they are worthier people because of their marital status.

The power of the ideology is evident in the pervasiveness of stereotypes of single people. It is the ideology, I believe, that has had a role in the overwhelming interest that scholars have shown in married life, and their relative neglect of single life. At a time when the social sciences have become increasingly sophisticated, methodologically, researchers studying marital status—and the reporters who write about their work—are making claims that their studies simply cannot support. We can never demonstrate definitively that getting married causes people to become happier or healthier because we cannot do the kinds of studies that allow strong inference about causality. But even when social scientists use some of the best methodological approaches they can muster, such as long-term longitudinal research, the results are often not at all what we have been led to believe. Getting married sometimes results in no changes in well-being, or only short-term changes, or only changes for certain subgroups. Sometimes it is the lifelong single people who do the best. Even if future research were to show definitively that people who marry (including those who do not stay married) do better than people who stay single in certain ways, that would not necessarily mean that single people would also do better too if only they were coaxed to marry—they are different people than the people who chose to marry.

Considering the many significant ways in which single people are stereotyped, stigmatized, marginalized, and discriminated against, and considering too the relentless celebrating of marriage and weddings and coupling that saturates contemporary life, it is even more remarkable that single people are doing as well as they are. That's what scholars need to address: How is it possible, despite all the singlism and matrimania, that so many single people are thriving? I have offered a preliminary set of answers, the beginnings of a positive psychology of single life, but some of my suggestions are speculative and need to be put to the empirical test, and there are far more ideas that need to be explored.

For too long, the ideology seems to have steered our scholarship toward the exploration of what is good and fulfilling about married life and what is problematic or lacking about single life. It has left us largely ignorant of the other half of the human equation: what is meaningful and empowering about single life and risky and limiting about married life. That needs to change.

The way we think about relationships needs to change as well. The ideological focus on the coupled relationship has relegated other deeply significant interpersonal relationships to the periphery of our scholarship (Fingerman & Hay, 2002). For example, adults are far more likely to have a friend than a spouse, and many friendships last longer than many marriages. The scant research that is available suggests that friendships can be conducive to well-being in important ways (e.g. Pontari, 2009; Schnall, Harber, Stefanucci, & Proffitt, 2008). Research on the supposed benefits of marriage should include comparisons to other relationships. Maybe results would show that the relationship most likely to contribute to our happiness and health is friendship.

Day (2016) argues that relationships researchers need to be proactive in countering the ideology and developing a new science of single life. They should, he suggests, "by default first consider research questions from non-marital standpoints, such as the perspective of singles and their various relationships." They need to "ensure that research questions are not being studied on populations because they are…perceived to be more important, perceived to have more benefits…" Further, researchers should be "committing to these changes on an upcoming project instead of sometime in the distant future."

Although I have focused on the many ways that single life can be meaningful and fulfilling, my goal was not to argue that single life is for everyone. Instead, I think that different people find different life paths especially rewarding. Fortunately, there are more opportunities today than ever before for people to lead the lives that suit them best (DePaulo, 2015a). It is not necessary for people to marry in order to support themselves, raise children, or live happily ever after (DePaulo, 2006).

There is little systematic research on the personal fit model that I am describing—that different people do better with different life choices about marrying. Some findings, though, are suggestive. For example, in a nationally representative sample of Americans aged 40 and older, the role of self-sufficiency differed for married people and lifelong single people (Bookwala & Fekete, 2009). For the single people, the more self-sufficient they were, the less negative affect they experienced. But among the married people, the reverse was true.

Finally, we need to acknowledge and study the diversity of experiences of single life. The prevailing focus on the stereotypically sad single people who are pining for partners is wildly misleading. There are more than 109 million unmarried people just in the United States (Census Bureau, 2016), so of course some of them are sad and lonely and yearning to marry. But research suggests that the proportion of such single people is far smaller than we have been led to expect. Instead of perpetuating false narratives about sorrowful single people, we should be inspired by a positive psychology of single life to recognize something else: Some people are single at heart. Living single is how they lead their best, most authentic, most fulfilling, and most meaningful life.

References

Amato, P. R. (2010). Research on divorce: Continuing trends and new developments. *Journal of Marriage and Family, 72*, 650–666.

Antonovics, K., & Town, R. (2004). Are all the good men married? Uncovering the sources of the marital wage premium. *American Economic Review, 94*, 317–321.

Averill, J. R., & Sundararajan, L. (2014). Experiences of solitude: Issues of assessment, theory, and culture. In R. J. Coplan & J. C. Bowker (Eds.), *The handbook of solitude: Psychological perspectives on social isolation, social withdrawal, and being alone* (pp. 90–108). Chichester, UK: Wiley Blackwell.

Bellas, M. (1992). The effects of marital status and wives' employment on the salaries of faculty men: The (house) wife bonus. *Gender and Society, 6*, 609–622.

Bookwala, J., & Fekete, E. (2009). The role of psychological resources in the affective well-being of never-married adults. *Journal of Social and Personal Relationships, 26*, 411–428.

Census Bureau. (2016, August 26). *Facts for features: Unmarried and single Americans week*: Sept. 18–24, 2016.

Cheung, E. O., Gardner, W. L., & Anderson, J. F. (2014). Emotionships: Examining people's emotion-regulation relationships and their consequences for well-being. *Social Psychological and Personality Science, 6*, 407–414.

Conley, T. D., & Collins, B. E. (2002). Gender, relationship status, and stereotyping about sexual risk. *Personality and Social Psychology Bulletin, 28*, 1483–1494.

Cwikel, J., Gramotnev, H., & Lee, C. (2006). Never-married childless women in Australia: Health and social circumstances in older age. *Social Science & Medicine, 62*, 1991–2001.

Day, M. V. (2016). Why people defend relationship ideology. *Journal of Social and Personal Relationships, 33*, 348–360.

Day, M. V., Kay, A. C., Holmes, J. C., & Napier, J. L. (2011). System justification and the defense of committed relationship ideology. *Journal of Personality and Social Psychology, 101*, 291–306.

DePaulo, B. (2006). *Singled out: How singles are stereotyped, stigmatized, and ignored, and still live happily ever after.* New York: St. Martin's Press.

DePaulo, B. (2011). *Singlism: What it is, why it matters, and how to stop it.* Charleston, SC: DoubleDoor Books.

DePaulo, B. (2015a). *How we live now: Redefining home and family in the 21st century.* Hillsboro, OR: Beyond Words.

DePaulo, B. (2015b). *Marriage vs. single life: How science and the media got it so wrong.* Charleston, SC: CreateSpace.

DePaulo, B. M., & Morris, W. L. (2005). Singles in society and in science. *Psychological Inquiry, 16*, 57–83.

Doherty, N. A., & Feeney, J. A. (2004). The composition of attachment networks throughout the adult years. *Personal Relationships, 11*, 469–488.

Etaugh, C., & Malstrom, J. (1981). The effect of marital status on person perception. *Journal of Marriage and the Family, 43*, 801–805.

Fingerman, K. L., & Hay, E. L. (2002). Searching under the streetlight? Age biases in the personal and family relationships literature. *Personal Relationships, 9*, 415–433.

Gerstel, N. (2011). Rethinking families and community: The color, class, and centrality of extended kin ties. *Sociological Forum, 26*, 1–20.

Gerstel, N., & Sarkisian, N. (2006). Marriage: The good, the bad, and the greedy. *Contexts, 5*, 16–21.

Gillespie, B. J., Lever, J., Frederick, D., & Royce, T. (2015). Close adult friendships, gender, and the life cycle. *Journal of Social and Personal Relationships, 32*, 709–736.

Government Accountability Office. (2004). *Defense of marriage act: Update to prior report.* GAO-04-353R.

Greitemeyer, T. (2009). Stereotypes of singles: Are singles what we think? *European Journal of Social Psychology, 39*, 368–383.

Hagemeyer, B., Neyer, F. J., Neberich, W., & Asendorpf, J. B. (2013). The ABC of social desires: Affiliation, being alone, and closeness to partner. *European Journal of Personality, 27*, 442–457.

Henz, U. (2006). Informal caregiving at working age: Effects of job characteristics and family configuration. *Journal of Marriage and Family, 68*, 411–429.

Hertel, J., Schütz, A., DePaulo, B. M., Morris, W. L., & Stucke, T. S. (2007). She's single, so what? How are singles perceived compared with people who are married? *Journal of Family Research, 19*, 139–158.

Johnson, M. K. (2005). Family roles and work values: Processes of selection and change. *Journal of Marriage and Family, 67*, 352–369.

Johnson, N. J., Backlund, E., Sorlie, P. D., & Loveless, C. A. (2000). Marital status and mortality: The national longitudinal mortality study. *Annals of Epidemiology, 10*, 224–238.

Kahn, J. R., McGill, B. S., & Bianchi, S. M. (2011). Help to family and friends: Are there gender differences at older ages? *Journal of Marriage and Family, 73*, 77–92.

Kahng, L. (2010). One is the loneliest number: The single taxpayer in a joint return world. *Hastings Law Journal, 61*, 651–686.

Kalmijn, M. (2017). The ambiguous link between marriage and health: A dynamic reanalysis of loss and gain effects. *Social Forces, 95*, 1607-1636.

Klinenberg, E. (2012). *Going solo: The extraordinary rise and surprising appeal of living alone.* New York: Penguin Press.

Krull, H., & Haugseth, M. T. (2012). *Health and economic outcomes in the alumni of the Wounded Warrior Project.* Santa Monica, CA: RAND Corporation.

Laditka, J. N., & Laditka, S. B. (2001). Adult children helping older parents: Variations in likelihood and hours by gender, race, and family role. *Research on Aging, 23*, 429–456.

Lamb, K. A., Lee, G. R., & DeMaris, A. (2003). Union formation and depression: Selection and relationship effects. *Journal of Marriage and Family, 65*, 953–962.

Long, C. R., & Averill, J. R. (2003). Solitude: An exploration of benefits of being alone. *Journal for the Theory of Social Behaviour, 33*, 21–44.

Long, C. R., Seburn, M., Averill, J. R., & More, T. A. (2003). Solitude experiences: Varieties, settings, and individual differences. *Personality and Social Psychology Bulletin, 29*, 578–583.

Lucas, R. E., Clark, A., Georgellis, Y., & Diener, E. (2003). Reexamining adaptation and the set point model of happiness: Reactions to changes in marital status. *Journal of Personality and Social Psychology, 84*, 527–539.

Luhmann, M., & Hawkley, L. C. (2016). Age differences in loneliness from late adolescence to oldest old age. *Developmental Psychology, 32*, 943–959.

Luhmann, M., Hofmann, W., Eid, M., & Lucas, R. E. (2012). Subjective well-being and adaptation to life events: A meta-analysis. *Journal of Personality and Social Psychology, 102*, 592–615.

Marks, N. F. (1996). Flying solo at midlife: Gender, marital status, and psychological well-being. *Journal of Marriage and the Family, 58*, 917–932.

Marks, N. F., & Lambert, J. D. (1998). Marital status continuity and change among young and midlife adults: Longitudinal effects on psychological well-being. *Journal of Family Issues, 19*, 652–686.

McAdams, D. P., & de St. Aubin, E. (1992). A theory of generativity and its assessment through self-report, behavioral acts, and narrative themes in autobiography. *Journal of Personality and Social Psychology, 62*, 1003–1015.

Morris, W. L., DePaulo, B. M., Hertel, J., & Taylor, L. C. (2008). Singlism—another problem that has no name: Prejudice, stereotypes, and discrimination against singles. In M. A. Morrison & T. G. Morrison (Eds.), *The psychology of modern prejudice* (pp. 165–194). New York: Nova Science Publishers.

Morris, W. L., & Osburn, B. K. (2016). Do you take this marriage? Perceived choice over marital status affects the stereotypes of single and married people. In K. Adamczyk (Ed.), *Singlehood from individual and social perspectives* (pp. 145–162). Krakow, Poland: Libron Publishing.

Morris, W. L., Sinclair, S., & DePaulo, B. M. (2007). No shelter for singles: The perceived legitimacy of marital status discrimination. *Group Processes & Intergroup Relations, 10*, 457–470.

Musick, K., & Bumpass, L. (2012). Reexamining the case for marriage: Union formation and changes in well-being. *Journal of Marriage and Family, 74*, 1–18.

Nock, S. L. (1998). *Marriage in men's lives.* New York: Oxford University Press.

Park, L. E., Young, A. F., Troisi, J. D., & Pinkus, R. T. (2011). Effects of everyday romantic goal pursuit on women's attitudes toward math and science. *Personality and Social Psychology Bulletin, 37*, 1259–1273.

Pontari, B. A. (2009). Appearing socially competent: The effects of a friend's presence on the socially anxious. *Personality and Social Psychology Bulletin, 35*, 283–294.

Rudman, L. A., & Heppen, J. B. (2003). Implicit romantic fantasies and women's interest in personal power: A glass slipper effect? *Personality and Social Psychology Bulletin, 29*, 1357–1370.

Rufus, A. (2003). *Party of one: The loners' manifesto.* New York: Marlowe & Company.

Sarkisian, N., & Gerstel, N. (2008). Till marriage do us part: Adult children's relationships with their parents. *Journal of Marriage and Family, 70*, 360–376.

Sarkisian, N., & Gerstel, N. (2016). Does singlehood isolate or integrate? Examining the link between marital status and ties to kin, friends, and neighbors. *Journal of Social and Personal Relationships, 33*, 361–384.

Schnall, S., Harber, K. D., Stefanucci, J. K., & Proffitt, D. R. (2008). Social support and the perception of geographical slant. *Journal of Experimental Social Psychology, 44*, 1246–1255.

Slonim, G., Gur-Yaish, N., & Katz, R. (2015). By choice or by circumstance?: Stereotypes and feelings about single people. *Studia Psychologica, 57*, 35–48.

Spencer, L., & Pahl, R. (2006). *Rethinking friendship: Hidden solidarities today.* Princeton, NJ: Princeton University Press.

Taylor, P. (2010, November). The decline of marriage and rise of new families. Pew Research Center, Social and Demographic Trends Report.

Toutkoushian, R. K. (1998). Racial and marital status differences in faculty pay. *Journal of Higher Education, 69*, 513–529.

Tucker, J. S., Friedman, H. S., Wingard, D. L., & Schwartz, J. E. (1996). Marital history at midlife as a predictor of longevity: Alternative explanations to the protective effect of marriage. *Health Psychology, 15*, 94–101.

Victor, C. R., & Bowling, A. (2012). A longitudinal analysis of loneliness among older people in Great Britain. *Journal of Psychology, 146*, 313–331.

Wenger, G. C., & Burholt, V. (2004). Changes in levels of social isolation and loneliness among older people in a rural area: A twenty-year longitudinal study. *Canadian Journal on Aging, 23*, 115–127.

White, J. M. (1992). Marital status and well-being in Canada. *Journal of Family Issues, 13*, 390–409.

White, L. (2001). Sibling relationships over the life course: A panel analysis. *Journal of Marriage and Family, 63*, 555–568.

Wolff, J. (2016, March 15). Why do philosophers make unsuitable life partners? *The Guardian.*

Wright, M. R., & Brown, S. L. (2017). Psychological well-being among older adults: The role of partnership status. *Journal of Marriage and Family, 79*, 833–849. doi:10.1111/jomf.12375.

16

POSITIVE PSYCHOLOGY INTERVENTIONS

Clinical Applications

Mariya Smirnova and Acacia C. Parks

Introduction

Historically, medicine has focused on eliminating negative symptoms or "what is wrong" with someone rather than what makes one feel healthy and promotes flourishing (Engel, 1989). Traditional forms of psychotherapy, for example, cognitive-behavioral therapy, often emphasize decreasing negative thoughts, emotions, and behaviors (e.g. Beck, 2011). General physicians who heal physical ailments also mainly focus treatment on the disease itself. Recently there has been an acknowledgment of an important gap in medicine and patient care. Humanistic psychology arose during the 1950s to address the pessimism of psychology and focused on personal growth and self-actualization (Maslow, Frager, & Cox, 1970). In 1946, the World Health Organization defined health as "a state of complete physical, mental and social well-being and not merely the absence of disease or infirmity" (WHO, 1946, p. 100), which showed a movement in medical care to acknowledging other aspects of health, such as happiness.

While people are predisposed to a certain amount of happiness from genetics and life circumstances (i.e. money, religious affiliation), happiness is also partially malleable and can be increased through intentional activities that can account for about 40 percent of one's happiness (Lyubomirsky, Sheldon, & Schkade, 2005). Intentional activities can include behavioral, cognitive, and volitional activities, such as, striving for personal goals, thinking optimistically, and engaging in enjoyable activities. Fordyce (1977) was one of the pioneer researchers on exploring how to increase happiness through intentional activities. He discovered that happiness can be increased through various activities that characteristically happy people do, such as, spending time socializing and developing optimistic outlooks. He found that actively pursuing happiness can actually increase it and this can be done on a self-study basis. Since this work, many interventions aimed at increasing positive emotions have been developed, researched, and have shown to be successful at not only increasing positive affectivity, but also alleviating depression and other negative symptoms in the process.

Positive psychological interventions (PPIs) are activities that aim to increase positive emotion, and thereby increase well-being and happiness. Increasing positive emotions is an important part of well-being because increased happiness has been linked to better immune system functioning, better cardiac functioning, increased longevity, and improved psychological health (Tugade, Fredrickson, & Barrett, 2004). While PPIs were originally intended for non-clinical populations, they have been shown to be feasible and effective in patient populations. These interventions are not intended to replace traditional medicine, but aim to supplement these techniques for a more robust increase in well-being. PPIs have been shown to significantly reduce depression and increase well-being (Bolier et al., 2013; Sin & Lyubomirsky, 2009). These interventions are appealing because they can be very easy to administer (i.e. self-help) and they have been effective in different types of clinical groups (i.e. depressed individuals, people with schizophrenia). There is also a vast variety of PPIs that can be tailored to different clinical populations and narrowed to each individual's therapeutic needs.

Types of PPIs

There are several types of PPIs, with different systematic components and different outcomes for certain individuals. These intervention categories include humor, gratitude, building character strengths, optimism, mindfulness, kindness, and active-constructive responding. Many of these PPIs themselves can be varied to modify to different clinical populations and adjusted to each person's optimal fit (Lyubomirsky & Layous, 2013). While some of these interventions are used alone, many are combined together throughout an extended period in a treatment plan.

Humor

Humor interventions are effective because they prompt positive emotion, which has been linked to various health outcomes posited by various theories. One way that humor interventions work is because they elicit amusement, a positive emotion that is linked to play, which cultivates exploration and creativity (Fredrickson, 1998). Humor is often associated with laughter, which is linked to increases in positive emotion and increase in immune system functioning (Agarwal, 2014). Humor is also classified as a character strength in Peterson and Seligman's (2004) Virtues in Action theory, and this character strength has been associated with pleasure and happiness (Peterson, Ruch, Beermann, Park, & Seligman, 2007). Furthermore, humor interventions have been shown to increase self-efficacy, positive affect, optimism, and perceptions of control (Wellenzohn, Proyer, & Ruch, 2016). Such interventions have been shown to be more effective in clinical populations by ameliorating depression and increasing happiness more than other PPIs in a group of people aged 50–79 years (Konradt, Hirsch, Jonitz, & Junglas, 2013; Proyer, Gander, Wellenzohn, & Ruch, 2014).

Various humor interventions have also been shown to be effective at lowering depression in all age groups (Wellenzohn et al., 2016). Examples of humor interventions include "three funny things," which involves writing down three funny things that occurred in a specified time frame, collecting funny things, counting funny things, applying humorous activities in a specified time frame (i.e. watching funny movies), and solving stressful situations in a humorous way (Wellenzohn et al., 2016). For example, when participants were asked to solve a situation in a humorous way, participants were instructed to think about a stressful experience and how it could have been solved in a humorous way. The rationale is to think about situations that went wrong, but acknowledging the positive outcomes. In the "collecting funny things" intervention, participants were instructed to remember funny past experiences and record them with as much detail as possible.

Gratitude

Gratitude interventions include both reflection and gratitude activities (Schueller & Parks, 2014). The basis behind using gratitude for increasing positive emotion is that it fosters savoring positive life experiences (see Kurtz, this volume); prevents people from taking good things in their life for granted; prevents "hedonic adaptation"; promotes stronger social bonds; and can be an adaptive coping strategy (Sheldon & Lyubomirsky, 2006). Inducing a grateful outlook has been linked to better psychological and physical health (Emmons & McCullough, 2003). Participants who counted their blessings reported less physical complaints, reported more exercising, had better sleep quality, and a decrease in negative emotion. In a more rigorous program for optimizing gratitude, participants had an increase in positive affect and were more likely to act in a prosocial manner. Gratitude interventions have been shown to be effective at alleviating depression in various clinical populations, including those with depression and cardiovascular disease (Huffman et al., 2011; Sin & Lyubomirsky, 2009). Not only might they be directly effective for clinical populations because of increases in positive emotion and well-being, but also because these individuals are building resources, such as social support. The practice of expressing gratitude to others helps to cultivate those social bonds, which is an important predictor of both physical and mental health outcomes

(Uchino, 2006). Examples of gratitude interventions include counting blessings in a weekly or nightly journal format, or writing a gratitude letter about another person and delivering the letter (see Lomas, Froh, Emmons, Mishra, & Bono, 2014).

Building Character Strengths

Character strengths are components of good character and they have been classified and organized by categories that can contribute to optimal development and well-being (Peterson & Seligman, 2004). There have been 24 character strengths identified that fall into six virtues, which include wisdom and knowledge, courage, humanity, justice, temperance, and transcendence. Some examples of character strengths are creativity, kindness, and humor. Giving participants feedback on what their strengths are and how to apply them in their life has been linked to a more fulfilling life (Peterson, Park, & Seligman, 2005). Certain character strengths are more closely related to well-being than others; they include, gratitude, hope, zest, curiosity, and love (Park, Peterson, & Seligman, 2004). Participants who used their signature strengths in a new way were more likely to report being happier and less depressed in a one-month and three-month follow-up (Seligman, Steen, Park, & Peterson, 2005). For example, a store clerk whose character strength is curiosity might take the time to chat more with her customers and learn more about them—something that is not required of her job, but may make it more rewarding for her. Using signature strengths in a new way was also one of the more effective interventions in a group aged 50–79 years, in increasing happiness and alleviating depression (Proyer et al., 2014). Discovering and building character strengths can help clinical populations by revealing their strong points, which can help them more effectively cope with their disease and build self-esteem.

Optimism

Optimism involves focusing on positive aspects of life experiences and having confidence that the future holds more positive events. Optimism has been linked to better physical health, better immune functioning, lower stress hormones, and better cardiac health (Peterson, Park, & Kim, 2012). Some optimism interventions include inducing a positive mindset, visualizing your "best possible self," and writing about positive experiences. These interventions are also often packaged with others.

Visualizing one's "best possible self" is an intervention that often includes viewing oneself in the best possible light and describing traits, behaviors, thoughts, and goals that are important to the individual. This activity helps improve self-regulation because it illuminates one's goals, strengths, and motives to oneself. Improving self-regulation is crucial to clinical populations, especially in those who have life-long diseases, because it has been linked to health promotion because of better maintenance of healthy habits (Bandura, 2005). Writing about a "positive self" was linked to increases in positive mood and increased subjective well-being 3 weeks after the intervention (Sheldon & Lyubomirsky, 2006). This intervention can be effective in individuals with clinical depression because it can increase positive emotion and increase optimistic thinking, both of which are often lacking in this population.

Writing has been shown to help trauma survivors' levels of well-being and health by increasing awareness of the benefits linked to the negative event (Ullrich & Lutgendorf, 2002). It was important for participants to recognize both emotional and cognitive aspects of their trauma to get full physical health benefits from the journaling intervention. Burton and King (2004) found that writing about intensely positive experiences can enhance positive mood and can also have health benefits, including fewer illnesses, which was measured by health center visits. Participants who wrote about intensely positive experiences were less likely to visit the university health center three months after the writing study compared to participants who wrote about a neutral event. Also, writing about the benefits of a traumatic experience, which included positive experiences, was linked to better health outcomes (King & Miner, 2000).

Being optimistic and writing about positive experiences has also been related to longevity. Nuns who had more positive emotional content in their brief autobiographies (written in their youth) were more likely to live longer than those with more neutral or negative content (Danner, Snowdon, & Friesen, 2001). This intervention can be relevant to clinical populations because many illnesses have stressful events tied to their disease, such as changes in self-image, financial burdens, and physical limitations. It can be potentially helpful for these patients to explore their disease in an optimistic light, using writing as a positive coping mechanism to relieve depression and anxiety and perhaps promote post-traumatic growth.

Mindfulness

Mindfulness involves decentering and having a non-judgmental presence of the current moment. It has been shown to promote increases in positive emotions by increasing presence for the present and by increasing compassion for oneself and others (Khoury, Lecomte, Gaudiano, & Paquin, 2013; see also Langer & Ngnoumen, this volume). Some examples of PPIs that use mindfulness as a technique include savoring activities and meditation. Mindfulness interventions have been effective at alleviating symptoms in clinical populations such as schizophrenia, cancer, and chronic pain (Carson et al., 2005; Casellas-Grau, Font, & Vives, 2014; Johnson et al., 2009).

Savoring—a form of mindfulness—focuses on prolonging pleasurable activities and promotes mindfulness to experience every aspect of the moment.

Savoring interventions have been linked to increases in happiness, life satisfaction, optimism, perceived control, and lower depression (Jose, Lim, & Bryant, 2012; Kurtz, this volume). They found that individuals who reported more momentary savoring responses in a daily diary study, experienced greater boosts in happiness as a result of the savoring. They also found that when people rarely experience pleasant events in their day, higher momentary savoring is consistent with enhancing positive mood more than is lower momentary savoring. Participants who reported savoring their pleasant events when they rarely had them benefited more from savoring those events than those who experience pleasant events often. This form of reflection can be helpful for individuals with depression who might perceive less pleasant events in their daily lives because it could help them savor the positive events that they do experience. Savoring interventions include savoring a moment in a designated time frame (e.g. watching a sunset) and concentrating on the activity with full attention. Components of savoring can also be found in other interventions such as counting one's blessings.

Mindfulness meditation involves full awareness of the present moment without making any judgments; there is an awareness of all thoughts and emotions and accepting all of them rather than trying to repress or block them. While there are various types of mindfulness meditation techniques that vary in their practices, most of them aim to manage negative emotions by increasing awareness for the present moment and learning to embrace the moment (Khoury et al., 2013). One type of meditation used as a positive intervention is loving-kindness meditation (LKM), which focuses on directing attention to the present moment and then to loving and feeling compassion for others and oneself. LKM begins like many other meditative practices, including closing one's eyes, breathing deeply and calmly and attending to the present moment (Johnson et al., 2009). Then, the participant focuses on someone that they care for and love, for example, their child or significant other. They are then instructed to project this warm feeling of love toward themselves. Toward the end of the practice, they are instructed to project this love to other people, often starting with people they know well, then to extended family and friends, eventually to all people and living things of the world. Most importantly, the benefits of LKM have been shown to increase over time because people don't become immune to its effectiveness. In fact, people who continued meditating were more likely to report more positive emotions even after a one-year follow-up (Cohn & Fredrickson, 2010). Positive emotion was also linked to minutes spent engaging in LKM. This intervention could be effective for clinical groups that report preoccupation with the past or future (e.g. panic disorder, social phobia, or generalized anxiety), because it can help them focus on the present moment and perhaps lower rumination and mind-wandering. Participants who implemented mindfulness meditation compared to a control and distraction condition had a lessening of dysphoria (Broderick, 2005). Meditation can be effective in populations where negative affectivity, dysphoria, and rumination are prevalent, such as depression and anxiety.

Kindness

Happy people are not only more likely to act kindly, but also pay more attention to the kindness that they receive and are more likely to desire to be kind (Otake, Shimai, Tanaka-Matsumi, Otsui, & Fredrickson, 2006). Participants who counted more kindnesses were happier, more grateful, and enacted more kind behaviors. Performing acts of kindness have been shown to increase life satisfaction (Buchanan & Bardi, 2010). Pressman, Kraft, and Cross (2015) found that participants who did acts of kindness, including acts such as offering a compliment, feeding a parking meter, and giving a gift, experienced an increase in positive affect, a decrease in negative affect, more optimism, gratitude, life satisfaction, and joviality. In this intervention, the givers of the act of kindness extended to the receiver the opportunity to "pay it forward." Receivers of the act of kindness who did pay forward their act of kindness, had an increase in happy emotions such as excitement and happiness. Kindness interventions include counting kindness (received and acted), pay-it-forward-style kindness, and random acts of kindness.

Mechanism

While the mechanism behind PPIs is still largely under-researched, there have been various theories that posit why these interventions are effective in clinical populations. One of these theories includes the broaden-and-build theory, which holds that positive emotions help us build resources that improve our well-being. Other mechanistic research behind PPIs suggests that positive attention redirection can increase well-being by redirecting from excessive attention to negative events, which is common in the many clinical illnesses, for example anxiety disorders and illnesses that produce a lot of anxiety, such as cardiovascular disease.

The Broaden-and-Build Theory of Positive Emotions

One theory of why PPIs are effective in various patient groups is because feeling more positive emotion creates an upward spiral that can increase well-being. Fredrickson's broaden-and-build theory (2001) of positive emotions states that positive emotions can broaden people's "thought-action repertoires" and build personal resources, including social, physical, psychological, and intellectual resources (see also Le Nguyen & Fredrickson, this volume). Also positive emotions undo the negative and narrowing effects of negative emotions, this is known as the *undoing hypothesis*. Positive emotions have been shown to reduce physiological arousal in negative situations and improve cardiac recovery from stress (Fredrickson & Levenson, 1998). Over time, positive emotions accumulate and build, broadening attention and helping the person fight adversity, which predicts future positive emotion. In patients with cardiovascular disease, not only is it important for these individuals to build personal resources to get help, but decreasing physiological arousal can be very beneficial for these patients where arousal is an important contributor to the progression and maintenance of their disease. Another clinical application where this theory is relevant is in anxiety disorders, where using positive emotions to lower arousal states can be an important factor in alleviating the stress from the anxiety. Happiness may also help lower the pain perception of the negative stressor by preventing a downward spiral of negative emotions.

Positive Attentional Focus

Another factor of why PPIs work on clinical populations to increase well-being could be that there is a shift of attentional focus in daily life to more positive events rather than negative events. People naturally focus and remember more negative events than positive events (Baumeister, Bratslavsky, Finkenauer, & Vohs, 2001). By focusing on positive events rather than negative events, one is less likely to catastrophize and ruminate on stressors, which are common cognitive processes in depression and anxiety. Seligman, Rashid, and Parks (2006) argued that using a combined PPI treatment plan was effective in a depressed population because the participants had an exaggerated tendency to focus on negative events and the intervention helped them refocus toward more positive events. Wellenzohn et al. (2016) found that using humor interventions seemed to help increase happiness and alleviate depression because people had a more "positive information-seeking bias" when they were told to look for or apply funny things throughout the day. Participants focused more on positive and humorous experiences in their day. Dickerhoof (2007) found that motivated participants who either did a gratitude or optimism intervention cognitively construed more satisfying experiences in their lives. These students were able to buffer naturally occurring stressful events (i.e. examinations, studying) better because they focused their attention onto more satisfying events.

Key Moderators

PPIs work best under different conditions depending on the best optimal "fit" for the individual (Lyubomirsky & Layous, 2013). Both features of the positive activity (i.e. dosage) and features of the person (i.e. motivation) matter for maximum well-being benefits and continued use of the PPI. Features of the activity can matter across activities, such as, dosage, variety, social support, and triggers.

Features can also matter within the same activities, such as time orientation (i.e. future, past, or present focus).

Activity Features

Features of the positive intervention that are relevant to its efficacy include dosage, length of intervention, and variety of the interventions. Dosage pertains to the amount of times the PPI is performed within a designated period of time. An example where dosage matters is in the "acts of kindness" intervention. When the acts of kindness are spread out, they are less potent than when they are all done in one day (Lyubomirsky et al., 2005). Similarly, counting one's blessings once a week was more effective in increasing well-being than counting them three times a week. Thus, these interventions appear to be more effective when they are performed once a week instead of numerous times a week.

Another important factor for the efficacy of a positive intervention is the length of the intervention and varying the positive activities. In a meta-analysis, Sin and Lyubomirsky (2009) found that the longer the intervention, the greater the increases in well-being. In a study of usage data from an iPhone app that gave users free choice between eight happiness activities, Parks, Della Porta, Pierce, Zilca, and Lyubomirsky (2012) showed that regardless of which particular activity users picked, more activities led to greater increases in well-being. However, they also found that users who selected a variety of activities reported more improvement than did users who repeated the same activity over and over. The authors posited that variation is important to avoid hedonic adaptation (i.e. becoming bored with the activity). Sheldon, Boehm, and Lyubomirsky (2012), too, found that hedonic adaptation can be slowed by increasing the variety of PPIs.

Person Features

Features of the person also matter for optimal person–activity fit; these features include motivation, personality differences, and demographics. Motivation to increase happiness is a driving factor for the effectiveness of many PPIs. Sin and Lyubomirsky (2009) found that individuals that self-selected to participate in positive interventions gained the most increases in well-being and decreases in depressive symptoms. Dickerhoof (2007) found that motivation was the most critical factor for the PPI to effectively increase well-being. Seligman and colleagues (2005) claim that individuals who self-selected to their website showed increased well-being for up to 6 months. In an 8-month study, Lyubomirsky, Dickerhoof, Boehm, and Sheldon (2011) found that motivation, or self-selection, was only half the battle. They found that participants who performed with more effort and persistence maintained increases in happiness.

Some demographics impact the effectiveness of certain PPIs. Older individuals seem to benefit more than younger ones (Sin & Lyubomirsky, 2009). However, PPIs have been shown to be effective in younger clinical groups, such as children with diabetes (Jaser, Patel, Rothman, Choi, & Whittemore, 2014). Cultural background can also impact PPI effectiveness. Boehm, Lyubomirsky, and Sheldon (2011) examined the effect of writing a gratitude letter and expressing optimism in Anglo-Americans and Asian-Americans. They found that both groups had increases in life satisfaction and well-being, however Anglo-Americans reported more happiness. This result can be explained by cultural differences with individualistic cultures putting more emphasis on self-growth and Asian-Americans coming from a collectivist culture putting less importance on individualism (Hofstede, Hofstede, & Minkov, 1991). However, cultural norms also could have dictated the way the participant responded (i.e. Asian-Americans might not want to report an increase in happiness because of cultural norms regarding modesty). This is an important consideration when treating individuals in a clinical setting because they might report important aspects of well-being, including various emotions and pain levels, differently because of their heritage.

Person–Activity Fit

There is an importance to match intrinsic values of the person of the activity so that the person can be matched well for maximum benefits from the activity (Layous, Chancellor, & Lyubomirsky, 2014). Individual personality differences are also important characteristics for the intervention to be effective and for the individual to continue to adhere to the activities. For example, people who are higher on extraversion and openness to experience seem to benefit more from positive activities (Schueller, 2012). Extraverts and introverts differed in their preferred positive activity. Extraverts benefited more from the gratitude visit and savoring exercises, while introverts responded better to the three good things, active-constructive responding and strengths exercises. Increased preference for the activity also is linked to better adherence for the intervention (Schueller, 2010). Adherence to interventions has been linked to happiness and depression scores (Seligman et al., 2005). Those who were the most adherent were the happiest and least depressed. Not only do person and activity features matter for the interventions to work, nuances such as time-focus of the activity can affect the outcome of an intervention.

Time-Focus

Wellenzohn and colleagues (2016) manipulated the time-focus for a humor-based intervention. They asked participants to write about three funny things that happened during the day on seven consecutive days and they varied the time-focus of this intervention by asking them to write about past funny things, present, or future funny events. They found that the future-oriented variation contributed more to an attentional shift and a more positive outlook, while the past-oriented variation increased more savoring of positive emotions. They also found that the present-oriented variation was the most effective for amelioration of depressive symptoms, while the past variant was the most associated with increased happiness. This shows that the orientation of time is important for different results in positive emotions. This is important when implementing this intervention in a clinical population because the time-focus can influence the effectiveness of the intervention. For example, someone with depression might benefit more from a present-oriented variant, while someone who is not depressed might benefit more from the past-oriented variant.

Clinical Applications

PPIs are not only useful for "healthy" individuals looking to increase their happiness, but these interventions can also be applied in a clinical setting. PPIs have been effective in helping individuals not only with psychological ailments, but physical ones as well. Some psychological conditions where PPIs have been shown to be effective include depression, generalized anxiety disorder, and schizophrenia. Physical impairments where PPIs have increased well-being include cancer, cardiovascular disease, diabetes, and chronic pain.

Depression

Using a meta-analysis, PPIs have demonstrated across multiple studies to increase happiness and alleviate depressive symptoms (Sin & Lyubomirsky, 2009). Positive psychotherapy (PPT) helps depression by not only reducing negative emotions, but also by increasing positive emotions, building resources for the individual to maintain positive emotions, and by building meaning in their lives (Seligman et al., 2006). There are three main components of PPT: (1) building a pleasant life by increasing positive emotions; (2) building an engaged life by increasing flow and absorption in work; and (3) building a meaningful life by using one's character strengths to work on something important to the individual on a spiritual level. PPT blended various PPIs, such as using strengths, three good things, obituary/biography (i.e. writing about what one would like to be remembered for), gratitude visits, active-constructive responding, and savoring. Patients in the PPT group scored in the non-depressed range of depressive symptoms after the intervention, compared to controls. After a year follow-up, those in the PPT group remained in the non-depressed range and also had an increase in life satisfaction. PPT also worked when added to traditional individual therapy. Patients had increased happiness, positive emotions, engagement, and meaning. PPT worked to alleviate depression because of various mechanisms. First, depressed individuals have an exaggerated tendency to focus on negative aspects of life. PPT helped individuals redirect their attention to more positive events, by interventions such as three good things where the individual focused on remembering good things in their day. Also, by showing individuals their character strengths, they were able to work more efficiently and to feel more flow.

PPIs have also been effective at alleviating depression in a geriatric population (Konradt et al., 2013). Patients with depression were given a humor intervention, where they learned about humor, laughing, and playfulness and applied those concepts throughout eight sessions and completed homework activities during the week. Those in the humor condition compared to the control group had a decrease in depressive symptoms and also had a decline in suicidal tendencies. The patients in the humor condition did not only feel an alleviation of negative symptoms, but also experienced increased satisfaction with life and state cheerfulness.

Generalized Anxiety Disorder

Generalized anxiety disorder is marked by persistent and unrealistic worry and fear about everyday events. Well-being therapy, when combined with cognitive-behavioral therapy (CBT), has been shown to have better outcomes for patients with generalized anxiety disorder (Ruini & Fava, 2009). Well-being therapy (WBT) occurs over multiple sessions. During the initial sessions, the patient is asked to identify instances of well-being and having the patient explore situations where they feel the most well-being. In the middle sessions, participants identify thoughts and beliefs that interrupt their well-being and the therapist encourages activities that can elicit well-being. Although this approach is similar to Rational-Emotion Therapy, it differs in that it focuses on promoting well-being rather than alleviating distress. In the later sessions, the therapist can specify where the patient is impaired the most, based on well-being dimensions according to Ryff's (1989) work. The six dimensions of well-being include: autonomy, personal growth, environmental mastery, purpose in life, positive relations, and self-acceptance. The goal of WBT is to achieve mastery in all six dimensions. Fava et al. (2005) compared the effectiveness of CBT as a stand-alone therapy, and CBT followed by sessions of WBT. They found that anxiety improved significantly more when the patient received both WBT and CBT. This may have occurred because patients focused more on maintaining a more positive well-being. Also all dimensions of psychological well-being increased in the CBT–WBT combination group.

Schizophrenia Spectrum Disorders

Individuals with schizophrenia spectrum disorders can individually vary in their intensity and prevalence of negative and positive symptoms. Some negative symptoms of schizophrenia include anhedonia, which is the diminished ability to anticipate pleasure, blunted affect, and asociality. Some positive symptoms include delusions and hallucinations. Various PPIs have been adapted to target both negative and positive symptoms in individuals with schizophrenia spectrum disorders.

LKM and mindfulness meditation have been shown to be a promising option for individuals with schizophrenia. Johnson and colleagues (2009) revealed through case studies that LKM can work to improve individual's negative symptoms, based on the mechanism of the broaden-and-build theory because positive emotions can improve anhedonia (lack of anticipatory pleasure), sociality, and motivation. Participants went to weekly group sessions that included discussion, skills training, and practice. The limitation of this study was that it was based on case studies, however they did show marked improvements in negative symptoms. Participants with previous experience in meditation had improved outcomes because their experience helped them learn and practice LKM more readily. Participants with no previous experience were said to perhaps benefit from basic mindfulness meditation first. A meta-analysis by Khoury et al. (2013) showed that mindfulness meditation can help individuals with psychosis, a prevalent positive symptom of schizophrenia. They found that mindfulness meditation can increase quality of life, reduce negative and affective symptoms, and improve distress from these symptoms. They found the effect sizes for positive symptoms were smaller, but meditation still showed to be helpful.

PPIs can work to help individuals with schizophrenia also by targeting well-being instead of focusing on getting rid of symptoms. These patients could benefit from building character strengths and resources to help them manage their illness better. Meyer, Johnson, Parks, Iwanski, and Penn (2012) adapted a version of PPT (Seligman et al., 2006), named Positive Living to fit individuals with schizophrenia. This intervention included six exercises, including using your strengths, three good things, biography, gratitude visits, active/constructive responding, and savoring. Participants also did an additional exercise called Positive Service, where they used their strengths to help, by promoting something "larger than themselves." In addition to the original intervention, they added a positive goal and mindfulness minute. Patients chose a goal that they wanted to work on during their treatment, and progress was reviewed at every session. Setting meaningful goals has been an important part of treatment for individuals with schizophrenia because it focuses on increasing hope and recovery. The mindfulness minute was also added to the Positive Living because mindfulness has been shown to be helpful for the treatment of psychosis (Khoury et al., 2013). The Positive Living intervention was effective because of high attendance rates and high levels of satisfaction with the intervention (Meyer et al., 2012). At the end of the interventions, participants reported higher levels of hope, well-being, savoring, and recovery, and their improvements were maintained at a 3-month follow-up. Despite the fact that this was an uncontrolled study (participants were doing other therapies), participants reported a decrease in paranoid, psychotic, and depressive symptoms. Interventions aimed at combining therapy as usual with Positive Living therapy could greatly increase patient recovery and well-being.

Cancer

Various cancers are common in society and are often paired with physical and psychological exhaustion, depression, and negative emotion (Bodurka-Bevers et al., 2000). Patients with cancer can benefit from PPIs, with most evidence mainly focusing on mindfulness meditation interventions and meaning-making interventions. In a meta-analysis by Casellas-Grau et al. (2014), they found that breast cancer patients can benefit from PPIs. They explored PPIs, such as mindfulness and hope therapy, as well as other interventions that fostered an increase in positive emotions. They found that positive therapies can help patients have an increase in satisfaction with life, self-esteem, optimism, and have an increase in sense of meaning.

A life of meaning can be an important route to increasing happiness (Peterson et al., 2005). Lee, Cohen, Edgar, Laizner, and Gagnon (2006) adapted a manual for coping with post-traumatic stress to cancer populations. Participants received individualized sessions where they learned to make meaning in their life. They reviewed their cancer experience as an autobiographical narrative embedded with other important life events. Patients also did tasks that included appraising their emotional and cognitive response to their cancer diagnosis, exploring previously used coping strategies and past life events on the present cancer experience, and lastly a discussion of life priorities. The meaning-making group had significant improvements in self-esteem, optimism, and self-efficacy. These improvements are important factors linked to future health and well-being because they can help individuals buffer the stress associated with the adverse effects of the treatment and cancer management.

Cardiovascular Disease

Many patients with various cardiovascular diseases have depression, which is linked to negative medical outcomes (Elderon & Whooley, 2013). Patients hospitalized for acute cardiac conditions (i.e. acute coronary syndrome or congestive heart failure) often have depression, which puts them at risk for another cardiac episode and increased mortality. Positive emotional states, such as optimism, are linked to better cardiac outcomes, such as lower incidence of coronary heart disease and mortality, and better adherence to treatment (DuBois et al., 2012; see also Carver et al., this volume). PPIs can benefit cardiac patients because these interventions can increase optimism and because of the beneficial link between positive mood states and cardiac health. Huffman and colleagues (2011) created a positive intervention plan to fit acute coronary syndrome patients and patients with congestive heart failure. Participants were randomized into a positive intervention condition, a meditation condition, and a control condition. Their intervention was delivered through the telephone and the patients were also given a booklet with homework assignments. For the positive intervention, participants learned various PPIs to foster various positive emotion strengths, such as gratitude and optimism. During weeks 1 and 2, participants focused on gratitude (three good things intervention and gratitude letter). During weeks 3 and 4, patients focused on cultivating optimism. They wrote about their best possible selves in their social relationships one week and about their best possible selves in their health the following week. Weeks 5 and 6 focused on doing three acts of kindness in one day. During weeks 7 and 8, patients chose which interventions they wanted to do from the previous weeks. Participants in the meditation condition did relaxation exercises shown to reduce anxiety and physical symptoms in this population. Participants in the recollection condition were the control condition and they just recalled events that occurred throughout the week. Participants in the positive intervention group had the largest increase in optimism, with the meditation group not far behind. Participants in the positive intervention group had greater improvements in depressive symptoms, anxiety, higher happiness, and better health-related quality of life compared to the other two groups. Meditation subjects also had improvements in happiness. This research shows the feasibility of helping cardiac patients using positive interventions and meditation.

Diabetes

Diabetes is a widespread disease that affects 29.1 million people in the United States (Centers for Disease Control and Prevention, 2014). Many factors can influence the progression of diabetes, such as medication adherence, exercise, and diet. Important factors that impact diabetes outcomes included psychological characteristics, such as, depression and anxiety, which are linked to poorer adherence to diet, diabetes-related complications, and mortality (Lustman & Clouse, 2005). While largely under-researched for this disease, PPIs have been shown to be a feasible and effective option for helping individuals with diabetes. However, while there is a large theoretical rationale and proof of feasibility, there is also a large gap in the literature showing disease-related health improvements.

Cohn, Pietrucha, Saslow, Hult, and Moskowitz (2014) created a PPI package for diabetes called the Developing Affective HeaLth to Improve Adherence (DAHLIA) intervention, which consisted of eight skills to increase positive emotion. The skills were: notice and recall positive events, savoring or capitalizing on positive events, gratitude, mindfulness, positive reappraisal, self-affirmation, and recognizing personal strengths, setting attainable goals, and performing acts of kindness. They found that depression scores dropped significantly in the intervention condition, however they didn't find a change in diabetes-specific psychological measures or health behaviors. The DAHLIA intervention showed that PPIs are a very feasible option for this population because there was a high completion rate. The intervention was easily administered using a website. Huffman, DuBois, Millstein, Celano, and Wexler (2015) also found that a positive intervention could be an easy and feasible option for adults with type 2 diabetes in both inpatient and outpatient settings. However, they also did not find evidence for PPIs to boost positive psychological states or modify health behaviors related to type 2 diabetes. One known study has found some increase in health behavior adherence in adolescents with diabetes.

Jaser and colleagues (2014) conducted a pilot study of a PPI in adolescents with type 1 diabetes. Adolescents were either assigned to the PPI or an attention control education condition. The PPI was designed to increase positive affect through gratitude, self-affirmations, small gifts, and parent affirmations. The adolescents did these activities when it was time to check their blood sugar levels. They found that higher rates of positive affect were related to overall adherence, and better self-reported glucose monitoring in the positive intervention group. This study showed that PPIs can have a promising effect on this population.

Chronic Pain

Chronic pain is a very pervasive and disabling condition that is often accompanied by depression. Flink, Smeets, Bergbom, and Peters (2015) had patients meet with a psychologist once a week and were assigned homework that consisted of the following interventions: three good things, savoring, seeing a silver lining, and the "best possible self" imagery. The interventions started out very simple and gradually grew more complex. They found that depression and anxiety improved for some patients. They found the biggest improvements in reduced catastrophizing and measures of disability. Disability was measured by a scale that is used to measure the degree to which everyday activities, such as sexual behavior and social activities, are hindered by pain. Outcomes showed that, after the intervention, people perceived less interference from pain in their everyday activities. There has been a link between higher optimism and lower levels of pain, with reductions in catastrophizing. This work might offer an important and relatively easy strategy for decreasing catastrophizing among people with chronic pain.

Loving-kindness meditation (LKM) also has been shown to improve chronic low back pain (Carson et al., 2005). Anger and resentment are very common emotions felt by chronic pain patients and these emotions actually contribute to increased pain. Redirecting attention from negative emotions, such as anger, to more positive ones, such as love, could help this group alleviate pain and have an increase in well-being. In the intervention, patients were training on loving-kindness practice to shift to more positive affectivity. They found that the intervention helped improve pain level and psychological adjustment. Patients in the LKM condition experienced less pain at the end of the intervention and reported less anger on the following day. There was also a direct relationship with the amount of meditation the participant engaged in and their response to the intervention.

Conclusion

PPIs have shown to be effective and beneficial for various clinical populations, including those with psychological (e.g. depression) and physical (e.g. acute coronary syndrome) illnesses. PPIs not only alleviate depression and other negative symptoms, but also increase happiness and satisfaction with life. With many diverse options of PPIs, they can be tailored to help many different people with different conditions. Research on person–activity fit helps us predict which interventions can work with specific individuals (Lyubomirsky & Layous, 2013). PPIs have been shown to help people in various age groups, not only college populations (Huffman et al., 2011; Proyer et al., 2014).

One large benefit to using PPIs is that they can be disseminated through various formats. PPIs can be administered through self-help, individual therapy, and group therapy. The majority of PPIs are utilized though a self-help format; these interventions tend to be short-term, but significantly help alleviate depression (Bolier et al., 2013). Since this method is so widely used, improving its efficacy is important. Delivery of the intervention also can vary, either in person, by telephone, or online. Also, increasing adherence to these PPIs will make them more effective. Increased preference for an exercise is correlated with increased adherence (Schueller, 2010), so it is important to tailor the treatment to the individual.

Self-help books are one important way that PPIs have reached the attention of the general public. One study found that a PPI self-help book (*The How of Happiness* by Sonja Lyubomirsky, 2008) reduced depressive symptoms among college freshmen at a rate that was comparable with a cognitive-behavioral self-help book (Parks & Szanto, 2013). Another relevant method of dissemination of PPIs is through technology, including cellphones and the internet. While once a luxury, cell phones have become an essential tool for people to connect to others, for gathering information, and for entertainment purposes. Currently 91 percent of adults in the United States own a cell phone (PEW Research Center, 2014). Parks and colleagues (2012) found that use of the iPhone app "Live Happy" for a longer length of time and for different activities was linked to increases in happiness. This is a very effective and also cost-effective method because most people already have cell phones and it would not be an extra cost to them to do these happiness exercises, rather than paying for individual therapy.

The next challenge, then, is to find ways to get PPIs—which research has established are effective in both non-clinical and clinical populations—into the hands of the general public. Research on the logistics and effectiveness of mass intervention dissemination is only in its infancy (e.g. Carpenter et al., 2016) but it provides a good beginning for this very important future work. A handful of papers has provided examples of PPIs delivered via the consumer marketplace—as self-help books (e.g. *The How of Happiness* by Sonja Lyubomirsky, 2008) or using technology, such as Live Happy (Parks et al., 2012) and Happify (Carpenter at al., 2016). In addition, other promising contexts, such as workplaces and health care settings, contain individuals with a wide range of stress and mental health symptomology—and are therefore potentially ideal for PPIs, which seem to have broad utility for wellness/stress management/prevention, as well as across numerous conditions and severity levels. However, more research is needed to evaluate interventions once implemented, and many PPIs have not yet been implemented in these contexts—there is much work yet to do.

References

Agarwal, S. K. (2014). Therapeutic benefits of laughter. *Medical Science, 12*(46), 19–23.

Bandura, A. (2005). The primacy of self-regulation in health promotion. *Applied Psychology: An International Review, 54*(2), 245–254.

Baumeister, R. F., Bratslavsky, E., Finkenauer, C., & Vohs, K. D. (2001). Bad is stronger than good. *Review of General Psychology, 5*(4), 323–370. doi:1037/1089-2680.5.4.323.

Beck, J. S. (2011). *Cognitive behavior therapy: Basics and beyond.* New York: Guilford Press.

Bodurka-Bevers, D., Basen-Engquist, K., Carmack, C. L., Fitzgerald, M. A., Wolf, J. K., de Moor, C., & Gershenson, D. M. (2000). Depression, anxiety, and quality of life in patients with epithelial ovarian cancer. *Gynecologic Oncology, 78,* 302–308. doi:10.1006/gyno.2000.5908.

Boehm, J. K., Lyubomirsky, S., & Sheldon, K. M. (2011). A longitudinal experimental study comparing the effectiveness of happiness-enhancing strategies in Anglo Americans and Asian Americans. *Cognition and Emotion, 25*(7), 1263 1272. doi:10.1 080/02699931.2010.541227.

Bolier, L., Haverman, M., Westerhof, G. J., Riper, H., Smit, F., & Bohlmeijer, E. (2013). Positive psychology interventions: A meta-analysis of randomized controlled studies. *BMC Public Health, 13*(1), 1–20. doi:10.1186/1471-2458-13-119.

Broderick, P. C. (2005). Mindfulness and coping with dysphoric mood: Contrasts with rumination and distraction. *Cognitive Therapy and Research, 29*(5), 501–510. doi: 10.1007/s10608-005-3888-0

Buchanan, K. E., & Bardi, A. (2010). Acts of kindness and acts of novelty affect life satisfaction. *The Journal of Social Psychology, 150*(3), 235–237. doi:10.1080/ 00224540903365554.

Burton, C. M., & King, L. A. (2004). The health benefits of writing about intensely positive experiences. *Journal of Research in Personality, 38*(2), 150–163. doi:10.1016/ S0092-6566(03)00058-8.

Carpenter, J., Crutchley, P., Zilca, R. D., Schwartz, H. A., Smith, L. K., Cobb, A. M., & Parks, A. C. (2016). Seeing the "Big" picture: Big data methods for exploring the relationships between usage, language, and outcome in internet intervention data. *Journal of Medical Internet Research, 18*(8), e241. doi:10.2196/jmir.5725.

Carson, J. W., Keefe, F. J., Lynch, T. R., Carson, K. M., Goli, V., Fras, A. M., & Thorp, S. R. (2005). Loving-kindness meditation for chronic low back pain results from a pilot trial. *Journal of Holistic Nursing, 23*(3), 287–304. doi:10.1177/0898010105277651.

Casellas-Grau, A., Font, A., & Vives, J. (2014). Positive psychology interventions in breast cancer. A systematic review. *Psycho-Oncology, 23*(1), 9–19. doi:10.1002/pon.3353.

Centers for Disease Control and Prevention. (2014). *National diabetes statistics report: Estimates of diabetes and its burden in the United States, 2014.* Atlanta, GA: U.S. Department of Health and Human Services.

Cohn, M. A., & Fredrickson, B. L. (2010). In search of durable positive psychology interventions: Predictors and consequences of long-term positive behavior change. *The Journal of Positive Psychology, 5*(5), 355–366. doi:10.1080/17439760.2010.508883.

Cohn, M. A., Pietrucha, M. F., Saslow, L. R., Hult, J. R., & Moskowitz, J. T. (2014). An online positive affect skills intervention reduces depression in adults with type 2 diabetes. *The Journal of Positive Psychology, 9*(6), 523–534. doi:10.1080/17439760.2014.920410.

Danner, D. D., Snowdon, D. A., & Friesen, W. V. (2001). Positive emotions in early life and longevity: Findings from the nun study. *Journal of Personality and Social Psychology, 80*(5), 804–813. doi:10.1037/0022-3514.80.5.80.

Dickerhoof, R. M. (2007). Expressing optimism and gratitude: A longitudinal investigation of cognitive strategies to increase well-being. *Dissertation Abstracts International, 68*, 4174 (UMI No. 3270426).

DuBois, C. M., Beach, S. R., Kashdan, T. B., Nyer, M. B., Park, E. R., Celano, C. M., & Huffman, J. C. (2012). Positive psychological attributes and cardiac outcomes: Associations, mechanisms, and interventions. *Psychosomatics, 53*(4), 303–318. doi:10.1016/j.psym.2012.04.004.

Elderon, L., & Whooley, M. A. (2013). Depression and cardiovascular disease. *Progress in Cardiovascular Diseases, 55*(6), 511–523. doi:10.1016/j.pcad.2013.03.010.

Emmons, R. A., & McCullough, M. E. (2003). Counting blessings versus burdens: An experimental investigation of gratitude and subjective well-being in daily life. *Journal of Personality and Social Psychology, 84*(2), 377–389. doi:10.1037/0022–3514.84.2.377.

Engel, G. L. (1989). The need for a new medical model: A challenge for biomedicine. *Holistic Medicine, 4*(1), 37–53. doi:10.3109/13561828909043606.

Fava, G. A., Ruini, C., Rafanelli, C., Finos, L., Salmaso, L., Mangelli, L., & Sirigatti, S. (2005). Well-being therapy of generalized anxiety disorder. *Psychotherapy and Psychosomatics, 74*(1), 26–30. doi:10.1159/000082023.

Flink, I. K., Smeets, E., Bergbom, S., & Peters, M. L. (2015). Happy despite pain: Pilot study of a positive psychology intervention for patients with chronic pain. *Scandinavian Journal of Pain, 7*, 71–79. doi:10.1016/j.sjpain.2015.01.005.

Fordyce, M. W. (1977). Development of a program to increase personal happiness. *Journal of Counseling Psychology, 24*(6), 511–521. doi:10.1037/0022-0167.24.6.511.

Fredrickson, B. L. (1998). What good are positive emotions? *Review of General Psychology, 2*(3), 300–319. doi:10.1037/1089-2680.2.3.300.

Fredrickson, B. L. (2001). The role of positive emotions in positive psychology: The broaden-and-build theory of positive emotions. *American Psychologist, 56*(3), 218–226. doi:10.1037/0003-066X.56.3.218.

Fredrickson, B. L., & Levenson, R. W. (1998). Positive emotions speed recovery from the cardiovascular sequelae of negative emotions. *Cognition and Emotion, 12*(2), 191–220. doi:10.1080/026999398379718.

Hofstede, G., Hofstede, G. J., & Minkov, M. (1991). *Cultures and organizations: Software of the mind* (Vol. 2). London: McGraw-Hill.

Huffman, J. C., DuBois, C. M., Millstein, R. A., Celano, C. M., & Wexler, D. (2015). Positive psychological interventions for patients with type 2 diabetes: Rationale, theoretical model, and intervention development. *Journal of Diabetes Research*, 1–18. doi:10.1155/2015/428349.

Huffman, J. C., Mastromauro, C. A., Boehm, J. K., Seabrook, R., Fricchione, G. L., Denninger, J. W., & Lyubomirsky, S. (2011). Development of a positive psychology intervention for patients with acute cardiovascular disease. *Heart International, 6*(13), 47–54. doi:10.4081/hi.2011.e13.

Jaser, S. S., Patel, N., Rothman, R. L., Choi, L., & Whittemore, R. (2014). Check it! A randomized pilot of a positive psychology intervention to improve adherence in adolescents with type 1 diabetes. *The Diabetes Educator*, 1–9. doi:10.1177/0145721714535990.

Johnson, D. P., Penn, D. L., Fredrickson, B. L., Meyer, P. S., Kring, A. M., & Brantley, M. (2009). Loving-kindness meditation to enhance recovery from negative symptoms of schizophrenia. *Journal of Clinical Psychology, 65*(5), 499–509. doi:10.1002/jclp.20591.

Jose, P. E., Lim, B. T., & Bryant, F. B. (2012). Does savoring increase happiness? A daily diary study. *The Journal of Positive Psychology, 7*(3), 176–187. doi:10.1080/17439760.2012.671345.

Khoury, B., Lecomte, T., Gaudiano, B. A., & Paquin, K. (2013). Mindfulness interventions for psychosis: A meta-analysis. *Schizophrenia Research, 150*(1), 176–184. doi:10.1016/j.schres.2013.07.055.

King, L. A., & Miner, K. N. (2000). Writing about the perceived benefits of traumatic events: Implications for physical health. *Personality and Social Psychology Bulletin, 26*(2), 220–230. doi:10.1177/0146167200264008.

Konradt, B., Hirsch, R. D., Jonitz, M. F., & Junglas, K. (2013). Evaluation of a standardized humor group in a clinical setting: A feasibility study for older patients with depression. *International Journal of Geriatric Psychiatry, 28*(8), 850–857. doi:10.1002/gps.3893.

Layous, K., Chancellor, J., & Lyubomirsky, S. (2014). Positive activities as protective factors against mental health conditions. *Journal of Abnormal Psychology, 123*(1), 3–12. doi:10.1037/a0034709.

Lee, V., Cohen, S. R., Edgar, L., Laizner, A. M., & Gagnon, A. J. (2006). Meaning-making intervention during breast or colorectal cancer treatment improves self-esteem, optimism, and self-efficacy. *Social Science & Medicine, 62*(12), 3133–3145. doi:10.1016/j.socscimed.2005.11.041.

Lomas, T., Froh, J. J., Emmons, R. A., Mishra, A., & Bono, G. (2014). Gratitude interventions: A review and future agenda. In A. Parks & S. Schueller (Eds.), *The Wiley Blackwell handbook of positive psychological interventions* (pp. 1–19). West Sussex: John Wiley & Sons. doi:10.1002/9781118315927.ch1.

Lustman, P. J., & Clouse, R. E. (2005). Depression in diabetic patients: The relationship between mood and glycemic control. *Journal of Diabetes and its Complications, 19*(2), 113–122. doi:10.1016/j.jdiacomp.2004.01.002.

Lyubomirsky, S. (2008). *The how of happiness: A scientific approach to getting the life you want.* New York: Penguin Press.

Lyubomirsky, S., Dickerhoof, R., Boehm, J. K., & Sheldon, K. M. (2011). Becoming happier takes both a will and a proper way: An experimental longitudinal intervention to boost well-being. *Emotion, 11*(2), 391–402. doi:10.1037/a0022575.

Lyubomirsky, S., & Layous, K. (2013). How do simple positive activities increase well-being? *Current Directions in Psychological Science, 22*(1), 57–62. doi:10.1177/096372141246980.

Lyubomirsky, S., Sheldon, K. M., & Schkade, D. (2005). Pursuing happiness: The architecture of sustainable change. *Review of General Psychology, 9*(2), 111–131. doi:10.1037/1089-2680.9.2.111.

Maslow, A. H., Frager, R., & Cox, R. (1970). *Motivation and personality.* Ed. J. Fadiman & C. McReynolds (Vol. 2, pp. 1887–1904). New York: Harper & Row.

Meyer, P. S., Johnson, D. P., Parks, A., Iwanski, C., & Penn, D. L. (2012). Positive living: A pilot study of group positive psychotherapy for people with schizophrenia. *The Journal of Positive Psychology, 7*(3), 239–248. doi:10.1080/17439760.2012.677467.

Otake, K., Shimai, S., Tanaka-Matsumi, J., Otsui, K., & Fredrickson, B. L. (2006). Happy people become happier through kindness: A counting kindnesses intervention. *Journal of Happiness Studies, 7*(3), 361–375. doi:10.1007/s10902–005–3650-z.

Park, N., Peterson, C., & Seligman, M. E. (2004). Strengths of character and well-being. *Journal of Social and Clinical Psychology, 23*(5), 603–619. doi:10.1521/jscp.23.5.603.50748.

Parks, A. C., Della Porta, M. D., Pierce, R. S., Zilca, R., & Lyubomirsky, S. (2012). Pursuing happiness in everyday life: The characteristics and behaviors of online happiness seekers. *Emotion, 12*(6), 1222–1234. doi:10.1037/a0028587.

Parks, A. C., & Szanto, R. K. (2013). Assessing the efficacy and effectiveness of a positive psychology-based self-help book. *Terapia Psicologica, 31*, 141–149.

Peterson, C., Park, N., & Kim, E. S. (2012). Can optimism decrease the risk of illness and disease among the elderly? *Aging Health, 8*(1), 5–8. doi:10.2217/ahe.11.81.

Peterson, C., Park, N., & Seligman, M. E. (2005). Orientations to happiness and life satisfaction: The full life versus the empty life. *Journal of Happiness Studies, 6*(1), 25–41. doi:10.1007/s10902-004-1278-z.

Peterson, C., Ruch, W., Beermann, U., Park, N., & Seligman, M. E. P. (2007). Strengths of character, orientations to happiness, and life satisfaction. *The Journal of Positive Psychology, 2*(3), 149–156. doi:10.1080/17439760701228938.

Peterson, C., & Seligman, M. E. (2004). *Character strengths and virtues: A handbook and classification.* Washington DC: Oxford University Press.

PEW Research Center. (2014). *Mobile technology fact sheet* [Data file]. Retrieved from: www.pewinternet.org/fact-sheets/mobile-technology-fact-sheet/.

Pressman, S. D., Kraft, T. L., & Cross, M. P. (2015). It's good to do good and receive good: The impact of a "pay it forward" style kindness intervention on giver and receiver well-being. *The Journal of Positive Psychology, 10*(4), 293–302. doi:10.1080/17439760.2014.965269.

Proyer, R. T., Gander, F., Wellenzohn, S., & Ruch, W. (2014). Positive psychology interventions in people aged 50–79 years: Long-term effects of placebo-controlled online interventions on well-being and depression. *Aging & Mental Health*, *18*(8), 997–1005. doi:10.1080/13607863.2014.899978.

Ruini, C., & Fava, G. A. (2009). Well-being therapy for generalized anxiety disorder. *Journal of Clinical Psychology*, *65*(5), 510–519. doi:10.1002/jclp.20592.

Ryff, C. D. (1989). Happiness is everything, or is it? Explorations on the meaning of psychological well-being. *Journal of Personality and Social Psychology*, *57*(6), 1069–1081. doi:0022-3514/89/SOO.75.

Schueller, S. M. (2010). Preferences for positive psychology exercises. *The Journal of Positive Psychology*, *5*(3), 192–203. doi:10.1080/17439761003790948.

Schueller, S. M. (2012). Personality fit and positive interventions: Extraverted and introverted individuals benefit from different happiness increasing strategies. *Psychology*, *3*(12A), 1166–1173. doi:10.4236/psych.2012.312A172.

Schueller, S. M., Parks, A. C. (2014). The science of self-help: Translating positive psychology research into increased individual happiness. *European Psychologist*, *19*(2), 145–155. doi:10.1027/1016-9040/a000181.

Seligman, M. E., Rashid, T., & Parks, A. C. (2006). Positive psychotherapy. *American Psychologist*, *61*(8), 774–788. doi:10.1037/0003-066X.61.8.774.

Seligman, M. E., Steen, T. A., Park, N., & Peterson, C. (2005). Positive psychology progress: Empirical validation of interventions. *American Psychologist*, *60*(5), 410–421. doi:10.1037/0003-066X.60.5.410.

Sheldon, K. M., Boehm, J. K., & Lyubomirsky, S. (2012). Variety is the spice of happiness: The hedonic adaptation prevention (HAP) model. In I. Boniwell & S. David (Eds.), *Oxford handbook of happiness* (pp. 901–914). Oxford: Oxford University Press.

Sheldon, K. M., & Lyubomirsky, S. (2006). How to increase and sustain positive emotion: The effects of expressing gratitude and visualizing best possible selves. *The Journal of Positive Psychology*, *1*(2), 73–82. doi:10.1080/17439760500510676.

Sin, N. L., & Lyubomirsky, S. (2009). Enhancing well-being and alleviating depressive symptoms with positive psychology interventions: A practice-friendly meta-analysis. *Journal of Clinical Psychology*, *65*(5), 467–487. doi:10.1002/jclp.20593.

Tugade, M. M., Fredrickson, B. L., & Barrett, L. F. (2004). Psychological resilience and positive emotion granularity: Examining the benefits of positive emotions on coping and health. *Journal of Personality and Social Psychology*, *72*(6), 1161–1190. doi:10.1111/j.1467-6494.2004.00294.x.

Uchino, B. N. (2006). Social support and health: A review of physiological processes potentially underlying links to disease outcomes. *Journal of Behavioral Medicine*, *29*(4), 377–387. doi:10.1007/s10865-006-9056-5.

Ullrich, P. M., & Lutgendorf, S. K. (2002). Journaling about stressful events: Effects of cognitive processing and emotional expression. *Annals of Behavioral Medicine*, *24*(3), 244–250.

Wellenzohn, S., Proyer, R. T., & Ruch, W. (2016). Humor-based online positive psychology interventions: A randomized placebo-controlled long-term trial. *The Journal of Positive Psychology*, 1–11. doi: 10.1080/17439760.2015.1137624.

World Health Organization. (1946). *Constitution of the World Health Organization*. Geneva: WHO.

17

SELF-DETERMINATION AND POSITIVE PSYCHOLOGICAL ASPECTS OF SOCIAL PSYCHOLOGY

Michael L. Wehmeyer and Karrie A. Shogren

The use of the self-determination construct to explain human behavior ranges from John Locke's late 17th-century speculations about free will and determinism to modern usages in psychology, with the construct applied in philosophy, psychology, social welfare, and education. Within psychology, self-determination has utility in motivational, personality, developmental, and social psychology. Given this, it is not surprising that self-determination, which refers generally to acting volitionally, was a foundational construct in the discipline of positive psychology. The January 2000 topical issue of *American Psychologist* on the science of positive psychology included an article on self-determination (Ryan & Deci, 2000).

The purpose of this chapter is to review applications of the self-determination construct in social psychology, examining current research and knowledge pertaining to self-determination as a central construct in positive psychology, from the standpoint of, and as a central construct in, social psychology. In this chapter, we discuss the application of the self-determination construct in positive psychology and social psychology, respectively, situating the construct in social psychology within general research and knowledge concerning action control. We then introduce Self-Determination Theory (SDT; Ryan & Deci, 2000), a motivational theory prominent in positive psychology, and examine current knowledge and recent research illustrating the importance of SDT to examining issues framed within social psychology. Next, we turn our frame to introduce Causal Agency Theory (CAT), which explains how people become self-determined, and overview current knowledge and recent research, particularly in the context of people with disabilities, that contribute to knowledge in social psychology. We conclude with a brief discussion of the development of self-determination, drawing from these two theoretical frames.

Self-Determination and Positive Psychology

Positive psychology is "the pursuit of understanding optimal human functioning and well-being" (Wehmeyer, Little, & Sergeant, 2009, p. 357). To engage in such a pursuit, researchers must account for the agentic nature of human action (Ryan & Deci, 2000), where agentic refers to the "state of being active, usually within the service of a goal, or of exerting power or influence" (VandenBos, 2007, p. 29). Human agency is "the sense of personal empowerment, which involves both knowing and having what it takes to achieve one's goals" (Little, Hawley, Henrich, & Marsland, 2002, p. 390). Theories of human agency share organismic approaches to understanding human behavior (Little, Snyder, & Wehmeyer, 2006), which view "behavior as volitional, goal-directed action" in which "individuals are inherently active and self-regulating and their actions are both purposive and self-initiated" (Little et al., 2002, p. 390). Importantly for social psychology, an organismic approach involves "an explicit focus on the interface between the self and context" (Little et al., 2002, p. 390).

The self-determination construct was co-opted by psychology from philosophical discussions about free will and the doctrine of determinism, which suggests that all events, including human behavior, are in some way caused. Self-determination "is a general psychological construct within the organizing structure of theories of human agency which refers to self- (vs. other-) caused action—to people acting volitionally, based on their own will" (Wehmeyer et al., 2009, p. 357). Self-determined action refers to the degree to which action is self-caused, volitional and agentic, and driven by beliefs about the relationships between actions (or means) and ends. Human agentic theories differentiate between self-determination as self-*caused* action versus controlling one's behavior; self-determined action does not imply control over events or outcomes, but that the person acted based upon his or her own volition.

Lopez and Gallagher (2009) noted that positive psychology provides a means to unify psychological research because constructs such as optimism, hope, and happiness, among others, require a focus from multiple psychological subdisciplines. This is true for self-determination, which, as mentioned, has applicability across psychological domains. To frame our discussion, we first situate self-determination within the discipline of social psychology.

Self-Determination and Social Psychology

Social psychology is "the study of how an individual's thoughts, feelings, and actions are affected by the actual, imagined, or symbolically represented presence of other people" (VandenBos, 2007, p. 868). Psychological social psychology emphasizes the internal psychological processes of the individual, including (among other factors) attitudes, perceptions, personality, emotion, mood, learning, and cognition (Baumeister & Vohs, 2007). In the *Encyclopedia of Social Psychology*, Baumeister and Vohs (2007) place self-determination under the heading of topics pertaining to *Action Control*. The term "action control" refers to the self-regulatory mechanisms "mediating the formation and enactment of intentions" and the "mechanisms mediating the final execution of a sequence of behaviors" (Kuhl & Beckmann, 1985, p. 2).

Because it is impossible to provide a comprehensive examination of the current research in self-determination in a single chapter and because some of that research is not relevant to social psychology, we have opted to include topics pertaining to self-determination that fall under the Action Control topic area, and which include the role of autonomy, decision making, problem solving, self-regulation, and goal-setting and attainment in conceptualizing and understanding self-determination and human behavior.

As indicated, human agentic theories emphasize the interaction between the organism (person) and the environment or context, and thus are important in social psychology to understand social interactions and the effect of psychological processes on such interactions and their outcomes. For example, research in developmental and personality psychology (reflected in CAT, to be discussed subsequently) has emphasized that becoming self-determined:

> ...means having the freedom (opportunity) to use one's resources (capacity) to pursue those ends in life that are (1) consistent with one's needs and interests and (2) expressed in a community that promises to respect those pursuits. In this sense, self-determination always occurs in a social context.
>
> *(Mithaug, 1998, p. 41)*

In research in motivation, the earliest research in Self-Determination Theory (SDT, also discussed subsequently) focused on the role of social contexts in supporting or thwarting intrinsic motivation and found that conditions fostering autonomy and competence were positively associated with intrinsic motivation. Thus, there is convincing evidence that extrinsic rewards (monetary, tokens, toys, food, prizes, etc.) undermine intrinsic motivation and reduce the probability that the person will engage in the action without some form of extrinsic reward (Deci & Ryan, 1985). Cognitive Evaluation Theory, which became the foundational meta-theory in SDT, "explains how and why external events such as rewards or praise affect intrinsic motivation" (Reeve, 2012, p. 156) and "reflects the social psychology of self-determination theory" (p. 157). Deci and Ryan (2012) observed that "motivated individuals exist within social contexts" (p. 86) and that "social contexts, whatever their level, have their impact on individuals by facilitating versus impairing satisfaction of basic needs" (p. 87). It is efforts to satisfy basic needs of competence, relatedness, and autonomy leading to autonomous motivation as explained by SDT that, in turn, energize (motivate) people to engage in causal action as explained by Causal Agency Theory.

People respond to challenges or opportunities in their context by employing causal and agentic actions, supported by action-control beliefs, that enable them to make or cause things to happen that fulfill basic psychological needs, sustain autonomous motivation, and, ultimately, become more self-determined.

So, self-determination at its core is about the interaction between the self and the context and provides social psychologists a means to consider the self-regulatory psychological processes leading to the initiation and execution of actions, or action-control sequences.

Self-Determination Theory and Recent Research

Self-Determination Theory (SDT) is a comprehensive, organismic meta-theory of motivation that "details the origins and outcomes of human agentic action" (Vansteenkiste, Niemiec, & Soenens, 2010, p. 106). SDT proposes three basic psychological needs—competence, autonomy, and relatedness—that are either supported or challenged by social contexts and the satisfaction of which leads to autonomous motivation, enhanced well-being, and healthy physical and psychological development (Deci & Ryan, 2012). The basic psychological need for *autonomy* describes the drive people have to be able to make choices and act volitionally. The psychological need for *competence* refers to the motivation to be effective within environments, which leads to behavioral responses that sustain and augment individual capabilities (Ryan & Deci, 2002). The psychological need for *relatedness* is the sense of connectedness and belonging with others. Environments that are supportive of the attainment of these needs enable people to become energized about engaging in actions for their own sake to meet their needs (Vansteenkiste & Ryan, 2013). In such environments, people are intrinsically or autonomously motivated, and act volitionally to address their needs. As Deci, Vallerand, Pelletier, and Ryan (1991) wrote, "social contexts that support people's being competent, related, and autonomous will promote intentional (i.e. motivated) action, and furthermore, that support for autonomy in particular will facilitate that motivated action's being self-determined (rather than controlled)" (pp. 332–333). However, under other circumstances, where behavior is directed and controlled by others or external circumstances, such as extrinsic rewards as mentioned previously, people are less autonomously motivated.

SDT consists of six mini-theories, each explaining a set of observed motivation phenomena in many domains (Deci & Ryan, 2012; Ryan & Deci, 2002). *Cognitive Evaluation Theory* explains the types of external events that enhance or diminish intrinsic motivation, identifies autonomy-supportive social contexts versus controlling social contexts, and explains the interactions of external events and social contexts and their effects on intrinsic motivation (Deci & Ryan, 2012). *Causality Orientations Theory* proposes three different personality orientations based on the source of initiation and regulation of behavior:

autonomous, controlled, and impersonal (Deci & Ryan, 1985). The autonomous orientation is associated with orienting toward internal and external cues in a way that supports ones' autonomy and the informational significance of cues, as when one acts based upon preferences, or "internalizes" external priorities as one's own. The controlled orientation is associated with perceiving internal and external cues as controlling and demanding (e.g. when someone's action is regulated by extrinsic rewards, externally dictated deadlines, directives of others that are not internalized as one's own). The impersonal orientation, illustrated by believing that some task or goal is beyond one's control, is associated with perceiving cues as indicators of incompetence and is linked with amotivation.

Organismic Integration Theory explains behavior that is externally motivated but also either controlled or autonomous (Deci & Ryan, 1985). Deci and Ryan (1985) proposed five types of motivation on a continuum from extrinsic to intrinsic: external regulation, introjected regulation, identified regulation, integrated regulation, and intrinsic motivation. *Basic Psychological Needs Theory* was formulated based upon findings that environments and contexts that support psychological needs satisfaction were associated with greater feelings of well-being, psychological health, and greater positive affect in both work and non-work related environments (Ryan, Bernstein, & Brown, 2010). *Goal Content Theory* posits that extrinsic goals are less likely to satisfy the three basic psychological needs than are intrinsic goals (Ryan, Kasser, Sheldon, & Deci, 1996). Finally, *Relationships Motivation Theory* (RMT) describes supportive elements that are most likely to lead to sustained and satisfying relationships and address the need for relatedness (Deci & Ryan, 2014).

Current Knowledge and Recent Research

SDT proposes that people are driven to engage in actions to fulfill their need for autonomy, relatedness, and competence, and that environments supportive of the fulfillment of these needs enable people to become energized about initiating and maintaining action and achieving goals. In social psychology, research questions might reflect upon what research in basic psychological needs satisfaction tells us about why people act to engage in volitional or causal action, how their relationships and other outcomes differ when they do, and what social and social interaction factors impact outcomes. Central to research pertaining to these questions are goal-oriented actions, and it is important to clarify the SDT approach to goal pursuits:

> SDT differentiates the content of goals or outcomes and the regulatory processes through which the outcomes are pursued, making predictions for different contents and for different processes. Further, it uses the concept of innate psychological needs as the basis for integrating the

differentiations of goal contents and regulatory processes and the predictions that resulted from those differentiations. Specifically, according to SDT, a critical issue in the effects of goal pursuit and attainment concerns the degree to which people are able to satisfy their basic psychological needs as they pursue and attain their valued outcomes.

(Deci & Ryan, 2000, p. 227)

SDT posits a continuum of behaviors (non-self-determined, self-determined), motivation types (amotivation, extrinsic motivation, intrinsic motivation), regulation types (non-regulation, external, introjected, identified, integrated, and intrinsic), and loci of causality (impersonal, external, somewhat external, somewhat internal, internal) that govern goal-directed activities (Deci & Ryan, 2000). A more detailed look at this continuum is beyond the scope of this chapter, but what is relevant is that SDT posits that "goal directed activities can differ in the extent to which they are autonomous or self-determined" and that "intrinsic motivation and well-internalized extrinsic motivation are the bases for autonomous and self-determined behavior" (Deci & Ryan, 2000, p. 237) and, thus, self-determined goal pursuit.

Deci and Ryan (2000) reviewed studies on the impact of regulatory styles (the "why" of goal pursuit, from non-self-determined to self-determined action and amotivation to intrinsic motivation) across multiple domains and found a link between autonomous regulatory styles and positive goal attainment. Within education, they concluded that "[s]tudents' pursuit of educational goals for autonomous reasons, relative to heteronomous reasons, has been positively associated with value endorsement, behavioral persistence, conceptual understanding, personal adjustment, and positive coping" (p. 240). In health domains, autonomous regulatory styles were related to better adherence to medication regimens and adherence to and achievement of weight-loss goals. The links between autonomous regulatory styles and positive goal attainment have been found in the attainment of new year's resolutions, goals related to changing behavior to protect the environment, and achieving sport-related goals.

Related research has also examined the role of social interactions in autonomous regulation and goal attainment. Deci and Ryan (2000) reviewed research that showed that when physicians are perceived by patients to be more autonomy supportive, patients were more likely to attain health-related goals. Ng and colleagues (2012) conducted a meta-analysis of 184 SDT-based studies applied to health contexts. Autonomy support within health care settings predicted higher levels of patient/client autonomy, competence, and relatedness, which in turn had moderate to strong effects on patient welfare, including physical and mental health. Ntoumanis and colleagues (2013) examined influences on goal striving by athletes. They first established that athletes with autonomous goal motives showed greater persistence when working to achieve a challenging goal. In a second study, Ntoumanis et al. replicated the first study, except for assigning athletes randomly to a priming condition in which they watched a video of an actor describing involvement in a research study but varying by goal motives (autonomous versus controlling). This study found a significant effect on goal persistence for participants being primed by a person elaborating autonomous goal motivations. In essence, athletes viewing people stating autonomy-regulated goals were more persistent to achieve their own goals.

Koestner, Powers, Carbonneau, Milyavskaya, and Chua (2012) reviewed literature showing that "social support can facilitate progress on personal goals because it enhances feelings of perceived competence…" (p. 1609), and that "autonomy support of goal pursuit may also be associated with improved relationship quality and personal well-being" (p. 1610). Koestner et al. conducted three studies examining the role of autonomy support (empathic perspective-taking on the part of another person), with directive support, (positive guidance). First, male–female pairs rated whether their partner provided autonomous and directive support with regard to academic, health, relationship, and friendship goals. Next, pairs of female friends rated the extent to which their friend provided autonomous or directive support in academic, health, and leisure goals. In both studies, Koestner et al. found that autonomy support of goal pursuits contributed to greater goal progress over time, which was not the case for directive support, a finding that held even when the goal was not self-generated. In essence, autonomy-supportive relationships enable people to achieve goals at higher rates. Further, participants showed increased perceptions of positive relationship quality when their partner or friend was autonomy supportive.

Autonomy-supportive relationships have been examined in the education context. Reeve (2012) noted that when students are in classrooms, they "live and interact in a social world that offers supports for and threats against their needs, goals, interests, and values" (p. 152). It is, of course, primarily the teacher (though also peers) who creates learning communities and influences that context, and interactions with teachers and students become critical elements in autonomy support and goal attainment. Research in SDT has clearly established the impact of autonomy-supportive educational environments and teaching practices on student motivation and positive outcomes. Deci, Schwartz, Sheinman, and Ryan (1981) found that autonomy-supportive teachers who created learning environments that enabled students to make choices and act volitionally were associated with higher levels of student intrinsic motivation, perceived competence, and self-esteem. Other research has linked autonomy-supportive teachers with enhanced self-regulation, learning and achievement, and engagement (Reeve, 2012). Reeve (2002) summarized several studies of autonomy-supportive teaching and concluded that:

> autonomy-supportive teachers distinguished themselves by listening more, spending less time holding instructional materials such as notes

or books, giving students time for independent work, and giving fewer answers to the problems students face.

(p. 186)

Autonomy-supportive teachers use a style that engages students and supports self-regulation. Research has shown that regulatory teaching practices result in enhanced student engagement (behavioral, emotional, and cognitive) and in more positive student goal attainment and academic progress (Reeve, 2016).

Ratelle and Duchesne (2014) conducted a longitudinal study of perceived psychological needs satisfaction with over 600 students from their last year of elementary school to graduation from high school, collecting data on basic psychological needs satisfaction and multiple indicators of school adjustment, including social adjustment ("student's perceptions of their socializing with peers and school professionals," p. 391). School and social adjustment was significantly higher for students who perceived that their basic psychological needs were fulfilled. In an analysis of the same dataset, Guay, Ratelle, Larose, Vallarand, and Vitaro (2013) found that students who perceived that adults (parents, teachers) were autonomy supportive achieved more positive academic outcomes than those who did not receive such support.

The development of one's identity is a central theme of adolescent development, and social interactions are obviously critical in this time. Research has shown that adolescents whose perceptions of competence and relatedness are relatively high have more positive social comparisons with their peers, and that competence and relatedness are associated with adolescents' feelings of autonomy within social groups (Griffin, Adams, & Little, 2017).

Mechanisms of autonomy support have been applied to examine dynamics in close personal relationships. Hadden, Rodriguez, Knee, and Porter (2015) reviewed literature pertaining to relationship autonomy (e.g. "fully endorsing one's involvement in the relationship," p. 359), and found it was associated with healthier, adaptive relationships. Hadden et al. concluded that SDT "provides an integrative perspective that elaborates and defines optimal development and true self-investment in one's close relationships" and that:

> relationships that facilitate both partners' feelings of autonomy, competence, and relatedness and those in which partners are engaged for relatively more integrated and intrinsic reasons, will be more likely to yield open, authentic, non-defensive behaviors and stances, especially during otherwise ego-threatening conflicts and other relationship events.
>
> *(p. 321)*

SDT has also driven research on relationships that are not close. For example, Legault, Green-Demers, Grant, and Chung (2007) found that subjects with more self-determined regulation had lower levels of implicit and explicit prejudice.

Thus, across domains of inquiry, research in SDT has established that autonomy-supportive relationships and autonomy-supportive social interactions improve outcomes, including academic achievement, goal attainment, positive health, healthy relationships, and athletic perseverance. Such interactions are, obviously, supportive, but incorporate problem-solving feedback and promote autonomy, relatedness, and competence.

Causal Agency Theory and Recent Research

The application of the self-determination construct in motivational psychology is the most extensive use of the construct, but not its sole use. The earliest use of the construct in psychology was by Andras Angyal who, in his 1941 text *Foundations for a Science of Personality*, proposed that an organism "lives in a world in which things happen according to laws which are heteronomous (e.g. governed from outside) from the point of view of the organism," but that "organisms ... can oppose self-determination to external determination" (p. 33). Angyal's approach was, essentially, an organismic one, in which the important tasks in developing a science of personality included identifying the principles of the *biological total process*, meaning the organism's trend toward autonomy.

Causal Agency Theory (Shogren et al., 2015) draws from research in motivational, personality, and developmental psychology to explain how people become self-determined and positions self-determination within the realm of personality and developmental psychology. Causal Agency Theory defines self-determination as a:

> dispositional characteristic manifested as acting as the causal agent in one's life. Self-determined people (i.e. causal agents) act in service to freely chosen goals. Self-determined actions function to enable a person to be the causal agent is his or her life.
>
> *(Shogren et al., 2015, p. 258)*

Within CAT, self-determination is conceptualized as a dispositional characteristic, referring to an enduring tendency used to characterize and describe differences between people. While the assumption is that self-determined people have a general tendency to act or think in a particular way, there is also a presumption of contextual variance (i.e. people behave in more or less self-determined ways as a function of the context or circumstance). *Causal agency* refers to the fact that it is the person who makes or causes things to happen in his or her life. It implies that the person acts with an eye toward causing an effect to accomplish a specific end or to cause or create change. Self-determined actions enable a person to act as a causal agent in their lives.

Like SDT, Causal Agency Theory is grounded in human agentic theories, which assume that action is self-caused. Self-determined action refers to the degree to which action is self-caused, volitional, and agentic, driven by beliefs about the relationships between actions (or means) and ends. The theory posits three essential characteristics—volitional action, agentic action, and action-control beliefs—that contribute to causal agency and the development of self-determination. These refer not to specific actions performed or the beliefs that drive action, but to the function the action serves for the person; that is, whether the action enabled the person to act as a causal agent and enhances the development of self-determination.

Volitional Action

Self-determined people act volitionally. Volitional action reflects one's personal preferences acting in the pursuit of goals. Thus, such action involves conscious choices (rather than simply hedonistic action) that are intentionally conceived, deliberate acts that occur without direct external influence. As such, volitional actions are self-initiated and function to enable a person to act autonomously (i.e. engage in self-governed action, such as pursuing a course of action counter to the will of someone else). Volitional actions involve the initiation and activation of causal capabilities—the capacity to cause something to happen—in one's life (Shogren & Wehmeyer, 2017).

Agentic Action

Agentic actions are the means by which something is achieved. They are self-directed, and goal-focused. When acting agentically, self-determined people identify pathways that lead to a specific end or cause or create change. The identification of pathways, or pathways-thinking, is a proactive, purposive process. Agentic action is self-regulated, self-directed, and enables progress toward freely chosen goals. Volitional actions involve the initiation and activation of agentic capabilities—the capacity to sustain action toward a goal.

Action-Control Beliefs

In applying volitional and agentic actions, self-determined people develop a sense of personal empowerment. They believe they have what it takes to achieve freely chosen goals. They perceive a link between their action and the outcomes they experience, and develop adaptive action-control beliefs. To account for these beliefs and actions, CAT incorporates basic tenets of Action-Control Theory (Little et al., 2002), which posits three types of action-control beliefs: beliefs about the link between the self and the goal (control expectancy beliefs; "When I want to do ____, I can"); beliefs about the link between the self and the means for achieving the goal (capacity beliefs; "I have the capabilities to do _____"); and beliefs about the utility or usefulness of a given means for attaining a goal (causality beliefs; "I believe my effort will lead to goal achievement" versus "I believe other factors—luck, access to teachers or social capital—will lead to goal achievement"). As action-control beliefs emerge, people are better able to act with self-awareness and self-knowledge in a goal-directed manner.

Causal Agency Theory was proposed to explain how people become more self-determined and to design interventions to enable people, and in particular (with regard to interventions) people with disabilities, to become more self-determined. Recently, Wehmeyer and colleagues (2017) proposed a sequence for the development of self-determination that draws from both SDT and CAT. Before describing this proposed developmental trajectory, we examine the research knowledge associated with self-determination as proposed by CAT.

Current Knowledge and Recent Research

As noted, CAT evolved as a means to understand self-determination as a dispositional characteristic, its development, and interventions to promote that development. Situated within the context of adolescent development, CAT framed research, assessment, and intervention efforts to promote the self-determination of youth and young adults, but particularly within the context of youth and young adults with disabilities. Historically, people with disabilities have not been provided opportunities to act volitionally and to become self-determined, in large measure because disability was understood in terms of disease and deficit (Shogren, 2013).

As Dunn (2015) described, modern conceptualizations of disability that move beyond historic models of disease and deficit are inherently social in nature. In the early 1990s, social-ecological models of disability began to emerge that emphasized disability as a function of the gap between a person's capacities and the demands of the environment (Wehmeyer, 2013). These models have led to strengths-based approaches to disability. Emerging simultaneously was a focus in secondary education for students to promote the transition from school to more positive employment, community living, and community inclusion outcomes, which included an emphasis on promoting the self-determination of students with disabilities as one means to achieving more positive transition outcomes (Wehmeyer & Palmer, 2003; Wehmeyer & Schwartz, 1997). The confluence of the emergence of social-ecological models of disability, a focus on transition and self-determination, and the rise of the positive psychology movement has led to the application of positive psychological constructs to the disability context.

As noted, self-determination refers to self-caused action and all "self-determined" or self-caused actions are in contrast with "other-caused" action (or, referring back to Angyal, reflecting heteronomous determinism). As Mithaug (1998) noted (quoted previously), there is a social context to self-determined action; it is self- versus other-caused action, and the "other" is usually the actions of another person. Thus, CAT has relevance to social psychologists to help answer questions about which social interaction and relationship factors influence and impact causal action and how acting as a causal agent influences how one might act in specific circumstances.

The primary focus to which CAT has been applied is the disability context. People with disabilities are historically marginalized, discriminated against, and lack opportunities to become self-determined. Dunn (2015) observed that "social psychological research dealing with disability adopts a focused view, one aimed at identifying those personal and situational factors that enhance the assessment, improvement, or treatment of those with physical, cognitive, mental or communicative disabilities" (pp. 4–5). We apply Dunn's lens, considering the role of self-determination pertaining to personal and situational factors that enhance understanding of ways to improve the lives of people with disabilities. To that end, research has established that people with disabilities, across disability categories, are not self-determined (Chou, Wehmeyer, Palmer, & Lee, 2017; Pierson, Carter, Lane, & Glaeser, 2008; Wehmeyer & Metzler, 1995) and that they have fewer opportunities to act volitionally, and are subject to controlling (rather than autonomy-supportive) relationships and environments (Stancliffe & Wehmeyer, 1995; Wehmeyer & Bolding, 1999, 2001). This research establishes that environments in which people with disabilities live, learn, and work offer far fewer opportunities to express and act upon preferences, and engage in individual goal pursuits (Stancliffe, 2001; Wehmeyer & Abery, 2013). It is clear that a significant factor in limiting or enhancing opportunities to act volitionally and autonomously in these environments is the number of people with whom one lives or the number of staff paid to support people. In both cases, the more people that are in the environment, the fewer opportunities for choice exist (Stancliffe, Abery, & Smith, 2000).

That what is at play here are interactions with people is evidenced by research on the phenomenon of *outerdirectedness,* a term used "to describe approaches in which individuals rely on external cues rather than on their internal cognitive abilities to solve a task or problem" (Bybee & Zigler, 1998, p. 435). It is, more specifically, a "motivational style of problem solving in which the child uses external cues rather than relying on his own cognitive resources" (MacMillan & Cauffiel, 1977, p. 643). Research has established that children with intellectual disability exhibit outerdirectedness at a greater rate than do typically developing children, likely due to multiple factors, including prompt dependency and overreliance, repeated experiences with failure, and task difficulty (Bybee & Zigler, 1998). This same body of research documents that outerdirectedness results in the lack of initiation of action, reduced problem-solving efficacy, and poorer school performance (Bybee & Zigler, 1998). In essence, interactions that are "other-determined" lead to a lack of self-initiation, limited engagement in problem-solving performance, and other less optimal outcomes.

It was this lack of autonomy and opportunities for self-governance that led to a focus on self-determination in the disability context. From the onset, these issues of self-determination were framed within an empowerment focus; people with disabilities were denied opportunities to live self-determined lives, and the response was to call for action with regard to both personal opportunities to make decisions in their lives, be free from the control of others, and act based upon personal preferences and interests; but, also, to have legally protected rights to self-governance. So, within a disability context, self-determination has always been equated with the right to basic human dignity. It is about others (and the interactions of people with disabilities with other people) respecting the choices, wishes, desires, and aspirations of people with disabilities.

There is clear evidence from the special education literature that providing instruction to promote component skills of causal action results in enhanced skills and greater self-determination for youth and young adults with disabilities. Two meta-analyses provided effective summaries of this line of research. Algozzine, Browder, Karvonen, Test, and Wood (2001) conducted group- and single-subject design meta-analyses of studies in which youth with disabilities had received some intervention to promote component skills of causal action as framed by CAT. These meta-analyses showed moderate (group design) and strong (single-subject design) effects of such interventions. Subsequently, Cobb, Lehmann, Newman-Gonchar, and Morgen (2009) conducted a narrative metasynthesis—a narrative synthesis of multiple meta-analytic studies—covering seven existing meta-analyses examining causal action skills, and concluded that there is sufficient evidence to state that interventions to teach or promote choice-making, problem solving, decision making, goal-setting and attainment, and self-advocacy skills result in enhanced skills in these areas.

Research has established causal relationships between promoting the self-determination of youth with disabilities and enhanced self-determination and positive school and adult outcomes. For example, Wehmeyer, Palmer, Shogren, Williams-Diehm, and Soukup (2012) conducted a randomized controlled study of the effect of interventions to promote self-determination in high school students with cognitive disabilities, and determined that students who received interventions to promote skills related to causal action showed significant growth in their self-determination, at higher levels than students with disabilities who did not receive interventions to promote self-determination. In a follow-up study of the students from Wehmeyer et al. (2012), Shogren, Wehmeyer, Palmer, Rifenbark, and Little (2015) found that self-determination status at the end of high school predicted significantly more positive employment and community access outcomes for youth with disabilities.

The primary intervention we have developed and evaluated, the Self-Determined Learning Model of Instruction (SDLMI), provides for teachers an autonomy-supportive instructional model to teach students (with and without disabilities) a self-regulated problem-solving process to enable them to set goals, create action plans to achieve those goals, and revise their plans or goals as needed. Randomized controlled-trial studies have shown that teaching students with disabilities to self-regulate problem solving leading to goal-setting and attainment enhances student achievement of academically-valued goals and enhanced self-determination (Shogren, Palmer, Wehmeyer, Williams-Diehm, & Little, 2012; Wehmeyer et al., 2012).

Of relevance to social psychologists, interventions such as the SDLMI not only improve student skills and self-determination, but change how others perceive and interact with them. As Dunn (2015) noted, disability means difference to most people... or at least, perceived difference. "The social psychology of disability is primarily concerned with the experiences of people who have a disability; how they think about themselves, interacting with others who have disabilities, and their relations with those who are not (yet) disabled" (p. 1). The perceptions of others about people with disabilities may dramatically impact the opportunities for them to live the lives they want more than the actual impairment that resulted in the disability. Shogren, Plotner, Palmer, Wehmeyer, and Paek (2014) found that teachers who implemented the SDLMI raised their expectations of students with disabilities as a function of the process of, and outcomes from, implementing the SDLMI.

Finally, a focus in the special education research has been to promote student involvement in educational planning. Such meetings are inherently social in nature; they include professionals, parents and family members, and sometimes (though not always) the student. Historically, these meetings were deficits-focused, emphasizing what the student could not do or had not achieved. A focus on self-determination in special education has begun to alter that. Research has found that students with disabilities can acquire skills to play a meaningful role in their educational planning process (Martin et al., 2006; Wehmeyer & Lawrence, 1995) and, when they do, they achieve more positive school outcomes (Wehmeyer, Palmer, Lee, Williams-Diehm, & Shogren, 2011) and enhanced self-determination (Seong, Wehmeyer, Palmer, & Little, 2015).

Development of Self-Determination

We close this chapter with a model of the development of self-determination that draws from both SDT and CAT (Wehmeyer, Shogren, Little, & Lopez, 2017). As noted, SDT posits three basic psychological needs for autonomy, competence, and relatedness. Satisfaction of these basic needs facilitates autonomous motivation, defined as intrinsic motivation and well-internalized extrinsic motivation (Deci & Ryan, 2012). The interplay between the context and the individual's psychological needs satisfaction is complex and reciprocal. When motives are salient, people are in a position to select goals on the basis of their expectations about the satisfaction of these motives (Deci & Ryan, 1985, p. 235). These psychological needs *initiate* a causal action sequence that, through interaction with environmental supports and opportunities, enables the development of a "synergistic set of action-control beliefs and behaviors that provide the self-regulatory foundation that is called upon to negotiate the various tasks and challenges of the life course" (Little et al., 2002, p. 396). Action-control beliefs about the link between the self and the goal (control expectancy beliefs), between the self and the means that are available for use to address a challenge (agency beliefs), and about which means are most effective for reaching one's goals (causality beliefs) (Little et al., 2002, p. 396), interact with and mediate volitional and agentic actions (as described previously), resulting in experiences of causal agency. Repeated experiences with the causal action sequence leads to multiple experiences with causal agency and enhanced self-determination.

Conclusions

Self-determination is a foundational construct in the discipline of positive psychology that is based in human agentic theories that view people as actors in their own lives, rather than being acted upon. Human agentic theories emphasize the interaction between the organism (person) and the environment or context, and thus are important in social psychology to understand social interactions and the effect of psychological processes on such interactions and their respective outcomes. Specifically, theories of self-determination can provide for social psychologists a means to consider the self-regulatory psychological processes leading to the initiation and execution of actions. There is evidence in motivation, personality, and developmental psychology across multiple contexts that research and practice in self-determination can enable social psychologists to better explain why and how volitional and agentic action impacts a person's interactions with her or his social environment and context.

References

Algozzine, B., Browder, D., Karvonen, M., Test. D. W., & Wood, W. M. (2001). Effects of interventions to promote self-determination for individuals with disabilities. *Review of Educational Research, 71*(2), 219–277.

Angyal, A. (1941). *Foundations for a science of personality.* Cambridge, MA: Harvard University Press.

Baumeister, R. F., & Vohs, K. D. (2007). *Encyclopedia of social psychology.* Thousand Oaks, CA: Sage.

Bybee, J., & Zigler, E. (1998). Outerdirectedness in individuals with and without mental retardation: A review. In J. A. Burack, R. M Hodapp, & E. Zigler (Eds.), *Handbook of mental retardation and development* (pp. 434–461). Cambridge: Cambridge University Press.

Chou, Y., Wehmeyer, M. L., Palmer, S., & Lee, J. H. (2017). Comparisons of self-determination among students with autism, intellectual disability, and learning disabilities: A multivariate analysis. *Focus on Autism and Other Developmental Disabilities, 32*(2), 124–132. doi:1088357615625059.

Cobb, B., Lehmann, J., Newman-Gonchar, R., & Morgen, A. (2009). Self-determination for students with disabilities: A narrative metasynthesis. *Career Development for Exceptional Individuals, 32*(2), 108–114.

Deci, E. L., & Ryan, R. (1985). *Intrinsic motivation and self-determination in human behavior.* New York: Plenum Press.

Deci, E. L., & Ryan, R. M. (2000). The "what" and "why" of goal pursuits: Human needs and the self-determination of behavior. *Psychological Inquiry, 11*(4), 237–268.

Deci, E. L., & Ryan, R. M. (2012). Motivation, personality, and development within embedded social contexts: An overview of Self-Determination Theory. In R. Ryan (Ed.), *The Oxford handbook of human motivation* (pp. 85–107). Oxford: Oxford University Press.

Deci, E. L. & Ryan, R. M. (2014). Autonomy and need satisfaction in close relationships: Relationships motivation theory. In N. Weinstein (Ed.), *Human motivation and interpersonal relationships: Theory, research and applications* (pp. 53–73). Dordrecht, NL: Springer.

Deci, E. L., Schwartz, A. J., Sheinman, L., & Ryan, R. M. (1981). An instrument to assess adults' orientations toward control versus autonomy with children: Reflections on intrinsic motivation and perceived competence. *Journal of Educational Psychology, 73*, 642–650.

Deci, E. L., Vallerand, R. J., Pelletier, L. G., & Ryan, R. M. (1991). Motivation and education: The self-determination perspective. *The Educational Psychologist, 26*, 325–346.

Dunn, D. S. (2015). *The social psychology of disability.* Oxford: Oxford University Press.

Griffin, L. K., Adams, N., & Little, T. D. (2017). Self-determination theory, identity development, and adolescence. In M. L. Wehmeyer, K. A. Shogren, T. D. Little, & S. J. Lopez (Eds.), *The development of self-determination across the life course* (pp. 189–196). New York: Springer.

Guay, F., Ratelle, C., Larose, S., Vallerand, R. J., & Vitaro, F. (2013). The number of autonomy-supportive relationships: Are more relationships better for motivation, perceived competence, and achievement? *Contemporary Educational Psychology, 38*, 375–382.

Hadden, B. W., Rodriguez, L. M., Knee, C. R., & Porter, B. (2015). Relationship autonomy and support provision in romantic relationships. *Motivation and Emotion, 39*, 359–373.

Koestner, R., Powers, T. A., Carbonneau, N., Milyavskaya, M., & Chua, S. N. (2012). Distinguising autonomous and directive forms of goal support: Their effects on goal progress, relationship quality, and subjective well-being. *Personality and Social Psychology Bulletin, 38*(12), 1609–1620.

Kuhl, J., & Beckmann, J. (1985). Introduction and overview. In J. Kuhl & J. Beckmann (Eds.), *Action control: From cognition to behavior* (Springer Series in Social Psychology) (pp. 1–8). New York: Springer.

Legault, L., Green-Demers, I., Grant, P., & Chung, J. (2007). On the self-regulation of implicit and explicit prejudice: A self-determination theory perspective. *Personality and Social Psychology Bulletin, 33*(5), 732–749.

Little, T. D., Hawley, P. H., Henrich, C. C., & Marsland, K. (2002). Three views of the agentic self: A developmental synthesis. In E. L. Deci & R. M. Ryan (Eds.), *Handbook of self-determination research* (pp. 389–404). Rochester, NY: University of Rochester Press.

Little, T. D., Snyder, C. R., & Wehmeyer, M. L. (2006). The agentic self: On the nature and origins of personal agency across the lifespan. In D. Mroczek & T. D. Little (Eds.), *The handbook of personality development* (pp. 61–79). Mahwah, NJ: Lawrence Erlbaum and Associates.

Lopez, S. J., & Gallagher, M. W. (2009). A case for positive psychology. In S. Lopez & R. Snyder (Eds.), *Handbook of positive psychology* (2nd ed., pp. 3–6). Oxford: Oxford University Press.

MacMillan, D. L., & Cauffiel, S. R. (1977). Outerdirectedness as a function of success and failure in educationally handicapped boys. *Journal of Learning Disabilities, 10*(10), 643–654.

Martin, J., Van Dycke, J., Christensen, W., Greene, B., Gardner, J., & Lovett, D. (2006). Increasing student participation in IEP meetings: Establishing the self-directed IEP as an evidenced-based practice. *Exceptional Children, 72*(3), 299–316.

Mithaug, D. E. (1998). Your right, my obligation? *Journal of the Association for Persons with Severe Handicaps, 23*(1), 41–43.

Ng, J. Y. Y., Ntoumanis, N., Thogersen-Ntoumani, C., Deci, E. L., Ryan, R. M., Duda, J. L., & Williams, G. C. (2012). Self-determination theory applied to health contexts: A meta-analysis. *Perspectives on Psychological Science, 7,* 325–340.

Ntoumanis, N., Healy, L. C., Sedikides, C., Duda. J., Stewart, B., Smith, A., & Bond, J. (2013). When the going gets tough: The "why" of goal striving matters. *Journal of Personality, 82*(3), 225–236.

Pierson, M. R., Carter, E. W., Lane, K. L., & Glaeser, B. C. (2008). Factors influencing the self-determination of transition-age youth with high-incidence disabilities. *Career Development for Exceptional Individuals, 31*(2), 115–125.

Ratelle, C. F., & Duchesne, S. (2014). Trajectories of psychological need satisfaction from early to late adolescence as a predictor of adjustment in school. *Contemporary Educational Psychology, 39,* 388–400.

Reeve, J. (2002). Self-determination theory applied to educational settings. In E. L. Deci & R. M. Ryan (Eds.), *Handbook of self-determination research* (pp. 183–203). Rochester, NY: University of Rochester Press.

Reeve, J. (2012). A self-determination theory perspective on student engagement. In S. L. Christenson, A. L. Reschly, & C. Wylie (Eds.), *Handbook of research on student engagement* (pp. 149–172). New York: Springer.

Reeve, J. (2016). Autonomy-supportive teaching: What it is, how to do it. In W. C. Liu, J. C. K. Wang, & R. M. Ryan (Eds.), *Building autonomous learners: Perspectives from research and practice using self-determination theory* (pp. 129–152). New York: Springer.

Ryan, R. M., Bernstein, J. H., & Brown, K. W. (2010). Weekends, work, and wellbeing: Psychological need satisfactions and day of the week effects on mood, vitality, and physical symptoms. *Journal of Social and Clinical Psychology, 29,* 95–122.

Ryan, R. M., & Deci, E. L. (2002). An overview of self-determination theory: An organismic-dialectical perspective. In E. L. Deci & R. M. Ryan (Eds.), *Handbook of self-determination research* (pp. 3–36). Rochester, NY: University of Rochester Press.

Ryan, R. M., Kasser, T., Sheldon, K. M., & Deci, E. L. (1996). All goals are not created equal: An organismic perspective on the nature of goals and their regulation.

In P. M. Gollwitzer & J. A. Bargh (Eds.), *The psychology of action* (pp. 7–26). New York: Guilford Press.

Seong, Y., Wehmeyer, M. L., Palmer, S. B., & Little, T. D. (2015). Effects of the *self-directed individualized education program* on self-determination and transition of adolescents with disabilities. *Career Development and Transition for Exceptional Individuals*, *38*(3), 132–141.

Shogren, K. A. (2013). Positive psychology and disability: A historical analysis. In M. L. Wehmeyer (Ed.), *The Oxford handbook of positive psychology and disability* (pp. 19–33). Oxford: Oxford University Press.

Shogren, K. A., Palmer, S., Wehmeyer, M. L., Williams-Diehm, K., & Little, T. (2012). Effect of intervention with the self-determined learning model of instruction on access and goal attainment. *Remedial and Special Education*, *33*(5), 320–330.

Shogren, K. A., Plotner, A. J., Palmer, S. B., Wehmeyer, M. L., & Paek, Y. (2014). Impact of the self-determined learning model of instruction on teacher perceptions of student capacity and opportunity for self-determination. *Education and Training in Autism and Developmental Disabilities*, *49*(3), 440–448.

Shogren, K. A., Wehmeyer, M. L., & Palmer, S. B. (2017). Causal agency theory. In M. L. Wehmeyer, K. A. Shogren, T. D. Little, & S. Lopez (Eds.), *The development of self-determination across the life course* (pp. 55–67). New York: Springer.

Shogren, K. A., Wehmeyer, M. L., Palmer, S. B., Forber-Pratt, A., Little, T., & Lopez, S. (2015). Causal agency theory: Reconceptualizing a functional model of self-determination. *Education and Training in Autism and Developmental Disabilities*, *50*(3), 251–263.

Shogren, K. A., Wehmeyer, M. L., Palmer, S. B., Rifenbark, G. G., & Little, T. D. (2015). Relationships between self-determination and postschool outcomes for youth with disabilities. *Journal of Special Education*, *53*, 30–41.

Stancliffe, R. (2001). Living with support in the community: Predictors of choice and self-determination. *Mental Retardation and Developmental Disabilities Research Reviews*, *7*, 91–98.

Stancliffe, R., Abery, B., & Smith, J. (2000). Personal control and the ecology of community living settings: Beyond living-unit size and type. *American Journal on Mental Retardation*, *105*(6), 431–454.

Stancliffe, R., & Wehmeyer, M. L. (1995). Variability in the availability of choice to adults with mental retardation. *The Journal of Vocational Rehabilitation*, *5*, 319–328.

VandenBos, G. R. (Ed.). (2007). *APA dictionary of psychology*. Washington, DC: APA.

Vansteenkiste, M., Niemiec, C., & Soenens, B. (2010). The development of the five mini-theories of self-determination theory: An historical overview, emerging trends, and future directions. In T. Urdan & S. Karabenick (Eds.), *Advances in motivation and achievement, vol. 16: The decade ahead* (pp. 105–165). UK: Emerald Publishing.

Vansteenkiste, M., & Ryan, R. M. (2013). On psychological growth and vulnerability: Basic psychological need satisfaction and need frustration as a unifying principle. *Journal of Psychotherapy Integration*, *23*(3), 263–280.

Wehmeyer, M. L., (2013). Beyond pathology: Positive psychology and disability. In M. L. Wehmeyer (Ed.), *The Oxford handbook of positive psychology and disability* (pp. 3–6). Oxford: Oxford University Press.

Wehmeyer, M. L., & Abery, B. (2013). Self-determination and choice. *Intellectual and Developmental Disabilities*, *51*(5), 399–411.

Wehmeyer, M. L., & Bolding, N. (1999). Self-determination across living and working environments: A matched-samples study of adults with mental retardation. *Mental Retardation, 37,* 353–363.

Wehmeyer, M. L., & Bolding, N. (2001). Enhanced self-determination of adults with mental retardation as an outcome of moving to community-based work or living environments. *Journal of Intellectual Disability Research, 45,* 371–383.

Wehmeyer, M. L., & Lawrence, M. (1995). Whose future is it anyway? Promoting student involvement in transition planning with a student-directed process. *Career Development for Exceptional Individuals, 18,* 69–83.

Wehmeyer, M. L., Little, T., & Sergeant, J. (2009). Self-determination. In S. Lopez & R. Snyder (Eds.), *Handbook of positive psychology* (2nd ed., pp. 357–366). Oxford: Oxford University Press.

Wehmeyer, M. L., & Metzler, C. (1995). How self-determined are people with mental retardation? The national consumer survey. *Mental Retardation, 33,* 111–119.

Wehmeyer, M. L., & Palmer, S. B. (2003). Adult outcomes for students with cognitive disabilities three years after high school: The impact of self-determination. *Education and Training in Developmental Disabilities, 38,* 131–144.

Wehmeyer, M. L., Palmer, S. B., Lee, Y., Williams-Diehm, K., & Shogren, K. A. (2011). A randomized-trial evaluation of the effect of whose future is it anyway? On self-determination. *Career Development for Exceptional Individuals, 34*(1), 45–56.

Wehmeyer, M. L., Palmer, S., Shogren, K., Williams-Diehm, K., & Soukup, J. (2012). Establishing a causal relationship between interventions to promote self-determination and enhanced student self-determination. *Journal of Special Education, 46*(4), 195–210.

Wehmeyer, M. L., & Schwartz, M. (1997). Self-determination and positive adult outcomes: A follow-up study of youth with mental retardation or learning disabilities. *Exceptional Children, 63,* 245–255.

Wehmeyer, M. L., Shogren, K. A., Little, T. D., & Lopez, S. J. (2017). *Development of self-determination across the life course.* New York: Springer.

Wehmeyer, M. L., Shogren, K. A., Palmer, S., Williams-Diehm, K., Little, T., & Boulton, A. (2012). The impact of the *self-determined learning model of instruction* on student self-determination. *Exceptional Children, 78*(2), 135–153.

18

APPLIED POSITIVE PSYCHOLOGY

Facilitating Multidimensional Flourishing

Tim Lomas

One of the most prominent and successful aspects of positive psychology (PP) is applied positive psychology (APP). APP is an overarching term for a burgeoning corpus of positive psychology interventions (PPIs), activities, and strategies designed to promote well-being. Thus, while PP might generally be conceptualized as the scientific study of well-being, APP could be defined as the scientifically-based practice of *enhancing* well-being. The emergence of APP is reflective of the fact that PP has always had, at its core, a spirit of *praxis*. In his *Nichomachean Ethics*, Aristotle (350 BCE/2000) divided human activity into three main types: theōria (contemplative endeavors); poiēsis (productive/creative disciplines); and praxis (practical occupations, featuring skillful application of theory). A more recent articulation of praxis was provided by Karl Marx (1845, p. 158), who famously wrote, "The philosophers have only interpreted the world, in various ways. The point, however, is to change it." This notion has been influential in the social sciences, where praxis is defined by Foster (1986, p. 96) as "practical action informed by theory." In the case of APP, this kind of "practical action" is specifically in the direction of improving well-being. This spirit of praxis has seen PP being applied across numerous practical domains, from psychotherapy (Seligman, Rashid, & Parks, 2006) to education (Seligman, Ernst, Gillham, Reivich, & Linkins, 2009).

In this chapter, I shall consider some of the key practices created or adopted within APP to promote well-being. Before this though, it is worth briefly touching on the contentious issue of how to actually define the remit and nature of APP. This includes asking questions around what exactly constitutes a PPI (and other such activities), and how these might be differentiated from forms of praxis in other areas of psychology (e.g. clinical psychology).

This is a rather tricky task, with considerable debate around what constitutes necessary and sufficient criteria for identifying an intervention as a PPI.

For instance, Parks and Biswas-Diener (2014) have identified (and critiqued) three broad definitions of PPIs. Content-level definitions conceptualize PPIs as interventions that simply focus on "positive topics." A weakness with such formulations is that this would encompass *any* subjectively pleasant activity, with no requirement that it leads to any beneficial outcome. Variable level definitions require that PPIs exert their beneficial effects via a recognized theoretical mechanism, such as Fredrickson's (2001) broaden-and-build theory of positive emotions. Although this definition is more selective, the concept of a "positive" outcome often remains vaguely operationalized.

A third type of definition conceptualizes PPIs as practices designed to promote wellness, rather than alleviate distress or fix dysfunction. However, this formulation overlooks recent developments around using PPIs for the treatment of psychiatric disorders, such as "positive psychotherapy" treatments for depression (Seligman et al., 2006). Moreover, all these definitions struggle to accommodate recent critiques of the foundational notions of "positive" and "negative" themselves (Lomas & Ivtzan, 2016). Critics argue that ostensibly negative emotions and thoughts may be conducive to well-being under certain circumstances, while seemingly positively-valenced qualia might ultimately be detrimental (see, for example, McNulty & Fincham, 2011). This recognition means it can be difficult to categorically designate a given quality or emotion as being intrinsically and unequivocally "positive." As such, seeking to establish a definition for a PPI on the basis that one of its components is "positive" is likewise problematic. For instance, consciousness-raising activities of the kind advocated by Paolo Freire (1972) might initially generate feelings of anger—for example, at societal iniquities—but, through leading to progressive social action, could ultimately improve well-being. Given that anger is generally appraised as a negative emotion, this would rule out such activities as being a PPI according to the definitions above, which would be unfortunate from a critical perspective.

Moreover, it may be tricky to appoint a particular intervention as being *exclusively* a PPI. For example, one of the most popular and prominent areas of interest within APP is an emerging range of interventions based around mindfulness (Ivtzan & Lomas, 2015). However, mindfulness-based interventions (MBIs) were pioneered and developed in clinical settings as treatments for physical (Kabat-Zinn, 1982) and psychological disorders (Teasdale et al., 2000). As such, it would be hubristic to claim mindfulness as a PPI (rather than, say, a medical or psychotherapuetic intervention). That said, recent years have also seen the extensive development and use of MBIs in non-clinical contexts, such as with school children (Burnett, 2011) or workers in various occupational settings (Shapiro, Astin, Bishop, & Cordova, 2005). Although such interventions fulfill many of the same functions as they do in clinical settings—like helping alleviate negative symptoms like anxiety—they also target positive outcomes, such as academic engagement and performance (Beauchemin, Hutchins, & Patterson, 2008). Interestingly though, this indeterminacy around what MBIs actually are offers a potential way of identifying PPIs. Specifically, PPIs might perhaps be defined not so much by the practices themselves as by the population they are applied to. That is, my colleagues and I have broadly defined PPIs as "empirically-validated interventions designed to promote wellbeing in a non-clinical population" (Lomas, Hefferon, & Ivtzan, 2015, p. 1349). I should add that this would not *stop* interventions that are classically regarded as being PPIs—such as gratitude-based interventions (Emmons & McCullough, 2003)—still being used in clinical settings and/or harnessed to address mental health issues, as per positive psychotherapy (Seligman et al., 2006) or positive clinical psychology (Wood & Tarrier, 2010). These latter examples remain a somewhat gray (and very important) area at the intersection of PP and fields like clinical psychology.

Nevertheless, this general definition does offer a potential heuristic for ascertaining what constitutes a PPI. My colleagues and I have found this definition useful when teaching about APP, and as such it is a definition that informs the present chapter. Of particular utility is the fact that this definition greatly expands the scope of APP, allowing it to draw on a wide range of theories and activities that can help facilitate well-being. Unfortunately, it is not uncommon to find discussions of APP being focused around a relatively small number of interventions that happen to have been developed by pioneering figures within the field, such as the gratitude-based tasks developed by Emmons and McCullough (2003), or the "three good things" exercise formulated by Seligman, Steen, Park, and Peterson (2005). While such PPIs are of course valuable, having been consistently found to enhance well-being (Sin & Lyubomirsky, 2009), it can be frustrating to see the field limiting itself to this narrowly circumscribed corpus of psychological techniques. In doing so, it risks overlooking the great wealth of practices—some of which were not developed within the context of PP *per se*—that may help to engender well-being.

For instance, PP has been criticized for largely overlooking the impact upon well-being of factors like the physical functioning of the body (Hefferon, 2013) and sociocultural processes (Lomas, 2015). However, the field has begun addressing these critiques, as seen with the emergence of paradigms such as "positive health" (Seligman, 2008) and "positive social psychology" (Lomas, 2015). As such, this chapter will attempt to give a sense of the newly expanding scope of APP, highlighting the diversity of strategies for enhancing well-being that can be regarded as within the remit of the field. In order to do that, I shall organize the presentation using a multidimensional theoretical framework that my colleagues and I have developed, namely the LIFE (Layered Integrated Framework Example) model (Lomas, Hefferon et al., 2015).

The LIFE Model

The LIFE model was created as an orienting framework and pedagogical strategy that enabled my colleagues and I to organize the diversity of interventions and activities within APP. It involves a multidimensional conceptualization of the person, and therefore offers a multidimensional approach to well-being. Such approaches to health and well-being are increasingly common. An early example is the World Health Organization's (1948) widely-cited definition of health as "a state of complete physical, mental and social well-being, and not merely the absence of disease and infirmity." This formulation recognizes three main dimensions to the person, and their health/well-being—physical, mental, and social—as does Engel's (1977) influential biopsychosocial model of health. By contrast, the LIFE model is based on a model of the person developed by the philosopher Ken Wilber (1997), which features *four* dimensions. These dimensions are produced by juxtaposing two common binaries, thereby creating a parsimonious and logically appealing framework.

The first binary is the contrast between subjective "mind" and objective "body/brain." This dichotomy has intrigued thinkers throughout the ages, often being referred to as the "mind–body problem" (Chalmers, 2004). While there are various philosophical perspectives on this issue, many assert a version of dualism, acknowledging the reality of both dimensions (even if there are disagreements around how they interact, as indeed there have been throughout history; Damasio, 2005). This is true of the dominant paradigm in contemporary consciousness studies, the neural correlates of consciousness (NCC) approach, which proposes that subjective mental states are accompanied by analogous neurophysiological states (Fell, 2004).

The second binary is between the individual and the collective. This reflects the idea that there are two fundamental modes of existence, referred to by Bakan (1966) as "agency" and "communion." Agency refers to the way people exist as discrete, autonomous individuals, whereas communion reflects the idea that people are *also* inextricably embedded in sociocultural networks. Traditionally, the study of these modes of being has tended to be somewhat compartmentalized, with psychology focusing on agency, for example. However, theorists have begun to recognize the limitations of studying these modes in isolation, and the need to explore their complex interactions, as reflected in the emergence of compound terms like "psychosocial" (Martikainen, Bartley, & Lahelma, 2002). Wilber's (1997) innovation was to juxtapose these two binaries—with the "subjective" and "objective" binary forming two columns (left and right respectively), and the "individual" and "collective" binary forming two rows (top and bottom respectively)—creating a two-by-two matrix of four quadrants, shown below in Figure 18.1.

The subjective-individual quadrant, at the top-left of the matrix, is the domain of the mind, an umbrella term encompassing all subjective experience, such as thoughts, feelings and sensations (as well as unconscious subjective dynamics, such as filters and biases). The objective-individual quadrant, in the top-right of the matrix, is the domain of the body/brain (i.e. physiological functioning and its link to behavior). The subjective-collective quadrant, in

SUBJECTIVE		OBJECTIVE	
SUBJECTIVE			OBJECTIVE
INDIVIDUAL	*Individual conscious experience*		*Correlated physical substrates*
		MIND	**BRAIN**
		CULTURE	**SOCIETY**
COLLECTIVE	*Relationships and shared meanings*		*Material systems and structures*
	INTERSUBJECTIVE		INTEROBJECTIVE

FIGURE 18.1 Schematic diagram of the four quadrants.

the bottom-left of the matrix, is the "intersubjective" domain, that is, people's subjective experience of being enmeshed within a shared culture (e.g. having similar worldviews and values, such as an "individualist" ideology). Finally, the objective-collective quadrant, in the bottom-right of the matrix, is the "interobjective" domain of society, which refers to the structural scaffolding of a culture (e.g. housing infrastructure or economic systems).

Wilber's framework represents a powerful tool for conceptualizing well-being in an integrated way. For example, Hanlon, Carlisle, Reilly, Lyon, and Hannah (2010, p. 307) have harnessed it in public health to understand the "maze of interconnected problems" which affect well-being. Consider, for instance, a person experiencing dysphoria in relation to being made unemployed. From the perspective of the mind, their plight could be appraised in terms of subjective distress, understood using cognitive theories of psychiatric disorder, and addressed through therapy. From the perspective of the body, it can be viewed in terms of brain dynamics, understood with neurochemical theories, and treated through medication. From a cultural perspective, their distress could be appraised in terms of the *meaning* of unemployment, understood through constructionist theories (e.g. concerning the valorization of work in Western societies, and the concomitant censure of being out of work; Cohen, Duberley, & Mallon, 2004), and tackled by challenging societal norms. Finally, from a societal perspective, their plight could be viewed in terms of socioeconomic factors that contribute to and result from unemployment, understood through economic and political theories, and addressed through efforts toward a fairer society. Essentially, Wilber's position is that none of these four perspectives can be considered the "right" one; all have something valuable to contribute to the situation, and ideally all could be engaged with, to most effectively address the person's plight. Thus, Hanlon et al. argue that all these "key dimensions of human experience need to be considered, harmonized and acted on as a whole" to fully address the well-being of the person (p. 311).

A particular strength of Wilber's framework is that it is "meta-theoretical." That is, the framework itself is "content-free," in that it does not prescribe or advocate the inclusion of specific theories. Rather, it provides scholars with a framework that they can use to situate concepts and theories from their *own* field. And, this is what my colleagues and I did, using the framework to organize the various material of interest within APP. However, we also found it useful to create our own adaptation of the framework, which we labeled the LIFE model. Essentially, our innovation was to stratify each of the dimensions into five distinct layers, where each level encompasses or supersedes the level below it, as shown below in Figure 18.2. There are of course many possible ways of carving up the domains; our way is merely one *example*—hence the acronym—of how it might be done. As explained further below, we stratified the mind into: (1) embodied sensations; (2) emotions; (3) cognitions; (4) consciousness; and (5) "awareness+." Then we stratified the body/brain into: (1) biochemistry; (2) neurons; (3) neural networks; (4) the nervous system; and (5) the body (as a whole). Finally, we stratified both culture and society using the supra-individual levels of Bronfenbrenner's (1977) experimental ecology—i.e. (1) microsystems; (2) mesosystems; (3) exosystems; and (4) macrosystems—plus an additional outer layer, namely (5) ecosystems.

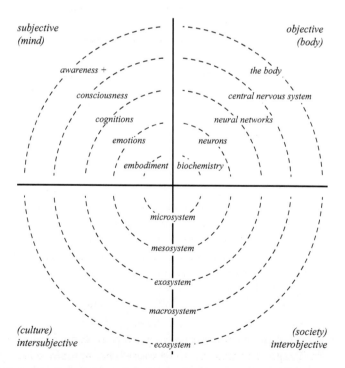

FIGURE 18.2 The Layered Integrated Framework Example (LIFE) model.

In the remainder of this chapter, I will show how this framework can be used to organize the various interventions and concepts within APP. That is, any given intervention can be situated primarily in a specific dimension, and moreover in a particular level within that dimension. For instance, MBIs might be placed within the subjective domain, specifically at the level of consciousness (i.e. awareness). In general then, PPIs that involve *psychological* techniques for enhancing well-being—for instance, the kind one could do sitting alone at home, such as mindfulness—can be situated in the subjective quadrant. By contrast, interventions involving physical actions (such as exercise) can be situated in the objective quadrant, whereas those concerning relationships (e.g. communication techniques) belong in the intersubjective quadrant, and those concerning structural features of the environment (say, its aesthetics or ergonomics) can be placed in the interobjective quadrant. In saying this, there are two key caveats. First, just because a PPI can be situated primarily in one domain does not mean that it does not also impact upon the other domains; indeed, the whole *point* of an integrated model is that the domains are interconnected. To return to the example of an MBI, even if we situate this in the subjective quadrant, such interventions will still have manifestations in the other domains, such as the neurophysiological correlates of mindfulness (situated in the objective domain), cultural norms relating to practice (situated in the intersubjective domain) and the physical environment in which practice takes place (situated in the interobjective domain).

The second, and related, caveat is that just because a PPI can be situated primarily in one *level* does not mean that it does not also involve the other levels. For instance, while MBIs involve the development of conscious awareness, evidently one can become aware *of* the other levels (i.e. embodied sensations, emotions, thoughts, and higher-level states). Thus, situating a PPI within a given domain, and describing it as targeting a particular level, is simply a heuristic device. We must therefore strive to remain cognizant of the complex interrelationships between the domains and levels. With that in mind, we'll take the dimensions in turn. Given that my colleagues and I have deliberately defined APP as having a large remit—namely, all initiatives and interventions "designed to promote wellbeing in a non-clinical population" (Lomas, Hefferon et al., 2015, p. 1349)—there are a great many practices that could be mentioned here. Clearly, it is far beyond the scope of this chapter to cover all such practices. Rather, the aim is simply to highlight indicative activities, thus indicating the great scope and potential of APP.

The Mind

In using the LIFE model to provide an overview of APP, we can start with the subjective domain of the mind. As noted above, here we can situate PPIs that work on the various levels of the mind via *psychological* techniques for enhancing well-being. More specifically, the LIFE model identifies five phenomenological "strata": embodied sensations, emotions, cognitions, conscious awareness, and "awareness+." Readers interested in how these levels were derived are encouraged to see Lomas, Hefferon et al. (2015) for more details. Suffice to say here that one might regard these levels as proceeding from "lower" to "higher," emerging in this order both in phylogenetic terms (i.e. the evolution of the species) and ontogenetic terms (i.e. the development of a person). From an APP perspective, we can examine PPIs and activities that "work on" the various subjective levels (while bearing in mind the caveat above that most PPIs impact upon more than one level).

Taking first embodiment, as noted above, PP has begun to respond to Seligman's (2008) call, in a paper on "positive health," for the field to become more than a "neck-up" focused discipline. Thus, we are seeing the emergence of activities aimed at helping people engage adaptively with their embodied experience. These include interventions based on practices derived from Eastern religious traditions, such as yoga (Khalsa, 2007) and Tai Chi (Adler & Roberts, 2006), as well as more contemporary therapeutic efforts, such as Pilates (Latey, 2001) and other such "Body Awareness Therapies" (Gard, 2005). Of course, many such activities pre-date the emergence of APP. However, following our expansive definition of the field—i.e. encompassing all activities/interventions that can promote well-being in non-clinical populations—these can, and arguably should, be considered as within the remit of APP, and/or as practices that the field ought to embrace. Moving "up" to the level of emotions, the importance of these to PP can hardly be overstated, with "positive" emotions being almost the defining feature of the field. In terms of situating PPIs at this level, though, this does not simply mean those that promote positive emotions as an outcome (as this is arguably the aim of *all* PPIs). Rather, emotion-focused PPIs are those that enhance participants' ability to *work with* their emotions. These can range from PPIs designed to cultivate specifc emotional qualities, like loving-kindness meditation (Fredrickson, Cohn, Coffey, Pek, & Finkel, 2008), to more comprehensive interventions aimed at engendering global skills, such as Mayer and Salovey's (1997) concept of emotional intelligence (e.g. Crombie, Lombard, & Noakes, 2011).

Moving to the cognitive level, as PP has developed a greater understanding of the impact of thoughts on well-being, this has led to the creation of cognitively focused PPIs. These include recalling positive events in discursive prose (e.g. gratitude journals; Emmons & McCullough, 2003), writing at length about positive memories (Burton & King, 2004), and developing meaningful/supportive narratives about past traumas or challenges (Pennebaker & Seagal, 1999). Other interventions include narrative restructuring exercises, where people are helped to engage with challenging events through activities such as creative arts, and thereby to develop adaptive narratives around these experiences (Garland, Carlson, Cook, Lansdell, & Speca, 2007). Stepping up to the level of conscious awareness, the exemplar PPI in this regard is mindfulness, as highlighted above. In the wake of Kabat-Zinn's (1982) seminal Mindfulness-Based Stress Reduction program, numerous MBIs have emerged. While some are specifically for use in clinical settings—and so by our definition are not PPIs *per se*—many others have been used in non-clinical settings, and so certainly fall within the remit of APP, including ones that specifically align themselves with PP (e.g. Ivtzan et al., 2016). Finally, meditation is also associated with the kind of advanced states of consciousness and/or spiritual experiences that fall under the rubric of "awareness+" in the LIFE model. In this final tier we can situate the various practices people worldwide have created to help them access such states and experiences. Indeed, researchers have already begun harnessing the power of these practices in contemporary interventions, including prayer (Mardiyono, Songwathana, & Petpichetchian, 2011) and contemplation of the sacred (Goldstein, 2007).

The Body

We now turn to the objective domain of the physiological body/brain. Here, the stratification is based on an evident hierarchical configuration, where each level is encompassed by the one above, as follows: biochemistry (i.e. subcellular mechanisms); neurons; neural networks; the nervous system; and the body "as a whole." (This configuration reinforces the point that the LIFE model is just one "example" of how stratification might occur. One could easily identify other physiological hierarchies, e.g. featuring more gradations or including other elements.) In terms of APP, in this domain we can situate interventions designed to act on each given level. Of course, in one sense, all interventions could be regarded as having an impact on physiology and analyzed as such. For instance, to return to our example of MBIs, there is a proliferation of research into their effects on various physiological outcomes, from immune system functioning (e.g. Davidson et al., 2003) to brain-wave activation (Lomas, Ivtzan, & Fu, 2015). Rather, the point here is to situate interventions that specifically *target* this domain.

Starting with the biochemical level, medical fields like psychiatry have developed a wealth of interventions designed to impact upon well-being by altering biochemical processes. A prominent example is pharmacological treatments for psychiatric disorders, such as selective serotonin reuptake inhibitor (SSRI) medications for depression (Ferguson, 2001). Currently, such interventions would not be considered within the scope of APP, because they tend to be restricted to clinical populations, and can only be delivered by licensed medical practitioners. However, it remains a theoretical possibility that, in future, biochemical treatments could fall within the remit of APP. For instance, Sessa (2007) argues that clinicians should consider using psychoactive substances not only to treat disorder, but also to actively promote well-being above and beyond an absence of mental illness (as per the goal of PP). Moving up levels, we find interventions that specifically target neural populations and networks. For instance, a subset of the aforementioned NCC approach is the "neural correlates of wellbeing" paradigm (Urry et al., 2004). This paradigm traces the associations between well-being and specific patterns of neural activity, like greater left-sided hemispheric activation (Davidson, 2000). Thus, from an APP perspective, there is the possibility of developing interventions that specifically facilitate these kinds of patterns. A pioneer in this regard is neurofeedback, in which participants—including even children—can be trained to self-generate patterns of electroencephalographic brain-wave activity that are conducive to well-being (e.g. Gruzelier, Foks, Steffert, Chen, & Ros, 2014).

Neural networks can be situated within the nervous system more broadly. As such, neurofeedback is likewise encompassed by the wider paradigm of biofeedback. For instance, research has suggested that physiological processes like Heart Rate Variability (HRV) play an important role in well-being; that is, HRV is regarded as, among other things, an index of regulated emotional responding, such as generating the emotional responses of "an appropriate timing and magnitude" from a clinical perspective (Appelhans & Luecken, 2006, p. 229). Consequently, we are seeing the creation of interventions that help people self-regulate such processes, such as that by Kleen and Reitsma (2011), who combined HRV biofeedback with mindfulness training.

Finally, in terms of the body "as a whole," here we are generally concerned with interventions and activities which impact upon physiological functioning more broadly (rather than being limited to any of the preceding levels). Perhaps the most obvious and important practice in this regard is sport/exercise. Research consistently shows that this not only impacts upon physical health—e.g. reducing the risk of diverse health conditions, from type-2 diabetes (Colberg et al., 2010) to cardiovascular disease (Vuori, 1998)—but also mental well-being. This effect is partly indirect, as physical health is itself associated with subjective well-being (Penedo & Dahn, 2005). However, it is also direct, since exercise is linked to positive affect via mechanisms like endorphin release, the so-called "runner's high" (Boecker et al., 2008). For all these reasons, Hefferon and Mutrie (2012) have described exercise as a "stellar" PPI. Finally, we might also mention the relevance to APP of factors such as food intake. As with exercise, diet not only indirectly affects mental well-being (i.e. via its impact on physical health), but also directly. For instance, Ford, Jaceldo-Siegl, Lee, Youngberg, and Tonstad (2013) observed an association between positive affect and consumption of a "Mediterranean" diet. Consequently, within the remit of APP are emergent non-clinical interventions aimed at helping people develop a healthy diet, such as Williamson et al.'s (2007) school-based obesity-prevention program.

Culture and Society

Finally, we'll end by considering the collective domains of the LIFE model, i.e. culture and society (the intersubjective and interobjective realms, respectively).

Focusing on these can help redress a prominent criticism leveled against PP, namely that it tends to "psychologize" well-being—i.e. to regard it primarily as an inner mental state over which the individual has control—and to overlook the sociocultural factors that impact upon it (Becker & Marecek, 2008), such as educational and economic opportunities (Prilleltensky & Prilleltensky, 2005). Learning from such critiques, PP can develop a more comprehensive approach to well-being by taking the collective domains into account. In the LIFE model, these are both stratified using Bronfenbrenner's (1977) experimental ecology, which identifies four sociocultural "levels" of increasing span: micro-, meso-, exo-, and macrosystems. These levels straddle both quadrants, such that one can analyze all levels from an intersubjective (e.g. shared values) and/or an interobjective (e.g. structural aspects of that level) perspective. In addition, the LIFE model adds an outer layer that encompasses all of these, namely the environmental ecosystem. Thus, in terms of APP, we can use these levels to situate sociocultural activities and interventions that impact upon well-being.

The microsystem is the immediate social setting of the person, e.g. their family or workplace. From an APP perspective, perhaps the most prominent microsystemic approach is practices that enhance the quality of relationships. I have already mentioned some relevant PPIs above; for example, by generating pro-social emotions, loving-kindness meditation can improve relational connectedness (Fredrickson et al., 2008). (Indeed, one could argue that the ability for a PPI to impact upon *multiple* domains in this way is an indication of its potency.) There are also practices that explicitly focus on relationship dyads; for instance, Kauffman and Silberman (2009) highlight the use of PP in couples' therapy to facilitate "growth-fostering relationships," such as teaching people effective communication strategies like "active-constructive responding" (Gable, Reis, Impett, & Asher, 2004). Such practices are transferable to other microsystems: e.g. active-constructive communication is promoted in positive organizational scholarship as an effective leadership strategy (Avolio, Bass, & Jung, 1999). Additionally, from an interobjective perspective, APP initiatives could involve improving the micro-setting environment. For instance, Gesler's (1992) work on therapeutic landscapes has shown that enhancing the aesthetics of one's milieu—especially via plants and natural light—has a powerful impact upon well-being.

Next, the broader mesosystem concerns the *interaction* between microsystems. This level recognizes that people "exist in inter-locking contexts" which together affect functioning (Sheridan, Warnes, Cowan, Schemm, & Clarke, 2004, p. 7). Meso-level PPIs involve working with clients across multiple settings in their lives. For example, in the case of children's well-being, Sheridan et al. point out that their two primary microsystems are home and school, which have a "bidirectional, reciprocal influence over each other" (p. 11). As such, Sheridan et al.'s "family-centred positive psychology" establishes partnerships between families and schools to address the "academic, social, or behavioural needs" of a child who is troubled in some way (p. 10). Similarly, the "Families and Schools Together" program is a successful school-centered intervention—endorsed by Save the Children—which builds protective factors for children by inviting families into the school to participate in co-produced activities. Then, broader still, is the exosystem, which refers to the broader structures in which microsystems are embedded, such as the local community. From an APP perspective, here we can situate the burgeoning range of community-based interventions that have been designed to promote well-being. For instance, in the UK, the Well London project is a co-produced initiative in which researchers work with marginalized communities in the more disadvantaged areas of the city to develop bespoke strategies to foster health and well-being (Wall et al., 2009).

The most all-encompassing of Bronfenbrenner's (1977, p. 515) levels is the macrosystem, namely "overarching institutional patterns" such as "economic, social, educational, legal, and political systems." Although consideration of such systems may seem far removed from the concern of APP, on reflection these are indeed very relevant to the field. The reason is that most of the practices outlined above depend upon macro-level processes. For instance, whether or not schools are enabled/encouraged to implement PPIs like mindfulness depends upon the educational policy of that country. As such, in terms of APP, we can begin thinking of macro-level interventions, such as shaping public policy according to well-being considerations (Evans, 2011). A pioneering example of this is Bhutan, which since 1972 has used Gross National Happiness as an index of social progress and to inform policy decisions (Braun, 2009). These types of considerations are beginning to be implemented more widely. For instance, prominent UN-commissioned analyses of global happiness levels have led to well-being-focused policy-level recommendations (Helliwell, Layard, & Sachs, 2013). Finally, the outer tier of the LIFE model is the environmental ecosystem. Again, this is of real relevance to APP, since human well-being depends upon the well-being of the planet, both in proximate terms (e.g. factors like air quality impact upon health) and in existential terms (we depend on a viable planet for our very lives) (Smith, Case, Smith, Harwell, & Summers, 2013). Thus, from an APP perspective, here we can include any intervention that helps to improve the environmental context in which people live. A nice example here is "active commuting" initiatives—e.g. encouraging people to walk or cycle to work—which not only help reduce carbon emissions, but have the added "multidimensional" benefit of improving the health of participants (Yang, Sahlqvist, McMinn, Griffin, & Ogilvie, 2010).

Applications and Future Directions

The chapter has outlined a comprehensive multidimensional approach to well-being, based on Lomas, Hefferon et al.'s (2015) LIFE model. The model identifies the four main ontological dimensions of the person—and hence of their well-being—namely, subjective mind, objective body/brain, intersubjective culture, and interobjective society. The model then stratifies these each into five levels, introducing further nuance to our appreciation of the dimensions. As this chapter has shown, this framework can then be used to organize the field of APP, i.e. by situating the various PPIs and practices within its different dimensions and levels. As a result, we are able to gain an overarching sense of the great range and scope of APP, allowing us to realize the diverse ways in which we can endeavor to improve well-being. This model can then be used to help improve people's well-being in real-life settings. That is, the central premise of the model—and indeed of the work of Ken Wilber (e.g. Wilber, Patten, Leonard, & Morelli, 2008), which inspired the model—is that well-being is a function of all the dimensions, and all the levels with these. Thus, as a broad generalization, the greater the extent to which all dimensions and levels are addressed and catered to, the better a person's well-being will be. Consider, for instance, a person who excels in the physical dimensions of well-being (e.g. being very healthy, with adaptive physiological functioning), but is faring badly in terms of the social dimensions of well-being. While their physical well-being certainly would be a boon, overall their flourishing would be enhanced if they could also improve their social existence.

The model therefore has implications for people looking to improve well-being, whether for themselves as individuals, or in terms of a broader organization of people, such as a school or a company. That is, a powerful way to engender these improvements is to engage in a wide range of activities/interventions—some of which have been outlined above—targeting as many dimensions and levels as possible. Indeed, this is the approach outlined by Wilber et al. (2008) in their notion of "integral life practice," and interested readers are encouraged to explore Wilber's work for practical examples of how a multidimensional approach to well-being might be implemented. Thus, for instance, a person looking to develop their well-being might not only take up a meditation practice (targeting the subjective domain), but also a program of physical exercise (targeting the objective domain) and become involved with a new social commitment (targeting the sociocultural domain). One might of course become even more specific, and target multiple levels within one domain. For example, in terms of the subjective domain, in addition to practicing meditation (which pertains primarily to the level of awareness), one might also take up a practice of Tai Chi (which pertains primarily to embodiment), a course on emotional intelligence (which pertains primarily to emotions), start a creative writing habit (which pertains primarily to cognitions), and explore forms of spiritual practice (which pertains primarily to awareness+). This multidimensional process can then of course be implemented on an organization-wide basis, e.g. harnessed by managers as a way of improving the wellbeing of people who belong to such organizations (e.g. companies or schools). Thus, for instance, a company manager might devise a program of activities for its employees, which taps into as many of these dimensions and levels as possible.

The model also has implications in terms of a research agenda, as the dimensions and levels of the model could be used to conduct a comprehensive assessment of well-being. That is, there are assessment tools that specifically pertain to each level within each dimension, as shown in Table 18.1 (together with the

TABLE 18.1 Table showing indicative assessment tools (and related theories) pertaining to the dimensions and levels of the LIFE model

Dimension	Level	Assessment Tools	Theory/Concept
Psychological	Embodiment	The Body Awareness Scale-Health (Gyllensten, Ekdahl, & Hansson, 1999)	Embodied awareness is a key aspect of well-being (Mehling et al., 2009)
	Emotion	The Positive and Negative Affect Scale (Watson, Clark, & Tellegen, 1988)	The ratio of positive to negative affect is the first of two components of "subjective [i.e. hedonic] well-being" (Diener, Sandvik, & Pavot, 2009)
	Cognition	The Satisfaction with Life Scale (Diener, Emmons, Larsen, & Griffin, 1985)	Judgments of quality of life are the second component of "subjective [i.e. hedonic] well-being" (Diener et al., 1985)
	Consciousness	The Mindful Attention and Awareness Scale (Brown & Ryan, 2003)	Mindful awareness is a "meta-skill" that impacts upon multiple aspects of well-being (Brown, Ryan, & Creswell, 2007)
	Awareness+	Spirituality at Work Scale (Ashmos & Duchon, 2000)	Spirituality is linked to meaning and purpose, which are key components of "psychological [i.e. eudaimonic] well-being" (Ryff, 1989)
Physical	Biochemistry	Cortisol secretion (Schulz, Kirschbaum, Prüßner, & Hellhammer, 1998)	Cortisol is a biomarker for stress (Schulz et al., 1998)
	Neurons	Activation of neurons in prefrontal cortex (PFC) (Newberg & Iversen, 2003)	The PFC plays a key role in the self-regulation of attention (Reid, 2011)

Dimension	Level	Assessment Tools	Theory/Concept
	Neural networks	Asymmetric activation of left hemisphere (Davidson et al., 2003)	Hemispheric left-sided asymmetry is associated with "approach behaviours" and positive affect (Davidson et al., 2003)
	Nervous system	Increased heart rate variability (HRV) (Kemp & Quintana, 2013)	HRV is a psychophysiological marker of physical and mental health (Kemp & Quintana, 2013)
	Body	Self-Rated Health Status (Miilunpalo, Vuori, Oja, Pasanen, & Urponen, 1997)	Self-rated health is predictive of morbidity and mortality (Miilunpalo et al., 1997)
Organizational	Microsystem	The Multidimensional Scale of Perceived Social Support (Zimet, Dahlem, Zimet, & Farley, 1988)	Perceived social support is a key stress buffer (Umberson & Montez, 2010)
	Mesosystem	The Readiness for Interprofessional Learning Scale (Mattick, Bligh, Bluteau, & Jackson, 2009)	Collaboration between different work teams or fields reflects the "bridging" dimension of social capital (Seibert, Kraimer, & Liden, 2001)
	Exosystem	Social Network Analysis (Cross, Borgatti, & Parker, 2002)	Social network analysis reflects the quality of network ties across an institution (Cross et al., 2002)
	Macrosystem	The Spirit at Work Scale (Kinjerski & Skrypnek, 2006)	Spirit at Work is one example of one's occupation aligning with a broader/deeper set of macro-values, such as religious orientation and expression (Kinjerski & Skrypnek, 2006)
	Ecosystem	Connectedness to Nature Scale (Mayer & Frantz, 2004)	Connection to nature is a key aspect of personal well-being, and at a systemic level is likewise vital to environmental well-being (Gesler, 1992)

background theory underpinning/informing that particular tool). These tools provide an indication of how people are faring in terms of that particular level. Thus, a global assessment of well-being—for instance of employees within a company—might involve using a range of such tools, covering as many levels as possible.

This table just includes one indicative example for each level; clearly, there are many more potential tools that could be used in this regard. Nevertheless, the key point of the table is to simply emphasize the value of a multidimensional analysis, and provide an example of how this might be done. That is, a global assessment of well-being would examine as many levels as possible, with well-being as a whole regarded as a function of all these levels. This is the kind of research agenda that is made possible by multidimensional frameworks such as the LIFE model. This agenda can then be allied with the practical agenda recommended by the model, namely endeavoring to enhance well-being by using activities and interventions pertaining to as many dimensions and levels as possible. Together, these practical and research agendas show a promising way forward for APP, and will hopefully be explored further in the years ahead.

References

Adler, P. A., & Roberts, B. L. (2006). The use of Tai Chi to improve health in older adults. *Orthopaedic Nursing, 25*(2), 122–126.

Appelhans, B. M., & Luecken, L. J. (2006). Heart rate variability as an index of regulated emotional responding. *Review of General Psychology, 10*(3), 229–240.

Aristotle. (350 BCE/2000). *Nicomachean ethics* (R. Crisp Ed.). Cambridge: Cambridge University Press.

Ashmos, D., & Duchon, D. (2000). Spirituality at work: A conceptualization and measure. *Journal of Management Inquiry, 9*(2), 134–145.

Avolio, B. J., Bass, B. M., & Jung, D. I. (1999). Re-examining the components of transformational and transactional leadership using the Multifactor Leadership. *Journal of Occupational and Organizational Psychology, 72*(4), 441–462.

Bakan, D. (1966). *The duality of human existence.* Chicago: Rand McNally.

Beauchemin, J., Hutchins, T. L., & Patterson, F. (2008). Mindfulness meditation may lessen anxiety, promote social skills, and improve academic performance among adolescents with learning disabilities. *Complementary Health Practice Review, 13*(1), 34–45.

Becker, D., & Marecek, J. (2008). Dreaming the American dream: Individualism and positive psychology. *Social and Personality Psychology Compass, 2*(5), 1767–1780. doi:10.1111/j.1751-9004.2008.00139.x.

Boecker, H., Sprenger, T., Spilker, M. E., Henriksen, G., Koppenhoefer, M., Wagner, K. J., … Tolle, T. R. (2008). The runner's high: Opioidergic mechanisms in the human brain. *Cerebral Cortex, 18*(11), 2523–2531. doi:10.1093/cercor/bhn013.

Braun, A. A. (2009). Gross national happiness in Bhutan: A living example of an alternative approach to progress. *Social Impact Research Experience Journal (Sire)* (pp. 1–142). Wharton: University of Pennsylvania.

Bronfenbrenner, U. (1977). Toward an experimental ecology of human development. *American Psychologist, 32*(7), 513–531. doi:10.1037/0003-066X.32.7.513.

Brown, K. W., & Ryan, R. M. (2003). The benefits of being present: Mindfulness and its role in psychological well-being. *Journal of Personality and Social Psychology, 84*(4), 822–848.

Brown, K. W., Ryan, R. M., & Creswell, J. D. (2007). Mindfulness: Theoretical foundations and evidence for its salutary effects. *Psychological Inquiry, 18*(4), 211–237. doi:10.1080/10478400701598298.

Burnett, R. (2011). Mindfulness in schools: Learning lessons from the adults, secular and buddhist. *Buddhist Studies Review, 28*(1), 79–120.

Burton, C. M., & King, L. A. (2004). The health benefits of writing about intensely positive experiences. *Journal of Research in Personality, 38*(2), 150–163. doi:10.1016/S0092-6566(03)00058-8.

Chalmers, D. J. (2004). How can we construct a science of consciousness? In M. Gazzaniga (Ed.), *The cognitive neurosciences*. Cambridge, MA: MIT Press.

Cohen, L., Duberley, J., & Mallon, M. (2004). Social constructionism in the study of career: Accessing the parts that other approaches cannot reach. *Journal of Vocational Behavior, 64*(3), 407–422. doi:10.1016/j.jvb.2003.12.007.

Colberg, S. R., Sigal, R. J., Fernhall, B., Regensteiner, J. G., Blissmer, B. J., Rubin, R. R., ... Braun, B. (2010). Exercise and type 2 diabetes. The American college of sports medicine and the American diabetes association: Joint position statement. *Diabetes Care, 33*(12), e147–e167.

Crombie, D., Lombard, C., & Noakes, T. (2011). Increasing emotional intelligence in cricketers: An intervention study. *International Journal of Sports Science and Coaching, 6*(1), 69–86. doi:10.1260/1747-9541.6.1.69.

Cross, R., Borgatti, S. P., & Parker, A. (2002). Making invisible work visible: Using social network analysis to support strategic collaboration. *California Management Review, 44*(2), 25–46.

Damasio, A. (2005). *Descartes' error: Emotion, reason, and the human brain*. New York: Penguin.

Davidson, R. J. (2000). Affective style, psychopathology, and resilience: Brain mechanisms and plasticity. *American Psychologist, 55*(11), 1196–1214.

Davidson, R. J., Kabat-Zinn, J., Schumacher, J., Rosenkranz, M., Muller, D., Santorelli, S. F., ... Sheridan, J. F. (2003). Alterations in brain and immune function produced by mindfulness meditation. *Psychosomatic Medicine, 65*(4), 564–570. doi:10.1097/01.psy.0000077505.67574.e3.

Diener, E., Emmons, R. A., Larsen, R. J., & Griffin, S. (1985). The satisfaction with life scale. *Journal of Personality Assessment, 49*(1), 71–75. doi:10.1207/s15327752jpa4901_13.

Diener, E., Sandvik, E., & Pavot, W. (2009). Happiness is the frequency, not the intensity, of positive versus negative affect *Assessing Well-being, 39*, 213–231.

Emmons, R. A., & McCullough, M. E. (2003). Counting blessings versus burdens: An experimental investigation of gratitude and subjective well-being in daily life. *Journal of Personality and Social Psychology, 84*(2), 377–389.

Engel, G. L. (1977). The need for a new medical model: A challenge for biomedicine. *Science, 196*(4286), 129–136. doi:10.1126/science.847460.

Evans, J. (2011). Our leaders are all Aristotelians now. *Public Policy Research, 17*(4), 214–221. doi:10.1111/j.1744-540X.2011.00632.x.

Fell, J. (2004). Identifying neural correlates of consciousness: The state space approach. *Consciousness and Cognition, 13*(4), 709–729. doi:10.1016/j.concog.2004.07.001.

Ferguson, J. M. (2001). SSRI antidepressant medications: Adverse effects and tolerability. *Journal of Clinical Psychiatry, 3*(1), 22–27.

Ford, P. A., Jaceldo-Siegl, K., Lee, J. W., Youngberg, W., & Tonstad, S. (2013). Intake of Mediterranean foods associated with positive affect and low negative affect. *Journal of Psychosomatic Research, 74*(2), 142–148. doi:10.1016/j.jpsychores.2012.11.002.

Foster, W. (1986). A critical perspective on administration and organization in education. *Critical Perspectives on the Organization and Improvement of Schooling*, K. A. Sirotnik and J. Oakes (Eds.) (Vol. 13, pp. 95–129). Netherlands: Springer.

Fredrickson, B. L. (2001). The role of positive emotions in positive psychology: The broaden-and-build theory of positive emotions. *The American Psychologist, 56*(3), 218–226.

Fredrickson, B. L., Cohn, M. A., Coffey, K. A., Pek, J., & Finkel, S. M. (2008). Open hearts build lives: Positive emotions, induced through loving-kindness meditation, build consequential personal resources. *Journal of Personality and Social Psychology, 95*(5), 1045–1062. doi:10.1037/a0013262.

Freire, P. (1972). *Pedagogy of the oppressed*. New York: Herder & Herder.

Gable, S. L., Reis, H. T., Impett, E. A., & Asher, E. R. (2004). What do you do when things go right? The intrapersonal and interpersonal benefits of sharing positive events. *Journal of Personality and Social Psychology, 87*(2), 228–245.

Gard, G. (2005). Body awareness therapy for patients with fibromyalgia and chronic pain. *Disability & Rehabilitation, 27*(12), 725–728.

Garland, S. N., Carlson, L. E., Cook, S., Lansdell, L., & Speca, M. (2007). A non-randomized comparison of mindfulness-based stress reduction and healing arts programs for facilitating post-traumatic growth and spirituality in cancer outpatients. *Supportive Care in Cancer, 15*(8), 949–961.

Gesler, W. M. (1992). Therapeutic landscapes: Medical issues in light of the new cultural geography. *Social Science & Medicine, 34*(7), 735–746. doi:10.1016/0277-9536(92)90360-3.

Goldstein, E. D. (2007). Sacred moments: Implications on well-being and stress. *Journal of Clinical Psychology, 63*(10), 1001–1019. doi:10.1002/jclp.20402.

Gruzelier, J. H., Foks, M., Steffert, T., Chen, M. J. L., & Ros, T. (2014). Beneficial outcome from EEG-neurofeedback on creative music performance, attention and well-being in school children. *Biological Psychology, 95*(0), 86–95. doi:10.1016/j.biopsycho.2013.04.005.

Gyllensten, A. L., Ekdahl, C., & Hansson, L. (1999). Validity of the body awareness scale-health (BAS-H). *Scandinavian Journal of Caring Sciences, 13*(4), 217–226. doi:10.1111/j.1471-6712.1999.tb00544.x.

Hanlon, P., Carlisle, S., Reilly, D., Lyon, A., & Hannah, M. (2010). Enabling well-being in a time of radical change: Integrative public health for the 21st century. *Public Health, 124*(6), 305–312.

Hefferon, K. (2013). *Positive psychology and the body: The somatopsychic side to flourishing.* Berkshire: Open University Press.

Hefferon, K., & Mutrie, N. (2012). Physical activity as a "stellar" positive psychology intervention. In E. O. Acevedo (Ed.), *The Oxford handbook of exercise psychology* (pp. 117–130). New York: Oxford University Press.

Helliwell, J., Layard, R., & Sachs, J. (Eds.). (2013). *World happiness report 2013.* Geneva: United Nations.

Ivtzan, I., & Lomas, T. (Eds.). (2015). *Mindfulness in positive psychology: The science of meditation and wellbeing.* London: Routledge.

Ivtzan, I., Young, T., Martman, J., Jeffrey, A., Lomas, T., Hart, R., & Eiroa-Orosa, F. (2016). Integrating mindfulness into positive psychology: A randomised controlled trial of an online positive mindfulness program. *Mindfulness.* doi:10.1007/s12671-016-0581-1.

Kabat-Zinn, J. (1982). An outpatient program in behavioral medicine for chronic pain patients based on the practice of mindfulness meditation: Theoretical considerations and preliminary results. *General Hospital Psychiatry, 4*(1), 33–47. doi:10.1016/0163-8343(82)90026-3.

Kauffman, C., & Silberman, J. (2009). Finding and fostering the positive in relationships: Positive interventions in couples therapy. *Journal of Clinical Psychology, 65*(5), 520–531.

Kemp, A. H., & Quintana, D. S. (2013). The relationship between mental and physical health: Insights from the study of heart rate variability. *International Journal of Psychophysiology, 89*(3), 288–296. doi:10.1016/j.ijpsycho.2013.06.018.

Khalsa, S. (2007). Yoga as a therapeutic intervention. *Principles and Practice of Stress Management, 48*, 449–462.

Kinjerski, V., & Skrypnek, B. J. (2006). Measuring the intangible: Development of the spirit at work scale. *Academy of Management Proceedings, 2006*(1), A1–A6. doi:10.5465/ambpp.2006.22898605.

Kleen, M., & Reitsma, B. (2011). Appliance of heart rate variability biofeedback in acceptance and commitment therapy: A pilot study. *Journal of Neurotherapy, 15*(2), 170–181. doi:10.1080/10874208.2011.570695.

Latey, P. (2001). The Pilates method: History and philosophy. *Journal of Bodywork and Movement Therapies, 5*(4), 275–282.

Lomas, T. (2015). Positive social psychology: A multilevel inquiry into sociocultural wellbeing initiatives. *Psychology, Public Policy, and Law, 21*(3), 338–347. doi:10.1037/law0000051.

Lomas, T., Hefferon, K., & Ivtzan, I. (2015). The LIFE model: A meta-theoretical conceptual map for applied positive psychology. *Journal of Happiness Studies, 16*(5), 1347–1364. doi:10.1007/s10902-014-9563-y.

Lomas, T., & Ivtzan, I. (2016). Second wave positive psychology: Exploring the positive-negative dialectics of wellbeing. *Journal of Happiness Studies, 17*(4), 1753–1768. doi:10.1007/s10902-015-9668-y.

Lomas, T., Ivtzan, I., & Fu, C. (2015). A systematic review of the neurophysiology of mindfulness on EEG oscillations. *Neuroscience & Biobehavioral Reviews, 57*, 401–410. doi:10.1016/j.neubiorev.2015.09.018.

Mardiyono, M., Songwathana, P., & Petpichetchian, W. (2011). Spirituality intervention and outcomes: Corner stone of holistic nursing practice. *Nurse Media Journal of Nursing, 1*(1), 117–127.

Martikainen, P., Bartley, M., & Lahelma, E. (2002). Psychosocial determinants of health in social epidemiology. *International Journal of Epidemiology, 31*(6), 1091–1093.

Marx, K. (1977/1845). Theses on Feuerbach: Thesis 11 *Marx Engels selected works.* London: Progress.

Mattick, K., Bligh, J., Bluteau, P., & Jackson, A. (2009). Readiness for interprofessional learning scale. In P. Bluteau & A. Jackson (Eds.), *Interprofessional education: Making it happen* (pp. 125–142). Basingstoke: Palgrave MacMillan.

Mayer, J. D., & Salovey, P. (1997). What is emotional intelligence? In P. Salovey & D. J. Sluyter (Eds.), *Emotional development and emotional intelligence* (pp. 3–31). New York: Basic Books.

McNulty, J. K., & Fincham, F. D. (2011). Beyond positive psychology? Toward a contextual view of psychological processes and well-being. *American Psychologist, 67*(2), 101–110.

Mehling, W. E., Gopisetty, V., Daubenmier, J., Price, C. J., Hecht, F. M., & Stewart, A. (2009). Body awareness: Construct and self report measures. *PLoS One, 4*(5), e5614. doi:5610.1371/journal.pone.0005614.

Miilunpalo, S., Vuori, I., Oja, P., Pasanen, M., & Urponen, H. (1997). Self-rated health status as a health measure: The predictive value of self-reported health status on the use of physician services and on mortality in the working-age population. *Journal of Clinical Epidemiology, 50*(5), 517–528. doi:10.1016/S0895-4356(97)00045-0.

Newberg, A. B., & Iversen, J. (2003). The neural basis of the complex mental task of meditation: Neurotransmitter and neurochemical considerations. *Medical Hypotheses, 61*(2), 282–291. doi:10.1016/S0306-9877(03)00175-0.

Parks, A. C., & Biswas-Diener, R. (2014). Positive interventions: Past, present and future. In T. Kashdan & J. Ciarrochi (Eds.), *Mindfulness, acceptance, and positive psychology: The seven foundations of well-being* (pp. 140–165). Oakland, CA: New Harbinger.

Penedo, F. J., & Dahn, J. R. (2005). Exercise and well-being: A review of mental and physical health benefits associated with physical activity. *Current Opinion in Psychiatry, 18*(2), 189–193.

Pennebaker, J. W., & Seagal, J. D. (1999). Forming a story: The health benefits of narrative. *Journal of Clinial Psychology, 55*(10), 1243–1254.

Prilleltensky, I., & Prilleltensky, O. (2005). Beyond resilience: Blending wellness and liberation in the helping professions. In M. Ungar (Ed.), *Handbook for working with children and youth* (pp. 89–103). Thousand Oaks, CA: Sage.

Reid, D. (2011). Mindfulness and flow in occupational engagement: Presence in doing. *Canadian Journal of Occupational Therapy, 78*(1), 50–56.

Ryff, C. D. (1989). Happiness is everything, or is it? Explorations on the meaning of psychological well-being. *Journal of Personality and Social Psychology, 57*(6), 1069–1081.

Schulz, P., Kirschbaum, C., Prüßner, J., & Hellhammer, D. (1998). Increased free cortisol secretion after awakening in chronically stressed individuals due to work overload. *Stress and Health, 14*(2), 91–97.

Seibert, S. E., Kraimer, M. L., & Liden, R. C. (2001). A social capital theory of career success. *Academy of Management Journal, 44*(2), 219–237. doi:10.2307/3069452.

Seligman, M. E. P. (2008). Positive health. *Applied Psychology, 57*, 3–18. doi:10.1111/j.1464-0597.2008.00351.x.

Seligman, M. E. P., Ernst, R. M., Gillham, J., Reivich, K., & Linkins, M. (2009). Positive education: Positive psychology and classroom interventions. *Oxford Review of Education, 35*(3), 293–311. doi:10.1080/03054980902934563.

Seligman, M. E. P., Rashid, T., & Parks, A. C. (2006). Positive psychotherapy. *American Psychologist, 61*(8), 774–788. doi:10.1037/0003-066X.61.8.774.

Seligman, M. E. P., Steen, T. A., Park, N., & Peterson, C. (2005). Positive psychology progress: Empirical validation of interventions. *American Psychologist, 60*(5), 410–421. doi:10.1037/0003-066X.60.5.410.

Sessa, B. (2007). Is there a case for MDMA-assisted psychotherapy in the UK? *Journal of Psychopharmacology, 21*(2), 220–224. doi:10.1177/0269881107069029.

Shapiro, S. L., Astin, J. A., Bishop, S. R., & Cordova, M. (2005). Mindfulness-based stress reduction for health care professionals: Results from a randomized trial. *International Journal of Stress Management, 12*(2), 164–176. doi:10.1037/1072-5245.12.2.164.

Sheridan, S. M., Warnes, E. D., Cowan, R. J., Schemm, A. V., & Clarke, B. L. (2004). Family-centered positive psychology: Focusing on strengths to build student success. *Psychology in the Schools, 41*(1), 7–17. doi:10.1002/pits.10134.

Sin, N. L., & Lyubomirsky, S. (2009). Enhancing well-being and alleviating depressive symptoms with positive psychology interventions: A practice-friendly meta-analysis. *Journal of Clinical Psychology, 65*(5), 467–487. doi:10.1002/jclp.20593.

Smith, L. M., Case, J. L., Smith, H. M., Harwell, L. C., & Summers, J. K. (2013). Relating ecosystem services to domains of human well-being: Foundation for a U.S. index. *Ecological Indicators, 28*(0), 79–90. doi:10.1016/j.ecolind.2012.02.032.

Teasdale, J. D., Segal, Z. V., Williams, J. M. G., Ridgeway, V. A., Soulsby, J. M., & Lau, M. A. (2000). Prevention of relapse/recurrence in major depression by mindfulness-based cognitive therapy. *Journal of Consulting and Clinical Psychology, 68*(4), 615–623. doi:10.1037/0022-006X.68.4.615.

Umberson, D., & Montez, J. K. (2010). Social relationships and health. *Journal of Health and Social Behavior, 51*(1), 54–66.

Urry, H. L., Nitschke, J. B., Dolski, I., Jackson, D. C., Dalton, K. M., Mueller, C. J., … Davidson, R. J. (2004). Making a life worth living: Neural correlates of well-being. *Psychological Science, 15*(6), 367–372. doi:10.1111/j.0956-7976.2004.00686.x.

Vuori, I. (1998). Does physical activity enhance health? *Patient Education and Counseling, 33*, Supplement 1(0), S95-S103. doi:10.1016/S0738-3991(98)00014-7.

Wall, M., Hayes, R., Moore, D., Petticrew, M., Clow, A., Schmidt, E., … Renton, A. (2009). Evaluation of community level interventions to address social and structural determinants of health: A cluster randomised controlled trial. *BMC Public Health, 9*(1), 207.

Watson, D., Clark, L. A. C., & Tellegen, A. (1988). Development and validation of brief measures of positive and negative affect: The PANAS scales. *Journal of Personality and Social Psychology, 54*, 1063–1070. doi:10.1037/0022-3514.54.6.1063.

Wilber, K. (1997). An integral theory of consciousness. *Journal of Consciousness Studies, 4*(1), 71–92.

Wilber, K., Patten, T., Leonard, A., & Morelli, M. (2008). *Integral life practice: A 21st century blueprint for physical health, emotional balance, mental clarity, and spiritual awakening.* Boston, MA: Integral Books.

Williamson, D. A., Copeland, A. L., Anton, S. D., Champagne, C., Han, H., Lewis, L., … Ryan, D. (2007). Wise mind project: A school-based environmental approach for preventing weight gain in children. *Obesity, 15*(4), 906–917. doi:10.1038/oby.2007.597.

Wood, A. M., & Tarrier, N. (2010). Positive clinical psychology: A new vision and strategy for integrated research and practice. *Clinical Psychology Review, 30*(7), 819–829. doi:10.1016/j.cpr.2010.06.003.

World Health Organization. (1948). Preamble to the Constitution of the World Health Organization. Geneva: World Health Organization.

Yang, L., Sahlqvist, S., McMinn, A., Griffin, S. J., & Ogilvie, D. (2010). Interventions to promote cycling: Systematic review. *BMJ: British Medical Journal, 341*, c5293. doi:10.1136/bmj.c5293.

Zimet, G. D., Dahlem, N. W., Zimet, S. G., & Farley, G. K. (1988). The multidimensional scale of perceived social support. *Journal of Personality Assessment, 52*(1), 30–41.

INDEX

Taylor & Francis eBooks

Helping you to choose the right eBooks for your Library

Add Routledge titles to your library's digital collection today. Taylor and Francis ebooks contains over 50,000 titles in the Humanities, Social Sciences, Behavioural Sciences, Built Environment and Law.

Choose from a range of subject packages or create your own!

Benefits for you

>> Free MARC records
>> COUNTER-compliant usage statistics
>> Flexible purchase and pricing options
>> All titles DRM-free.

Benefits for your user

>> Off-site, anytime access via Athens or referring URL
>> Print or copy pages or chapters
>> Full content search
>> Bookmark, highlight and annotate text
>> Access to thousands of pages of quality research at the click of a button.

REQUEST YOUR FREE INSTITUTIONAL TRIAL TODAY

Free Trials Available
We offer free trials to qualifying academic, corporate and government customers.

eCollections – Choose from over 30 subject eCollections, including:

Archaeology	Language Learning
Architecture	Law
Asian Studies	Literature
Business & Management	Media & Communication
Classical Studies	Middle East Studies
Construction	Music
Creative & Media Arts	Philosophy
Criminology & Criminal Justice	Planning
Economics	Politics
Education	Psychology & Mental Health
Energy	Religion
Engineering	Security
English Language & Linguistics	Social Work
Environment & Sustainability	Sociology
Geography	Sport
Health Studies	Theatre & Performance
History	Tourism, Hospitality & Events

For more information, pricing enquiries or to order a free trial, please contact your local sales team:
www.tandfebooks.com/page/sales

 Routledge
Taylor & Francis Group

The home of
Routledge books

www.tandfebooks.com

Made in the USA
Las Vegas, NV
20 May 2021